THE HOUSE OF
OF
Corelli

THE HOUSE OF Corelli

Marilyn Milley

PRIMIX
PUBLISHING
THE WRITE CHOICE

Primix Publishing
11620 Wilshire Blvd
Suite 900, West Wilshire Center, Los Angeles, CA, 90025
www.primixpublishing.com
Phone: 1-800-538-5788

Published by Primix Publishing: 08/18/2023

ISBN: 978-1-957676-86-9(sc)
ISBN: 978-1-957676-87-6(e)

Library of Congress Control Number: 2023914162

Contents

Chapter One

A S THE SHIP ROLLED and pitched, Angela held her daughter tightly in her arms. The child nestled on her mother's lap, her head firmly tucked under Angela's chin. Christina was almost five years old, and even at such an early age the promise of great beauty shone in her luminescent deep green eyes and became all too apparent in her perfect bone structure. They did not speak for a few moments; Angela was preoccupied with thoughts of her future and Christina was content to be held within the loving circle of her mother's arms.

She twisted her head so that she could look up into her mother's eyes and said, "Mama, tell me again what Papa said about our new house in Canada? Will I really be able to have a puppy and a kitten?" The last question was accompanied by a coy smile, and mischief shone in her eyes.

Angela replied, "Papa said, 'the house is warm and comfortable, and has as much room as we will need for the three of us. It has a large backyard stretching down to a small creek with lots of tall, shady trees. I have made a swing for Christina to play on, as well as her own playhouse. At the back of the house the yard is all grassed and very clean. If Christina wants a puppy and a kitten, I think we just might be able to get them for her.'" She paused momentarily then continued, "Now, my little one, it's time for lunch. Are you hungry?"

A smile transformed the child's face and brought forth squeals of laughter as she jumped from her mother's lap and skipped her way across the deck. Angela caught up to her and Christina tugged at her mother's hand with all of her strength.

"Can we sit at the table that looks out the window, Mama? Can we sit with my new friend Tonio?"

"Yes, we can sit by the window, and yes, if Tonio is in the dining room we will sit with him," she replied.

They had finally embarked upon a new life, one that would include her husband, Frank. He and his brothers had left Italy just before the war had ended, fearful of their lives, as they had been active members of the Italian underground. About to be arrested, the leader of the group had ordered them to pack a few belongings, say their goodbyes, and hastily board a ship sailing to Canada. Angela had been devastated. Left with a small child to care for and her handsome, wonderful husband thousands of miles away, she could only hope that Frank would send for them as soon as he had promised. She had waited months into the new year of 1945 living for the letters, which arrived on schedule. As she pored over the lines of each letter, Frank painted a picture of a bright and prosperous new life for them in a new land that was just beginning to emerge as a developing country of great resources. The coal mines were a sure thing, promising prosperity for at least fifty years. He loved his work; he had made many new friends, many of which were Italian families, as well as Polish and Czechoslovakian ... hardworking and honest as the day was long. He had written:

"I know, mi amore, that you do not speak English too well, but you will learn. Everyone here is in the same predicament and we all try to help and teach one another. Christina will learn quickly as well, if we all agree to speak English throughout the day. I cannot tell you how excited I will be when I see you both again and am able to share my dreams with you in person. I loved you before, I love you now, and I will love you all the days of my life, Angela, that I promise you."

Your loving husband, Frank.

The distance between them had not driven them apart or cooled their passion, it had merely strengthened the bond of their family unit. The expectations of a new life in a strange country merely heightened her anticipation and resolve to be held once again in Frank's arms. She had missed him dreadfully, lost in the expanse of their double bed. The absence of his warmth and slow, steady breathing had been very hard to bear as she reached out to reassure herself that he was there at her side, only to awake in despair and disappointment. She had borne the ensuing months after his departure surrounded by the loving circle of her parents, her sisters and their families, her grandparents and the many friends that their closely-knit Italian community afforded. They kept her busy with many tasks and her spirits remained high. Angela had gained much comfort through the church, and with such thoughts she wondered if there was a Catholic church in the small mining community Frank had described. She could not recall him mentioning anything in his letters. Perhaps he had overlooked this fact in his excitement to describe his new work and the future that awaited them.

The voyage to Halifax harbour in Canada would take them approximately three weeks to a month, depending upon the wind and the weather. Thus far, the captain of the tramp steamer had been optimistic and the long journey had only ridden out one rather nasty storm. Angela and Christina had remained in their tiny quarters, seasick and miserable for a few days, but they soon recovered. The child's natural curiosity and delight returned as she made friends among the other passengers, sharing her dreams and telling everyone who would listen about her wonderful Papa Frank, who was going to meet them in Halifax.

As they ate their lunch in the crowded dining room, Angela and Tonio's mother were engrossed in friendly conversation, sharing parenting problems, past struggles, and their relatives in Italy, but always returning to the immediate future. The children played sea games as they looked out upon the large expanse of ocean. Christina said, "Tonio, do you know how deep the sea is? I bet it's a trillion miles deep and a trillion miles wide," and she stretched her arms as wide as she could.

Already the worship for this beautiful tawny-haired little girl shone in Tonio's eyes as he answered, "Maybe not a trillion miles but it could be a million, I bet." He was six and a half years old and four inches taller than Christina, and he felt that he had to protect her from everything. The coincidence that their mothers had become friends on board, and were actually destined for the very same community in the Rocky Mountains of Western Canada, defied logic. Both were Italian mothers who had been left behind in Italy, but Teresa had been alone with her son Tonio for a period of three years. It had been a very long time and she was worried about her feelings for her husband, Gino. She wondered if he had been faithful to her during his long absence. She knew he was a deeply passionate man and needed the company of a warm and loving woman. Teresa confided her thoughts to Angela as they became close friends early on into their voyage. With only a few days remaining before their arrival in port, her worry deepened. Angela attempted many times to reassure her by saying, "Perhaps what you don't know can't hurt you. Had Gino's letters been as warm and happy and full of hope as Frank's?"

Teresa said they had, and at that point the two women said in unison, "Then we have nothing to worry about."

Christina tugged on her mother's arm, interrupting the conversation. "Mama, can Tonio and me go play?"

Angela replied, "Yes, but don't go too far away, and don't climb up on the railing." She turned to the older boy and said, "I'm counting on you to look after her, Tonio."

"I will, Mrs. Corelli."

Teresa and Angela promptly returned to the subject at hand and poured a last cup of tea. The dining room was not as crowded as it had previously been, and they began to relax in one another's company, a bond of friendship forming as they exchanged experiences.

An hour passed almost as quickly as it had begun. Suddenly, Angela remembered the children. They usually ran in and out of the dining area, ready to report on what they had seen or heard on their ramblings throughout the ship. Teresa's forehead creased with worry as they searched one another's faces. Angela spoke, "We must find the children. It's not like them to be gone this long. It's almost two o'clock and we haven't heard or seen them for over an hour."

Teresa nodded and the two left the dining room together. "I'll go around this way and you go around on that side and circle the ship. I'll meet you on the bridge, and if we haven't found them we can call the Captain." Hastily they parted company, not having voiced their worst fears, those being that the children had fallen overboard. Angela dared not think such thoughts, not wanting to comprehend such a nightmare. Surely, someone would have seen them. Children never played quietly for very long. They laughed and chatted, skipped and ran about, only to be disciplined by one of the crew as they were cautioned to stay out of harm's way.

Within a very short while Angela and Teresa met on the bridge, each seeking assurance from the other that the children had been found. The sky was cloudless, the sea was calm; the ship was cruising at an average rate, the sun shone down on the frightened mothers. They rushed into the Captain's quarters unannounced, both speaking at once. Captain Spirillo realized that he had to deal with two women on the edge of hysteria. "Ladies, please ... now, what seems to be the trouble? Here, sit down. Can I get you anything?"

"Our children are missing. We've searched the decks, upper and lower, and we can't find them anywhere!"

"How long have they been missing?" At this point he spoke into the intercom, "This is the Captain speaking. All crew on alert. Two passengers are reported missing. One is a little girl, approximately five years old, and a boy about seven years. All crew members are to begin a thorough search. First mate, report to the bridge, immediately."

A flurry of activity began. Fellow passengers joined in the search. Another hour passed with no one having seen the children. Again, the Captain broadcast, "Continue searching all areas of the ship. If anyone has heard or seen anything please report immediately to the Captain."

Angela and Teresa were in tears, comforting one another between episodes of convulsive sobbing. Teresa crossed herself, turned her eyes upwards and whispered a silent prayer, "Please God, not the children. Please, not the children."

Angela had tried to keep her emotions in check, realizing that she was not helping the situation, but knew that she, too, was on the verge of collapse. An Italian mother in emotional distress would only worsen the situation, so she turned her eyes upward and joined Teresa in silent prayer.

They were unaware of how much time had passed as they kept their vigil. Their heads bent in worry, they wrung their hands and rocked back and forth. Their distress did not go unnoticed by their fellow passengers, as a few stopped to offer words of encouragement and reassurance that the children would be found safe and sound.

A strong hand placed upon Angela's shoulder brought her to attention. She turned about and looked up into the Captain's eyes. Expecting the worst, her eyes filled with tears as all the colour drained from her face. She could not speak; she was too terrified to ask.

"Mrs. Corelli, Mrs. Marcellus, we've found them. They are just fine. Nothing has happened to them." Teresa's sudden cry of relief as Angela's shoulders slumped forward caused Captain Spirillo to react quickly, as he fully expected her to pass out. He held onto her, bracing her fall. "Allow me to explain. They were found sleeping under a tarp in one of the lifeboats. The crew searched the boats but did not realize that, being as small as they are, they were able to wriggle under the tarp where it had come loose. They said they went there to lie down, watch the clouds, and guess at the shapes of the cloud formations. They became tired of playing, and after their lunch, with the warm sun shining upon them, they crawled under the tarp and fell asleep. Really, they are just fine." At this point, the two sleepy-eyed children were carried in by members of the search party. Angela reached out to embrace Christina, who was unable to understand why her mother was so upset. Tonio was clutched in his mother's arms as the tears ran down her cheeks.

"Mama, mama, why are you crying?" Christina asked, her own eyes filling with tears.

"Oh, angel, Mama's fine now. I thought you had fallen off the ship and into the water and had drowned. I'm so happy that you're all right that my tears are tears of happiness."

"You told us not to climb on the rail and we didn't, did we, Tonio?" Christina's childlike assertiveness was something to watch as her little form stood firm. Her stature, all of three and a half feet, seemed to grow as she proudly reported that she and Tonio had obeyed orders. "We climbed up into the little boat so we could lie down and look up at the clouds."

Tonio added, "We couldn't lie down on the deck because people would step on us; that's why we climbed up in the boat."

Teresa hugged him, and then shook her finger in his face. "You must never go away from me for so long and you must never, ever climb into anything on this ship again. Capice?"

Tonio reverted to Italian as he answered, "Capice, Mama, I understand. I'm sorry."

Angela apologized to Captain Spirillo, thanked everyone around them, and vowed that the children would not leave their sight for the remainder of the voyage. At least they had only a few days left at sea. Teresa nodded in assent as she, too, promised fervently that the Captain and his crew would no longer be troubled.

Exhausted from the afternoon's events, the women parted company, each with a child in hand, and entered their quarters to rest and reflect on the afternoon's near tragic events.

Angela spoke very earnestly to Christina, saying that maybe they should not mention this to Papa when they saw him. Why worry him for no reason? It was past and done with, and they had much more to talk about. Christina agreed, happy that her mother was no longer crying. They soon fell asleep on the small cot, the child resting against the warmth of her mother's body curled snugly in a foetal position, secure in the knowledge that her mother loved her dearly.

Chapter Two

T HE REMAINDER OF THE sea voyage passed without incident. On an early morning in late July of 1945, Angela and Christina Corelli, along with Teresa and Tonio Marcellus, said their goodbyes to the Captain and crew, and descended down the ramp with their personal belongings in tow to the dock and throngs of anxious relatives waiting below. A number of official-looking people were milling about, most likely from immigration, and there was a fenced area where friends and relatives were awaiting the ship's docking. Angela searched the front of the crowd behind the fence but did not see Frank's handsome face. Perhaps he had been delayed. It would be at least two hours before they could clear immigration and be processed, so she knew that he had time to come and collect them. If not, she would wait in the outer waiting room until he arrived. Her broken English served to identify them and an interpreter did the rest. Soon her papers were processed and stamped, and she was done with Pier 21, having become a newly landed immigrant in this strange new land called Canada. Where were all the people? In Italy, the streets and shops were ever so crowded, but this place seemed deserted once the ship had unloaded its passengers and they had embarked upon their business. Christina asked, "Where is Papa? Did he forget about us, Mama?"

"No, angel, I'm sure he hasn't." Suddenly, her attention was drawn towards a crowd of people parting a path for a very out of breath, worried, and extremely agitated young man. His dark curly hair was awry, and his forehead beaded with sweat as he attempted to part the crowd. It was Frank. After all the months that had passed between them, it all seemed to melt away, as their eyes locked and a smile transformed them.

"There's Papa, there's Papa," Christina shouted. In seconds, Angela found herself crushed in her husband's arms and heard him murmur, "Mi, amore, mi amore, thank God you are finally in my arms." Christina was crushed in the same embrace and all that could be seen of her were her shoes and part of her legs sticking out from under her mother's long coat. The glow of happiness was unmistakable. Breaking apart, searching each other's faces, looking for change, neither spoke for a moment, captured within the circle of love.

"Franco, how I have missed you," Christina whispered as she returned his embrace. We've missed you so very much," with the emphasis placed on "we".

They moved over to a bench in the waiting room where Angela had left their personal belongings. Frank had to wait to retrieve the luggage from the checkout counter. The ship had first to unload. She surveyed the waiting room and caught sight of Teresa and Tonio as they made their way towards them. Angela introduced them to Frank as Teresa spoke, "Would you mind very much if we traveled with you and your husband to our new home? I do not speak as good English as you and I don't think I can follow directions. I'll probably get on the wrong train or something. My husband, Gino, could not get away to come all this way to greet us."

Frank said, "You're Gino Marcellus' wife? Well, I'll be damned. I work with Gino. He's one great guy, Mrs. Marcellus."

"Then, it's all right I come with you?" she asked again.

"Yes, yes, of course. Give me your baggage checks and I'll get us a taxi. We have to stay overnight in this city. Our train leaves in the morning. It will give us a chance to rest before we begin the final part of our journey. It will take at least two nights and three days to reach the mountains."

"This country is that big?" Both women looked at one another and began to laugh.

Now that everything was being taken care of Teresa and Angela relaxed. Teresa said, "He's so handsome. My Gino is not so handsome but he loves me very much and that's what counts. I can't wait to see him," she added. Angela hugged her as they followed Frank out of the waiting room to the waiting taxi. The cab driver had tied some of the luggage onto the roof, as there was more than expected. Personal belongings for two families were not his normal fare. The two women listened to Frank as he explained the route they would be taking. All Angela wanted to do was have a long hot bath, the same treatment for Christina, and a hot meal that was not prepared by the ship's cook.

Frank looked deeply into her eyes and saw the promise of passion, and his spirits soared. Finally, his wife was here at his side and they would become one throughout the long night ... remembering past times and making love in the dim light of the street light which shone into their room. Christina would sleep for a long time, exhausted from the day's events, missing the constant roll of the ship.

They awoke the next morning early, too excited to sleep, to what promised to be a very hot and humid day. Angela dressed Christina in a light cotton frock, hoping to keep her cool throughout the journey. Air conditioning on the passenger train consisted of opening a window and getting a face full of black soot from the engine's smokestack as it drifted over the cars. By nine a.m. the four passengers were seated in a comfortable compartment with enough room to stretch out and thus avoid cramped muscles.

Angela had filled Frank in on all of the family's news. She had kissed him at least fifty times and shaken his hand in fun for all of the relatives back in Italy who sent him their blessings and good wishes. Frank said he wished he had a hundred more. The children watched the passing landscape and laughed as they counted the cows grazing in the fields, waved to people waiting at the crossings, and kept themselves occupied, delighted at experiencing their very first train ride.

Angela removed some family pictures from her carry-on carpet bag and shared them with Teresa.

Frank, now done with the catching up, began to describe their new community. He included Gino, Teresa's husband, as often as he could.

"Tell us about the town, please, Frank?" They asked.

"It's known as Cranston and it sits on the crest of a hill near the base of the most prominent mountain in the valley. The air is clear and fresh in the early morning and the mountain flowers are everywhere."

"How many people live there? Is there a department store?"

He continued. "There is a main street with shops on both sides. We have a bank, a general store, a courthouse, a meeting hall, a lumber and feed store, a drugstore, and a hardware store. Oh, yes, there is a theatre with a balcony and behind the main street is the schoolhouse."

"Is there a church, Frank?" Angela asked, worried that there might not be a place for her to worship.

"Yes, in fact, we have two churches. The Catholic one is on the rim of the hill overlooking the valley, and the United Church is in the smaller community just a mile or so away. The miners and businessmen have built a ball field with bleachers, and there is talk of building an indoor ice arena. We have an outdoor rink, but the Canadian winters are so long and bitterly cold that it's too hard for spectators to stay and watch the games. Our company, Cardiff Collieries, takes fifty cents a pay from every miner, matches it and pays for our Sports Association."

As Frank painted the bright picture of the community, a light began to shine in Angela's eyes as she imagined a life filled with prosperity and happiness.

"What about our house, Frank?" she asked.

"I described it to you in my letters. It has two bedrooms, a large kitchen with running water, a tiny bathroom, a pantry, and a sitting room. Most of the single men's units have outhouses, and no running water."

Teresa spoke, "Have you been to my house, Frank? I mean, Gino's?"

"Yes, of course. I'm sorry, Teresa, I should have mentioned something. What I'm trying to say is that all of the houses, except the mine manager's and the owners', are all the same. They are called row houses and some are attached to one another. Ours is a single, as well as yours and Gino's, because we have children."

"How do we heat the house in winter?" Angela asked. They laughed when Frank said, "We burn coal, silly."

By this time Frank had exhausted his descriptive capabilities and it was time for dinner. He had scrimped and saved for months to pay for his ticket, as well as Angela and Christina's passage, but he had made sure that they could afford to eat in the dining car. It was an experience for Christina that would stay in her memory forever.

"Christina, Tonio, wake up. It's time for dinner." Angela spoke gently as she shook the children awake.

Christina was the first to awake, sitting up and rubbing her eyes. For a moment she did not remember that they were on the train. Her beloved Papa reached across the seat and picked her up in his arms. Tonio left the compartment trailing behind his mother, and Angela followed, bringing up the rear. As they left the passenger car, the sudden clash of the metal wheels and the rush of warm air were frightening and Christina clung tightly to her father, hiding her eyes against his chest. Three cars later, they entered the dining car.

Christina was amazed. The small tables were set with white linen tablecloths, gleaming cutlery, and linen napkins reflected in the glassware. All this luxury was impressive for a little girl on her first adventure.

Again the children hogged the window seat, occupied by the ever-changing landscape. Angela checked the menu and the prices as she commented, "Frank, we can't afford these prices, can we? Why, they're double what the hotel restaurant charged."

Teresa commented, "They really are very high."

Frank admonished them as he suggested they order. Teresa chose the cheapest and most nourishing meals for herself and Tonio, and Angela allowed Frank to order for her and Christina. The children were ecstatic. "Wait 'till I tell Nona that we ate and rode on the train at the same time." They laughed, but Christina became sad, because her Nona, or Grandmother, was now so very away.

Frank changed the subject. He said, "And, my little bambino, you can sleep on this train tonight and when you get up in the morning our journey will be half over."

Mountains, to Christina, meant land almost like home in Italy. The Italian Alps were in the distance from their old village and the vineyards and olive groves terraced their way halfway up the slopes to the tree line high above the village. She asked, "When will we see the mountains, Papa?"

"Not until another day and another night have passed, angel."

After lunch, Frank napped, the women chatted quietly, and the children played card games. Angela worked on her latest creation, a knitted sweater for Frank. She promised she would teach Teresa how to knit.

The following morning, the small entourage changed trains in the city of Winnipeg, Manitoba. The long journey across the Canadian prairies weighed heavily upon the children and they soon became bored and cranky. They quarrelled and slept a lot. The steady pitch and clack of the train was almost second nature to them as they ran out of conversation and decided to make friends with their fellow passengers. Not too many people were going to their particular destination, but to the port of Vancouver, British Columbia on the shores of the Pacific Ocean.

Christina was about to give up hope that they would arrive in Cranston when her Papa said, "In two hours, angel, we will be in the mountains and in Cranston." She could hardly sit still.

Chapter Three

PERHAPS IT IS BEST that people cannot know the future. If they could, then the small entourage that had disembarked from the passenger train would have waited for the next train back to Halifax and gotten on another ship to return to Italy. A new life in a new country is the biggest challenge anyone can face. Combined with learning a new language and a whole new culture, as well as being confronted with racial slurs and discrimination can dull anyone's enthusiasm.

Her belongings scattered around her and Tonio, Teresa scanned the station platform and parking lot. Gino was nowhere in sight. Frank noticed her face change from happiness to disappointment, then to sadness. He had a good idea where Gino was, and exactly what he was doing, but couldn't speak the truth to Gino's family. Instead he said, "Teresa, I think I know where to find Gino at this hour. He was working nightshift and probably slept in. He has to work again tonight and I'll bet his partner forgot to wake him. We don't have telephones in the houses yet, but that will change soon." His lame excuse was accepted with a wan, but expectant, smile. He continued, "If everyone will wait here for about twenty minutes, I'll go get him. He should be here to help you collect your baggage and take you home." Angela smiled and nodded assent, only slightly disappointed that they had to wait to see their new home. She reasoned that they had the rest of their lives in this place, and she could wait another twenty minutes or so.

Frank literally took the span of railroad tracks in leaps and bounds, maintaining a steady pace as he ran towards the center of the town, and accessed the street going north towards the crest of the hill. A few more blocks and he had reached the street of row houses that had become so familiar to him. Gino's was the one next to his and Angela's. He ran up the wooden sidewalk and onto the front porch, and didn't bother to knock as he entered and called out, "Hey, Pysano, where the hell are you?"

A commotion from the front bedroom caught his attention. He turned on his heel and made his way through the tiny sitting room, the door standing ajar to the bedroom. There he found Gino, disengaging himself from a very naked Rosie, the waitress from the hotel restaurant downtown.

Frank said, "I might have known you'd be grinding your ass in bed instead of sleeping." "Yeah, yeah, what's so important that a guy can't finish what he started?"

"I'll tell you what's so important. Your wife and kid are standing on the platform at the railway station wondering where the hell you are."

At the sound of this news, Gino leapt from the messy bed, grabbed his pants, quickly put them on, and, as he tucked his shirt into his trousers, he yelled at Rosie. "Rosie, you've got to get the hell outta here. My wife and kid are here from Italy. Come on, get a move on." He handed her her shoes and nylons, quickly scanned the sloppy room for any traces of Rosie, and took the photograph of his small family from the bureau drawer, placing it on the haphazardly dusted surface of the night table. Frank grabbed his arm as he urged Gino to move. The two men slammed out of the house, banging the screen door, and ran towards the station. As he ran Gino combed his fingers through his curly black hair and asked Frank to check his face for traces of Rosie's lipstick. After being assured that he was half-assed presentable, they made their way to the station. A little more than twenty minutes had passed, as Frank had promised. When Gino saw his beautiful wife Teresa and his son Tonio, now grown from a small three- year-old into a good-looking boy, Gino's eyes filled with tears. It had been so long since he had held her in his arms. Teresa was crushed within his embrace as Tonio held back, unsure and shy at the sight of his father. Gino held Teresa at arm's length and drank in the sight of his child bride. Together they turned to Tonio, and Gino grabbed him and threw him in the air as though he were a three-year-old. Tonio squealed with delight. With his father before him, Tonio's sense of security returned. The separation had been long and difficult.

Because it was not too far to walk the distance to their neighbourhood, the four adults managed to gather up all of the baggage and the children helped by each carrying a small suitcase.

Angela began a survey of their new surroundings. As they walked through the town, Frank showed them the hotel and pool hall that he had failed to previously mention. He also didn't mention the fact that the miners spent almost every Friday night drinking beer until the bar closed at midnight, spending money that should have gone to their families. They believed that it was therapeutic to wash down the coal dust that accumulated in their throats during the week with beer. For some unknown reason, water just didn't do the job. Another building that was situated at the end of the main street on the north side contained a doctor's office and a residence. Frank said that this was where the miners' hospital and doctors' offices were located. Relieved that they would be able to get medical care within the community, Angela went on to ask about their house. She felt grimy from the long train ride and wished to freshen up with a long hot bath, since her last one had been at the hotel in Halifax. Frank said little about their new home. As they rounded the corner to the street of row houses he studied her face. "What is this place, Frank?" she asked.

He replied, "It is the street where we live, Angela. Here we are, home at last," and he opened the gate and led them up the wooden sidewalk to the veranda. Angela could not believe her eyes. The yard was mostly dirt; a few patches of grass attempted to pass for a lawn. There was rubbish, no doubt blown from the street and lodged in the hedge and fence. The sidewalk was dirty, with black footprints ground into the wood. The front steps leading up onto the veranda were about to fall apart and the veranda itself was covered in a film of black dirt. It was everywhere. The clapboard siding had once been white but it was in a state of disrepair. The paint had peeled and flaked, leaving bare wood showing in patches. The paint that remained had turned to a dingy grey.

Frank urged Angela to put down her belongings as he lifted her up into his arms. Christina opened the screen door and Frank carried Angela across the threshold. He put her down gently, and was reluctant to have her leave his embrace. She smiled shyly and said, "Frank, later. Not in front of Christina. Let me look through the house."

The kitchen was a disaster. Frank had attempted to keep it in order but it definitely needed a woman's touch. He didn't have curtains on the dirty windows, just an old green pull blind that blocked out the sunlight. The windowsill was coated and streaked with coal dust. The stuff was everywhere. Angela ran her hand over the kitchen counter and table; her hand came away very black and grimy. "This stuff is like soot, Frank. When did you wipe the table last?"

"Don't worry about the table, Angela, come and see the rest of the place. There is an upstairs with storage space and two bedrooms. We can use the bedroom downstairs or upstairs, it's up to you." He added under his breath, "I don't care which bedroom, just so we do it in a bed." He had not been as obviously unfaithful as his friend Gino, but he had frequented the local whorehouse in the adjoining community. The brick house had housed a few good whores in the past and it was still a place to gamble and drink, as well as dip your wick for many a lonely miner with money in his pocket and no woman at home. He knew that not one of his mining friends would ever tell Angela, or that she would hear it from any of the other wives. They had accepted the fact that the whorehouse existed and prayed that their own husbands were done with that life.

Christina decided that she had had enough of the interior of the house and dashed out the back door onto another open porch smaller than the front veranda. She almost tripped on the broken steps but the lush green lawn that spread before her was a welcoming sight. In the corner of the fenced lot grew an enormous shade tree and from a very sturdy extended branch hung a little girl's dream. A very tall swing with a comfortable wooden seat was suspended from the large poplar. Across from the swing in the opposite corner of the yard was a playhouse complete with shutters and shingles. A wooden sidewalk extended only a short distance from the house to create the illusion that it was a replica of her family's house. She was so pleased with the back yard that she could hardly contain herself. She couldn't decide what to do first: explore the playhouse, or swing as high as the rafters with her Papa pushing her higher and higher until she could see into all of the back yards up and down the street. Angela stood quite still, a small smile tugging at the corners of her mouth as she watched the two most precious people in her world enjoy one another's company at long last. Six months alone with her immediate family, with only Christina for company, had felt like six years. She was disappointed in her new surroundings; she missed the golden sunlight of Italy streaming down upon the olive groves and touching the red roofs of the houses and shops of the village, where everything was clean and bright. Already she felt grimy from the constant presence of the coal dust. It lay everywhere, and she knew that much of her future would be spent doing endless housework and laundry. How could she hang out a beautiful clean wash to blow about in the summer breeze, when the coal dust would settle in the creases of the towels and sheets and streak her cotton blouses before they were even worn? She shrugged off the despondency before it threatened to become a permanent part of her psyche. So long as she, Frank, and Christina were together, they would make their way through life content in the knowledge that they were in a new world with so much promise for wealth and luxury. She thought about how one must begin at the beginning, and left the stoop to join Frank and Christina. "Can I have a puppy, Papa? You promised," Christina begged.

Frank's broad smile was a good enough answer until he said teasingly, "Maybe a little girl would like a bunny instead?"

"No, Papa, a puppy first, then maybe a bunny."

"Doesn't a bambino have a birthday coming up very soon?"

Angela interjected. "That would be a perfect present, Frank. The puppy could be housebroken before winter sets in. Just don't make it a big and hairy one. They are really a lot of work."

Fatigue set in as the excitement of their new surroundings began to wear. Frank encircled Angela's tiny waist, bent his head, and inhaled the scent of her beautiful, rich hair and the fragrance of his woman. Christina asked if she could stay outside and play until supper, and they both agreed. Entering the house together, Frank could feel his rising passion, his member becoming larger and tighter within the confines of his trousers. He knew he must control his feelings until evening. Angela, too, felt the well of passion rise within her as her love for Frank was returned in kind.

"I love you, *mi amore*," he whispered. She replied, "I love you too, Frank."

Angela opened the cupboards, withdrew a few items, asked Frank for the can opener, and started preparing the evening meal. He proudly showed off the icebox and its contents. He had asked a neighbour to shop for supplies and to ensure a fresh block of ice was delivered that day. Actually, it had been Rosie who had been so kind and, although he didn't share Gino's passion for the woman, he knew that she was a generous and helpful person who seemed to be able to lend a hand and whatever else that might add to his comfort.

Chapter Four

ANGELA MADE FRIENDS VERY quickly within the neighbourhood and throughout the shops in town. She was, in her own right, an extremely attractive woman; voluptuous, not too tall, with an hourglass figure that even the dowdiest housedress couldn't conceal. Her snapping dark eyes matched her dark, luxuriant long hair, and next to Frank's dark blonde good looks they were two opposites. Plans were in the works for Christina to start school in the fall, even though she was just past five. The puppy was well-ensconced in the house and backyard. Frank had gone so far as to build a doghouse next to the playhouse, as the puppy spent very little time there. His black-and-white good looks matched his nature, and the little girl and her puppy became inseparable. She wanted to bring him along with her to school every day. Christina made friends with most of the children her age, but her very best friend was Tonio. He adored her more and more every day. Teresa and Angela commented upon the fact that Tonio was not only her slave, but had become her self-appointed guardian.

The first day of school was a bright and glorious one. The weather had co-operated and the children had only to wear a sweater over their new clothes to keep the morning chill from their bones. September arrived in all of its glory. The morning frost painted the leaves in colors of golden yellow, deep orange, and red. Frank described the season as Indian summer, the last warm days to enjoy before the long and bitter cold Canadian winter descended upon them.

Christina blossomed in the company of the school group. She learned her lessons quickly, as she was bright and intelligent. Her teacher realized that she was special in many ways. The child had a talent for drawing and color, and she encouraged her in every way. Christina became close friends with a new girl, Rebecca Sanders. Dark-complexioned and tiny, she was a year older than Christina, but the little girl had begun to shoot up and outgrow her clothes so that she caught up with Rebecca, and would no doubt surpass her in height. They were opposite in nature, but they respected and trusted one another with their little girl dreams. Mrs. MacLeod was pleased to witness the bonding of her two special pupils into what she believed would become a lifelong friendship.

Their first winter in the Canadian Rockies proved to be as severe as promised. The fall colors of Indian summer faded quickly, and the leaves were blown about by the terrific winds that blew readily through the Pass and left the landscape both bleak and dull. Freshly fallen snow coated the surrounding hills and mountain peaks. The snow that accumulated on the streets of Cranston and the other valley towns became covered with the ever-present coal dust that drifted from the Cardiff Coal yards and the tipple, which processed the coal. The freight train, loaded with finely crushed coal, passed through the community. On its way to market it always lost a good two inches of fine coal dust as the top layer of the coal hopper car was not sprayed with a chemical that would harden and keep the coal from being lost on the sides of the rail bed. The siding on the houses absorbed its share of the black stuff and by the time spring arrived, cleaning began in earnest on the outside windows, and a fresh coat of paint was added on the houses and fences. It was a never-ending battle for the women of Cranston. Laundry was especially a chore. The Cardiff Coal Company arranged to stockpile the coal instead of processing it in the tipple where it was washed, crushed, screened, and loaded, so that the women could hang their wash out on the clothesline on Mondays. After that, it was business as usual.

Angela and Teresa became fast friends and entered into a routine of enjoying coffee together in the mornings, often planning their days. The children had taken to the English language and were often found correcting their mothers in daily conversations. They were planning the Christmas concert held in conjunction with the school. Everyone was looking forward to the company party that would mean plenty of good food, lots of music and dancing, and a chance to touch base with everyone in the community, as the whole town, including the business people, was invited to the shindig. Politics and business, the current coal market, and who was sneaking around with another person's husband or wife, were hot topics. The children would meet Santa in the school gymnasium on Saturday morning, each receiving a present from Santa by way of the Company president. Christina couldn't understand why Santa had to make two trips instead of just one, and Angela really couldn't come up with a reliable answer.

A knock at the back door roused Angela from her daydreaming as she put the clothes through the wringer washer. "Come in, it's open," she called out as she hastily dried her hands.

"Good morning, Angela, it's just me," Teresa said as she appeared in the kitchen doorway. "Hi, come in and sit down. I have fresh coffee." Angela reached up into the cupboard, removed a large mug, and filled it to the brim. She topped up her own coffee mug, and as the next load of washing swished and swirled around in the washing machine beside the kitchen sink, she sat down opposite Teresa. "You look as though you didn't get much sleep last night. Is something wrong?"

"I don't know. It's Gino. Sometimes I think he doesn't love me anymore. He's been so distant lately."

Angela asked, "Have you talked to him about it?"

"Yes, but he just says I'm being silly and that I'm the only woman for him, but he just can't seem to look me in the eye."

"You don't think he's fooling around, do you?" Angela hated to use the dreaded word adultery or infidelity, so she chose her words carefully.

"I don't know. They say a woman always knows when her man has been sleeping with another woman. He makes love differently ... something like that." Teresa's brow was creased in a perpetual frown and she swirled her coffee absent-mindedly in the large mug.

Angela reached across the table, placed her hand on Teresa's arm, and tried to reassure her, "I don't think he has time to fool around. He works shift work, sleeps most of the time, and only goes out on Friday night with the other miners. Frank goes out as well, and comes home as pickled as the rest of them."

When Frank's name was mentioned, Teresa suddenly blurted out, "You wouldn't mind asking Frank if he knows anything? Please, oh could you ask him? I just have to get rid of this feeling I have about this whole situation. I hate being suspicious, but I have to know."

"Oh, so now it's become a situation. Really, Teresa, don't get so worked up. Where has all of this come from in the first place?" Angela waited for the answer.

"Actually, I overheard a conversation in the ladies wear section of the general store. I was trying on an outfit when I heard two women discussing the waitress, Rosie, who works at the Restaurant Inn on Main Street. They were saying that she played fast and loose with any miner who looked her way, and recently she had taken up with just one in particular. I know the women lowered their voices at that point, but I could have sworn they said Gino's name."

"Are you certain, or are you just guessing?" Angela had been the brunt of gossip in the community over a small incident in the past, and the whole thing had been blown way out of proportion by the time she heard the tale. In keeping with the growing spread of gossip, she did not listen or indulge in story telling unless she had firsthand information or had seen for herself the truth, and she never passed it on.

"I don't know. Maybe I'm making too much out of this. It just keeps nagging at me." "Well, if you ask Gino and he denies it as well as says he loves you, then you just might have to leave it at that. Should I ask Frank? He gets pretty annoyed if I ask about his mine cronies."

"No, it's okay. I'll just have to put it behind me," Teresa answered and tried to put on a brave smile. Their topic of conversation turned to the children and school, and the two women began their English lessons in earnest. They were far ahead of many of the other women, and could read and write quite well. Angela wrote her letters to her family in Italian, but in Canada the family spoke English all day, every day, and had enjoyed a measure of pride in this accomplishment.

Teresa left soon after, and Angela began her housecleaning in earnest. The wash was hung out to dry in the frosty winter air, and a brisk breeze froze the clothes to the line. They would take longer to dry, but the smell of the outdoor air came indoors as Angela folded and piled the sheets and towels in the linen shelves in the spare room. Monday passed almost as quickly as it had begun, and she looked forward to Christina's return from school. The puppy had grown into a clumsy stage, and he never failed to track in the coal dust from the back yard as he raced to greet Christina as she came through the front gate and into the house. She had named him Rocko, and they were inseparable. The bunny hadn't materialized, as well as the kitten, and Angela was glad of this fact as she was the main caregiver during the day while Christina attended school.

Christina's happy voice rang out as she slammed the front door closed. "Mama, I have some news. Mrs. MacLeod picked me to play an angel in the school play. I need a costume, and she was wondering if you could sew one for me?"

Her pride shining in her eyes, Angela answered, "I think we can come up with something. I have an old white satin nightgown that's just too cold to wear in the winter, and it would make a beautiful robe for my little angel."

Frank came in shortly, his eyes perpetually coated with coal dust eyeliner and his moustache gleaming from the wash house shower he took every workday. He learned the news of Christina's part in the school nativity and smiled his pleasure. A look of disappointment fleetingly crossed his face from time to time. They had tried to have another baby, as Frank longed for a son, but so far nothing had happened. Angela sensed his frustration and had remarked that perhaps they were trying too hard. Upon hearing this, he had become angry and stormed out of the house. Angela wondered why men always said it must be the woman's fault if she couldn't conceive.

Frank had news that evening and he told it over supper. His two brothers, Tony and Joe, had asked him if he wanted to get out of working underground in the mine and go into the trucking business with them. He would have to borrow a good deal of money from the bank, but they had been promised by the company a coal haul contract that would bring the coal down from the mountain at the higher elevations from inside the mine and dump it at the tipple downtown. They would be paid in tonnage as well as a wage, and the tonnage earnings would be used to pay for the trucks and repairs. It sounded too good a deal to pass up. They had decided that Corelli Trucking was as good a name as any, and that any decisions could be made amongst the three of them with the odd man out accepting the collective decision. Angela asked, "Just how much money are we talking about, Frank? You know money's always an issue, after the company takes out the rent and we pay the grocery bill at the company store. It's a good thing that I can sew most of our clothes and mend your work clothes."

"I know what you're saying, Angela, but I feel it in my heart. When the trucks are paid for we can buy more and hire drivers. Many of the men are scared working underground and only do it under contract mining so that they can make a decent living. I don't like working in the semi-darkness. I feel just the way a gopher must feel. Day in and day out, one loses track of time."

"I didn't know you felt that way, Frank," Angela answered.

"Well, I do. And I'm telling you, this is a helluva opportunity. We would have to borrow at least ten thousand dollars for the new truck, fit it with a special box that would hold the maximum tonnage that we are allowed to carry. The company will widen the road up to the mine and maintain it so that it is safe."

Angela's face changed. Ten thousand dollars in 1946 was a lot of money. More than she could possibly imagine. "When do we have to pay it back?"

"The bank said we could take it in payments and pay it back in five years. I'm damn sure we can pay it back sooner and if we do, then the interest will be lower and our credit rating will be established. Corelli Trucking should have six trucks on the road in three years, we figure."

She nodded her head. "On one condition, Frank: that we put a little aside every week for our savings."

"I promise you, Angela, and I also promise you that I will build you the finest house next to the company's owner, that is, in whatever part of town you choose."

She felt some trepidation as she uttered the words, "I'll hold you to that, Frank Corelli, the house of my dreams, and no more rent to pay to the company."

Christina sat through all of this adult conversation drinking in the hopes and dreams of her parents, secure in the knowledge that if Papa said it would happen, then it would happen. He never made a promise that he couldn't or wouldn't keep. She smiled happily as she stroked Rocko's coat, listening to the music on the radio and drawing, always drawing pictures of fine ladies in beautiful clothes. She designed and colored clothes, raised and lowered the hems, ballooned out the skirts, dropped the necklines and added accessories. She was very good at such a young age. Her very best friend Rebecca, whom she called Becka, asked her once why she didn't draw animals, country sides and such, but Christina replied that she just wasn't interested, as everything was the same. With designing clothes they could be changed at will to suit her whim and imagination.

Life at the Corelli's was soon to undergo enormous changes. Frank would work long hours with his brothers and the wives would keep one another company, solving the children's problems as they arose and maintaining a warm and happy atmosphere. Finally their husbands returned from the makeshift garage where they changed brake linings, greased and oiled and trucks, changed tires and talked about how many trucks they would soon own.

Christina reached her ninth birthday and began to grow. She shot up at least six inches and her joints and muscles ached from the rapid growth. The only doctor in town was Dr. Martin Sanders, and he had assured Angela that her daughter was just suffering from "growing pains" and should level out by the time she reached puberty. Then, the growth rate would be gradual. Angela didn't believe him. In her heart she believed that Christina was suffering from something deadly and fretted and fussed about it until Frank told her that she was worrying for nothing. Hadn't the doctor told her that Christina would be a very tall, slim and exceptionally attractive young woman when she had reached full maturity? Angela had replied that yes, he had, but all she could see was her daughter growing out of her clothes every six months. She couldn't keep the dresses at knee length for very long and had sewn them with generous hems. Even so, Christina's pants were made into shorts for the summer as they were too new to throw away or hand down.

Throughout this rapid growth, Christina became self-conscious of her height. She was a head taller than the tallest boy in school, and standing beside Becka, she looked like her much older sister, even though the two girls were just months apart.

Rocko had grown into a handsome dog. He was well behaved and Christina's guardian during all of her waking hours. When Christina attended the Saturday matinee with her friends, he would pace the back yard, peering through the picket fence as he strained to catch a glimpse of his owner. If Mr. Dickens had allowed it, Rocko would have been at the movies along with the girls.

Chapter Five

ONCE THE ICE BEGAN to melt and the mountain meadow flowers sprang forth, Christina's spirit was renewed and she and Rocko took long walks together as the evening daylight hours lengthened. During these walks she recalled conversations she had overheard of her parents, aunts, and uncles discussing, often heatedly, the issues and labour disputes that were prevalent both locally and in the news. Talk of a possible miner's strike was cause for alarm for the prosperous Corelli Trucking company. The brothers talked of branching out and investing in other ventures and talk of a saw mill within the community was always a good subject. The Corellis, although not filthy rich, were well on their way to prosperity. Her father's long term vision of a fleet of trucks had materialized. The Corelli Trucking Company had purchased a one hundred and sixty-acre piece of land on a natural plateau tucked away on the lee side of the mountain's abutment. The location meant the prevailing west wind didn't howl as loudly or gust as strongly so as to bend the aspen trees into a permanent lean. They built a large six-bay garage and maintenance center for their operation, and hired many mechanics and drivers.

The 1950's had arrived and the post-war boom began in earnest. Talk of large subdivided tracts for housing was rumoured, and market malls, swimming pools, and a recreation complex kept the council buzzing with activity. Already a Federal building was in use, housing the post office, customs offices and Unemployment Insurance Commission. The Courthouse and jail were also housed within this two-story edifice. Beside the courthouse were the telephone exchange and the Municipal

Library. Administration made up the entire square of new buildings where once stood the awful row houses and two-story mine houses. As the occupants became more prosperous they had secured long-term mortgages and moved their families out of the direct line of the coal dust. The sale of building permits skyrocketed and tradespeople began moving into the Cranston Valley.

A Corelli family meeting was held and the brothers agreed to sell a one hundred and twenty- acre parcel for development but retain forty acres for themselves. On a very prominent site, Angela chose the place of her dreams. The mountain creek meandered through the property and shade trees abounded in groves amidst the grassy slopes. Her sisters-in-law decided that they, too, would live nearby. Christina was a little sad because this would mean that she would not live as close to Rebecca's house, but Becka's father was also considering a new clinic and home closer to the newly proposed subdivision. The new hospital was a joy to work in and everyone in the community felt that they had all of the amenities a prosperous community required. Now all that was needed was a few more doctors to join Dr. Sanders and Jones in a professional corporation known as the Cranston Associate Clinic. Everyone felt the ever-changing pulse of the community, and the future was bright.

At school, Christina's grade six class had almost doubled in size and her teacher was having difficulty controlling some of the bigger boys. At home, she was somehow pushed aside as her parents pored over house plans, consulted architects, met with builders, then changed their minds and began all over. The trucking company had made a very large profit on the sale of the land. It would pay off all of the outstanding debts and each brother could build a fine new home. Joe was contemplating running for a council seat in the next election. He had felt very strongly about the street of dirty row houses that had become more dilapidated each year. He had urged the Cardiff Coal Company to bulldoze the street as soon as each house became vacant. Joe's work had not gone unnoticed, and many prominent citizens decided that he would be a strong member of the local governing body. He had been adamant about the amount of dust drifting from the processing Tipple and loading dock. That too had been cleaned up, and the amount of dust had been reduced by at least fifty percent.

Telephone lines had been strung throughout the valley. Tonio's mother had been trained as an operator and loved her job. Gino and Teresa also had only one child and Teresa had become bored with her life, with Gino still working underground in the mine as well as shift work. He had been offered a job with the trucking company, but he made more money contract mining and got along well with his partner.

Many a family sported a spanking new sedan, washed and polished to be driven and shown off in the church parking lot. Sleek lines, pastel colors, whitewall tires and plenty of chrome gave pedestrians a reason to turn and stare as the cars cruised past. Gasoline was twenty-five cents a gallon and it appeared to be plentiful, keeping two service stations very active. The local whorehouse across the river continued to entertain the lonely, and bootlegging was a viable second home-based business. The hotel watering hole closed at eleven p.m., so if one needed more liquor to continue a party at a neighbour's home, everyone chipped in and paid the bootlegger's exorbitant price. In many instances the police were inclined to look the other way, as long as the purchaser went straight home with his illegal booze.

Christina moved with her family to their elegant house on the hill during the summer of nineteen fifty-two. She was twelve years old and soon would become a young woman, or half girl and half woman, definitely a teenager. Rocko was getting on in years and missed his old yard and doghouse. He eventually grew accustomed to the new place and took to wandering away, down to the creek to wade and drink the cool, sweet water.

Tonio and Rebecca made up their threesome. Tonio had become even better looking but now was at least three inches shorter than Christina, even though he was two years older. Becka was petite and probably wouldn't be much taller than five feet. Christina was five feet and six inches tall, and very self conscious of the fact.

Their evening ritual was nearing its end as she made her way through the lavish iron gates and up the driveway, Rocko plodding along beside her panting in the summer heat. As she entered the house, she heard her mother call, "Christina, come in the living room. I want you to meet someone." Christina turned and entered the large bungalow-style living room and dining room combination. A sophisticated, dark-haired woman in her late twenties sat across from Angela, holding a cup of tea. She studied Christina as the tall, very beautiful, too slim, and clumsy young girl shyly approached. As she was so much taller than her friends, Christina had taken to slouching to diminish her height, a habit not uncommon with tall people.

Angela spoke, "Christina, this is Miss Darby. She is opening a dance academy and local live theatre. I've asked her here today for your sake."

Miss Darby smiled and the stark, sharply honed features of her face were suddenly transformed as her broad, even lips parted and revealed a set of perfect teeth. She delicately placed her teacup onto the saucer and deftly returned it to the coffee table. The act was almost in one continuous motion, it was so graceful.

Christina was about to sit beside her mother on the elaborate sofa, when Miss Darby spoke. "Christina, please stand up straight, walk away from me to the end wall, turn, and come back." Surprised at the firm tone, Christina did as instructed. Angela studied the woman as she watched Christina do her walk and return. Miss Darby clucked her tongue in slight disapproval, then smiled quickly as Christina drew herself up to her full height. As she walked towards them, Miss Darby exclaimed, "She has such style for one so young. With a few months' work, Mrs. Corelli, your daughter will walk and move like royalty. She has such bone structure and color I have not seen in a very long time. She has the makings of an extremely beautiful woman, and I promise you that she will turn the heads of every man, both young and old. All she requires is instruction in poise, posture, and wardrobe. The clumsiness will vanish when she learns the coordination of dancing." Angela beamed. Christina listened, almost as an absent party, excluded from the conversation. Still, she liked the part about her bone structure and drop dead emerald eyes.

Miss Darby and her mother continued talking and Christina excused herself and walked rather gentile, or so she thought, out of the room. Once out of sight she took the stairs two at a time and dashed down the hall into her fairy godmother bedroom. She walked over to the full-length mirror, studying herself as she approached. She stood tall, hands on hips, turned left, looking into the mirror, turned full face, then right. Her shape had begun to change. Tonio, although he worshiped her, had remarked rather slyly that she resembled his mother's ironing board in both shape and size. The subtle curves were beginning to take shape, her waist was defined, and a rounding of her buttocks was apparent.

She pulled her luxuriant long hair back and up to show the curve of her neck. It was long and thin, but in proportion to the breadth of her shoulders and head. Suddenly her shoulders slumped and quick tears filled her eyes. Who was she kidding; an ugly out-of-proportion duckling looked better than she did. She thought her Mama must be mad, that she did look like Teresa Marcellus' ironing board. Miss Darby sure had her work cut out for her.

She brushed the tears from her eyes as her attention turned to the latest romance novel she had taken to reading, and her mood lifted. Soon bored with the whole thing, she reached for the white princess phone on her night table. It had been a gift from her father, as well as a transistor radio equipped with headphones. The television was firmly ensconced within the living room despite Christina's pleas for a set of her own in her private domain. She absolutely adored the new house. After all of her stuffed toys and treasures were placed in appropriate areas of her room, she still had room to prance about and entertain her girlfriends as they experimented with make-up, hairdos, and clothes. Growing up, thus far, had not been too difficult a task, she mused. She dialled. To the "hello" at the other end of the line she asked, "Mrs. Sanders, this is Christina, may I please speak to Rebecca?"

"Why certainly, Christina. One moment, I'll get her." Christina waited as Mrs. Sanders called her daughter.

"Hi, Christina. What's up?" Becka's cheerfulness was ever-present, even at the worst of times.

"It's Saturday tomorrow, let's go rafting. We'll get Tonio to come along and he can do most of the poling."

"Right on," Becka replied. But then her tone became serious as she changed the subject. "Tell me honestly, Christina, do you think Tonio likes me? I mean, you know, really likes me?"

"Of course he does, silly. Why wouldn't he?"

"No, I mean like a boy likes a girl. You know. He totally worships you," she sadly added. "Maybe he does, but I don't worship him. Okay?"

"I wonder if he'll ever care about me, the same way I care about him."

"You worry too much. Now, I'll meet you and Tonio at eleven where the creek runs into the big pond. Rocko can fit on the raft too, if we're careful. Don't forget to wear shorts as we may have to wade. In case you fall off the raft," Christina chided. "Oh yes, you have a much nicer figure than I have, remember. Tonio must have noticed that you already need to wear a bra." They laughed together, sharing secrets, talking for another twenty minutes, mostly about the other boys and girls they knew from school … who was allowed to wear lipstick and did they make out on dates. They referred to the older girls, of course, as no one in their crowd was allowed out on a formal date. Did Becka know about the drive-in theatre that was being built on the outskirts of town? "We probably won't be allowed to go there with a boy until we're old ladies, I'll bet," said Christina.

Finally, Christina heard her father come into the house, and her mother called her to supper. They always waited to eat together as a family unless work kept Frank out late. This just didn't happen very often, and Christina knew that her parents loved one another as deeply as they had when they first married. He had promised to love her all the days of his life, and so far this was exactly what he was doing. They were an openly affectionate family; hugs and kisses occurred often and spontaneously. Frank enjoyed coming home after work. It was the best part of his day. They drank wine with their meal and then relaxed; Frank retired to the living room where he read the paper and Christina and her mother watched the Ed Sullivan Show on television. She didn't stay up for Playhouse Theatre but that didn't bother her. Christina said goodnight, kissed her parents and retired for the night. A new adventure awaited her down at the pond in the morning.

Chapter Six

C HRISTINA AWOKE TO A beautiful, warm, sunny Saturday morning. There was not a cloud in the sky and the prevailing west wind had decided to take the day off. She stretched, yawned, and arose from her bed. She could hear her mother downstairs in the kitchen, so she hadn't missed breakfast. The family always lingered over breakfast on Saturday mornings for sometimes up to two hours. On many occasions they would be joined by other relatives or friends, and the coffee pot never stopped percolating.

She dressed in a tank top, shorts, crew socks, and saddle shoes. She tied her hair back in a pony tail and, satisfied with her image, bounded down the staircase.

"Good morning, everyone."

"Good morning, dear. Would you like waffles this morning?"

"Sounds delicious, Mom," she replied.

Her father studied this only child of his. His thoughts were reflected by the proud glint in his eye and the expression on his face. She was a joy to behold. He often wondered what the future had in store for the family. They seemed to be almost too lucky. Nothing had happened to them other than prosperity and happiness. As a premonition during his reverie, a chill passed through his body, all the way down his spine. He shuddered and shook off the feeling, telling himself not to tempt fate, but think good thoughts.

Teresa came through the kitchen with fresh cinnamon buns, still warm from the oven. She had not come by in quite some time, as she didn't always have the use of the family car. Gino was usually off somewhere with his cronies and she could no longer walk to the Corelli's. All in all, when she did show up it was always a welcome surprise. She adored Christina and was glad that she and Tonio had remained friends. "Good morning, Mrs. Marcellus," Christina said. "Did Tonio tell you that we're going down to the Big Pond to raft and picnic this morning?"

Frank frowned into his cup, took a sip of coffee and said, "I hope you don't intend to go swimming, young lady. We have a brand new swimming pool in town that could be put to good use."

"Yes, Papa. We just want to sit on the grass, have our picnic, and do a little rafting. Becka is coming along with us."

Angela joined the conversation, "It will be all right, Frank, it's not like they haven't done this before."

The adults changed the subject and Christina, her breakfast done with, dashed upstairs and tidied her room, in case her mother came up later to check. She would be grounded on Sunday if the room was messy. She obeyed the rules and life was fun, but if she didn't she soon lost her privileges.

Christina went outside and played ball with Rocko, walked down to the creek with him and dangled her feet into the cool running water. He paddled in and out, retrieved the ball from the shoreline, and panted about her feet. Finally Rocko was too tired to play, and the two decided it was time to return home. Christina checked the time when she got home and had just enough time to pack a lunch and tuck a large towel and afghan inside her drawstring beach bag. She wheeled her bike out of the garage and was soon speeding down the paved driveway at her usual breakneck pace. It was at least a fifteen minute bicycle ride from her home to the Big Pond, but Tonio and Becka only had to cycle approximately five minutes. She reached the grassy shoreline of the Big Pond, spread the afghan blanket upon the ground under the large poplar tree, and waited for her friends. Within a few minutes the two arrived, parking their bicycles in the shade. They stood together on the shore and tried to locate the old raft. Someone had left it unanchored and it had drifted west and come ashore quite a ways from where they were standing. Christina said, "Tonio, why don't you go and get the raft and pick up Becka and me over here? We don't want to walk through all those willows and weeds."

"No way. You can come along with me and we can get on the raft down there and bring it back here together," he replied.

"Well all right," they agreed. A noise turned their attention to a shape moving in their direction. It was Rocko. He apparently wasn't too tired to follow Christina down to the Pond. "We'll just have to take him on the raft with us, or else he'll bark until he's hoarse if we leave him on shore."

That decided upon, the group made their way through the thickets of willows and weeds and burst forth on the other side of the pond right where the raft was marooned. Tonio took hold of the large pole and handed another to the girls. They looked at him as though he had lost his senses until he said, "You'll have to take turns then, because I'm not doing all the work." This agreed upon, they seated themselves at each corner of the raft, with Rocko close to Christina. Tonio knew that in order to cross the pond he would either have to follow the shoreline or venture out into the deeper part of the pond, hoping that the pole would be long enough to reach the bottom. He decided that the shortest route would be to cross the water at the bottom end and then follow along the shore.

The sun felt good on their bodies. Tonio was just past fourteen and he had begun to muscle up. He began to sweat and calmly removed his T-shirt. The sun shone on his upper torso and the deep tan from summer showed off his physique to the maximum. Christina heard a sharp intake of breath from Becka as she admired Tonio's body. She smiled mischievously, aware of the attraction. Tonio poled away and Rocko rested upon the raft, content to be in the company of his favourite people. They reached the halfway point and Tonio noted that the long pole was becoming quite short when he tried to move the raft. The wind had come up and was helping him in his efforts to reach the shallower end of the pond. Christina began to fool around on the raft. She began to rock the old boards to and fro, hoping to scare Becka into Tonio's arms. Becka cried out, "Christina, stop fooling around. You're going to dump us into the water."

As Tonio reached for the extended end of the pole, Christina was by his side. Their combined weight caused the raft to tilt precariously. Rocko stayed as still as possible but Becka began to slide on the wet boards. The three occupants tried to stop the momentum of the raft as it dipped, but there was nothing to hang onto. Tonio went into the water first, followed by Becka. Christina tried to grab onto the outside board, and slipped. Just as she was about to enter the water, she banged her head on the edge of the raft. Tonio and Becka surfaced at the same time and began to swim for the raft. Becka looked about and screamed, "Tonio, where's Christina? She's not on the raft. Find her, Tonio, she must be underwater. Oh God, Christina."

Tonio didn't waste any time. He dove down and looked about in the murky water. He could not see Christina anywhere. He surfaced, gulped more air, and dove again. This time he caught a glimpse of her long pony tail and frantically reached for it. Successful, he pulled as hard as he could and kicked his way to the surface. They emerged quickly, but Christina was unconscious, either from water in her lungs or from the now bleeding blow to her temple. Becka tried to remain calm, but she was near hysteria. Tonio yelled, "Becka, help me get her to shore. We can't put her on the raft. She's not conscious and I can't tell if she's breathing." Becka jumped back into the water, leaving Rocko on the raft. She caught up to Tonio as he used his life-saving skills and towed Christina's limp body to shore.

The two pulled her up onto the grassy slope and Becka said, "Turn her over, Tonio. Push on her lungs. Maybe we can get the water out of her that way. I saw it on T.V."

Tonio turned Christina's pale, limp form over and sat astride her as he leaned his body forward, his hands placed over her lungs. He applied pressure and was rewarded with a coughing sound. Becka noted that water was coming from Christina's mouth. Tonio bent forward and noticed her chest rising and falling. They turned her over and covered Christina with the afghan as Becka said, "She's not conscious, but she is breathing. What should we do?" Before Tonio could answer she said, "Take my bike, Tonio, and go and get help. My Dad is home today and he'll come in the truck. Hurry, Tonio, please, please, hurry." Without a backward glance, Tonio flew down the road as fast as his legs could pump. Becka sat with Christina's head cradled in her lap, her lips moving in silent prayer. "Oh please, Christina, don't die. You mustn't die. I couldn't stand it if you died. Please, God, don't let her die."

A barking sound interrupted Becka's hysterical praying, and she realized that Rocko was still out on the raft. He was barking excitedly, unable to decide whether to jump and swim to shore. Becka called out, "Jump, Rocko, come here, boy." The dog bounded from the raft and was soon swimming strongly towards shore. He came to the girls, shook his wet coat all over them, and began to whimper. Christina's breathing was shallow and her color was not good. The blood oozed from the cut on the right side of her head. Becka's tears splashed down onto Christina's face as the dog lay down beside his mistress knowing instinctively that all was not well.

"Please hurry, Daddy. Please, someone, come and help us," Becka said to no one in particular. It seemed like hours, but it was just a matter of minutes until the wail of the ambulance and rescue siren could be heard fast approaching. Becka felt Tonio's arms about her shoulders as he lifted her up from the grassy slope. Christina had been placed upon a gurney and the rescue team was working on her in the ambulance. Becka was soaking wet and shivering from shock, so Tonio placed the afghan around her shoulders. The picnic lunch was forgotten as the ambulance roared away, taking their beloved Christina to the hospital. Tonio and Becka decided to put their bicycles in the back of the rescue truck and ride home with the firemen. When she reached the security of her home, Becka ran straight for her mother's arms. "O Mama, Christina's going to die, I just know it. I feel so awful." The tears were nonstop, and Mrs. Sanders did her utmost to assure Becka that her and Tonio had saved Christina's life. "Someone has to phone her parents, Mama. Will you do it?"

Becka's mother nodded and picked up the phone. "Angela, it's Jean Sanders. There's been an accident. Christina has been taken to the hospital. My husband is there now and will fill you in. I don't know all the details, but Tonio and Becka pulled her from the water and brought her to shore." Attempting to answer the rapid questions coming from the other end of the line, Mrs. Sanders kept her composure and assured Christina's father, who had grabbed the phone from his wife's hand just before she collapsed into a chair.

"Can I go to the hospital, Mom?" Becka begged, the concern for her friend growing deeper with the passing of each minute.

"Wait, dear, I'll ring the hospital. The nurse at the main desk will be able to tell us something." She dialled and spoke, "Hello. This is Mrs. Sanders. Barbara, can you tell me how Christina Corelli is?"

"She was just brought into emergency. Apparently they were able to stabilize her in the ambulance but she still remains unconscious. It seems she sustained a very hard blow to her temple as she entered the water. Dr. Sanders will call you when he is through examining her."

"Thank you so much, Barbara, I'll tell my daughter. It should help calm her down. Can she come down to the hospital later?"

"Yes, Christina will be admitted after she's had X-Rays."

The conversation ended and Mrs. Sanders relayed what information she had obtained to Becka. The young girl let out a long sigh and sat down collapsing on the kitchen chair. Her mother poured her some hot coffee, hoping to relax her and stop the frantic shaking that came in waves to Becka's petite frame. About ten minutes elapsed and Becka was appearing much calmer when the phone jangled at her elbow. She grabbed the receiver and heard her father speak, "Becka, honey, it's Dad. Christina seems to be doing fine, but she hasn't regained consciousness. She has a cracked skull and a severe concussion. We'll have to keep her here for now."

"Daddy, can I come and see her? I'll be quiet. I just want to be beside her. I feel so awful, Daddy. I think it was my fault that the raft tipped. I couldn't hold on when it began to rock and I slipped on the wet boards. I'm sorry, Daddy. I just want to tell Christina that I'm sorry."

"Honey, you have nothing to be sorry about. I talked to Tonio and he explained what happened. It was just an accident. It was no one's fault."

"If you say so, Daddy," Becka said through her intermittent sobs.

Jean took the phone from Becka's hand and lowered her voice. "Martin, the girl is far too upset. I'm bringing her down there right now. She won't calm down until she sees Christina for herself. We'll be right along. Bye." To Becka she said, "Come, darling, change your wet clothes and I'll meet you in the driveway." Jean didn't have to urge Becka to make haste; the girl was changed and in the car within five minutes. "Dad said that Christina wasn't going to die. You must believe that. He also said that the concussion was severe and that means that she won't regain consciousness until the swelling goes down in her brain. C'mon honey, dry your eyes, we're there." Becka left the vehicle the moment it stopped and raced up and through the main entrance as fast as she could. The nurse at the desk motioned her to Christina's room and urged her to slow down before she knocked someone over in her headlong dash to see her friend. She stopped suddenly outside the partially closed door, brushed the tears from her eyes, squared her shoulders, and gingerly looked into the room. Angela was holding Christina's hand and Christina's eyes did not open.

Frank and Angela remained vigilant over Christina throughout the following days, with no noticeable change in their daughter's condition. On the morning of the third day, the nurse noted occasional stirring, hand movements, and leg positions. Dr. Sanders checked her twice daily for changes in her pupils, but he could detect nothing that would indicate that she would soon awaken from her coma. The cut on the side of her head was healing well, and the swelling had gone down, so why hadn't she regained consciousness?

Becka could only come to visit Christina for short periods in the evening, staying about ten minutes, always praying silently as she held onto Christina's hand and spoke about the things they had to do that involved growing up together and sharing new experiences. She missed her friend dreadfully and the stress was beginning to show. Becka had lost weight, and shadows were beginning to show under her eyes as each day wore into the next.

On Saturday morning, a week after the accident, Becka sought out Tonio and asked him to accompany her to the hospital. They could spend more time talking to Christina and perhaps the two of them could break through the comatose state. Becka was willing to try anything. Tonio had stayed away, not wishing to intrude upon the parents' grief and worry. Inwardly, he could not bear to see his childhood sweetheart lying almost near death. He could not imagine a life without Christina. Together they entered the hospital, Becka speaking first, "Tonio, just don't expect too much, okay?" She attempted to prepare him for the imminent visit.

"Okay, Becka. What do you do when you see her?"

"I talk to her as though she was awake. The nurse said that many people in comas actually hear what is going on but are unable to answer."

Tonio's sharp intake of breath, and a change in his pallor, was noted by Becka as they went into the private room. It was empty of visitors, so the two friends approached the bed quietly. They sat on respective sides of the patient and in turn began to talk. It was one o'clock in the afternoon, eight days after the accident. Tonio spoke first. "Hi, Christina.

It's me, Tonio. Can you hear me? Becka and I are here. We found Rocko down by the pond guarding the picnic basket and resting his head on your beach bag. He hasn't been the same since you were brought to the hospital. Your mother told us that he just mopes about the house, looking for you everywhere. He doesn't even want his special treats."

Becka responded in kind. "Tonio's right, Christina. We miss you so much."

A nurse came into the room to take Christina's pulse. Suddenly all three visitors were stunned when the patient moved and began to mutter. Becka began to cry and Tonio smiled as Christina's eyelids began to flutter. The nurse calmly said, "Good afternoon, young lady. Can you tell me your name? Do you know where you are?"

"Christina, and no, I don't know where I am. The incredible emerald eyes opened wider and she took in the sight of the two best friends she had in the world. "Why are you crying Becka? Tonio, what are you doing in my bedroom?" The room filled with laughter and a collective sigh of relief as the nurse assured them that Christina would fully recover. She left the room to report to the doctor and call Christina's parents. Becka and Tonio crowded around her and began to tell her what had happened.

"You saved my life, Tonio." A new respect for the young man shone in her eyes as she tried to thank him.

"It was nothing, Christina. Becka helped too, and Rocko, if you really want to know."

They stayed for a few more minutes, noting that Christina's eyes kept closing. She would sleep the sleep of the exhausted, and awake fully refreshed to the news that her concussion was gone and she would be released from the hospital in twenty-four hours after a thorough neurological check.

Chapter Seven

THE FOLLOWING DAY JUST after lunchtime, Christina was released from hospital. Although Dr. Sanders had given her a clean bill of health, Angela decided that it would not do any harm to coddle Christina for a few more days by insisting that she rest at home. Her father, now that the crisis was over, resumed his obsession with making money. She saw him briefly that evening when he came up to say goodnight, and he was gone early before they had breakfast.

"Good morning, darling," Angela said. "Did you sleep well?"

"Yes, Mama. It was nice to be back at home in my own bed. The hospital beds are not that comfortable," she added.

The doorbell rang and Angela noted the time as eight thirty. Aloud she wondered, "Who could be calling at this time of the morning?" Christina remained seated in the corner of the sunny kitchen breakfast nook, leafing through a magazine and nibbling on her toast. Another voice joined that of her mother's, and Christina was surprised to see Teresa enter the kitchen.

"Good morning Christina. How are you feeling?"

"Fine, thank you, Mrs. Marcellus," Christina replied. The women made polite conversation for a few minutes while Angela filled two cups from a fresh pot of coffee. Finally Christina decided to watch a little television, as she was still lethargic from her hospital stay. She excused herself and settled on the sofa. She did not turn the up the volume on the set and could make out a little of the conversation drifting from the kitchen.

"I know I shouldn't burden you with my problems, Angela, but I feel closer to you than anyone in this town, other than my husband, Gino."

"That's all right, Teresa, tell me what's wrong, and if I can help I will. What are friends for?"

"It's Gino. He is very much involved in the Coal Miners' Union and spends most of his time either at the Union Hall or in the bar drinking beer and discussing Union business. I don't see much of him as it is because I work shift work at the telephone office. We just seem to be strangers passing in the night. He hasn't touched me for a few months, and that is definitely not like my Gino."

"Have you tried talking to him, Teresa?" Angela asked.

"When we have dinner together, Tonio is there and the two of them have begun to argue constantly. Gino wants Tonio to go to college and not to work in the mine. He wants a better life for his son. By the time the two of them are through arguing, Gino is up and out of the door before I've finished cleaning up after our supper."

"What about when he comes home? Can you talk to him then?"

Teresa's eyes filled with tears. "It's no use. He's usually too drunk to reason with or to discuss anything. He falls into bed and is asleep almost as soon as I get his shoes off. I don't know what to do. He says I worry too much, and not to get too worked up. How do you tell an Italian woman not to get too worked up? The worst part of all of this is that I have smelled the traces of another woman's perfume on his clothes. He says it's from the barmaid at the hotel, but I just can't believe him."

By this time, Teresa was crying in earnest, her beautiful brown eyes sorrowful and despondent; windows that were testimonial to the state of her heart and soul. Angela's manner was all sympathy. She tried to reassure Teresa that her worst thoughts were just ... thoughts. However, her own life had taken a downturn. Frank wasn't to be accused of keeping company with other women; his new mistress was money. He had investments in so many ventures that it required all of his energies to keep on top of it all. Some of the new business proposals didn't include his brothers or the Corelli Trucking Company. He was a third partner in a large sawmill destined to open soon at the other end of the valley. It would diversify the community's economy so that if there was a sudden slump in the coal markets, then the lumber mill would take up the slack. Taking all of this into consideration, Angela found herself alone more and more, especially in the evenings. They did not spend much time together as they had in the early years of their marriage. If Frank was home, it was to entertain many of his new friends and their wives. Angela did not consider these new couples as friends, rather just acquaintances

... not to become too familiar, just polite strangers. Christina was growing up and becoming a lovely young lady, leaving Angela with much time on her hands. She had turned to the church and the Catholic Women's League, helping out at potluck suppers and fund-raising activities. With these thoughts in the back of her mind she tried a little advice. "Have you tried talking with Father Perinni?"

"I thought about it, but I can't get past the usual confessional. I just haven't had the courage," Teresa replied. "If only I was back at home in Italy. There, everyone knows your business, but at least their advice is reliable and if a husband is committing adultery the family steps in and deals with it."

Angela's heart skipped a beat as she fondly remembered the family discussions she had listened to as a child and young girl growing up in Italy. Teresa was right.

"Could you talk to Frank for me?" Teresa asked. "What would I say?"

"I don't know. Maybe he knows what's going on? If he is out as much as you say, he may have seen Gino with someone, or heard the men talking?"

Angela hated to refuse her best friend's request, but she could not say that the two men traveled in different circles. Frank hobnobbed with the business community and upper level management, while Gino was of the Union, blue-collar club. Teresa said, "You have this beautiful home, and a husband that cares about you. I have a son that is not too interested in anything, a husband that cares about his looks and cronies, and I have a job that keeps me sane. What else could a woman want, ironically speaking, of course?"

Angela was surprised at the comparison. However, she did give Teresa some insight into her own loneliness as she replied, "All this means nothing to me if my husband is not here to share it with me. We are drifting ... me, trying to amuse myself with church activities and community charities, Frank with his obsession with money. If only we could go away on a holiday together, but he always has some other deal to close or a new one opening up. I swear I almost wish it was another woman. Then, maybe, I could deal with it all."

Although nothing was resolved, Teresa felt a whole lot better for having opened her heart to Angela. She dried her eyes, thanked Angela with a hug, called a goodbye to Christina from the back door, and left as quietly as she had come. Angela watched as Teresa drove around the curved driveway, slowed at the wrought iron gates, and entered the main thoroughfare. She shook her head, poured a final cup of coffee and sat sipping it slowly, staring off into space, preoccupied with her private thoughts. Life had been much happier in that dirty little row house eight years ago. She loved her new home and garden. The cleaning lady Frank had hired for her came three times a week, leaving Angela with more time on her hands. Miss Darby had been a breath of fresh air when Angela had introduced her to Christina. Classes would begin in the fall along with the school year. Perhaps Angela could participate in some way with the theatre group. It was worth a thought. She could not solve Teresa's problems but she decided that maybe, just maybe Frank could help her out.

Christina overheard much of the conversation, not understanding all of it, but she had heard enough to know that Tonio's life was not to be compared to her own. He had become moody lately, but would not confide in her or Becka. Becka was beginning to feel shut out, but Christina assured her that her feelings for Tonio were strictly big-brother. She agreed with Becka that he was the best-looking boy in their school but that didn't mean much to Christina. Her own looks were already beginning to turn heads, but having grown up with this, it meant nothing to her. She was only interested in how her friends treated one another; if they were truly sincere, or just being nice to get something out of being the friend of one of the richest families in Cranston. She knew her father was worth a lot of money but she had no idea how powerful he had become. He was not yet forty and felt he had only just reached his stride. After hearing how lonely her mother was, Christina tried to be around much more, even inviting her on her walks with Rocko, but Angela began to withdraw from her family. A letter had arrived from Italy and the news was not good. Her beloved grandmother was very ill and wished to see them once more. This being her maternal grandmother, Christina stood by watching helplessly as Angela became morose, losing interest in her surroundings. Finally, Frank became concerned. He had tried to help out with the problem of Gino and Teresa but he did not wish to blow the whistle on Gino. The man had been doing Rosie for many years, and just maybe had moved on to someone else. It was none of his business. Now he had problems of his own. He could not leave just yet to go to Italy, but decided that Angela needed the trip. Whirlwind arrangements were made, and after eight years of absence, Angela and Christina were on their way to Italy. Frank promised to call when he could join them, but there remained just three weeks before the school year began and Christina must return.

After a tearful goodbye at the airport, Christina was soon airborne for the very first time, Transoceanic at that. It was a fourteen hour flight, but mother and daughter had much to talk about. Angela asked Christina what she remembered about Italy. "I remember Nona, she was so beautiful. I remember her smile and how she would hold me tightly in her arms when I fell and hurt myself while playing. I remember all of the aunts and uncles at the table when Nona cooked her wonderful pasta. The smells from her kitchen are part of me." As Christina recalled her childhood memories, Angela's heart warmed. She had not realized how much of a wall she had formed around her heart by shutting out these wonderful memories. "I remember the sunshine on the olive groves, and the warmth of the people in the town. Whose wedding was held in the town square, where everyone drank vino and danced all night?"

"That was your uncle Guido's. He married my friend Maria. She was as close to me as you and Becka. I think that if we have time we will stop and visit them in Toronto, perhaps on our way back. Her letters are always filled with their happiness and prosperity, but letters are not enough. She and Guido have three children, two older boys and a girl a year younger than you. Maria mentions in her letters that Nona's recipes for Italian bread and pastry have been the backbone of their bakery business. Guido has just opened two more bakeries within the city and the boys are helping out with the delivery vans. It just sounds so different from our lives. The last letter was filled with such hope. Maria said that Guido had promised her a new home in the suburbs, but he had just opened the two new businesses so perhaps she could wait a few more years. The apartment above the bakery in the heart of their Italian community in Toronto was filled with smells from the bakery below, and the rooms filled with the daily sounds of the street. It sounded more like a neighbourhood tying people together, celebrating their culture and living their lives to the fullest." Angela experienced a few pangs of envy and they crept into her voice.

"Are you unhappy, Mama?" Christina asked.

"Sometimes, my angel, I am. It's only because I miss my family. My father must be getting old, and my sisters are still in Italy. Maybe if some of my side of the family lived closer to us, I wouldn't be so homesick for Italy. Your father's family is all right, but it's just not the same. Do you understand?"

"I think so. I know I would be very unhappy if I couldn't see you and Papa every day, or if I lived very far away from everybody." Little did she know, the warmth and security of her fairy tale life was beginning to wane, and a crack was forming in the cocoon that surrounded her. The flight attendant announced on the Public Address System that they could watch an in- flight movie or retire for the night. They would arrive in Rome at six a.m. From Rome to their town was an hour's bus ride to the south. Angela knew that hour would be the longest, as their anticipation ran high. She could hardly contain her excitement, and not being able to fall asleep, she opted out for the movie. Christina slept the deep sleep of youth, and Angela marvelled at the innocence and beauty of her daughter. They had given up on having any more children and she knew that Frank blamed her for this. However, Angela was through caring; her love and direction focused upon the child God had given them. The movie wasn't too exciting, and Angela finally drifted off to sleep, attempting to relax in a reclining position with very little leg room afforded by first class.

* * * * *

ROME WAS AN INCREDIBLE place. Christina marvelled at the fact that everything, though so old, could look so magnificent. She did take note of the lack of flamboyant neon signs and garish billboards that were so prevalent in Canada and America. She promised inwardly that she would one day return to explore the wonders of this city and its surrounding countryside. The taxi ride was an experience in itself and her mother and the driver conversed in rapid Italian all the way to the hotel. They would have to stay overnight at the Palazzio D'Italia before boarding the connecting bus to the town of Marino a hundred kilometres south of Rome. She drank in all of the sights and sounds, not saying a word as the open markets flashed by. The traffic slowed in congested areas and she was able to get a glimpse of the heart of Rome. The hotel was old, world class, and very chic; they were greeted as though they had stayed there countless times. They ate a light lunch at a sidewalk café situated along the Piazza then strolled along the narrow streets, stopping involuntarily at the shop windows. Angela promised herself that she would indulge in one very expensive designer suit complete with accessories, and some twenty-four carat gold jewellery and leather goods for Christina. It didn't take long for the two to be laden down with packages, and, it being but a short walk to the hotel, they were able to manage. A few Italian men had stopped to offer help but Angela refused politely, although very pleased that she had been approached. They had not purchased anything for their relatives, their visit being one of a sombre nature. Perhaps another time would be more appropriate.

The view from the tiny balcony's third floor window afforded them a fantastic panorama of the city and the lifeblood that flowed well into the evening hours. They watched as the lights came on all over Rome and nightlife began in earnest. Christina was fascinated. She felt as though she had been picked up and transported to another world, as indeed she had. Angela regretted having to retire for the night, but the day ahead would be fraught with emotion.

They were awakened by the hotel concierge at 7:00 a.m. and a continental breakfast was served out on the balcony. "Mama, I never want to leave this place. It is too beautiful. The sun seems brighter and the smiles of the people wider. I just can't believe I am here."

Angela smiled, proud that Christina had taken such an interest in their homeland. She too felt the strong pull, as her cultural roots brought once-forgotten memories to the forefront of her mind. The taxi arrived to take them to the bus terminal. They were soon on their way out of Rome and Angela relaxed in her seat, glorying in the lush countryside. Christina became quiet, almost pensive, as the sights flashed past. She began to study the other passengers. People cuddled babies, pulled out picnic baskets and bottles of wine. It was considered a privilege to be offered a share of their repast. Angela, fluent in the language, fit right in, and everyone was excited to learn that she was from Canada. They wanted to know everything there was to know, especially the truth about the severe winters. Angela, in turn, wished to be brought up to date on her beloved Italy, and the conversation flowed back and forth from topic to topic. Christina was soon lost in the dialogue, unable to understand the rapid Italian, so she amused herself with watching the children. What would her life be like in the future? Would she marry a handsome, warm and loving man? Would God grant them children? She was knowledgeable in the facts of life and couldn't wait until she was fully matured. Most girls her age were interested in the present and didn't dream about the future until some boy happened to catch their eye.

The bus pulled into the town square in Marino, and a crowd of people approached. As the passengers left the bus, each in turn was snatched up and hugged and kissed interminable times, as tears flowed freely. Angela heard her name called and her face was transformed. There stood her father next to her Aunt Sophia, who she hadn't quite recognized, and she left Christina's side rushing into the arms of her Papa. Christina stood on the outskirts of the group waiting her turn. This happened almost immediately, as with arms intertwined they turned to where she was standing. She was surrounded by bodies, hugs and kisses all around, and felt her ribs about to crack. Angela laughed as she introduced the relatives. She remembered her Nono, or grandfather. He had held her on his knee when she was very young and had become her surrogate Papa. She loved this man very much, and tears of joy filled her eyes. A sombre attitude changed the group as Angela asked, "Papa, how is Mama?"

Sadness filled his eyes as he answered, "She is waiting for you, Cara Mia, but do not be shocked. She is very thin and not at all as you remember. Her heart is not strong, and the doctor says she must rest. He says that she will most likely die in her sleep, peacefully, with very little pain." His voice broke with emotion, as he continued, 'It is very hard to imagine a world without your Mama. I cannot."

She placed her arm about his waist and together, father and daughter and granddaughter left the square. Sophia and the other relatives followed closely behind, carrying the luggage. A car awaited them and they were soon piled into the back seat, the luggage stored on the roof. Carlo drove at breakneck speed, his usual pace, which scared the wits out of Christina but did not raise an eyebrow of the other occupants in the vehicle. They approached a long hill with a slightly winding lane, passed vineyards, olive groves, large shade trees growing wild, and stone fences and finally came to rest at the doorstep of a large stone house. A few more relatives were there to greet them. Within minutes Angela and Christina were taken to Nona's bedside. Her happiness shone through the paleness of her complexion. Angela was definitely shocked at her appearance, despite being forewarned. The eyes had not changed. The deep brown depths of her mother's beautiful eyes drank in the sight of her Angela. Christina stood tall, slightly behind Angela. Her mother disentangled herself from her grandmother's embrace, and said, "Mama, here is Christina, do you remember?"

Choked with emotion, Nona smiled through her tears, "Mi bambino, bella, bella."

Christina could not remember this frail woman. How could this be her Nona, who had loved her, scolded her and taught her the Old Italian songs in her spacious kitchen? But, in truth, it was she. She hid her astonishment and returned the embrace. "Nona, it is so good to see you."

Their trip to Italy had begun in earnest, and Angela vowed to stay for as long as she could. A thought occurred to her. No one had asked her about Frank. Perhaps when they dined around the enormous table out on the patio with the relatives and family, someone would remember to ask. Her brothers brought their wives and children, Nona came out to join them all for a few minutes basking in the warmth of the late afternoon sun. Christina had never felt such family love. It was intense and enveloping, almost overwhelming.

Finally, they all sat quietly as Angela described their life in Canada. She showed them where the valley was and had brought pictures of their home, Rocko, and the trucking firm as well as of Frank, Joe, Tony, and their wives and children. Christina retired around ten o'clock after looking in on her grandmother. She left a fresh rose by her bedside, touched her cheek gently so as not to awake the frail old woman. Her thoughts were filled with all she had experienced and witnessed during the past two days but sleep did not claim her for a very long time.

Chapter Eight

As HE TURNED THE key in the lock, Frank could hear the phone ringing. He managed to pick up the receiver after the fifth ring. "Hello. Yes Operator, this is Frank Corelli. Yes, I'll accept the charges." There was a pause and then, "Angela, is that you, honey?"

"Yes Frank, can you hear me?"

"Is everything all right, Ange? Christina okay?"

"We're fine, dear. I just wanted to hear your voice. We miss you terribly."

"Me too. How is everyone over there?" A wave of memories flooded his mind as he thought of his old home and the village of Marino.

"Nona is getting weaker as the days pass. The doctor says it is her heart. She's nearly seventy, and that's old by any standard. She's worked hard all of her life and her body is wearing out. I don't know if I can stay and watch her linger. It's too hard, Frank."

He heard the catch in her voice and imagined the tears coursing down her cheeks. Frank replied, "Try to be strong, Angela. I'm doing my best to clear the business so that I can join you, but right now it doesn't look too promising."

"Frank, Christina and I need you. Please try, it's so important. Everyone is asking for you.

Your relatives have been calling every day hoping that you will be here."

The operator broke into the conversation, "Your three minutes are up, Madam. Do you wish to continue talking?"

Something happened to the connection, and the line went dead.

Frank spoke into the empty receiver, but soon realized that the overseas call was terminated. A rush of longing for Angela coursed through him, and his disappointment filled the room. He sat down heavily, awash with loneliness. They had not been apart for one night since Angela had arrived from Italy and this was hard to take. He had not eaten yet, and it was now past eight p.m. Cook had left his dinner warming in the oven, but after two hours the delicious meal had become dry and tasteless. He decided that he could not face a long evening in the empty house. He showered quickly, changed into casual clothes, retrieved a jacket to ward off the evening chill, and decided to go down to the Inn. The place was renowned for its fine food and clientele. Most of Frank's business colleagues and friends dropped in on a daily basis to touch base with one another. Many a business deal had been closed over a glass of fine wine.

Within minutes he reached the Inn, found a parking place and turned off the motor. He tossed his jacket on the front seat as he left the vehicle. The evening was as fine as ever. The mountain air was clean and crisp and the stars shone clearly above the tall peaks as the moon's rays turned the limestone rock to a soft dove grey. He loved this valley and had never regretted the move to this wonderful country. At thirty-seven, he was on his way to making his first million and beyond. Frank's obsession with money and power had not waned. In fact, it had grown stronger as the business ventures he supported grew. He was richer than his brothers, Joe and Tony. They were content with the prosperity of the trucking firm. As he approached the bar, Frank was greeted by the owner.

"Good evening, Mr. Corelli. How are you this fine evening?"

"Good evening to you, Sam. Just fine, thank you. I think I'll have something at the bar while I wait for a table. Call me when you have one ready, will you?"

"By all means, Mr. Corelli," Sam answered.

Frank surveyed the occupants at the long curved bar. Towards the end, seated at the short side of the counter against the wall, was his business partner's wife, Sharon Nesbitt. Five of them had entered into the business relationship and owned the new mall. Sharon had hosted many a party for them, along with the other wives. She was as different from Angela as night from day. Sharon was a platinum blonde, with the face of an angel. Her pale blue eyes gave away nothing. He had thought upon first meeting her that she reminded him of the original "ice" queen.

However, she overturned that impression when she smiled at him. It was slow and seductive; the eyes changed, deepening in intensity, promising and teasing. He smiled warmly as he approached her, "May I buy you a drink, lovely lady?"

"Why, Frank Corelli. How nice to see you. Of course, vodka martini, very, very dry." "What is a lovely lady like you doing in a place like this all alone?"

"It's a long story. I just felt like a night out. That big house on the hill was stifling. Dave is home but on the phone to some corporation overseas, and I couldn't stand another minute of his wheeling and dealing."

The drinks arrived and Frank was amazed at the large gulp she took to finish off the previous drink and taste the new one. He sipped on his rye, deftly swirling the ice around inside the glass. The conversation between the two became more personal after two more rounds. The waiter came over to Frank and announced that his table was ready. He said to Sharon, "Have you eaten? Care to join me?"

"I thought you'd never ask," Sharon replied. As they walked through into the dining room, a few heads turned in recognition, but many in admiration. Frank's good looks complemented his partner's. He held the chair for her as she chose the seat nearest the wall. Frank sat beside her, but at an angle that afforded him the opportunity to bend forward and speak quietly and intimately, and admire her scent. They ordered from the menu. Sharon ate like a bird, which attested to her fine, willowy figure. Frank was ravenous and ordered a large T-bone steak. She watched him eat with gusto, relishing each bite. "I can't remember when I watched a man eat with such enjoyment," she remarked. "You certainly have a large appetite."

"I have a large appetite for lots of things, especially with a beautiful woman looking on." This was the first opening in the conversation that suggested that there just might be more to this evening than they had both counted upon.

Sharon smiled, studied the wine glass, and raised it to her lips. She sipped delicately, her eyes half lidded, and studied Frank. He certainly was a lot more appealing than her blasé husband. After five years of marriage, Sharon had no children and was totally bored with her life. The incessant rounds of parties to entertain their business acquaintances left her empty and friendless. Whether the other wives saw her as a threat to their marriages, or were envious of her perfect body and stunning good looks she did not know, but she was alone with no one to confide her dreams and expectations. So she began to hide her loneliness in a bottle. Vodka left no trace on her breath and she could, by this time, put away a number of them before she began to stagger or slur her words. Frank hated a drunken woman and this she knew, so she had switched to the white dinner wine, nursing the large goblet throughout the meal.

The evening wore on and an orchestra arrived, playing background dance music. Frank and Sharon did a few turns on the tiny floor, and the closeness of her willowy body sent the usual messages to his maleness. He hoped that the casual trousers he wore were baggy enough to hide his aroused state. Sharon felt the hardness against her thigh as they moved slowly to the music. Their eyes met. Frank felt the change in her mood and read the promise in her eyes. Perhaps the combination of the wine, the music, and the dinner had relaxed and lifted her spirits.

"You are terrific. Do you know that? Do you have any idea what you're doing to me?" "I believe I do, Frank. What do you suggest we do about it?"

Without waiting for her to have a possible change of heart, Frank gestured to the waiter for the check, retrieved her coat, and they were in the parking lot within moments. He drew her into the shadows and enclosed her in an embrace that took her breath away. The passion grew between them. Frank did not take any liberties out in public, but he couldn't wait to get his hands on her. He opened the car door for her and she slid onto the leather seat, swinging her legs around in one motion.

He walked around the back of the car, stopped momentarily and checked his wallet. He had a few condoms with him, which he carried around for the hell of it. It had become a habit when he was a young man and he was glad now that he had not changed. Sharon was in his arms almost before he had the door closed. Her lips burned on his, and his tongue opened and sought the inner recesses of her mouth. Her tongue worked with his and the level of passion rose. His hands stroked her breasts until her nipples peaked. She shed her clothes deftly, removing her dress in one fell swoop. The lace bra was next, and the matching panties got in his way until she drew them off her thighs and down so that they caught on one slender ankle. She was a true blonde, this he noted before he entered her. She was a screamer. Angela made love intensely, expertly, and moved in gentle rhythm with Frank. This woman was a wild one. She shrieked in passionate pleasure as he moved strongly in and out, the motion of lust and sexual fantasy. Their coupling was over almost as soon as it had begun. Frank had used the condom and excused himself as he left the car for the shadows of the hedge. He removed the condom and threw it over the hedge, belted his pants, and took a few gulps of the crisp evening air. He thought about what had just happened, and how he had been unfaithful to his wife. The guilt overwhelmed him momentarily, but he shrugged it off and realized that he still had to drive this woman home. Sharon had dressed and was repairing her makeup when Frank re-entered the car. He sat holding the steering wheel and turned his head. Sharon slowly lifted her head and met his eyes. The spark between them returned. She was the first to look away. Frank spoke. "Sharon, I'm sorry. I didn't mean for it to go that far. Really. I'm sorry."

"Don't be sorry, Frank. I've wanted you for a very long time. It just happened, that's all."

Surprised at her reply, Frank continued. "We can't do this again. I'm married. You're married."

"You're absolutely right, Frank." With these words echoing on her lips, she reached across the seat and stroked his penis through his trousers. "You're very good. Did anyone ever tell you?"

Surprised and beginning to become aroused again, he placed his hand over hers and said, "As nice as that feels, young lady, don't you think you'd better be getting home? It's past eleven and your husband will be worried."

"Worried? Not in a million years. He's probably still on the phone or asleep on the couch in front of the television set." She became serious. "Frank, can we do this again? Maybe next time we can rent a room?"

Frank was thrown off guard. Should he begin an affair, or keep this as a wonderful chance meeting; one occasion only! Looking into those pale blue eyes, touching the perfect alabaster skin, how could he refuse? "Angela won't be back until the day before school starts, so call me?"

She smiled her delight, secure in the knowledge that her seductive charms had not failed, and this time on a man that she had fantasized over more than once. He had no idea that during one of her fabulous dinner parties, she had singled him out and imagined the two of them naked as jay birds, entangled in ecstasy while everyone around them made polite conversation and nibbled on their food. Sharon was not what she appeared. Ice, yes, but fire underneath. It was a fire that now burned brightly for Frank Corelli. Contrary to everything he believed in, Frank soon realized that he couldn't get enough of Sharon Nesbitt. They met and had sex whenever possible, trying to remain discrete but unable to control the tide of emotion that engulfed them. Frank reluctantly agreed to take her to his home, where they could make love without fear of interruption. Knowing full well what he was doing to his marriage, he was beyond redemption. Whatever fire burned within Sharon Nesbitt had totally mesmerized him. He never, ever thought of Angela during his sexual encounters, and felt little or no remorse afterwards. All he could think about was when they could meet again. Sharon enjoyed every minute and every day during the ensuing two weeks. She knew full well that they would have to cool their relationship once Angela and Christina returned, but she had no intention of breaking off the affair. She thought they would meet and be together in the future, and damn the consequences. She had done this same thing once before and the exhilaration she experienced was almost better than the sex. The sneaking, lying, and cheating were all part of the game, and she had become well versed in all aspects of a hot affair. Frank was hers and hers alone, at least for the time being.

Chapter Nine

ANGELA'S FACE LIT UP as she recognized Frank's figure threading his way through the crowd. He looked tired, and he had lost some weight. She quickly thought how that would all change now that she and Christina were home. He held her tightly in his arms, perhaps a little longer than usual. This was their second separation from one another during their twelve year marriage. He felt the love engulf him as she returned his embrace. Christina held back shyly as her parents embraced, then joined in the collective hug. She, too, noticed that her Papa looked tired, somehow older than his years. The truth of the matter was that neither one of them would ever guess that the center of their world had been engaged in extramarital activities so much so that his health was suffering.

The return trip home to Cranston took a little over two hours by car and Angela and Christina, chatted away bringing Frank up to date on their extended Italian relatives. Nona was not expected to live much longer and the two had steeled their hearts and left, tears coursing down their cheeks, knowing that they would never again see her alive. Her heart was worn out and nothing short of a miracle would keep it beating. Angela had begged to stay, but her mother had insisted that she wished her daughter to remember her as she saw her now, not lying cold and pale in a coffin. Besides, there was the fact that Christina must begin the new school year. She had looked at the pictures they had brought along a thousand times over and Angela had answered her questions again and again with great pride. She always finished their session with, "But you know, Mama it is not as beautiful as Italy." A trace of tears appeared in the old woman's eyes but pride and love shone through. Her glance would switch to Christina and she would comment, "*Bella, bella*, Angela. She is so beautiful, this granddaughter of mine."

"What's wrong, Frank?" Angela asked. "You seem so far away."

His manner became serious as he replied, "Nothing's wrong, Angela. I'm just tired. It's been a long two weeks. I've had many long and late business meetings as well as early morning meetings with the bankers and financial advisers trying to put this deal together. If the miners do strike, and it lasts as long as they expect, we have to be prepared. Corelli trucks do not stand still. We are retrofitting out trucks to carry long haul goods and the coal boxes will be kept in storage in the warehouse. We have contracts to haul lumber and container products from rail terminals and dockyards to destinations in the U.S.A. Joe and Tony are handling the labour shortage. Good drivers are hard to come by and many of ours belong to the United Mine Workers' of America, so they will be joining the picket lines. It's a helluva mess, but I think we have our end under control. We can't afford to have a cash flow interrupted while the mall is under construction. That won't bring any income to our accounts until next spring. It just might prove to be a long and lean winter."

Angela heard all of this and took it in her stride, but she still believed that there was something else; an underlying something that Frank wasn't telling her. Perhaps it was her imagination, but she definitely knew this man she had married. She allowed her emotions to slip away, promising to question him later when they were alone.

They stopped once at a gas station and restaurant combination, and ordered a light lunch as Frank downed at least four cups of coffee. Angela said, "You drink too much of that stuff, Frank. It can't be good for you."

"Stop fussing over me, Angela. Coffee is not my problem."

She was hurt by the sharp outburst and finished her sandwich, withdrawing from the conversation. Christina shared her impressions of Italy with her Papa, and Frank nodded occasionally while in truth he was only half listening. At one point, he was overcome with guilt, as images of Sharon's nudity and flamboyant sexual gyrations flashed through his mind. He shook his head and willed himself to focus upon the conversation at hand. His face gave him away, and the movement and shift in his position had not gone unnoticed. Angela was sure that he was keeping something from her. She would bide her time.

Frank's major guilt stemmed from the fact that they had done it in Angela's bed. He had not consented to this until Sharon had begged and teased him, running naked through the upstairs rooms, finally throwing herself across the expensive satin bedspread. Throwing caution to the wind, he had indulged himself to the fullest. He had to shake the thought. He actually was experiencing a male arousal. As Frank smiled at his wife, Angela caught the look of passion and her heart beat rapidly. She had missed Frank's lovemaking and the thought of him being so many thousands of miles away had only increased the longing.

They picked up Rocko from Tonio's and the dog was overcome with happiness at seeing his mistress. Christina endured a face wash, loud barking in her ear, and a frenzy of jumping up and about her heels. He jumped into the car and sat beside his mistress on the back seat. His family was back.

Was it Frank's imagination, or had Teresa Marcellus looked at him suspiciously? He shrugged it off, thinking it was just her way. In actual fact, Teresa had looked at him in just the way he had thought. Frank had no idea that he had been seen in the company of Sharon Nesbitt. Teresa had just gotten off an afternoon shift from the telephone exchange and was walking home when she passed the Inn. Frank and Sharon were walking close together, arms entwined about one another, definitely not as acquaintances but a lot more than that. The implication was there for anyone to see, and Teresa's heart ached for her dear friend Angela. She had decided that perhaps she was reading too much into the incident until she looked back and saw Frank and Sharon in a long embrace, kissing hard and passionately in the shadows afforded by the tall hedge. She had no idea what to do with the information. Her first inkling was to confront them both, accusing Frank of adultery and calling Sharon Nesbitt any number of dirty names. Instead, she did nothing. She had long suspected her own husband, Gino, of carrying on with another woman, but she was not a brave person. What if it was true and Gino chose his mistress over her and Tonio? Teresa was not a person that enjoyed living alone and she loved him far too much. She had decided long ago to let it alone. What she didn't know couldn't hurt her. Her only goal in the whole matter was to protect Tonio from the truth, if indeed it was true. She knew in her heart that it probably was, and this attributed to the sadness that often threatened to consume her.

"I've missed you so much," she said as Angela kissed her on the cheek.

"Me too. We'll meet soon and I'll tell you all about our trip. It was wonderful, but it's good to be home," Angela replied.

They were gone almost as soon as they had arrived. Teresa watched the car grow smaller and finally disappear around the corner. She shrugged her shoulders and shook her head. Should she tell Angela what she had witnessed, or keep the knowledge to herself? Teresa did not decide at that particular moment what to do. She had her own problems to contend with. Tonio was becoming a handful, staying out longer and longer and not being completely honest as to what he was doing. Gino worked shift work, and was either out drinking with his buddies or too tired to deal with a teenage son with raging hormones. Angela's problems would surface in their own time.

Chapter Ten

THE CORELLI FAMILY'S LIFE lapsed into a routine within a few weeks of their return from Italy. Christina was in grade seven at school and had been enrolled in Miss Darby's live theatre and dance classes. She had managed to convince Becka's mother that being a part of Miss Darby's school was the best thing for Becka as well. The girls learned how to walk with poise and grace, practice proper table manners, how to arrange and set an attractive dinner table, and to converse on matters of world importance. Their creativity became apparent when they were given parts in the latest play, a mystery filled with suspense, horror and murder. Becka found that she had definite talent in this area. Christina had overcome her shyness. She was able to walk down the runway with such sophistication during the Fall Fashion Show sponsored by the Women's Church Group that many of the participants found jealousy a monster difficult to disguise. She had been instrumental in putting the show together and choosing the ensembles that were loaned to the models from the different clothing outlets within the community.

The dialogue for the fashion show was created and delivered by Miss Darby in her most eloquent voice, and the show had people talking for many days afterwards. Angela had not been this enthused about anything since her return from Italy. However, their elation was not to last. A phone call from overseas came from her father. His voice breaking with emotion, he told of her mother's death. Christina attempted to comfort her mother, but within weeks Angela had begun to withdraw. Her father tried to cheer Angela, but he was much too occupied with his business dealings, as well as his chronic affair with Sharon. He had tried to break it off when Angela returned, but to no avail. His need for Sharon had only grown stronger. Now the elements of dare and intrigue added to the excitement, and the few hours they managed to share together were heightened by the fact that they were doing something not acceptable within the community. Sharon had had an affair before, but it was all very new to Frank. He had almost confessed to his brother Tony on one occasion, but decided that a moment of bragging was not worth jeopardizing the relationship.

Doing some soul searching had only brought out a small fact: Angela was withdrawing from the world. Had his affair somehow changed him in that he made love hastily and with no emotion other than a need to satisfy? In many instances he was the partner who begged off, using fatigue as an excuse. Little did his wife know that the excuse was not a lie. He was having trouble satisfying two women, so he chose Sharon as his sexual release and Angela began to fade into the background. She still attended church on a regular basis but no longer volunteered within the structure of the charities that she had once found so rewarding. Christina became worried, thinking that the problem lay with her mother's grief over the loss of Nona. In exasperation one morning she asked, "Mama, Miss Darby is swamped with work at the dance academy and theatre. I explained to her that you are able to sew just about anything when you put your mind to it. Do you think you could help us out with costumes for the play? We have to get the programs printed for opening night and rehearse at least three nights a week. Miss Darby works all day Saturday and Sunday every weekend but she can't seem to get ahead. Please Mama, come with me today."

Perhaps it was the pleading look in her daughter's eyes, or perhaps the promise of becoming occupied with something other than her home and family, but a spark of interest returned to her mother's eyes as Angela replied, "Yes, I'll come with you. If I can help in any way, I'll do my best. What time do we have to be at the theatre?"

"Ten o'clock and you can expect to be there until at least four."

"That just gives me time to prepare dinner for us. Your father will be home by five or so, he promised."

Christina's spirits lifted. It would still take a concerted effort to keep her mother's interest sharp, but bringing her out of her small world and into the community was a good start. She knew that Angela had much respect for Miss Darby and it had grown over the past few months as she witnessed the change in Christina. Now that she had been invited to become a part of the group, Angela began to see that her world had indeed become very small. Frank had become his own man, coming and going with little or no thought to her comfort or feelings. He had no idea that he was slowly destroying their relationship and only the bonds of the church and Christina were keeping them together. Angela required an outlet for her loneliness and despair. She had begun to sympathize with Teresa, knowing now how it felt to be second best.

Thank goodness for Miss Darby. Christina could not believe how her mother took to the theatre. She worked long hours on the costumes, fitting and designing many of them. Christina helped with choosing the colors and a few of her designs were worn by the cast. The mystery show was held during the weekend of Halloween and was a tremendous success. The theatre and balcony had been filled to capacity, and Becka did especially well. She had a natural talent for acting and had captured the hearts of the audience. Christina was one of the first to congratulate her on opening night. The girls had found their niche, Christina with her design and artistic ability and Becka in expressing her emotions on stage. Tonio had somehow faded into the background, his interests lying in making money, playing pool, drinking beer and hanging out, or cruising the streets trying to pick up girls. Becka remained convinced that he was still the boy for her, but she was too young to be out late at night and could not participate in activities not approved by her parents. She wished that she was at least seventeen, but that wouldn't happen for at least three years. Tonio was fifteen, almost sixteen, and was getting a bad reputation. Christina said, "Becka, I think I saw Tonio in the audience tonight."

"Really, well I hope he didn't find the performance too boring. Was he alone? Or was he with that awful Cynthia? The one that goes out with any boy who asks her and does who knows what until the wee hours of the morning?"

Christina answered, "I couldn't see. I think he was actually there with his parents. I did see Mrs. Marcellus in the lobby at intermission but I didn't speak to her. My mother stopped to chat for a minute. Why do you think he would bring Cynthia to our show? I hear he only takes her to the drive-in theatre and out to the Big Pond for a big night out."

"Thanks a lot. That really makes me feel good. Everyone knows what happens at drive-in theatres and out at the Big Pond." Her words were filled with much emotion; sarcastic and bitter to say the least. "Change the subject please, Christina. I don't want to talk about or even think about Tonio Marcellus ever again."

* * * * *

Two Years Later

"MOTHER, CAN YOU DO me up? My zipper's stuck." Christina called from the upstairs landing. Angela put down her sewing as she replied, "I'll be right there, dear."

Christina was fast approaching her sixteenth birthday and had been invited to the prom. She was only in grade ten, but her personality and poise made her appear to be older than her years. She was very tall, hopefully reaching her full height of five foot nine inches. She towered over most of her young teenage admirers and had reluctantly agreed to attend the dance with a very nice boy, who was the same height as Christina, so long as she didn't wear heels. Angela had argued that high heels made a young girl look out of place and wouldn't allow her to wear them. The dress she had made was one of Christina's design, and in 1956 it was all the rage to wear a dress with a fitted bodice, tiny straps, and a voluminous skirt with a net can-can slip underneath. The deep green chiffon was breathtaking against her golden complexion and enhanced the depth of the color in her incredible emerald eyes. Christina's eyebrows and eyelashes were darker than her hair, which had been streaked golden by the warm rays of the sun. June had been unseasonably warm and the family had spent much time outdoors. Her mother had bought her tiny dress flats and they had covered them in the same material as the dress. Christina was only too happy to wear them, knowing full well that she would be at least the same height as her date. David Foster had emerged as a very nice looking young man after puberty had set in. Before that he had just been another skinny, pimply-faced boy who sat behind her in class and tormented her at every turn. He had the locker next to hers and Becka's, and on many occasions had left notes squeezed between the cracks of the locker door. Finally he had mustered his courage and asked her to the prom. Much to his surprise, Christina had agreed. Now she wasn't so sure. She didn't have any real feelings for David, other than as a friend, but going out on a very important date would put their relationship on a different level. She was determined not to change their friendship status. Her mother had cautioned her as to what boys were all about, and to avoid being alone with one for any length of time. Safety in numbers was the best advice Angela could come up with, though her own courtship and romance with Christina's differed so much.

"Well, I'm ready, mother."

Frank was home for a change and as he glanced up from his newspaper he could not take his eyes from the beautiful young woman coming down the stairs. Was this his daughter? She moved with such grace and elegance, the dress affording the final touch, that it took his breath away. His pride shone in his eyes as he said, "Is that my little girl? You look incredibly beautiful."

"I'm not a little girl, Papa, or haven't you noticed?" The mischief was all too apparent in her tone.

"I should say you're not. When did all this happen?" he asked

"Under your very nose, Frank Corelli," said Angela. "Now, go and answer the door. It must be Christina's date."

Frank opened the door to a very shy, nicely dressed young man. "Good evening, sir, I'm here to pick up Christina."

"Come in, my boy," Frank gestured. The young man stepped over the threshold and was amazed at the opulence of the home. Christina stood poised at the base of the stairs, while her mother came through the hallway with her wrap. David handed Christina a beautiful yellow rose corsage, knowing beforehand that her dress was green. This information had come from Becka. Angela pinned the corsage on the dress, securing it with the pearl studded pin, before she said, "Will you take just a minute, dear? I'd like to take a few pictures. You both look so wonderful. How about one alone with your father? Come on, Frank, stand a little closer, put your arm around her."

Frank did as instructed, his pride in his daughter all too apparent. Then David and Christina posed for Angela. Finally, David took the last picture of Christina with her parents. "Mother, we'll be late. No more pictures! We have to go."

David took the advice to heart as Frank stated, "No later than midnight, young man. And drive carefully."

"Yes sir, I will. Fine sir, I'll have her home by midnight."

They were gone. The house felt empty. Frank studied his wife of seventeen years, taking a long look at her, as though he had just discovered her all over again. She was still very attractive, a striking woman, and he felt long-hidden emotions welling inside. Angela was quiet after the couple had left. She felt a little old. Here was her little girl, almost a grown woman, out on a very important date. A change came over her face. Her shoulders slumped as she walked to the kitchen to get a fresh cup of coffee. Frank watched her figure retreat and he was overcome with such guilt that he had to sit down. What the hell had he been doing for the past few years? That goddamned Sharon had taken over his life. His wife and daughter needed him, especially his wife. There was the operative word: Wife! He vowed to break it off as soon as possible. No doubt Sharon would move on. Her husband turned a blind eye to her extracurricular activities and couldn't give a damn what she did with her spare time, so long as she was the gracious hostess for his elaborate business dinners. She was deprived of companionship and a soul mate. Hell, their relationship could be best described as an intimate business partnership, so Frank had been an easy outlet. He would tell her tomorrow.

Chapter Eleven

THEIR ARRIVAL AT THE dance did not go unnoticed. A young man of eighteen lounged beside the buffet along the east wall of the gymnasium watching the new arrivals. He was new to the community, his father being Dr. William Carmichael, a new partner added to the growing clinical practice in Cranston. Adam could not take his eyes off the tall, willowy young woman who had entered on the arm of a rather nondescript partner. She was in a class by herself. He vowed that he would meet her before the evening ended.

David took Christina's wrap and checked it. They joined a group of friends already waiting on the sidelines for the band to begin playing. A glass of punch was pressed into Christina's hand and she welcomed the distraction, still feeling a little embarrassed at the stir their entrance had caused. Her mother's catching dress design had been a definite success. From time to time her old shyness would encompass her and she would have to steel herself to stand tall and not stammer. As Christina surveyed the room, she made eye contact with a very good-looking stranger who was obviously studying her every move. He was tall, a quality she always took note of first, but he also had sandy, slightly red hair and his eyes were a pale grey-blue. His face was thin, rather long, but with strong lips and perfect jaw line. She could not take her eyes from him ... until finally David broke the spell when he asked if she would care to dance. The band had started up opening with a brisk fox trot, and the room came alive with swirling figures as couples stepped lively and in sync with the music. The attractive stranger did not dance with anyone; Christina noticed rather gladly that he had not chosen anyone other than herself.

What a strange thought! She was David's date for the evening, but he would not be one to monopolize her time if she was asked to dance with someone else. After the first round of dances, David found them a quiet corner to sit out the lively polka, all of the crowd waiting for the new Rock & Roll Jive to be played. They were not disappointed. The next round of dances left everyone in higher spirits and slightly out of breath. Glad of a reprieve, Christina sipped her glass of punch, and over the rim of her glass she made eye contact again with the newcomer. David followed her glance and commented, "That's the new doctor's kid, just moved to town. No one seems to know much about him, only that he will be graduating at the end of June. He transferred here from the city. He sure seems interested in you, Christina."

She answered, "I don't think so. But still, he is making me feel a little uncomfortable as he keeps staring at us. Why don't we just ignore him for the time being? Perhaps he'll forget about us."

"Good idea," David replied, and they turned their attention to the friends in their immediate circle. "Why isn't Becka here tonight?"

"She has a bad case of the flu and her father finally put his foot down and ordered her to rest in bed. She was not looking forward to this dance because Tonio would not be here. I don't think she'll ever get over him."

Sally added, "I saw him out with Cynthia last night. I don't think Becka has a chance unless she agrees to play fast and loose, if you get my meaning."

Her date nodded in agreement. Christina felt badly for Becka, knowing the depth of emotion that kept her hoping that someday Tonio would notice her as a female companion and not as a childhood tomboy friend. She had almost given up in despair and had dated a few of the boys from her class. They paled in comparison to Tonio; he was by far the best-looking boy in school. Becka was no slouch in the looks department but she would not cheapen herself just to gain his attention. Christina had promised to deliver a blow by blow description of the dance; especially who had paired up with whom and what the girls were wearing.

David had disappeared momentarily as the band began to play a slow waltz. She felt someone by her side and turned to find herself in the company of the stranger. He said, "You are, Christina Corelli, by far the best looking girl in this room. Will you dance with me?"

"Only if you tell me your name," Christina could think of nothing else to say. "That's easy. My name is Adam Carmichael ... now will you dance with me?"

He encircled her waist with one arm and expertly held her with the other. She pulled away from the closeness of the dance, keeping her head a few inches from his shoulder. He was actually taller than she was; she thought he must be at least six feet. The music was having a definite effect upon them both. Chemistry was happening; she had never felt so alive. They moved in unison, almost instinctively in rhythm, slow stepping, their bodies finally moulding to one another. Christina fitted perfectly to his frame, and his male physique was that of a mature young man, not a boy. She looked up as their eyes met. He did not speak; he was afraid to break the spell. Christina was aware that her heart had accelerated and she was almost breathless. She knew her color was high, but somehow it didn't matter. Had she come home, safe and secure, in this stranger's arms? She wondered where that thought had come from. He smiled and a shock went through her body, right down to her toes. She smiled back, saying nothing. Finally, after the first waltz came to an end, he held her hand and they strolled slowly around the dance floor until the next waltz began. The feeling that coursed through that hand contact was absolutely amazing. She had held hands with boys before, but never with this effect. What was happening to her? She suddenly wished Becka was there so she could rush to the powder room and share her thoughts. Was this what Becka felt for Tonio?

"Are you going steady, Christina?" he asked. "No, I'm not. David and I are just good friends."

"Thank goodness for that, because I really hate to have to share you with anyone."

Before replying she thought how he certainly didn't waste any time, then said, "That remains to be seen. I'm really not interested in keeping steady company."

"Then I'll just have to change your mind, now, won't I?" He smiled again and she was compelled to meet his eyes. For an instant she became dizzy and lost her step. His strong arms tightened their hold and she regained the rhythm of the dance. They did not speak further. David stood on the sidelines watching as the love of his life, although she did not know it, became lost to him forever. He witnessed firsthand their growing attraction, and couldn't help but admire how well they looked together. This Adam Carmichael had stolen his Christina, just when he thought he had finally made some headway. The evening still belonged to David and Christina, and he decided to cut in on the couple. "Excuse me, Christina, mind if I reclaim my date?" This was addressed to Adam.

The reply was, "Yes, I do actually, but I see I have no choice." To Christina, he said, "I'll see you later."

The contact was broken and Christina experienced a sharp loss as she changed partners. David's presence held no magic, no pull as their bodies moved together in unison as old friends. Now she knew the difference. She danced with David one more time before they rejoined the group in the corner. Sally slyly asked her, "Who was that dreamboat you were dancing with, or are you going to keep him all to yourself?"

Christina, a little miffed by the implication, answered, "His name is Adam Carmichael and his father is Doctor Carmichael. They just moved here a week ago and he thought it would be a good idea to meet the graduating class before the end of June. He seems really nice."

"I noticed he couldn't take his eyes off you."

"Don't be silly. I'm David's date and I just couldn't leave him in the lurch for a complete stranger," Christina said, hoping that Sally would change the subject.

It never happened. She quickly surveyed the room and sure enough, Adam was watching them from the far side of the room. Christina wished that he would dance with someone else so she could regain her composure. Butterflies were dancing in her stomach and her knees felt weak. She sat down on the bench against the wall and arranged the voluminous can-can slip under the heavy taffeta skirt; anything to take her mind off of her raging emotions. Her mother had not prepared her for anything like this. David was at her side and they began another round of dancing. For some reason she wished the dance would end, but then again, she longed to be held in Adam's arms, whirling about the dance floor, a circle of emotion generated by two people brought together by fate. The band took a break and a light buffet lunch was served. Christina looked about the room but could not see Adam anywhere. Perhaps he had left. No, there he was, just coming back into the gymnasium with two other fellows. This time he paid no attention to her or the group she was with, and she was definitely disappointed. Lunch over, the tables were cleared and the dancing resumed. A hand on her elbow sent an electric shock through her body as a voice spoke softly in her ear. "I told you I would see you later. May I have this dance, Christina?"

Without a word, she found herself in his arms. The emotion was even more intense and their eyes locked as the lights in the gym were lowered. The music played softly, enveloping them in the rhythm. The striated brilliantly lit ball above them sent myriads of light darting past them, coming to rest as fluorescent polka-dots on the dance floor, and the couples locked in motion. The magic of the dance was almost hypnotic and when the music ended abruptly, she was reluctant to leave the warmth of Adam's embrace. Before the lights were turned up, impulsively he bent his head. She returned his kiss without realizing that her emotions were betraying her and she had lost her usual composure. The soft contact of his lips as they moved with hers made her head spin and they momentarily forgot that they were in the middle of the dance floor. David saw the embrace and his face fell. The full realization hit him and he had never felt so helpless. She would never look at him that way, not in a million years. David glanced at the time and as the final half hour of the dance wore on, he finally claimed Christina from Adam's arms for the last set. Christina was extremely quiet on the drive home. David had attempted to pull her close beside him on the front seat as they drove to her house, but Christina resisted. She had meant to discourage David at all costs, and meeting Adam only reinforced her resistance. He was very disappointed, but knew in his heart that this was probably the one and only date that they would ever share. He fervently hoped for a good night kiss, but it never happened. Christina had thanked him, gave him a soft brush of her lips on his cheek, and was out of the car before he could offer to walk her to the front door. He sat there for quite some time, the letdown eating him alive. Finally, he put the car in gear and drove slowly down the driveway, through the elaborate brick and wrought-iron gates, and swung the car in the direction of his neighbourhood. He would remain Christina's friend, he could not bring himself to cut her off completely. He would admire her from afar, secure in the knowledge that he had once dated Christina Corelli.

Christina did not call Becka when she entered the house that evening; for some reason she did not wish to share her emotions just yet. Her thoughts were too private and full of great expectations. Adam

Carmichael was the love of her life, and the idea scared and thrilled her both at the same time. She did not wish to voice her thoughts, thinking that perhaps this would dampen her spirits or dull the emotion. She spent a few minutes downstairs with her mother, explaining that the dance had been wonderful, everyone enjoyed themselves and it had been over all too soon. Angela was relieved that she was home on time as Frank had stated, but she did detect a light in Christina's eyes that mystified her. Knowing full well her ties to David were just friendship, Angela wanted to question the girl, but Christina didn't give her the chance. She feigned tiredness, when in truth she was so wound up that she knew she wouldn't fall asleep for many hours. Within minutes she was under the covers, the moonlight streaming into the room through the open window. She shook her head to clear the raging scenes, fantasizing about things that were better left unspoken. She had, on a few occasions, imagined herself in the arms of a young man, actually making love with total abandon. The young man no longer was faceless. It was Adam Carmichael that held her lovingly, encircling her and covering her body with his weight. She was suddenly very warm under the light blanket and threw it off. She punched and rearranged the pillows, tossed and turned for another hour and finally fell asleep, to dream the remainder of the evening into the early dawn.

She promised she would call Becka first thing in the morning, a little guilty that her best friend was not feeling well and had missed the most memorable night of Christina's life. She would make it up to Becka.

Chapter Twelve

WHEN CHRISTINA AWOKE ON Sunday morning she decided to take Rocko for a walk to the Big Pond. He was twelve years old and no longer spry, but he continued to enjoy attention from his mistress. Her parents were in good spirits, talking and laughing over breakfast. Her mother decided that early mass would have to wait, as they were expecting company before lunch. The object of the meeting was to plan a surprise. Christina had not seen her parents so talkative and attentive to one another in a very long time. She hoped it would continue, as her mother had languished for many months occupying herself with mundane tasks, almost as though she were marking time. Christina decided that it was all too grown-up and complicated for her to worry about. She said very little about the dance, reported upon the crowd, what the chaperones wore, and other usual stuff that always satisfied her mother's curiosity. She said nothing about Adam. For the time being she intended to keep the magic of their meeting and strong attraction for one another a secret. She hugged the knowledge as she went over the scenes one by one relishing the hidden meaning in a look, a glance, a compliment, and then storing each anecdote away for future reference. The walk to the Pond took longer than usual, but Christina didn't mind. She knew Rocko's days were numbered and only wished to make them as pleasant and comfortable for him as possible. Last winter had been extra hard on the old dog. His joints stiffened and became chronically sore; the veterinarian had urged them to put him down, but Christina didn't have the heart. She gave him his medication for arthritis daily and he lay in the sunshine warming his body whenever the opportunity arose. They met no one on the walk, as it was still quite early. Upon her return, she realized that she must call Becka as she had promised.

"Hi, Becka it's me. Are you feeling better? Is it okay if I come over?"

"Christina, yes, I'm not contagious. Dad just made me get more rest than I probably needed. You've got to fill me in on the dance. I'm dying to hear all about it. See you in a bit."

The girls found that chatting on the telephone wasn't nearly as much fun as day-dreaming in the privacy of one another's totally overcrowded bedrooms. Christina still rode her bicycle when she needed to get over the small acreage to Becka's across town. Rocko did not lift his head when she passed him in the yard. He laid quite content on the front verandah against one of the large round columns, a favourite place he had chosen for himself.

"Well, how was your date with David?" Becka asked, expecting some little tidbit. "Oh, David. It wasn't anything, really."

"So I'm dying to know. Was Tonio at the dance? Was he with anyone?" Christina saw the despair in her eyes, fully expecting a yes to both questions.

"No he wasn't there. But Cynthia was there so that means that at least Tonio wasn't out with her."

"What about David? Did you kiss him goodnight?" "No, I told you, we are just friends."

"Christina Corelli. I know you too well. Something about you has changed. I don't know what it is, but you look different." Becka had put her finger on it.

"Okay, you win. I met the most incredible guy at the dance. No, you don't know him because he just moved to town. He is two years older than I am, because he said he is graduating with the class at the end of the month. His father is the new doctor in town"

"So, what else?" Becka prompted.

"So, early into the evening he came over and introduced himself, having asked my name in advance from someone. He almost pulled me away from David and we danced a sensational slow dance. He didn't pull me close until the third waltz, but when he did, I can't explain what happened. It was as though we were the only two people in the room. No one else mattered. I didn't want the music to stop or the dance to end, not ever. Becka, I think I'm in love."

Becka gasped. She hadn't expected such a burst of emotion from Christina. She stared at her as though she had encountered a stranger sitting on her bed. "How can you be in love in a matter of hours? Are you absolutely sure of this?"

"I think so, Becka. I have to see him again to see if this feeling is real. I didn't get much sleep last night. I kept going over and over in my mind the way he looked at me, the things he said. No one has been that attentive to me ever before."

"Maybe it's just a line. You know how these older guys are. We've heard how older guys have a line just to get a girl going. You know what I mean."

Christina continued. "He's at least three inches taller than I am, and when we danced, I fit snugly under his chin and against his chest. Our feet moved in perfect rhythm; it appeared as though I were floating. I can't describe it. I just knew I belonged there. Do you understand Becka?"

"I understand, all right. I have to see this Adam for myself. You haven't even described him. What does he look like?"

"Actually I don't think it would matter, but he is very good looking. He has light sandy red hair, and his eyes are the lightest blue grey, soft and teasing and penetrating, as if they are looking right into my soul and reading my thoughts, God forbid."

"I guess I'll have to be content with that ... a tall stranger, with blue gray penetrating eyes," Becka teased.

The subject changed to what everyone was wearing. Becka's dress would have to wait to be worn on another occasion. The ravages of the influenza attack showed in the prominent dark circles under her violet eyes. She was still a little pale, but no longer tired. They dressed in T-shirts, shorts, bobby socks, and saddle shoes the craze of the month. Christina was preoccupied throughout the remainder of the morning. They parted company around noon, and Christina made her way back home. She rode her bicycle slowly through the main street, stopping to gaze into the department store windows. The council had beautified the street by planting shady trees along the wide sidewalks. They were in full leaf and added a final touch to the street improvements. The town of Cranston promised to remain clean and beautiful with sustained growth, keeping up with its growing pains as new industries and businesses found a niche within the community. She loved her town.

Later that afternoon, Christina and Becka decided to wander over to the local fast food outlet. A&W had come to town and it had become the local hangout for all the kids. They found a comfortable booth and sipped on the tall iced mugs of root beer. Suddenly, Christina stopped talking, her lips suspended as she lowered her head. "What? Why did you stop talking?" Becka asked.

"It's him. It's Adam. How do I look? Is my hair mussed?" "For goodness sakes, get a grip Christina. Where is he?"

"He's just coming in with half the football team. Oh God, Becka, he's coming over."

The high flush that appeared and painted Christina's cheeks only heightened her beauty and the excitement shone in her eyes as Adam strolled over to their booth as a young man with a purpose. "Hello again, Christina. And who might this be?" His eyes were on Becka.

Her mouth hung open. She stammered something that sounded like, "You must be Adam.

Christina told me she met someone new at the dance last night."

He motioned to the group he had come in with and they seated themselves across the room in another row of booths. Adam slid deftly into the booth and his body rested against the warmth of Christina's. He turned and looked into her eyes. Becka watched in fascination as she was made a spectator, since they forgot she was across from them in the crowded booth. She cleared her throat and attempted conversation. Finally she said to no one in particular, "I'm just going to the washroom, I'll be back shortly." Christina nodded and Adam ignored her.

"How about coming out for a drive with me tonight, Christina? We can watch the baseball game and then come here for a hamburger afterwards." He smiled and it went right down to her toes.

"I don't know if I should. I really don't know you that well now, do I? Besides, I promised Becka we'd do something together tonight."

He was ready for her excuse. "We'll bring Becka along. How about if I bring along a blind date for her, or just bring one of the guys, and they can keep one another company? The main thing is that we would spend time together. I promise we won't be alone if that's what's worrying you."

She had to admit, he had all the angles covered. She nodded, unable to answer, believing that her voice had deserted her. They focused upon the approaching figure of Becka and waited until she was seated opposite until they asked, "Would you like to come for a drive tonight and watch the baseball game with us, Becka? Adam says he'll bring along one of his friends, if that's all right with you." She kicked Becka under the table and gave her a severe look. A look that said, Say yes, or I'll be really angry with you.

Becka had dated any number of boys but still kept her options open for Tonio, so she had no problem with keeping company with one on a friendly basis. She said, "It sounds okay with me. What time will you two pick me up?"

Adam rose from the seat and said, "How about six o'clock? The game starts then, but we don't have to stay for the whole nine innings." Before Christina could answer, he said, "Don't worry, I know where you live. I'll see you then."

Perhaps it was a good thing that Christina was seated because she blurted out that her knees were like jelly and probably wouldn't support her if she attempted to stand. Becka was impressed. He was certainly smooth, this Adam Carmichael. She could actually see why Christina was so taken by him. They suited one another. Becka couldn't put her finger on why she thought this, but it just popped into her head. The girls studied the guys from afar, not looking directly at them but glanced over between sips and whispered conversation until they had finished their drinks. It was well into the afternoon when they left the A&W, Christina on her bicycle, which suddenly made her appear quite infantile, or so she thought, and Becka on hers. At the end of the main street they each turned to go their respective ways with a "See you tonight."

Thus began a summer of a young love that becomes the envy of all who have never experienced it. Adam did not rush her; instead, he kept his intentions in check. They included him within their circle and he entertained them with stories of his former home.

Chapter Thirteen

CHRISTINA EXPLAINED TO HER mother that she had met some new friends and that they were going out for a drive and would probably take in the ball game. Angela asked, "Will your father and I get to meet these new friends of yours?"

"I expect so. Becka will be along as well so I won't be alone. You needn't worry, Mother."

She had taken to calling her Mama by the more formal term Mother, as Miss Darby had insisted it was a sign of respect. She still called her father by his pet name, Papa. She fully intended for them to meet Adam and pass judgment because, in spite of her own instant attraction, she felt that she needed a detached impression of him. Whether their objections, if any, would be taken into consideration, well that was a different matter. Christina realized that a two year difference in their ages, especially at this stage of development, would be a challenge, and with his city-wise ways, she was a little intimidated. She would have to establish the ground rules for their dates. She laughed inwardly; she believed that they would become a couple, and that this was not just a casual date.

As the time approached for Adam to collect her, she had tried on everything in her closet at least twice over. She had called Becka to ask what she was going to wear, and the answer was "the usual." Christina had to make the best impression ever, so she chose a soft, short sleeved sweater with a matching cardigan, which would protect her from the chill of the evening air. She decided on a fitted skirt, which flared out at the bottom four inches in box pleats and allowed the illusion of a sensual sway to her walk. The usual bobby socks and saddle shoes, which were cleaned and polished to perfection, added the finishing touch. She decided to tie her long hair back in a pony tail secured with the latest fashion statement, white fur pom-poms. She was pleased with the effect. The skirt was a break from the norm as most of her crowd wore blue jeans, rolled up just below calf level. She added a touch of color to her lips, smoothed out her eyebrows, gave her bangs a final comb through and was ready for her date fifteen minutes early. Seven o'clock arrived and so did Adam. She was totally impressed as she watched the strange car cruise along the driveway. It was a deep turquoise blue 1956 Ford Monarch, the newest model with all of the trimmings. Lots of chrome and white-walled tires enhanced the unusual color. Adam was a perfect gentleman, impressing her parents to no end. Her father was a little sceptical until Adam told him he would be entering University in the fall as a Pre-med student. Angela was happy to learn that he came from an excellent family, being that his father was the newest doctor to move to their community. Throughout the introductions and questioning Christina had stayed in the background, saying nothing. Her shyness had returned and she felt like pinching herself to see if she was dreaming. Finally they left the house, her parents waving from the porch.

Another young man was waiting in the car for them as they approached. He opened the passenger door and got out. "Hi Christina, I'm Steve."

She nodded a hello and slid onto the luxurious white leather seat. Steve got in beside her and they sped away. They swung by to pick up Becka, and Christina could see that Steve was quite impressed with Becka's striking good looks. He was no slouch in this department but Christina only had eyes for one man: the driver. Within an hour they were talking and laughing as though they had known one another for a long time. Becka relaxed in Steve's company in the back seat and Christina had been persuaded to remain in the center of the front seat, her shoulder just making contact with Adam's arm as he drove along the road to the ball field. They stayed at the game for an hour or so until someone suggested they might grab a bite to eat at the drive-in. No one wanted to leave the camaraderie of the car so they decided to order curbside. Adam was very attentive; he catered to Christina's every need. She was almost embarrassed at the attention and wished for the cloak of darkness. So did Adam. He bent his head close to her ear and whispered, "I can't wait until it gets dark. Then I can kiss you without an audience from the back seat."

Her heart did a flip-flop but she met his glance straight on and smiled. Whether he took this as an invitation, his arm slid across the back of the seat and she was pulled even closer to his side. It felt good. She could not describe the surging emotion, but it felt as though she had come home. She belonged there. The evening wore on and Christina and Adam did do some light necking, not heavy enough for him to make a pass. She had enjoyed the fact that she did not have to fight him off, which she had experienced on previous dates. Becka and Steve were also getting along very well and Christina was surprised because she knew in her heart that it would take a lot for Becka to forget her loyalty to Tonio. Christina didn't think Becka owed Tonio anything.

By ten p.m. the party of four was tired. The girls had to be in by ten thirty. They decided to drop Becka off first, then swing around and take Christina home. For a brief moment she wished that Adam would take Steve home and then leave her off last, but then again she did not trust herself to be entirely alone with him in the car on their first date. He seemed to know exactly how to treat her; not too demanding, not pawing her, just being together. She hadn't enjoyed herself so much in a very long time. He decided not to walk her to the door but promised to call the next day. Christina had set the ground rules until school was out. There would be no dates during the week until exams were over and they would finally be out of school for summer vacation.

Her mother met her at the door. Angela was delighted that Christina had found someone so suited to her daughter. His manners had been impeccable, but not too smooth. Christina gave her mother a rundown of where they had been and Angela was satisfied that the young man had been a perfect gentleman.

Becka called, and the two girls chatted from their bedrooms. Steve was a lot of fun. Although he wasn't Tonio, he just might be all right for the summer months. Tonio was working at the bike shop after school and hustling pool in the evenings. He had taken to wearing a black leather jacket, and combed his hair in the latest ducktail cut. Becka didn't like the change; she preferred Steve's brush cut to brylcreamed perfectly groomed locks. Tonio dressed in blue jeans and a white T-shirt and blended in with his crowd.

"Do you think Tonio noticed us when we drove by the pool hall?" she asked.

"I didn't notice, and neither should you," Christina admonished. "If he cared so much for you then he would be around more, don't you think?"

"I don't think my parents care too much for Tonio anymore. His reputation is getting quite bad and my Dad always hears the latest rumours from his clinic receptionist. She's quite the gossip."

"What do you think of Adam? Wasn't he just too much?"

"Oh yes, too much. I think you'd better take it easy in the feelings department. You both have it pretty bad."

"I'll talk to you tomorrow. Good night, Becka." "'Night, Chris."

July first saw the foursome attend the Miners' Picnic and Christina tasted her first bottle of beer. She had been brought up on wine, and the beer was a new experience. After two bottles she was light-headed and silly, the warm summer sunshine adding to her dizziness. Becka urged her to eat something as that would help offset the effects of the alcohol. Adam was only too happy to see her let down her hair. He asked her, "Do you think we can be alone tonight? Let's take Steve and Becka home early. Then it's just you and me, what do you say?"

Before she realized the implications of his question, she answered, "Sounds good to me."

His eyes filled with passion, and it was all he could do to not crush her in his arms right then and there as the crowd pressed past them. Knowing the promise she had made, for the remainder of the day they acted as though they shared a big secret. That evening, as promised, Becka and Steve were dropped off at nine and Adam and Christina had an hour to share, alone at last. He drove out to the Big Pond. The community had improved the pond of her childhood. A paved road now encircled the lake pond; the large poplar trees were left as sentries to guard the groomed paths and grassy slopes. Sand had been trucked in and a good-sized beach sporting a long wooden dock had been constructed. It barely resembled the dark waters and weedy bottom of the old site that had nearly taken her life. She no longer dreaded coming out to the Pond. A few cars were parked along the lakefront and couples were drinking and necking. Soft music played from the car radios as windows were opened to allow the fresh night air to drift through the car interiors. Adam opened the sun roof of his car. They moved the seat back and reclined to gaze up at the stars. The silence was choking her. If he didn't take her in his arms soon, she would make the first move. He must have read her mind. She found herself pressed to him, her body pinned against his wide chest. He kissed her forehead, her lips, and her neck, and began to plant soft kisses at her throat and neckline. The blouse she wore buttoned in the front and he was slowly undoing one button at a time, their eyes locked in shared passion. Her lips quivered as she attempted to brush his hand away from her breast, but it felt so good. A raging fire was burning within her and she did not want him to stop. A voice from somewhere within finally made her pull away. Adam released her with a groan. "Do you have any idea what you're doing to me?"

"I know it's hard. But Adam, I just can't. It's not right."

"Christina, you know how I feel about you. I love you. What's not right?"

"I didn't mean that." Her heart absorbed the words and locked them in memory forever. How could something, which felt so right, be so wrong? She wondered. She knew other girls had gone all the way, but Christina could not bring herself to take the step. Adam got out of the car, and she welcomed the reprieve. She straightened her clothing, fixed her hair, and applied fresh lipstick. She watched as Adam walked along the dock, the glow from his cigarette rising and falling as he relaxed. She decided to join him. They walked to the far end of the dock; no one else was there. They did not speak. Adam did not put his arm around her as they sat together at the end of the dock. He didn't trust himself to be able to keep his emotions in check. Abruptly he got up, took her by the hand and said, "I have to take you home now, Christina Corelli, or I swear I won't be responsible for my actions."

She nodded, unable to speak, and followed him wordlessly as he pulled her along the dock. They drove to her home in silence. He did kiss her long and hard, then almost roughly pushed her out of the car and drove away faster than usual. She didn't care. Adam loved her and she loved him. That was all that mattered. This knowledge she would keep to herself. Later she would share her secret with Becka.

It promised to be a very long hot summer, and with her emotions running high, Christina believed that in her mind, she would be able to resist the final temptation. But would her body betray her?

Chapter Fourteen

A WEEK PASSED AND CHRISTINA heard nothing from Adam. Had she done something wrong? Was he seeing someone else? Had Becka been out with Steve and Adam? The answers to all of the questions came up as a definite no. They were well into another week of hot summer weather when Adam re-appeared. His explanation was that he had returned to the city with his parents to make permanent arrangements for his entrance into University. Open house had been held and his classes were now set. Tuition had been paid and his marks had been excellent. His life was all planned out for the next seven or so years. Christina was disheartened at the news. Adam would be leaving come September and the possibility of a long distance romance became very bleak. He promised her fervently that he would write as often as he could, and he would be home for all of the long weekend vacations. She put everything out of her mind, deciding to deal with his absence when the time came. Becka continued to spend time with Steve and they had become good friends. She spoke of Tonio less and less and Christina actually believed that her best friend had gotten over Tonio Marcellus.

The long weekend of August was to be a huge surprise, but Christina had inadvertently overheard her parents secretly planning Christina's sixteenth birthday celebration. Her relatives from Toronto, Guido and Maria Corelli, along with their family, would be flying out for the event. Her mother had a week to hire a caterer, rent an outdoor white tent and furniture, as well as have a professional gardener arrange huge urns of fresh flowers placed categorically so as to complement the ambience of the outdoor affair. Christina had no idea that the party planned in her favour was to become so lavish. She had always enjoyed her birthday parties, but this was almost a coming-out party.

The population of Cranston had swelled to sixteen thousand and was becoming a very popular tourist destination, as well as an economically viable place to live and raise a family. This was thanks to the Corelli brothers and a downtown business association who had vision. She was no longer as intensely involved with Miss Darby's theatre group but she kept up her design and drawing. This was a release from the tension that was building between her and Adam. She had tried not to be alone with him on most occasions but he had managed to arrange a few of their dates so that they could be alone. He had promised to come to her party, realizing that it was intended to be one of the most important days of her life.

Early Saturday morning, the dawn of her sixteenth birthday, promised to be bright and sunny. Christina had slept fitfully. She had tossed and turned throughout the long night, going over in her mind her date with Adam. Over and over again she recalled the longing in his voice as he said, "Christina, how can we keep going on this way? You know I love you. Why can't we make love?"

She had almost surrendered, her heart torn apart by his desperate need. He had been angry, unable to understand why she would not succumb. So much for her high moral standards; he was definitely wearing her down, and she was afraid she would lose him if she continued to resist. She just had to talk to someone. She walked over to Becka's that morning, promising her mother that she wouldn't be gone too long. By ten a.m. the large expanse of back lawn and garden was swarming with professional people. The patio was being transformed into a floral paradise, with colourful lights strung effectively in order to afford the guests room to move about with ease. Her father had suggested installing a swimming pool, but with the climate being what it was in the area, he had changed his mind. They really were as wealthy as everyone said. Christina cared less about money, never having had to worry about the lack of it. Her clothes were no fancier or expensive than her friends', and she never put on airs as to what her parents had recently purchased or were about to purchase. It just didn't matter.

Becka greeted her warmly. "Hi, Chris, what's up? You sounded a little upset on the phone.

By the way, happy birthday."

"Thanks, Becka. I just came over to talk to you about Adam. If you thought our feelings for one another were intense when we first met, you should know that they were nothing compared to what we feel now. I can't stand being apart from him. It's as simple as that. I hate when he drops me off and I have to spend the night alone."

"It sounds like you really are in love with him."

"Sounds like? I never want to spend time with anyone else, ever."

Becka did not miss the despair and longing in Christina's voice. She decided to let her talk it all out. "Go ahead, I'm listening."

"I know he wants us to make love, and I know how he suffers after we've been making out.

I don't know how much longer I can hold out. I feel so sorry for him."

"Sorry for him … that sounds pretty lame as a reason to make love." Becka was unsure of her territory, not having made out with a boy as of yet. She still maintained that Tonio Marcellus was the man for her and she would bide her time.

"It's hard to explain. I guess what I'm really afraid of is that if we do go all the way, then he will no longer find me interesting and will move on."

"You really don't believe that he loves you?"

"Oh, yes I do, but then I have these guilty feelings and I doubt him. It's gotten so that we begin a date on a happy note and part a few hours later so miserable and frustrated that I wonder if it's all worthwhile."

"What's all worthwhile?"

"You know … remaining a virgin."

"I think we had better change the subject before you make a very important decision and blame me for pushing you in the wrong direction. Whatever you decide, it has to remain your decision, yours and Adam's. I just can't be a part of this, Christina."

"I understand, Becka … thanks for listening. I'll see you at six. By the way, your dress is lovely."

She walked aimlessly in the direction of home, meeting a few people along the way as she stopped to window shop downtown. She returned home at lunchtime and managed to pinch a few canapés from the catering trays left cooling in the refrigerator. The gap left by her pilfering she rearranged by moving the canapés further apart on the tray. Angela was in her glory. She called from the back yard, "Christina, is that you? Come meet your Aunt Maria. Your father and uncle have gone downtown to make some last minute arrangements."

Her Aunt Maria could not disguise her open admiration of the beautiful, tall, willowy young woman standing before her, a shy smile transforming her face. "Is this really my little niece, Christina?" She kissed Christina on both cheeks, hugging her at the same time. "I just can't believe it. She is so attractive."

Angela had long gotten over Christina's beauty by living with it on a daily basis, and was not surprised by Maria's remarks. Instead she said to her daughter, "I hired Miss Darby to come and do your hair and help you dress for the party ... I hope you don't mind, Christina?"

"Sounds wonderful, Mother, I haven't seen Miss Darby for quite awhile. I trust and respect her taste."

As Christina left the room, Angela turned to Maria and began explaining whom Miss Darby was and what she did. She wandered about the yard, taking in the flurry of activity. This must be costing her Papa a bundle. He really knew how to impress people. It was too bad Christina had never had a sister or a brother. Sometimes she felt pressured by the affection and dotage lavished upon her. Perhaps her parents could lighten up a little and allow her some room to breathe. Now, where had that come from? She had freedom to date, freedom to choose her friends, freedom to wear whatever she wished, freedom to pursue her creativity, so what had prompted these thoughts? Again, the unresolved situation began with Adam. She vowed not to dwell upon her decision, whether she would or wouldn't go all the way.

* * * * *

Miss Darby had worked her magic. Christina's hair was arranged to offset her features, the regal curve of her neck, and the cut of her chiffon dress. She had applied make-up as an artist challenging a blank canvas, and soon realized early on that Christina's natural beauty required little or no enhancement. She darkened and framed the emerald eyes with eyeliner, and chose a soft earthen color of eye shadow and soft brown liner for her eyebrows. The golden tan needed no blush on the cheeks. A soft touch of natural cocoa pink to brighten and shape

Christina's lips added the final touch. She was a joy to behold. Sixteen years old and the world awaited her.

Approximately fifty guests were lounging about the estate, enjoying the setting. Angela's face was set in a permanent smile, so happy was she to see that everyone had chosen to attend. Frank took her aside and said, "Everything's all set. When it gets dark, I want you to bring Christina out to the front porch so I can give her the present. Do you want to see it before hand?"

Angela knew what the present was, so she decided to wait and enjoy the surprise and happiness when Christina saw it. "It's okay, Frank. I'll wait." She watched as he left her side, mingling and charming all of the guests. He stopped to chat with a group of his business partners, and she noted that Sharon Nesbitt was at his side. Angela's heart stopped for a split second as she watched from a distance. Was that worship she saw on Sharon's face as she listened to Frank? Sharon seemed to be mesmerized by Frank as Angela watched, unable to shake the suspicions from her mind. She had suspected Frank of having an affair when she had returned from Italy, but that was months ago. He had changed significantly last May, and she knew that the old Frank had returned. She had not asked him outright, but had kept her suspicions to herself. Now she wasn't so sure. Someone at her elbow proffered a tray of tall glasses of champagne and Angela politely took one, sipping on it absentmindedly. She refused to dwell upon a possible connection between Sharon and Frank.

The music swelled and drifted out onto the expanse of lawn as Adam and Christina walked about. He said, "You look absolutely stunning. I can't take my eyes off you."

"What about Becka? She looks gorgeous, don't you think?" "I don't love Becka. I love you, Christina Corelli."

A fanfare from the band summoned the guests to the front entrance of the home. Angela waved to Christina to attract her attention. She quickly left Adam's side and joined her mother.

"Come, Christina. It's time to open your presents. But first we have to go to the front of the house. Your Papa insists."

Humouring her mother, Christina joined her Papa and guests on the front porch. Her father circled her waist and held something in his right hand. A distinctive pause caught the crowd's attention and a collective gasp was soon heard as Adam drove up the driveway in a Robin's Egg

Blue, hard-top 1956 Thunderbird. Christina looked to her parents and back to the magnificent automobile. Her eyes rested momentarily on Adam's smiling face as he held the door ajar and waited for her to get behind the wheel. Tears of happiness welled in Christina's eyes as she heard her Papa say, "Happy birthday, my Angel." He pressed the spare set of keys into her hand and Christina kissed her father on both cheeks, breathlessly trying to find the words to thank him. She skipped down the spacious front steps to the crowd's delight and slid behind the wheel. The guests clapped, some clucking and whispering as to the cost of the luxurious automobile.

Christina called from the car, "Does this mean that I have to give up my bicycle, Papa?"

They all laughed at her teasing. The guests began returning to the back of the house and to the food that promised to tease the most discerning of palates. The fanfare was predominantly Italian, but catered to everyone's tastes.

Adam beamed at her. "This is the best, Christina. My car is nice, but this ... hell, I never imagined anything like this. This is the Motor Trend car of the year. My dad says it'll go from zero to sixty in 6.4 seconds. You are one lucky girl." For a brief moment, Christina was replaced by her new car. She enjoyed the depth of his jealousy but knew that he was only expressing his amazement and happiness for her gift.

They left the birthday gift parked in the driveway and rejoined the party. Christina opened the remaining gifts and, with tears in her eyes, thanked everyone over and over again. When the guests began dancing, Christina approached her father and asked, "Would you mind if Adam and I took the car for a spin? We only want to take it for a cruise through town. I promise we won't be gone long. You and mother enjoy yourselves. Thank you, Papa, this is the most wonderful party I ever had. I love you."

Frank was a little embarrassed by the words but he hugged Christina and replied, "Go and enjoy. Love you too."

It was a toss-up as to who should drive. Adam insisted that it being her car, she should be the first to drive it. Christina agreed, but only if they took turns. She drove down the driveway, through the iron gates, made the comment that she hadn't ever so much as scratched a fender, and whisked them away through light traffic. They cruised through town; a few wolf whistles came from the corner of the pool hall where Tonio's crowd hung out. A self-satisfied smile curved her lips as she rounded the corner to the main street. There weren't many people about, and the ones that were on the street had stopped to window shop and chat with friends and neighbours. No one seemed in any particular hurry. She drove about for about a half hour then angle-parked in front of the restaurant. She got out of the car and traded places with Adam. He backed out and sped towards the Big Pond. In the back of his mind, fuelled by raging adolescent male hormones was a plot to break the car in properly. They were parked under an enormous shade tree and the radio had been fine tuned to the local favourite rock and roll station. Adam fumbled for the seat control and pushed it back as far as it would go. He reached for Christina, almost with the same motion. The kiss lasted longer than usual and he began to probe with his tongue opening her lips and teeth as the French kiss became endless. Christina began to fidget and squirm and finally pulled away. His passion was high and he reached for her again. His tongue began its magic, but Christina groaned and pulled away. Adam said nothing. He sat upright, behind the wheel, turned the key and started the car. Christina realized that they had gone one step further to actual intercourse. She redid the clasp on her bra, covered herself with the bodice of her dress, and fixed her hair, all the while not speaking. Adam lit a cigarette and put the car into gear.

"Where are we going?"

"I don't know about you but I'm driving me home. I can't take this anymore, Christina. You have no idea how I suffer after an hour of heavy necking. Perhaps we should cool it for awhile?"

"What do you mean, cool it? If you mean not see each other anymore than say it, why don't you?" She all but screamed at him. Little did he realize, her emotions were also running high.

"Yes, that's exactly what I mean. This is getting us nowhere. I've told you I love you but that doesn't seem to be enough for you, does it?"

"Well what about me? Just because we love one another doesn't give us the right to sleep together. I distinctly remember my parents saying that you don't do it until you're married."

"Wake up, will you? Half our friends have already done it, with more than one partner, if I may add."

"Well my friends don't speak for me, Adam Carmichael."

"See you around, Christina." Without a backward glance he stormed up the walk to his house leaving her in despair. She was still angry but tears clouded her eyes. She brushed them away as she got behind the wheel. She drove home slowly, trying to make sense out of what had just happened. Maybe her mother was right. All boys wanted from girls was one thing ... sex. How could she have been so wrong about Adam? She brushed past the lingering guests and sought sanctuary in her room. She soaked in a long, hot bubble bath, the tears mingled with the soapy water. A half hour later she felt better, but the sadness lingered. Her phone rang on the night table but she did not answer. It was either Becka or Adam and she did not want to speak to anyone. She just wanted to be alone with her misery.

The following morning Christina put on a happy face, came down to breakfast as usual, and remained resolved to forget Adam Carmichael. Maybe she would give up boys altogether. She intended to meet with Miss Darby and throw herself into the summer theatre for the remainder of the summer. She had to return to class in two weeks, and Adam would be off to University and that would be the end of it. Somehow the thought was too painful to bear, and she felt the tears welling up in her eyes. Her parents were acting rather unusual this morning. The atmosphere was icy, her mother going through the motions. Had something happened after she had left the party? It really wasn't any of her business. They had quarrelled before this and had made up. Besides, she had her own problems.

Two weeks passed. On one occasion Becka had been with her in the new car as they stopped for a hamburger at the A&W. A familiar teal-green Monarch was parked just two cars down from where they had stopped. Christina could not take her eyes off the occupants. Was that Cynthia's platinum hair resting in the curve of Adam's arm? Becka tried to distract her, but she failed. "Don't pay any attention to them, Christina. You know Cynthia's reputation. She thinks she's Marilyn Monroe, all grown up with the morals of an alley cat."

By degrading Cynthia, Becka only worsened the situation as the implication was there staring them in the face. Christina hadn't given in to Adam, so he was getting it elsewhere. She was devastated and choked on her hamburger, the sobs in competition with the food. Recovering from her coughing fit, she asked Becka if they should leave. "I don't think we should give him the satisfaction, Christina. Let on that you're not bothered by their presence. Was that Steve in the back seat with a girl? I could care less, so why should you?"

"I guess you're right, Becka." They stayed for another half hour, finishing their food. By half past ten, Becka and Christina decided to call it a night. Adam and his passengers had left the drive-in heading in the direction of the Big Pond, which made Christina all the more determined to put the matter out of her mind.

She threw herself into the staging and preparations of the summer theatre finale and Miss Darby remarked how much she had learned over the past few years. Christina's costume designs and color suggestions were a welcome respite from the same tired old backdrop and settings they had used for the past two summers. Christina put Adam away in the back of her mind but he still filled her heart. She knew that there would never be another such as Adam Carmichael, and she had not turned to another boy to seek comfort. She had to get over one relationship before starting another.

As the final days approached for Adam to leave Cranston, Christina thought he would call to say goodbye, but by the eleventh hour of the eve of his departure, she had heard nothing. The Sunday evening had begun as usual, with a cruise through town to see what everyone was doing. Becka kept the subject neutral, talking about the theatre's Saturday night performance. The production had opened to a capacity crowd and the thunderous applause had been well worth the effort. Miss Darby beamed with joy. She had Christina, and her staff, take bows and a final curtain call. It was a culmination of a long and happy summer.

Becka decided she would call it a night, so Christina drove her home. They did not linger over small talk; Becka left with a, "call you tomorrow."

As Christina drove slowly home she thought that she was being followed. A car was definitely behind her, about a block or so away. She checked her rear view mirror but could not identify the vehicle, so she shrugged it off and continued the drive home. She parked the car and was about to leave the garage when headlights broke the evening darkness, flooding the garage and silhouetting her figure. She was momentarily blinded by the lights until she heard a voice call out. As she approached the driver's window she recognized the car, it was Adam. He said, "Get in, Christina."

Wordlessly, she did as she was told. He drove expertly, a little faster than usual, and Christina thought he had been drinking. She could not smell liquor on his breath or in the car, so that couldn't be the reason for his speed. His face looked pale in the moonlight, his mouth set in determination. "Where are we going, Adam? What's going on? Did you drop Cynthia off, then come looking for me?"

He turned and glanced at her, concentrating on the road ahead, "No, I didn't drop Cynthia off. I haven't seen her since that night at the drive-in. I only did that to make you jealous. After taking you out, do you think that Cynthia could hold a candle to you? You still don't get it, do you?

"No, I guess I don't, Adam. Perhaps you'd better explain it all to me. Why you hurt me so, and left me when I wouldn't do what you wanted."

He had reached the Big Pond, parked, and turned the car lights out. The light from the dash radio reflected on his face, and his longing and despair matched hers. She could not resist. She was in his arms, crushed to his body, as he covered her with kisses. She matched his passion one on one. "Christina, please, I can't go away, wanting you this much. Please, please, Christina, I love you so much. I will love you all the days of my life, and all the Cynthia's in the world won't change the fact."

She was lost. Their passion mounted until she could no longer think. She felt her clothes being removed, and shivered in the breeze coming through the window. He rolled the window up and they began in earnest to make love. Adam was gentle with her until she matched his rhythm. She had cried out with the pain when he first entered her, but it didn't last. They were lost in the wonder of their love. Christina wondered if it had lasted longer than five minutes. It seemed that they had been here at the Big Pond for hours. He did not speak. He just watched her as she dressed in the semi-darkness. He put his shirt on, straightened his jeans, and they sat, not touching, well aware of what had just happened. He turned to her. "God Christina, you were incredible. I'm sorry if I hurt you. I love you."

He brushed the tears from her eyes and kissed her cheeks and lips, his passion spent. "Did you mean it, Adam?"

"Mean what?"

"That you really love me. That you will love me all the days of your life?"

"Yes, my love. I have never told any girl that I loved her, and I never will. That is, except you."

She had to be happy with that. He was, after all, leaving in the morning and she wouldn't see him until Thanksgiving weekend. He noticed that it was after eleven and reluctantly drove her home. They remained in the car for a while longer, each not wanting to break the spell. Finally Christina opened the car door and left. Adam drove away with her standing forlornly silhouetted by the outdoor lanterns shining from the front columns of the house. So she had become a woman. She could not wait to climb the stairs to her room and face herself in the mirror. Someone had once remarked that when you lost your virginity it always showed in your eyes. Well, they were wrong. She looked no different than last night. The small voice of her conscience nagged at her, but it was too late, there was no going back.

Chapter Fifteen

CHRISTINA SLEPT FITFULLY THROUGHOUT the next few weeks. She missed Adam dreadfully and the new school term did not fill the gap. The weather remained warm, reluctant to say goodbye to the summer solstice. At times she wondered if she and Adam had made love, then reality struck home when she was late with her period. She could not accept the possibility and allowed things to slide until another one passed. It was now the beginning of November, and she was experiencing symptoms that were related to early pregnancy as described in the family physician reference her mother kept in the study. Unable to keep such drastic news to herself, she decided she must confide in Becka. Her parents were the last people on earth she could turn to. She drove to Becka's that fateful Saturday morning, begging off joining her parents for breakfast, knowing full well that the meal would not stay down. She was thankful that the weather was cold and crisp with frost and she could wear her bulky coat. Christina could see the changes in her body and disguised her thickening waist with oversized sweaters over her blue jeans, as the top waist side button no longer fastened. When she arrived at Becka's, Mrs. Sanders greeted her as a member of the family; she had such respect and affection for Christina. Dr. Sanders was about to leave for hospital rounds and his smile was also one of warmth and affection.

It took all of her courage to return the smile and to look directly into Mrs. Sanders face as she said, "Good morning, Mrs. Sanders, Doctor."

Doctor Sanders, with the discerning eye of a physician, thought that Christina looked rather pale. He asked, "Are you feeling all right,

Christina? You look a little tired. Not coming down with a cold or anything now, are you?"

She blushed, stammered and was overcome with nervousness as she managed to reply, "Not really sir, I'm fine, really. Well, I'd best go up to see Becka."

At the top of the stairs, Christina paused to catch her breath and compose herself. Becka heard her on the stairs and called out, "Hi Christina, I'm just getting dressed. Come in."

Christina approached the foot of the bed, smiled wanly and watched as Becka dressed, combed and teased her hair, put on a soft layer of lipstick, examined her teeth in the mirror, then, seeing the expression on Christina's face, she stopped midway. "Christina, what on earth? You're crying! What's wrong?"

She could no longer contain the awful truth so she blurted it out. "Becka, I'm pregnant. I just know I am. I missed two periods and strange things are happening to my body."

Becka sat down beside her at the foot of the bed and the two stared at one another in the mirror across the room. Becka's look of shock and concern sent shivers through Christina's body, and she began to cry in earnest.

"Let me guess. You said your last goodbye to Adam by letting him have his way.

Whatever were you thinking, Chris?"

"I wasn't thinking. It just happened. Famous last words! We just couldn't help ourselves.

The question is, what am I going to do?"

"Have you told your parents?"

"No ... and I'd rather not, but I can't hide this forever. Oh, Becka, how could I have been so stupid?"

Becka was quiet for a few minutes, thinking of what to say that would offer encouragement and hope to her best friend. "The first thing we have to do is to talk to my dad. When he comes back from the hospital, we'll catch him in the infirmary before my mother gets back from shopping."

Christina paled at the thought at having to share her secret with one more person. She said, "Do I have to?"

"Yes, you do. He'll want to examine you and advise you how best to handle the situation. You won't be the first unwed mother to come through those doors. Dad will not judge you; he'll only do what's best for you. I know him."

After the decision had been made the two girls amused themselves with other topics, skirting the issue but coming back to it from time to time. All the while, their ears were fine- tuned for the sound of Doctor Sanders' car in the driveway. An hour later, he arrived.

Becka hurried to the top of the stairs and called out, "Dad, can we talk to you?"

As her father looked up, she added, "Not here, in the infirmary. It's Christina. We need your help."

The examination was routine, perhaps a little embarrassing for Christina, but she didn't flinch. As they sat across from the doctor, Becka held Christina's hand tightly. Her father said, "Well, young lady, you are definitely pregnant. My guess from what you have told me is that you will probably have this baby the last week of May. You are a little run-down but we will fix that. I have some vitamin supplements that you must take in order for you to produce a healthy child and remain healthy yourself." He continued to outline the course of prenatal care and made an appointment for the next month.

"Thank you, Dr. Sanders. I guess I'd better go home and break the news to my parents." "Would you like me to set up an appointment with them and we can tell them together?" "That's very kind, but no, I have to do this on my own. You've been wonderful. I thought you might be rather harsh with me for what I have done, but you have only shown that you care about me and my baby. I can't thank you enough."

"It's not my place to judge, Christina. I am a little disappointed in you, but situations happen and I'm here to help."

Becka had remained silent as her father and her best friend conversed. It all seemed like a dream. Christina was going to be a mother, for God's sake. It was just too much.

Finally, just before noon Christina walked into the kitchen and broke the news that would change their lives forever. Her father looked up from his proverbial Saturday morning newspaper; her mother lifted her coffee cup to her lips. Christina sat across from them both and said, "Mother, Papa, I've just come from Doctor Sanders' office. I'm pregnant."

The look on her father's face was of shock, and then total disgust.

Her mother paled and could find nothing to say. Her father spoke first. "You're pregnant. You dirty little slut. What the hell's wrong with you? How did this happen? Angela, didn't you tell the kid about the facts of life?"

Angela shook her head, unwilling to believe what Christina had just said. Her baby was going to have a baby. No way. She heard very little of Frank's tirade, suddenly stricken by the devastation and despair on her child's face. The tears were streaming down her face but no sobs issued forth. The silent crying was the reaction to her father's condemnation. "Who the hell did this to you? Tell me, and I'll break his neck."

"No, I won't tell you. Not in a million years."

Then her father said the cruellest thing he had ever said to her in her entire life, "You mean to tell me you don't know who the father is? How many guys have you slept with, you slut?"

At that point Christina felt her heart break. Her father looked at her as though she had just crawled out from under a rock. He continued, "You will have this baby, but it won't be in this community. You will leave next week after we have made the arrangements for the home for unwed mothers in the city. The nuns can look after you for the next seven months. I don't want to see your face, or hear your voice, until this is all over, do you understand? Your mother and I will make some excuse to our friends and the gossips won't have a heyday. You will not keep this baby. It will be adopted as soon as it is delivered."

Christina's heart felt like it was choking her as it beat rapidly in her breast. She felt the panic rise as her mind heard each word and her heart absorbed the cruel blows. So she was not to keep her baby. It had not become real until this very moment. She would have to part with this new life. All thoughts of Adam were erased from her mind; she still refused to tell her father who the father of this child was. She vowed she would not even tell Adam. He had not written or called since that last night before he left for University. That too, was something she had to contend with ... the fact that he had abandoned her. She felt dirty. Perhaps her father was right. During these thoughts, her father's tirade began to fade, her mother's face swam before her eyes and Christina passed out. She bumped her head on the kitchen floor and remembered nothing after that. She awoke on the sofa, her mother by her side pressing a cold cloth on her forehead as the color returned to Christina's face. Her tears splashed upon her daughter's face, and her own face looked ten years older. Christina noted that her father was no longer in the room. For this she was grateful.

Whirlwind arrangements were made after her parents had confirmed her pregnancy with Doctor Sanders. For one brief moment during her sad goodbye to Becka, Christina wished that she could abort this child and everything would return to normal. Being a devout Catholic she had been consumed with guilt at the very thought ... and divorced it from her mind forever. Her parents drove her to the convent, a five and a half hour drive from their community in the mountains. She was introduced to Mother Superior and led away. Her parents neither hugged her nor kissed her in farewell. Her father stood very tall, his face set in stone, his eyes emotionless. Her mother would not look directly into her eyes as she coldly said goodbye. A tiny, barely five foot nun put her arm about Christina's waist and in the softest of voices said, "Come my child. I'll take you to your room and you can meet the other girls. Referring to her parents she said, "Don't blame them. They are as overwhelmed as you. In God's good time they will come around, but this is not the time."

She led Christina through a long hallway and up a flight of stairs to a large dormitory. Christina was shocked to see so many young girls in various stages of pregnancy. No blame showed in their faces as she was introduced to her new surrogate family. The girls wanted to hear all about the latest fashion fads and news from the outside. Christina turned to the tiny nun and looked deeply into the deep brown eyes, filled with compassion. "Thank you, Sister Rose."

The nun smiled and excused herself, promising to keep an eye on this new girl. She had never seen anyone so beautiful and unaware of her great beauty. The pregnancy had already begun to manifest itself in the inner beauty of this teenager. When her situation was resolved, Sister Rose believed that she would reach full maturity, and her beauty would be further enhanced by the ordeal of childbirth. She had taken an instant liking to Christina Corelli, but had only distaste for her father. Because it was against her religion to form personal opinions, or to pass judgment but for her private thoughts, Sister Rose said a few Hail Marys and the Act of Contrition after regular prayers that evening. Christina was welcomed into the life of the convent without anyone pointing fingers or blaming her in any way. She was in a predicament that required love, understanding, help, and later, guidance as her child was taken from her.

Christmas was a week away and Christina had not heard from her parents. It was as if she had some serious contagious affliction and they wanted no contact with her. Reputation and status in a community should not come to mean more than your own flesh and blood, or so Christina had been led to believe. The days had begun to merge one into the other as her body changed and her pregnancy became obvious. She did not intend to become close with any of the girls as they left within a week of delivering their babies, forlorn and empty. They were all teenage girls who entered the home, but left as grief-stricken, forsaken and alone with the wisdom of experience forever etched on their faces and a look in their eyes that was definitely worldly.

Sister Rose spent many of her personal breaks with Christina, teaching her the arts of embellishment, fine beading and lace trim, after she had seen Christina's designs. They used the convent sewing room and, although Christina would not be keeping her baby, she managed to make a wonderful layette to be presented to the adopting parents. Sister Rose was not much older than Christina, having entered the convent at the age of sixteen and two years later had become a full-fledged member of the Sisters of St. Martha. It was not a cloistered convent, and the nuns were trained as nurses, caregivers, teachers, or whatever they could creatively turn a hand to. Sister Rose was studying nursing and personal care. One day. the subject of Christina's perusal walked softly down the corridor with a letter in her hand. She greeted the girls as she approached Christina's room.

"Good morning, Christina. I have a letter for you. It came in the post late last night." Christina could not contain her excitement. Perhaps it was the long-awaited letter from Adam. But how could he know her whereabouts? She had sworn Becka to secrecy and her parents would not tell a soul the truth about her new residence. She thanked Sister Rose and hugged the letter to her heart. It was from Becka.

> *Dear Chris,*
>   *I cannot tell you how terribly much I miss you. You are as close to a sister as I will ever have and it just seems so unfair that this has happened to keep us apart. I have*

THE HOUSE OF CORELLI

some news about Adam but I'm not sure you're ready for it. He is home from University until just after New Year's. I don't think he was going to call me personally but we met unexpectedly and it would have been rude of him to ignore me. We put our differences aside (I still blame him totally for your condition, I believe that you were taken advantage of just to satisfy his male pride). He offered me a ride home and we talked about you. No, don't worry, I didn't tell him where you are … I only told him the story that your parents concocted … that you were in Toronto, helping out your relatives while your Aunt Maria recovered from surgery. He did ask if you had quit school, and I told him you were taking correspondence courses and attending night school. He is much thinner; the long hours of studying and classes have taken their toll. I have enclosed a gold locket that Adam purchased for you, hoping to see you during Christmas vacation. He asked that I give it to you with his love. He really does care deeply for you, Christina, and I could not help but feel that he is quite lost without you. He told me he was very angry at first to hear that you had left Cranston without a word to him or a letter to tell him what was happening. I defended you, saying that you had not heard a word from him since that night, not even a phone call to say goodbye. He did not come home for Thanksgiving because of the severe weather. Silence from you meant only that you no longer cared for him so he buried himself in the books.

It was so difficult not to tell him our secret. Believe it or not, I actually felt sorry for him until I reminded myself that it was not him that was living with strangers and awaiting the birth of a baby. My dad asks about you from time to time. My parents miss you as well.

I bought a gift for you as well, Christina. It's not much, but I thought a diary might help you sort out your thoughts and feelings. It comes with a tiny gold key and I had it engraved. We will think of you during the holidays and I hope that yours will be pleasant. I have not seen your *parents for a few weeks. I don't know what I would say to them. It's all so unfair.*

I will write again soon Christina. I love you and miss you terribly. Your very best friend,
Becka.

Christina finished the letter, but the last words were blurred from the torrent of tears. Her heart ached for her old life ... the worry free, everyday problems of adolescence were now replaced with mature decisions and adult situations. The locket from Adam was beautiful. The heart was engraved with tiny filigree leaves encircling a rose etched into the gold. She opened it and inside there was the picture of the two of them taken at the Big Pond. She could not take her eyes away. It seemed as though a lifetime had passed. She abruptly closed the locket and opened her bureau drawer. She put it away in the back of the drawer, wishing she had never opened it. She cried herself to sleep that night. Becka's letter she stored in the new diary, still not having decided whether to record her miserable and boring life on a daily basis.

As winter turned into spring, Christina's body was now swollen with child. Being so tall, she had plenty of room to carry the baby, and her clothes had fit her for up to the seventh month, loose blouses taking the place of fully pleated smocks. She had worked diligently upon the layette, choosing mint greens and soft yellows, not knowing the sex of the unborn child. She gained weight rapidly after her second trimester and was now quite uncomfortable. Easter had come and gone and Christina had a month to go before her delivery date. She had received a cursory card from her mother just after New Year's, but not a word or a phone call from her father. She had long since given up hardening her heart to the fact that he had washed his hands of her. She no longer referred to him as her Papa, vowing never to call him by the adoring title. He was her father and that was the extent of it. As for her mother, Christina had not sorted out her feelings. They had promised to come for her after the birth of the baby and she would return home as though nothing had happened. She could not accept the future as readily.

She awoke on the first Sunday in May in shock. Her bed was soaking wet. She called out to Sally in the next bed when the first pain took hold. Sister Rose was by her side within minutes and Christina began the long hours of labour, two weeks early but, ironically, on Mother's Day.

Sister Rose stayed with her throughout the fourteen hours, reading to her, praying, holding her hand and encouraging Christina to push, breathe or hold back, working with the contractions. Having no previous experience Christina relied upon the wisdom of the staff around her and did as she was told. The doctor expressed his concern for the length of the labour, but his patient was in good health; young and strong and holding up well. The baby arrived at eight p.m. She was a perfect little girl, just over six pounds. A few minutes later, much to everyone's surprise, another baby girl was born, identical to the first, at an even six pounds. This was so unexpected, as no one had the foggiest idea that Christina had been carrying twins. Doctor Jenkins explained that the first baby's position had most likely masked the heartbeat of the second baby during the monthly examinations. Christina had been anaesthetized for the last half hour of labour and had no knowledge of the second baby. She had smiled at the news of the firstborn and succumbed to the anaesthetic. When she awoke a few hours later, she was in the hospital ward with Sister Rose by her bedside. In a panic she felt her stomach. It was flat, and the full realization of her labour brought her fully awake.

"Sister Rose. Where's my baby? Can I see my baby girl?"

Because she was under strict orders from Mother Superior, Sister Rose chose her words carefully, but in her heart she knew that Christina had to be told the truth. She said, "You mean your baby girls? Yes, Christina, you were delivered of twin girls, both perfect in every way. How do you feel?"

"Twins. Oh my God. I can't believe it. Where are they?" "They are in the nursery and doing fine."

"When can I see them?"

Sister Rose fought back tears as she quietly said, "I'm afraid that isn't allowed. You cannot see them. It only makes it that much harder on you when they leave the hospital."

The hysteria rose in her throat. She fought to control it as she struggled with the truth.

"Please, Sister, I'm begging you. How can I go through life without having seen the faces of my children? I have to have something to remember them by. If I could I would keep them, you know that. Please, just fifteen minutes. I have to hold them, and say goodbye. I'll never forgive myself if I can't do this. I have to see them." She clutched onto the nun's robe and would not let go. Sister Rose's heart was breaking for this young woman, whom she had grown to love. It was against all the rules but the desperation and hysterical sobbing were too much. She cautioned Christina to be still and dry her eyes as she bent forward and whispered, "I'll bring them to you tonight just after night shift, when the staff is giving turnover report. That will give you a half hour to see them and hold them, and to say goodbye. I could be severely punished if we are discovered. "

The grateful smile that welcomed these words was all that the nun needed. She knew God would forgive her even if Mother Superior would not. It was the least she could do for Christina. The fact that this young girl was a victim of her own circumstance was of no consequence ... she had a right to a half hour of holding the children she had nurtured for nearly nine months and borne the pain of labour. The half hour must last a lifetime as the possibility of ever seeing them again was unheard of. The records of adoption would be sealed for life and the twins would be lost to Christina forever. Why not give her these few minutes of happiness? She had every right to hold these babies, to examine every inch of their bodies, to inhale the baby smell, and cradle them to her heart.

Christina rested under the sedative administered but was awake well before the allotted time. Sister Rose carried in two tiny sleeping bundles snugly wrapped in their receiving blankets, both sound asleep. She placed each one on either side of the new mother. Christina's eyes opened in wonder. She could not take her eyes from her babies. The nun unwrapped each baby and Christina made comments as she touched and fondled the infants. She looked carefully at each, and discovered that they had identical triangular birthmarks on their respective shoulders, identical to the one that Christina bore. She kissed their tiny hands, counted their toes, and marvelled at the soft reddish-blonde and darker brown hair that covered each head, respectively. Sister Rose watched in awe. She would never again find herself in the presence of such love. This was so natural, as well as heartbreaking.

The half hour passed without incident, and it was all the nun could do to not allow Christina further time with the babies. Their eyes met, and Christina's changed. The light went out of her eyes. It was as if her soul had left her body and was replaced with despair. The nun felt a shiver run down her spine as she carefully wrapped the infants in their blankets. They were not sleeping but they were still quiet. Perhaps the warmth from the fondling and touching had kept them quiet. Christina could not turn her head away as she slowly left the room, the babies cradled in each arm. She heard the swish of the nun's long robe and the metal and pearl jingle of the heavy cross and rosary that dangled from the sister's habit. Her eyes blurred with tears and she quickly brushed them away. They were no longer in her line of vision, and Christina's body was wracked with sobs. She did not cry out; these were the tears of such deep agony and loss that the body poured forth a torrent. After much soul searching, Sister Rose could not bring herself to return to Christina's room. She knew not the words of comfort. Instead, she went to chapel and prayed for the new mother and the hope of a bright future for the twin girls that would not grow up as sisters, and without the love of their birth mother. She had to accept the ways of the world, but that didn't make it right in her heart.

Chapter Sixteen

T HE WEEK AFTER CHRISTINA's twins' birth passed by in a blur. She had not called her parents, but they arrived on the seventh day to take her home. She had said her goodbyes to her roommates, not at all encouraged by their well wishes and prayers. Christina's one regret was her poignant last meeting with Sister Rose. The nun had spent as much time as was allowed with her, to see that she was healing well, and attempted to lift her spirits at every turn. The time had come for her to leave. Christina's few belongings were packed; she had left her maternity clothes for some other unfortunate unwed mother and was wearing the outfit she had made under Sr. Rose's instructions. She knocked upon Mother Superior's office door and was asked to enter. Her parents stood as she came into the room, but Christina focused upon the figure behind the desk. Her father spoke first, "Hello, Christina, your mother and I are here to take you home."

When she heard the word home, Christina felt a lump form in her throat but choked it back. Home had nothing to offer her after what she had been through. Her home was with her children. She merely nodded, smiled wanly, and shook Mother Superior's hand, thanked her while speaking softly, and turned to leave. She did not look at her parents, but left the room ahead of them. She heard her father thanking the nun, followed by footsteps coming up behind her. Sr. Rose approached her from the foyer and Christina wanted to hug her, but this was not allowed. The dark brown eyes were filled with compassion for the young woman, and she took Christina's hands in her own and pressed something into the palm of her right hand. With a look that said, Don't read it now, she said instead, "Take care, Christina, I will always remember you in my prayers. God go with you."

Christina bravely fought back the tears. She brushed them away and stood tall, her spine rigid as she walked through the front entrance into the beautiful spring day. Why was it that the weather had to be so incredible when she was so sad? Rain and drizzle and cold would have been the setting for this movie, so why was the sun shining so brightly when her future looked so bleak?

From the front seat, her mother attempted to make small talk as they traveled south. Christina rested her head back, lifted her feet, and fell asleep. She had not fully recovered from the childbirth and required rest. She drifted in and out and vaguely heard snatches of conversation between her parents. None of it held the slightest interest for her. In her dreams she relived the last half hour when she had held and kissed her girls. If only she had a picture of them, but the rules of the convent were far too rigid. One of the girls, who was early on in her pregnancy and helped out in the office, actually saw one of the couples who had adopted one of the twins. She described them to Christina as being very well heeled, apparent by the outward look of things. The woman had cried, filled with happiness, and her husband had beamed when he held the baby. She had no access to the file as Mother Superior kept them locked in her inner office. She regretted that she had no news of the other child. So the children were split up, to be raised in different cultures and different religions and regions. Assured that they would be placed in carefully selected homes did nothing to ease her pain or fill the void. She would live with this for the remainder of her life. They reached Cranston and Christina begged off from further contact with her parents, using fatigue as her excuse.

Becka was the first to call when she was finally back in her old room. Christina wasn't sure if she wanted to see anyone, but Becka begged and pleaded until Christina agreed. Shortly thereafter, Becka drove up in a bright yellow Volkswagen Beetle, proudly saying that her parents had given it to her on her seventeenth birthday. Christina accepted the offer of a drive about the community. She would do anything to get away from the evasive attitude of her parents.

"You look different, Christina; older, but much prettier than I remember."

"Becka, it's so good to see you. I guess I'm still a little pale from being in the hospital, but once I get out in the sunshine, that should change. Thanks for coming. I feel that I'm nothing but an embarrassment to my parents. They are walking on eggshells around me. God, I hate that. Why can't they just come out and say what they feel?"

She felt foolish. This was her best friend Becka for goodness sakes, Becka who knew all about her, so what the hell were they doing talking small talk? She broke the ice. "Becka, I've missed you so very much. If only you could have seen them. They were so beautiful."

"What do you mean, see them? That's against the rules, isn't it?"

"Yes, it is, but I made friends with Sister Rose and she allowed me a half hour with the babies, a half hour that has to last me a lifetime. She pressed a message into my hand before I left and I read it when I was in the car on the way home. She wrote: Christina, if you ever need me for anything, you can reach me at the address below. The phone number is my real sister's and she is closest to me. Promise me that you will keep this close. God bless you, Christina. Becka, I put it in the tiny side pocket in the diary you sent me at Christmas." She said nothing of the babies' pictures that the nun had also provided. They were in the locket beside Adam and Christina's pictures. "I'm sorry I didn't get you anything but we were not allowed out to shop. Sister Rose purchased some material for me and showed me how to sew my new outfit, but other than that, we just stayed on the grounds and helped out with light duties. Please, let's change the subject."

"I have to tell you that I haven't seen or heard from Adam since Christmas. I don't think he came home at Easter, and I heard that he accepted a road construction job in British Columbia. The workers stay in camp and the money's good. Maybe he didn't want to relive old memories."

Christina weighed her words carefully. "My feelings for Adam will have to lie buried for the rest of my life, Becka. Compared to what I just went through, he pales in comparison. Those babies didn't deserve what we did to them, and I don't want him to ever know. My parents certainly won't tell anyone, and I know you and your Dad won't. I wish I could leave Cranston but I have my exams to write in June. I won't be attending school, I'll write them as part of the correspondence courses I took. That should complete grade eleven at least. I just don't think I could relate to school activities, they all seem so silly now. I guess that sounds snobbish, doesn't it?"

"Not really, Christina. I'm trying to understand, but it's not easy." "How is Tonio?"

Becka's face fell at the mention of her secret love. "Same as always. He works at two jobs, takes care of his motorcycle, plays pool and goes to school. He doesn't date anyone in particular."

"Do you want me to talk to him?"

"No, Christina, you just might be the cause of his unhappiness. He has always loved you, since you met as little kids. He did ask me if I had heard from you, as well as the reason for your sudden departure. I think he believed the reason we concocted, but he didn't look very happy when I told him I had no idea when, or if, you would be coming back."

"I'm sorry, Becka. If I could change the way he feels, you know I would."

They had pulled into the driveway and Christina got out of the car. She did not look back, but made her way slowly up the walk to face another long afternoon and evening in her room. She avoided her parents as much as possible and saw them only at mealtimes. Her depression was all consuming and she soon lost interest in everything.

Her seventeenth birthday came and went; she had turned down all plans of a celebration. Finally, at the end of August, Angela and Frank were so concerned for her health and well being that they consulted with Dr. Sanders. As they described Christina's despondency and total lack of interest in her surroundings, the doctor advised a complete change of scenery for the young woman. Putting their heads together, Frank and Angela decided that they would send her to Toronto to live with Guido and Maria. The city of Toronto offered many challenges and possibly a brighter future for Christina. Arrangements were made over the telephone and within a few days, Christina had only hours to say goodbye to Becka, leave a note for Tonio to be given to him by Becka, hug her old dog Rocko, and be driven to the airport. Her mother gave her a last minute hug, but her father offered no fond farewells. He said, "Christina, call us if you need anything. Otherwise, obey your aunt and uncle. They are looking forward to your coming to live with them. Make the most of it."

She replied, "I will, father."

Had he tuned into the formal address of father? Christina cared less. She felt nothing for this man. He was her father in name only and she couldn't very well trade him in for another model. They had lost all hope of reconciliation when her "Papa" had chosen his place and reputation in the community over her happiness and well-being. Rather than support her in her time of need he had called her a slut, and her blood had run cold. It remained that way to this day.

Within weeks, life in Toronto became routine. The winters were slightly milder than in Cranston, and Christina grew to love the smells and sounds in her relatives' bakery. She worked in the front, serving customers, and began to make friends. Christina had decided not to return to school; instead she enrolled in night school and pursued a career in fashion design. Her days and nights were filled with activity and her aunt and uncle's warmth and love began to thaw the icy wall around her heart. She was mature beyond her years, but the little girl impishness shone through when she interacted with her cousins. Carmella became Christina's shadow and imitated her in make-up, dress, and manner. It was the family joke, but Christina at least had an outside interest. The babies' faces began to fade and it alarmed Christina, but she had no control over the fact. Memories fade, and emotions dull, but they do not totally leave the heart. As a distraction Christina developed a strong attraction to movie going. Christina's interest in the lavish extravagant movie productions of nineteen fifty-eight grew. She often met her cousins Veno and Carmella after early evening classes and they would sit through the second feature with her. The Broadway musicals and the costumes designed by Edith Head held a certain fascination for her and she just couldn't afford to miss any of the new releases. It was soon Valentine's Day and the bakery had been particularly busy as they sold cookies and cakes fashioned into cupids, hearts, and arrows. She had written to her parents last Christmas and exchanged a few gifts, but the card from her mother was terse and cold. Christina had long since given up trying to measure up to their expectations and had decided that a career in fashion design would satisfy her completely. At least she had a goal. Her aunt Maria had feared for her niece when she had first come to live with them. Where was the bright-eyed, vivacious, full-of-life teenager? In her stead had appeared a listless, blank-eyed, aged-beyond- her-years young woman with no purpose in life other than to make it through the day. Something dreadful had to have brought this drastic change.

As they emerged from the movie theatre one evening, the lights from the marquee shone directly over them, bathing Christina in a beam of light as though she was in her own spotlight. The group huddled from the cold as Veno walked to the parking lot to bring the car around and pick the girls up. A well-dressed man in his late twenties approached the girls. Carmella noticed him first as she said, "Christina, do you know that man? He's been staring at you for the past five minutes. Oh no, he's coming over."

"Maybe he just wants to ask directions, silly."

"Excuse me, Miss. My name is John Cole and I have to tell you that you are the most beautiful young woman I have ever seen."

Christina was embarrassed by the stranger's open admiration and said nothing. Before she could think of a reply, he quickly continued, "I run a modeling agency with my sister Maggie here in Toronto. Wait, don't go ... here's my card." She felt the small card thrust into the palm of her hand.

"What has any of this to do with me?" Christina met his glance.

"You are probably the most sensational discovery I have ever made in my ten years as an agent. I would appreciate it if you could come to our studio at the earliest possible date ... tomorrow, perhaps, and we'll see how the camera likes you. You have nothing to lose, and I will pay you for your time. The number is on the card and the address is uptown. Shall we say nine a.m.? By the way, I don't know your name."

When Carmella gently gave her the elbow, prompting Christina to speak, she did so by stammering that she was Christina Corelli and that she lived with her relatives above the Corelli Bakery. He beamed as he said, "We wouldn't even have to change her name. She's a natural."

By this time Christina had to take him seriously, otherwise this would become nothing more than a very cruel joke. He had found her Achilles heel ... fashion, magazines, movies, glamour

... everything that was of any interest to her. Veno called from the curb side and the girls piled into the car.

"Was that guy bothering you?" he asked.

"No Veno, the strangest thing just happened." Christina related the conversation and if she left anything out, Carmella filled in the gaps. "I don't know if he really meant what he said or if he's one of those perverts we hear about all the time that try to get young girls to pose nude while promising them the moon. He sounded so sincere."

"He didn't look like a pervert, and he didn't dress like a pervert, but then again, I've never met a real pervert," Carmella added.

When they were all back in the apartment, Veno broached the subject and they talked it over with Guido and Maria. Guido had long since formed the opinion that Christina was a beautiful girl, but seeing her every day he took her for granted, as well as everyone around them did. Perhaps this was worth pursuing. Maria was overprotective of her niece but was won over when she saw the light shining in her deep emerald eyes. The hope and wonder of it all, and the wishful dreaming, was not lost on her aunt. She said, "Papa, maybe we should look into this, for Christina's sake. What do you think?"

They all said, "Yes, we think, yes."

Veno said, "And when Christina is famous, she will remember that we were the ones who made her go to the interview. I'll go with you, Christina, just in case this guy isn't honest. Can I borrow the car for a coupla' hours, Papa?"

"For Christina, sure you can borrow the car, but you will have to make the afternoon deliveries in the van."

Christina was so keyed up that she did not fall asleep until after midnight. Nevertheless she awoke bright and early, studied the business card for the hundredth time and hugged herself. She chose a comfortable outfit of soft wool, a matching cardigan, and a string of pearls. She very seldom wore earrings as they made her neck appear longer than it actually was. She arranged her hair pulled back behind one ear secured by a gold clip and allowed the rest to cascade over her right shoulder, a copy of Rita Hayworth, a famous and beautiful movie star of the period.

She ascended the stairs with Veno a few steps behind. The Cole Modeling Agency was bright and airy; carpets covered the waiting room floor and the furniture was both modern and expensive. A few perfectly groomed young women smiled at the two newcomers as they found seats. The receptionist greeted them, but surprisingly motioned Christina to approach her desk. Quietly she said, "You must be Christina Corelli. After Mr. Cole's description of you this morning I couldn't miss you for the world. He wanted to see you the minute you arrived. Please follow me."

Christina did as she was told, glancing back at Veno, who made a circle of his thumb and index finger, a gesture of good luck. What followed was nothing short of a whirlwind of cameras, costume changes, hair and make-up, seating and posturing. She was aware of the few comments made by Maggie as she watched the two-hour proceedings. "She carries herself like a queen. Have you noticed?"

John's reply was, "I told you she's a natural. Have you ever seen such skin?"

"You say she's past seventeen. There's something … a look, a sadness … that gives her a more mature look, and then she switches to an adolescent girl. I can't put my finger on it. Do you see it, John?"

"Maggie, I don't care how old she is. This girl is going to make us all rich, mark my words." The developing process of the many color photos would take a few days, and Christina was urged to return to the studio to see her portfolio. They had not tied her to any contract, unsure as to what the pictures would portray. The camera didn't lie, but sometimes the most beautiful of women did not photograph well. John trusted his instincts and assured his sister that the photo shoot hadn't been a waste of time and money.

When Christina finally emerged from the inner recesses of the spacious studio, she found her cousin Veno nervously pacing and checking his watch every few minutes. He was so relieved that she was okay that he forgot his anger at having been made to wait for two hours. The receptionist had assured him that these things took time, especially where Mr. Cole was concerned.

Christina was so excited and energized from the photo shoot that Veno just let her talk, all the way back to the Bakery. His parents were waiting, almost as excited as Christina. The family celebrated Christina's good fortune that evening even though they had no idea as to the outcome. It didn't take much for the Corellis to sit down to a big family dinner with friends and lots of wine. They talked of fame and fortune, prestige and travel. Maria said, "And I will save every magazine that has your picture on it, especially if you are on the cover."

Christina blushed, unable to believe that this just might happen. She didn't think it was likely for her to be on a cover. The two days of waiting dragged on and she did not get a call from Mr. Cole. Her aunt urged her to call the studio and speak with Maggie Cole, but Christina was too shy. She said, "It was all a cruel joke, Auntie, they weren't happy with my pictures, I just know it."

"No, no, that is not true, bambino. Maybe I could call them for you?" "Oh, would you, Auntie?"

With the phone already in her hand, Maria read the number from the card and dialled the agency. "Allo, please I speak to Mr. Cole. Mr. John Cole?" She waited. "He is not there?"

She turned to Christina, a question in her eyes. Christina took the phone from her and asked, "Can I please speak with Maggie Cole? Thank you, I'll wait. This is Christina Corelli and I'm calling about my portfolio."

Maggie Cole's voice came on the line, "Christina, thank goodness you called. John left town unexpectedly on a shoot and he forgot to leave your number with the receptionist. I have your pictures on my desk and they are perfect. Can you come in this afternoon? I think you had better bring your uncle with you, and a lawyer, because we're talking contracts, big contracts. I'll see you at one."

Christina sat down on the chair beside the hall phone. Maria asked, "What, what did she say? What's wrong?"

"Oh Auntie nothing's wrong. It couldn't be better. It looks as though I'm going to be a model. Starting tomorrow, if Uncle Guido will act as my guardian." Suddenly the image of her parents popped into her head. Should she ask their permission? She squared her shoulders and decided that they had made enough decisions in her life, and look where they had gotten her. No, her aunt and uncle would be the ones to help her make her decision and make certain that she would not sign anything that could be used in an inappropriate manner. No risqué pictures, suggestive poses, or semi nudity. She had very high standards imposed upon her and drilled into her by Miss Darby. She had taught Christina to conduct herself in a ladylike manner at all times, be polite and patient and kind and respectful, and not to do anything that would cheapen her reputation. A one-time mistake with Adam had not taken this away and she intended to maintain her moral standards.

Christina returned to the Cole Modeling Agency a few days later with her lawyer at her side. Uncle Guido called Angelo, whose son was a lawyer and agreed to represent her. She could see by his manner that he was very impressed. They presented a very professional, businesslike manner. Maggie and John, after reading her contract changes, were convinced that the newest addition to their client list was not only drop-dead beautiful but intelligent as well.

She did ask one favour of her new employers, a rather unexpected one, but not unreasonable. She was so impressed by the portfolio the studio had put together of her different poses that she wanted copies for her parents and her relatives in Toronto. That solved, Christina and Vito left the studio. The paperwork was now being processed and a passport application had been included in all of the employee and contract negotiations. Maggie and Christina had taken an instant liking to one another, and John only added to the secure "everything is on the up and up" feeling that Christina had first noticed.

She was to be groomed, instructed, and made over in the popular image of the day. She had the latest hairdos, colour of eye shadow, and was dressed down and dressed up because, unknown as yet to Christina, she would soon be a welcome feature on the runways of Paris and Milan. If the promotion of Christina Corelli went fully as expected, she would become an overnight success.

With her portfolio tucked under her arm, she entered the waiting cab with Vito, her lawyer. He asked if he could see the photos under the guise that he had to judge them to see if she had been compromised in any way. His eyes took on a glow as he studied the glossies, one by one, unable to take his eyes away. The camera loved this woman ... he had to refer to her as a woman because she had all the right parts in all the right places ... and yet the photographer had managed to capture the little-girl look in a few of the photos. He was totally impressed as he said, "If these don't make you a star and a household word Christina, nothing will. I can't believe that a little make-up and the right expertise could create and bring out your inner beauty. I will be following your career closely because, friend of the family or not, you are incredible."

Impulsively she hugged Vito embarrassing them both as she answered, "You are my newest fan, probably my only one, Vito, thank you so much."

"May I offer a little advice?" "Of course, Vito."

"Just don't let the big city and its' worldly ways change you. People have a way of hurting you, and in no time you can surround yourself behind a wall and the camera will pick up on it. My mother told me once that if you are camera shy, keep a picture of something very dear to your heart in your mind and smile into the lens. Remember the eyes are the windows of your soul and reflect your personality. Well, I guess that's it, except that I wish you all the success in the world and when you are famous and rich I can honestly say that I drew up Christina Corelli's first contract."

Christina's eyes filled with tears as she listened to Vito's wise words. She was deeply moved, especially when the image of two tiny infants swam before her eyes. The pain and rush of love was etched on her face as she smiled sadly through the blur of tears. "That is very good advice, Vito. How did you get so wise? You're not that old."

They laughed together and sat through the remainder of the cab ride in comfortable silence. Vito dropped her off in front of the bakery, and sped off to his office on Yonge Street. Her Aunt Maria was just finishing the icing on a cake and smiled as she greeted her niece. "Christina, you don't have to work today. You have to pack and get ready for your trip to New York. Come tell your auntie what happened today."

Christina felt as close to this warm hearted woman as she had not felt to her own mother in many, many years; not since she was a small child. She had nothing but a bad taste in her mouth when she thought of her parents. Their place in the community meant more to them than two helpless newborn, flesh of their flesh, their first grandchildren, and, as Christina vowed, possibly their last. The tightly-knit Italian family unit meant nothing when wealth and reputation were in the picture. She had replaced her mother with her aunt and in doing so suffered no remorse. She said, "Would you like to see my pictures, Auntie?"

As Maria washed and dried her hands, she tucked a few unruly curls behind her ears and cleared a place behind the counter. As she studied each of the large photos she was absolutely amazed. "It is really you, Christina? You are so beautiful. *Bella, bellisimo.* Again, such a look! I am so proud, bambino."

Christina smiled and accepted the compliments without guile. If that was what the camera saw, then so be it. She had only to focus on the last moment she had gazed upon the twins, and the look was captured forever on film. Her uncle Guido came into the front of the shop and he, too, could not contain his admiration as he looked through the portfolio. "Have you called your parents, Christina? Your aunt and I did not want to call them without telling you."

"No, Uncle Guido. I haven't. Maybe I'll call them from New York. It looks as though I won't be back in Canada for quite some time. Maggie told me today that after I have worked in New York and been seen in all the right places, I will probably be going to Europe. Maybe we should just use the time left to get together and celebrate. If I flop in New York, I'll be back behind that counter the next day, I promise you both." The aunt and uncle that stood before her at that moment could not have been prouder of her than if she were their own daughter. They were all crying and laughing when a few customers came into the store, watching in open admiration the aura of happiness that emanated from the trio.

That evening, Christina penned a long letter to Becka. She had not written since Christmas vacation and Becka had dropped a short note soon into the New Year promising to write more at a later date. With the news she was about to share, Adam's face swam before her eyes, unexpectedly and poignantly. Her emotions had a way of betraying her, and she became angry. She had hardened her heart in the love department, as so far that had not gotten her very far.

She was a mother, biologically speaking, abandoned and banished by her parents, and forced to keep a secret that threatened to break her heart. She paused in her writing and made a solemn vow to throw herself into her career and give it all she had. Maybe then, the memories of those two precious faces would find a special place deep in her heart and she could live with the consequences of her actions. No one had remarked that her body had carried and borne a pregnancy. Being as tall and long-waisted as she was, stretch marks hadn't materialized and Christina's body was that of a fully mature young woman. She was rounded and curved, her breasts high and firm, not overly endowed but in perfect proportion to her thighs.

She was delighted with the surprise party given in her honour. Everyone she had grown to love and admire was in attendance and the party lasted long into the night. She had never seen or tasted so much food. Hopefully, it wouldn't add to her weight. She would have to watch every pound; if she was too thin her complexion would become sallow, too heavy the plump deposits under her cheekbones would take away from the hollowness that the photographer so admired. This was actually the only total responsibility she had over the control of her body. Everything else was soon decided. In New York her hair was trimmed, shaped, sun streaked, and lightened, her eye shadow brought out the emerald of her eyes, and dark liner made them look larger than ever. In some instances she hardly recognized herself. Maggie and John acted as though she was the find of the century. She soon learned the language of modeling, style, and marketing. Within two months, it became second nature to her. She had very little time to herself, which was fine, and she had purposely put off telling her parents. Guido and Maria only spoke to them about twice a year, and she had every intention of telling them of her new career and rising success before long. She did not mail the copy of the first portfolio. Instead she kept it on a shelf in the closet of her New York apartment.

Chapter Seventeen

C HRISTINA NEVER DID CALL her parents to inform them of her career change. When guilt reared its ugly head she shrugged it off, banishing it from her mind, using the image of a terrified young woman in labour without the benefit of her mother's care and attention. Perhaps it was tit for tat, but Christina decided that her parents wouldn't be interested in a slut's career. Wouldn't her father just shrink and hide if she did decide to pose nude? However, this would not be the case. Within the inner circle of the modeling world and the who's who of advertising, she earned the reputation of being the ice maiden. The tabloids had begun hounding her and the paparazzi kept vigil outside of her New York apartment. She had done numerous shoots in and around New York and traveled to Montreal and Florida, but she looked forward to the runways of Milan, Italy.

Becka had written a few times filling Christina in on all the local gossip. She had dated Tonio Marcellus a few times, but for some reason they were unwilling to commit to a more permanent relationship. Becka would enter Nursing School in the nearby city for a three year term, something her parents had both wanted, especially her father. Christina remembered him with affection. If only her father had as much compassion as Dr. Sanders. But then again, life has a way of taking its own turns, not necessarily in a straight line. Maggie and John Cole were on top of the world, so proud of their new protégée and the prestige she brought to the New York agency.

The money rolled in and Christina soon realized that modeling was a very lucrative business. She decided that she would learn everything she could about the business from the inside out. Her designs were becoming very creative both in concept and color. She was just a bit too radical. The norm of the runways entailed the models to project elegance as perfectly coiffed, perfumed, made-up Barbie dolls. Christina's height was a plus when they worked the private salons. The Park Avenue crowd could not take their eyes off her when she entered the room. With a turn here, a smile there, and a glance into the crowd, the heavy green taffeta gown with its fitted bodice and matching stole kept the Mrs. Park Avenues riveted on her form. As the new lines were introduced, Christina became aware that she was always the first model to be requested.

She made friends quickly with her co-models but she was aware of the unmasked jealousy. At one point in her life this would have bothered her, but no longer. Christina's heart was encased in a hard wall of defence and it would take a stronger force than mere jealousy to break it down. The day of her eighteenth birthday was fast approaching, and Christina made the decision to call her Aunt Maria and Uncle Guido in Toronto. She had sent them both cards and memos, as well as a few photographs and gifts from Florida, but she had been in and out of New York so much that in most cases her mail caught up with her two weeks later.

When she heard her aunt answer the phone, she smiled to herself as her aunt's face, always so loving and dear to her, entered her mind. "Christina, it's so good to hear your voice. Where are you bambino?"

"I'm here in New York, Auntie. We are leaving for Italy next week and I wondered if you had any messages for the relatives. If I get some time I could drive down to Marino after the show. "

Her aunt's voice was full of undisguised love and pride. "I already wrote them about you. The last time they saw you was when your Nona died. Your grandfather passed away a few years later, after you left home, but the rest of the family remembers you with love. I even sent them the magazines that you are in, especially the cover ones. They can't read English but they recognize you right away. What about your birthday, Christina? Your uncle and cousins were wondering about holding a big family party. Do you think you can come to Toronto?"

"Thank you, Auntie, but I will be Milan by then. You could still hold the party and I could call long distance and speak with all of you. I know how much you like giving parties. I have to go now, Auntie, I love you both very much. Ciao, Auntie. "

John and Maggie began working solely out of the New York office and hired a manager to oversee the Toronto offices. Maggie had become Christina's surrogate mother. She had no life outside of the agency and Christina had been like clay in her hands. Maggie taught her the financial side of the agency, all about contracts, which were Johns' forte, as well as how to arrange and close an advertising shoot. The staff admired her interest and soon recognized that she would, without a doubt, become a shrewd businesswoman able to compete with the best. Christina did not date any one man in particular. She had been seen around New York and Manhattan with numerous handsome male escorts, mostly arranged by the studio. Maggie had landed her a perfume contract that paid a highly inflated dividend. The company arranged shoots in all of the high priced boutiques, cosmetic outlets, and Park Avenue shops. Chanel No. 5 was the most expensive perfume on the market, and Christina was delighted to be the model of choice. Her present challenge was to capture the hearts and minds of the couturiers in Europe. Maggie had suppressed the growing anxiety as the fall and winter collections of the Manhattan fashion houses were put together. Thirty thousand dollars for a runway afternoon show was a small price to pay for the monumental coverage during the showing of the collection. Christina was slated to wear three outfits during her debut. She would wear day wear, formal evening, and had been selected to wear the bridal gown. It was the highest honour for any model and Christina was amazed that she had been chosen. Apparently the Italian designer had asked for someone new and fresh, not one with the plastic look of the proverbial mannequin that most models were slated to become; their most elegant facial expression being one of boredom.

When they were aboard the airplane, Christina extracted a rather fat envelope from her carry-on. The contents were composed of various notes and birthday cards sent from the many places she had made friends. She recognized the handwriting and chose Becka's letter to read first.

> *Dear Christina;*
> *I don't know when this letter will reach you but I have some rather bad news and I find it very hard to write it down. It would be much easier if I could face you and tell you but I know it is impossible.....*

For God's sake, get on with it, Christina thought.

There was a serious explosion and cave-in at the Cardiff mine and at least twenty men were buried alive. When the rescuers finally reached the level where the cave-in occurred they found no survivors. Tonio's father Gino was one of the miners killed. He had been working at the face with his partner when a large slab broke loose from the roof above them. Although the shaft had been shored and timbered, the slab moved and the seam shifted. The whole roof caved in on the men. Hopefully, they died instantly and did not linger for the two days it took to reach them. Tonio is beside himself. I was very surprised when he called at the house on the weekend when I was home visiting my parents. I didn't know what to say, but he seemed to draw some comfort from just talking about it. I did get some time off to attend the funeral. He just seemed so lost.

Your parents were in attendance and you would have been proud of your mother. She took much of the burden from Teresa by arranging everything, and your father took Tonio under his wing. They seemed to hit it off really well; it was almost as if your father was trying to be a substitute father for Tonio. I don't know where exactly all of this will lead, but it would be a load off my mind if Tonio had finally found something or someone that he could work at and look up to. Funny it should turn out to be your dad. Tonio said they were going to get together next week and maybe he'll be working for Corelli Trucking soon. He's twenty-one now and needs some new direction. His mother is totally devastated. The entire community has lost a good chunk of their male population; fathers, sons, uncles, grandfathers ... all gone in a few minutes.

I realize this is not much of a birthday present, Christina, but I do wish you well. Eighteen is supposed to be special in some way, but I didn't feel any different. Good luck on your trip to Milan ... I'm so proud of you.

As ever, Becka.

Maggie studied Christina's face as she watched her read the letter. She asked, "Is it bad news, Chris?"

"Yes, in a way. It doesn't affect my family directly, but remember when I told you about my boat trip to Canada when I was young? Well the young boy, Tonio, has just buried his father. He was trapped in an underground cave-in and died with his co-workers. He has no brothers or sisters and Becka is really worried about him." She did not mention her parents' part in all of the proceedings; she never mentioned her parents to Maggie, or anyone else for that matter. Maggie had broached the subject either out of curiosity or to make conversation, but Christina had closed the door after the first question and Maggie had gotten the hint. So her father had finally taken some notice of Tonio. Well he always wanted a son, now maybe he could put this longing to good use. Heaven knows, Tonio had been treated as more of a pal, rather than as a son by his own father. Gino Marcellus, in mind and spirit, had never passed the age of thirty and was now no longer among the living at the age of forty.

She decided to fill the ensuing hours of the trip with a long letter to Becka, opening her heart and mind for the first time in many months. Well, since the birth of the twins. She sorted through the rest of the mail but found nothing too exciting. It was nothing that couldn't keep. They landed in Rome without incident and were soon speeding through traffic in a cab driven by a Kamikaze pilot.

She had been in Rome at one time in her life but the memories were dim. The architecture throughout Italy was the same and the only change that she could discern was that the traffic had increased tenfold. The cab drivers on any given day could qualify to drive in the American Indy 500. Maggie and Christina were breathless by the time they reached their hotel. The plan was to rent a car and drive to Milan in the morning. This day would be used for the group to energize themselves, shop, browse, snack, or dine. Christina particularly enjoyed a demi-tasse of European Espresso coffee. It was so thick and strong that she got quite a buzz after only one cup. She taught Maggie some conversational Italian, laughing at Maggie's attempts at pronunciation. Maggie spoke, "Okay, so I wasn't born here, that doesn't mean you have to make fun of me, *capice?*"

They dined late into the evening. The onset of summer heralded warm breezes and the smell of flowers reached the street below from the hanging baskets precariously perched on balconies. The streets were filled with flower merchants during the day and roses were sold to passers-by in the late afternoon and evening. As Christina strolled with her group along the narrow cobblestone streets, she was approached by a handsome young Italian wearing a smile that showed perfectly even, very white teeth in a dark-complexioned face under a moustache. *"Scusa, Senorina*, a rose for such a beautiful lady."

Christina turned to face him and her surprised expression changed to one of delight. *"Graci,* it is very beautiful," and she pressed the rose to her nose and inhaled the fragrance released by the touch of the petals against her face. He said no more, his eyes merely registered a degree of adoration reserved solely for the very beautiful.

Maggie remarked, "Already, a secret admirer. I guess we'll have to keep you under lock and key while we're over here or some handsome young gigolo will whisk you away for a week of love."

"Don't be silly. I'm not interested in any man, Maggie, you know that."

Maggie did not reply, but she did wonder why Christina rarely dated, and only went out if the evening had been arranged by the Agency for publicity purposes. It was unusual ... very unusual. They entered the open air restaurant under soft lights and live music. Their table was long and seated at least twenty people. Their group numbered a dozen, but they were soon joined by other patrons, bringing their bottles of wine to the table and introducing themselves. No one minded. They would not talk shop. They were out on the town in a city of magic, so why not indulge in a little Italian immersion? It was well past ten when the group called it a night. Some took taxi cabs to the hotel, while others decided to walk off the heavy meal and the heady wine. Christina remarked, "If only life was as simple as this, what could be better?" Everyone around her agreed. Someone began a song while they walked along the street and, they were soon joined by others. It was one of the most pleasant evenings Christina would remember.

Chapter Eighteen

M AGGIE AND HER ASSISTANT were waiting in the lobby, their bags loaded into the boot of an open car. The morning sun shone brightly as they sped away from the busy streets of Rome and out into the countryside, along the winding roads of Italy. Christina took the scenery for granted, and they discussed the upcoming runway show. If all went well, Maggie hoped that Christina would capture the hearts and eyes of the most famous couturier houses in Europe. Christian Dior, Gucci, Coco Chanel and many others would be showing their fall and winter lines over the following three days. Everything was in readiness for their arrival, and all that remained for Maggie to do was ensure that Christina and the other models were well rested and fresh for the show. One of her models, Suzanne, had become an overnight party girl once she had been signed on with the Agency. Maggie had covered for her a few times and hesitated to bring her along to this shoot, but John had insisted. She was an asset to the Agency but at the rate she was burning the candle at both ends, her beauty would not last. The camera picked up on fatigue, wrinkles, lacklustre eyes, and sallow complexion long before the discerning eye of an agent. Make-up could do wonders but eventually nothing would fool the camera. She had imparted all of this to Suzanne, but it had fallen on deaf ears. Maggie had rescued Suzanne from the male predators who frequented the hotel lobbies and fashion shows. They would brag that they had been the first partner for many of the girls. Virgins were a prize to be lauded over at breakfast the next day. Many of the girls had been released into the care of their agents, but some of the agents were well paid, providing some very old men with insatiable sexual appetites for young bodies and firm flesh for an overnight fling. Maggie was not one of these agents and she had vowed that she would revoke Suzanne's contract if she didn't behave herself during this very important make-or-break show. Suzanne was jealous of Christina at first sight, but the two had become rather good friends, Suzanne being the bold one. This had helped Christina overcome her initial shyness when meeting new people. She amazed Christina with her open familiarity with strangers. Suzanne said, "What the hell, Chris, we're all in the same business. They aren't really strangers, now, are they? Would you like to meet some handsome guys after the show for dinner tonight?"

"No thanks, Suzanne. I'm not interested."

"I don't get it. You're drop dead gorgeous. All the men that see you want you. I pale by comparison. Are you still a virgin?"

Christina did not reply. The question was far too painful, as well as personal. She remained cool to Suzanne.

Maggie and Suzanne chatted with John, Teresa, Candy, and Della. Christina remained quiet, content to be part of the background and not directly involved. She put her hand to her throat and removed the locket from under her blouse. She stroked the soft gold metal, while long- buried memories surfaced. With a soft sigh she replaced the locket on its chain to rest between her breasts, never far away from her heart.

It all happened so fast. The car in front of them attempted to pass the large cargo van ahead on a curve. As the car crossed the center line and entered the passing lane, it was directly in the path of an oncoming vehicle. The car swerved to the left and disappeared over the embankment. The oncoming vehicle had swerved to miss it and was immediately in their path. John yanked the wheel to the right and applied the brakes. He attempted to steer the car as it approached the ditch against the mountain. The oncoming traffic had averted them, but was still traveling in the wrong lane. The car behind the one they were riding in collided head-on with the oncoming vehicle. A loud explosion filled the air. Everyone in the open car held their breaths; one of the girls screamed as they collided with the rock abutment. Christina was on the outside passenger's seat and was thrown sideways and forward, striking the side of her head and shoulder, which rendered her unconscious. Maggie pitched forward onto the dash, breaking the windshield. The steering wheel slammed into John's chest as the car came to a halt. Chaos ensued. Both lanes were blocked by the head-on behind them; the cargo van had kept on going, unaware of the tragedy that had just occurred behind them.

John managed to extract himself from behind the steering wheel and staggered across the road. He looked down the embankment and saw the smoking, steaming vehicle at least two hundred feet below, on its roof. Nothing stirred. He then turned and looked back at the head- on. His crew and staff were involved in this, the most serious accident. He made his way to the cars, attempting to determine if anyone was alive. He heard someone say, "Help me, I'm trapped under the front seat. My legs are jammed and I can't get out." He looked through the window and was horrified at the blood splattered about. The driver was dead or unconscious, and John could do nothing for him. He approached the passenger side of the car and managed to open the door. He helped the injured man from the front seat and laid him on the grassy slope of the ditch. He was joined by the third vehicle of their entourage, the cube van that carried the collection, as well as additional staff and crew. They were unharmed, and had been privy to the entire four-vehicle accident as it had unfolded. They soon realized that John was in shock and attempted to calm him down.

Two men ran to the convertible, which still held Maggie and the models. The only two injured appeared to be Maggie and Christina. She was still unconscious, bleeding from the wound above her left ear, and Maggie had a huge gash across her forehead. She moaned with the pain and drifted in and out of consciousness. A blanket was wrapped around Christina and she was transported to the cube van where a place was cleared for her to lay down. She was joined by Maggie. John was dazed and in shock, but except for the pain in his chest he was not critically injured. The models in the back had braced themselves, and put their heads down as though prepared for an airplane crash. They were bruised and shaken but not bleeding. A passing car slowed, and a very excited Italian gestured that he would call for help. By this time it was determined that the oncoming car contained no survivors. Two people were dead, as well as the occupants of the car that had gone over the embankment.

John climbed into the back of the cube van to see how Maggie and

Christina were faring. Everyone stood about, helpless and confused. No one seemed capable of organizing and controlling the traffic until one of the photographers stepped forward and took charge of the situation. They could not direct traffic; it appeared that both lanes would remain closed. The convertible blocked passage on the mountain side, and the head-on had placed the oncoming vehicle crossways in the oncoming lane. To drive around it would mean that traffic would be precariously close to the steep embankment and no one wished to attempt it. Within an hour the traffic was backed up on both sides of the accident for a mile. The ambulance arrived shortly after the accident had been reported; they were only about twenty minutes from Rome. As many as could ride in the ambulance without having to lie down were jammed in, and another ambulance had been dispatched for the overflow. Christina had drifted in and out of consciousness and attempted at one point to sit up but the pain in her head was too great and she fell back with a groan. John calmed her, telling her that she would be all right, just to lie still. He said, "Maggie is hurt. She hit the windshield and has a very bad cut on her forehead; probably a concussion as well."

"How are you, John?" Christina asked through waves of pain.

"I think I may have a few cracked ribs. The steering wheel gave me quite a jolt. I really feel beat up but I'm not bleeding anywhere."

She smiled faintly and allowed the black waves of unconsciousness to claim her. She came to when they met and passed the second ambulance rushing to the scene. Within minutes Christina was lifted and transported into the hospital. She could understand the language and answered in Italian as the doctor examined her and asked her questions. He assured her that the blow to the head was severe and she would have to stay overnight in the hospital, along with a few others of their group. John was taken to X-ray and diagnosed with a few cracked ribs and a bruised sternum. He was fine otherwise. He asked for a telephone and, with Christina's help, managed to contact their people in Milan. As he explained the details of the accident and their injuries, Christina whispered a silent prayer of thanks that they had been spared. It could have been the end of everything. She cared less about the next day's runway show, but John was already making arrangements for them to be pre-empted and decided that they would be available on the last day of the show. That would give everyone three days to recuperate and re-organize. They had lost a photographer and a prop assistant. Other than a few broken bones, he believed that they would be able to cope with this severe setback. They had traveled such a great distance and their careers and livelihoods were hanging by a thread. Maggie would remain in the hospital, unable to travel for a few days. John promised that he would keep in touch and they would pick her up on the return trip to New York. She was so terribly disappointed, but they relied upon one another and she knew that John would come through for them all.

Christina had not noticed that the hospital foyer was filled with photographers, paparazzi with cameras flashing in rapid fire. The hospital staff had attempted to keep them out of the treatment rooms, but to no avail. They could not treat the injured and simultaneously escort the curious and parasitic news reporters out of the hospital. The police had also arrived and it was chaos all over again. Christina's vision was momentarily blinded by a flashbulb, as the photographer just inches from her face leaned over the gurney to get a good headshot. He was removed immediately from the treatment room, but left with a backwards, "Thanks for the picture, beautiful. I've got me tomorrow's headline picture."

Maggie and Christina were admitted to the same semi-private room on an upper floor. They were both thankful for the peace and solitude and drifted off to sleep under the influence of the strong sedative, which had been administered in the emergency room.

Needless to say, the newspapers and tabloids had a heyday reporting the horrific accident. Christina's face was plastered on the front page of all the major dailies, some alluding to her as a famous American model, others as a rising star. All attested to her great beauty and the hospital was bombarded by the press seeking an interview with Maggie and Christina. John had said goodbye earlier that morning as he set out again for Milan with what remained of their entourage. Maggie awoke with a helluva headache, but remained brave in the face of it all. She promised to remain behind to attend to funeral arrangements for the photographer and prop man they had lost in the head-on collision. Christina's head throbbed but she felt much better for having rested overnight. She planned to leave later on that day and meet with John and the group at the hotel in Milan later that evening. The doctor entered the room with a nurse in tow. He was pleased to have been the admitting physician for these two famous people. Maggie smiled at the allusion to the word "famous." They could not leave yet, but by all accounts very soon. Christina would be allowed to leave the hospital around noon but Maggie agreed to stay until at least four o'clock. Christina was to be discharged and escorted through a rear exit to avoid the news group. Maggie knew the publicity would do them no harm, but she insisted that some cloak and dagger tactics would be good for their image in the long term. It all added to the mystery and kept the news media interested.

Christina and her chauffeur were approaching the scene of the accident. Christina unconsciously braced herself for the shock of impact but all vestiges of the crash had been removed from the scene. The mountains stood majestic in the early afternoon sun, the sky was deep blue with a few high clouds, and summer was in full bloom. Once past the bad place in the road, Christina reclined against the back seat and allowed herself to drift. She fondled the locket around her neck, and her thoughts took her to memories of home. It had been almost a year since she had left her parents in their respectable setting of Cranston and she was surprised at the realization that she missed nothing about it except perhaps Becka and Tonio. Adam was in medical school and far removed from her life. She wondered if their paths would ever cross again. The possibility was very remote, as Christina traveled in opposite circles at opposite ends of the world. If the runway show was successful in Milan, Maggie and John had promises of Christina working for Christian Dior, so the next stop might just be in Paris, France. She crossed her fingers and whispered a prayer. The face of her mother swam before her eyes. She knew she had disappointed her parents, but for her mother to turn her back on her only child hurt Christina more than she could ever imagine. After all, it was her wonderful Mama, who had loved and protected her for as long as she could remember. They had closed their hearts and minds to her and she was truly out in the world on her own. Without Maggie and John, she shuddered at what could become of her, given the proper circumstances.

Although the accident had put a damper on the upcoming show, Christina found John to be in good spirits. He had checked with the hospital and Maggie was just fine. The gash on her forehead would leave a scar, but she suffered no permanent damage. He was delighted that Christina had reached Milan without incident. Together they rehearsed the line-up, John trusting Christina's judgment, knowing that Maggie had been grooming her to learn all of the facets of modeling as well as the business end of the Agency. It certainly proved to be a boon. The first two days of the show seemed endless, but everyone was amazed at the success of the whole thing. Maggie joined them within two days, and the paparazzi had followed them. She could not remain in Rome. There she was, once more featured on the covers of their tabloids and newspaper headlines, this time on the runway in all her glory and charm.

In the small town of Marino, Christina's maternal relatives studied the newspapers. They passed the paper around to one another and finally came to the conclusion that this had to be Angela and Frank's girl, Christina. Certainly they had not seen her since Nona died, when Christina was a child, but the face had only matured; it remained Christina. They studied the magazine covers, which Maria had sent them. With much excitement, one of the aunts, Rina, placed a long distance call to Toronto to speak with Guido and Maria. By this time the "Expose" had picked up the article and run it. Maria had seen it but had said nothing to her husband. She had called the hospital in Rome, and was relieved to learn that Christina was fine. She hoped that the tabloid would not be seen by Angela and Frank. However, she was wrong. The call came that evening. As Maria recognized Angela's voice she became very nervous. "Angela, is that you? It is good you called."

"Maria, Frank and I have a tabloid in front of us and the picture of the model looks like Christina. Where is she? Is it Christina?"

"Put Frank on, Angela. I'll explain."

Frank shouted, "Maria, what the hell is going on? Why isn't Christina in Toronto, with you and Guido?"

"She didn't tell you?" Maria asked, acting as surprised as the man at the other end of the connection.

"Tell us what?" Frank's voice was becoming impatient and a little angry.

"She is going to be a very famous international model, Frank. An agency signed her up in February and she has been living and working in New York. The runway show in Milan is meant to launch her career."

"Maria, this is all news to us. Have you any idea how we can reach her? We have to talk to her as soon as possible. What the hell were you thinking of, allowing her to go off to New York by herself?"

"Franco, we didn't just let her go off to New York by herself. She had a lawyer, we met the owners of the Agency, we talked it over with everyone. Christina said she would be the one to write and let you know, I can't help it if she didn't."

"You're right, Maria. Is she all right? The paper didn't go into the extent of her injuries, but were more interested in her background and the fact that she could be someone famous from America."

"Christina called us from the hotel in Milan yesterday. Here is the number. The group should still be in Milan until Friday. If I hear from her I will tell her you called. That's all I have to say, Frank. Try talking to your daughter for a change instead of waiting for strangers and relatives to tell you how she is doing. Goodbye."

Frank realized that Maria was miffed by his tone of voice and the burden of blame he had laid upon her, but he was worried about Christina. He said he would place the call for Angela's sake, but in his heart he needed to hear her voice. They had parted under such bad circumstances, and the word "slut" still rang in his ears. He had not meant to be so cruel, as he recalled the shock and hurt that registered upon his angel's face. She had died a little before his eyes, and he now realized he had destroyed the one last part of her childhood and innocence. If she became hardened to the ways of the world it could be attributed to their last encounter. She had withdrawn from them and her surroundings until they had reached the decision to send her to Guido and Maria. Thank goodness for Maria's warmth and understanding. But this ... to allow her to go to New York to become a model! Anything could happen to her in a city of that size. As they waited for the overseas operator to call them back, Frank and Angela paced in turn, not really meeting one another's glance, skirting the issue at hand, filling the hours with small talk. The operator called to say that Miss Corelli was unable to come to the phone, she was on the runway. Should she continue trying?

Frank shouted into the receiver, "Yes, of course, you keep trying. You keep trying until I hear my daughter's voice on the telephone, *capice?*"

"Yes, sir, I will continue to try your call."

At long last, the telephone rang. Frank picked up the receiver and said, "Yes, this is Frank Corelli."

"We have your party on the line, Mr. Corelli, go ahead."

"Hello, Christina. This is your Papa. Are you there, Christina?"
"Yes, father, I'm here." She waited.

"What the hell is going on, Christina? Your mother and I have a right to know. How could you do this to us? At first, we thought you might have been killed or crippled. What the hell is the matter with you? Do you know what this has done to your mother?"

As Christina listened to the tirade at the end of the line, she thought how he had not asked a word about how she really was. Was she badly injured? No ... he only talked about how this had affected them. She said, "I didn't think you cared what I did with my life. The last time we talked you called me a slut, and I've set out to prove you wrong. What's so wrong about that?"

The words hit him separately, like blows from a sledgehammer. So he had hurt her. The wounds were very deep and never to be forgotten. He said, "Here's your mother."

Angela grasped the receiver with shaking hands as she said, "Christina, angel, are you okay? We were so worried when we saw the newspaper and couldn't reach you. Aunt Maria gave us your number. Tell Mama you're fine."

"Yes Mama, I'm all right. Funny thing is, you didn't worry as much when I gave birth to the twins, did you? But then again that wasn't publicized, was it? I really have nothing more to say, except that I'm fine and happy, as happy as can be expected. Goodbye Mama."

"No, Christina, don't hang up." But the only answer to Angela's pleas was the line going dead. With tears in her eyes, she turned to her husband. "We have lost her, Frank. She spoke to me as though I was an acquaintance, not her mother." She could no longer speak, the wrenching sobs took over and she collapsed in despair on the sofa. Frank stood by helplessly, unable to cope with such emotion. He was pale and shaken, as the full realization of what they had done to Christina finally sunk in a year and a half later. There was no going back. All they could do was hope that over the next few years, Christina's heart would soften and she would return to them as their daughter. Angela's weeping continued.

Angela slipped into chronic depression over the next few months. Frank attempted to follow Christina's career as she catapulted to fame, her picture gracing the cover of Esquire, Vogue, Cosmopolitan, the European magazines, Fashion Daily. The woman that stared out at him was breathtakingly beautiful, enhanced by the best make-up artists in the world. Her clothes were almost regal, from the best couturier houses in France and Italy. The European tour had lasted until fall, when Christina returned to New York. She had not written to her parents, using the excuse that she was too busy and did not have a return address for them to receive a reply. She decided that she would write to Becka instead.

Chapter Nineteen

They were in the city of Cannes in the south of France. Never had Christina seen a place so beautiful. From her third floor balcony overlooking the sea, she drank in the scent of her surroundings, wafting on the light breeze as it sped through her very spacious suite.

The phone jangled with an unfamiliar sound and Christina answered.

"Christina, it's Maggie. Will you be ready for a late dinner around eight or so? John and I have a great deal to discuss with you, it's very important."

"What's very important? For goodness sakes, Maggie, don't leave me dangling. It's hours yet before eight."

"I know that, but we had to be sure that, having the evening off from the photo shoot, you wouldn't go exploring as you usually do. Don't worry, it's all good news, I promise." On that note the connection was broken, and Christina's expression became pensive. They had come to Cannes for the spring film festival; the opportunity to mingle with the rich and famous was too great to miss. Four magazines had used their agency for feature articles, and a famous European line of designer fashions had scheduled a runway and photo shoot. They were booked for at least two weeks, and Christina wished that it would extend for at least two months. She had been working very hard over the past three years. Maggie and John were becoming very rich, as the agency landed large bookings and contracts. John had married Ellen, and they fit together like a well-worn pair of leather gloves. Ellen complemented John, and John relied upon her to tie up all the loose ends as he travelled extensively for the agency. On many occasions Ellen had accompanied him and, in her very quiet, composed, and efficient manner had managed to convince clients that John and his sister were the best in the business. Christina had little doubt that the two would remain married forever.

She dressed that evening in a pale peach silkscreen print dress that featured a fitted bodice, halter top, and bare back below the bra line, flaring out from the tiny waist in beautiful gores that moved with each step of her long, darkly tanned legs. She wore matching high heeled sandals and her long sun streaked hair was tied back secured by a headband of matching print. She was dressed to perfection, simply and elegantly, and all heads turned as she entered the open air restaurant behind the waiter. "Hope I'm not late. I couldn't wait after your phone call, Maggie. That was pretty mean of you to keep me guessing all afternoon. Well, I'm here now, what's up?"

Maggie laughed as she turned to John and Ellen. She apologized as she said, "Well, John, I had to ensure that she would have dinner with us, but I didn't tell her anything."

Christina faced the three of them, waiting with a slight smile upon her lips. The late evening sun was just sinking into the sea and they were bathed in golden light that never failed to make even the shabbiest place appear beautiful. Ellen spoke, "Perhaps we should tell Christina our good news first, John."

He ordered champagne for them, and as he raised his glass to touch theirs, he said, "You're looking at the proudest parents-to-be in the history of mankind."

At the news, a shadow crossed Christina face, but she quickly hid her feelings as the memory of those two infant faces swam before her eyes, and she lifted her glass and drank. She smiled through the tears as she said, along with Maggie, "That's wonderful. I'm so happy for you both. When will this tiny bundle arrive?"

John answered, "It will be a Christmas present for Aunt Maggie."

Maggie was speechless. They had kept this from her in order to share it at once. She couldn't be happier. Although Maggie was a striking looking woman in her own stead, she had never attempted to compete with her models. Instead, she had used the tricks of the trade to make a pointed chin appear rounder, a long nose appear shorter, and eyebrows and lashes to die for. Her shoulder-length honey blonde hair always looked windswept, but it suited her. She dressed for the business as a professional, well groomed and almost never casual. Christina admired her immensely for her poise, presence of mind, and assertiveness in all of their business dealings. She had become Christina's mentor and role model in the business end of the agency.

"Now that's out of the way, shall we order?" This came from John, who was always hungry, but never overweight.

"Please don't keep me in suspense any longer." Christina tried to appear stern. "My curiosity is beginning to hurt."

They all laughed. John turned to Maggie and said, "Will you tell her or shall I?" "Tell me what?" Now she was begging.

"Let's tell her together."

Maggie began. "Christina, you know how much we need you as part of our business. You have brought in more money and profit that any other model. Although it's a few months away from your twenty-first birthday, John and I are offering you a full partnership in the agency."

For a moment, Christina could say nothing. This was the next best thing that had ever happened to her. She had dreamed of some day owning her own business, but to be brought into the firm by the two people she respected and admired most was incomprehensible. She stuttered, "I ... I ... don't know what ... to say."

"Say yes, silly, and we can get on with our dinner."

"All right then, yes, oh, yes, I can't believe that you really want me!"

"Of course we do, we talked it all out in New York and decided to ask you here in Cannes.

What better place to make memories?"

"What exactly do you want me to do? Will I still be modeling?"

"Yes, nothing at that end will change. You will have more say in what we contract, and I'd like to use more of your designs. The fashion scene is changing so fast, a whole new line is emerging from Carnaby Street in England. It's scary. The colors are mismatched, the skirt lengths are all over the map, and what didn't go before is now in. Even hairdos are outlandish. We need a lot of help in this area if we intend to keep on top."

Ellen spoke. "Christina, I hate to change the subject, but there is a very handsome young man just to your right against the wall. He has not taken his eyes off you from the time you entered the café. Don't everyone look at once. Oh, oh, he's coming over to our table."

Christina kept her eyes focused upon the food in front of her, suddenly shy and at a loss for words. She had formed no relationships, still unable to trust her male counterparts in the language of love, and had dated sporadically. She was on uncertain ground in this area of human relationships. No one could touch her or affect her when she was on the runway. She was just someone to be admired from a distance and thus far she had been able to control her emotions. The pain of the past still occupied a very large part of her psyche and laid buried deep within.

The waiter precluded the stranger. *"Excuse moi, Mademoiselle.* This gentleman wishes to be introduced to you if you so wish."

Christina turned and looked up into the deepest sky blue eyes fringed with dark lashes that would be envied by many women. His smile flashed a row of teeth whitened in contrast to his deep tan. He was the handsomest man Christina had ever seen. Her heart skipped a beat, and her breath came in rapid gasps. As he leaned forward to take her hand, his rich black hair fell forward and a lock escaped from the carefully combed, perfectly groomed look of the present. "A rose, for one so beautiful. I could not resist, Mademoiselle." His French accent was unmistakable but soft and pleasant as he wrapped his tongue around the English pronunciations. As she extended her hand to take the rose, he grasped her hand and she felt his soft lips brush the surface of her hand. She was slightly embarrassed, as no man had ever kissed her hand before. She looked up and their eyes met. The electricity began to flow. If anyone had been watching Maggie, they would have seen a look of consternation cross her face. She couldn't see how anyone could resist this incredible stranger. She could feel herself being pulled in by his charm, and no doubt Christina was already lost.

"My name is Evan D'Argent. I am from Cherbourg on the coast. I have never seen such loveliness. You are Christina Corelli, non?"

"Yes, I am Christina." The reply seemed rather lame but she could think of nothing else to say, and she had learned that when one is at a loss for words, less is best. She allowed him to continue.

"Forgive me, but I have been staring at you for the past half hour. I could not allow you to leave without our having met, and now that we have, would you have lunch with me tomorrow? I would be honoured to show you Cannes as only someone who has been here many times can do."

Christina could not have said no, even if the word was printed on cue cards in block letters two feet high. She felt herself drawn to this man, pulled as a moth to lamplight, his charm a magnet that compelled her to reply, "I would like that very much, Monsieur D'Argent."

"Please, call me Evan. My driver will pick you up at your hotel at noon. You are staying at the Palais du Mer *n'est ce pas?* Say around eleven?"

"That would be wonderful. I look forward to it." Christina replied, still rather shaken by her emotions.

When he left the café, to Christina everything went flat. The moon had begun its ascent, and the stars sparkled intensely in the deep navy blue sky. The moonlight danced upon the sea and the warm breeze drifted through the villa-type restaurant, softly touching the patrons and moving on. She suddenly felt a chill, an omen perhaps, but the new emotions invoked by the meeting of this stranger were too strong and she shook off the warning of her conscience. Maggie and John chatted on as usual about the unexpected meeting, Maggie chiding her that if they made a photo shoot couple, she couldn't say who would grab the most attention. He was some hunk, according to Maggie's New York description. "I'll just bet he has a title. Or he is so rich, it's decadent."

The evening had been one with many twists and turns. Christina now had an assured income from the agency, a career path to pursue once her looks had faded, and with people whom she both trusted and loved. Maggie had quickly become Christina's surrogate mother when the two had met. Now she would be entrenched even deeper in Christina's life. Maggie was never a person to judge; she took what fate threw her, decided what course to follow, and kept on going. Christina had almost, on more than one occasion, blurted out the truth about the birth of her twins and the adoption. Perhaps she had not spoken because it would somehow diminish Maggie's respect for her. It was just too complicated and too emotional for Christina to discuss. She had not told her too much of her parents either; Christina kept them locked away in another compartment of her heart, unable to forgive them for what they had done. She remained a polite but aloof stranger to them, calling or writing sporadically until the cards had been exchanged only on special occasions, holidays and such. Becka was her one link to Cranston, her parents, and the hurtful memories.

After Evan and his party had left the restaurant Christina appeared to lose interest in the conversation. She played with her food, smiled occasionally, and interjected a yes or no from time to time, but she was definitely pre-occupied. Maggie finally decided to call it a night, much to Christina's relief. The talk had turned to the future prospects of the Agency, and although Christina would become a full partner when she signed the papers in New York, she had resisted the conversation. Maggie had noticed but said nothing, deciding Christina was most likely tired from the many appearances she had made over the past week. They still had a ways to go to honour their contracts in Cannes, and Maggie yearned to go to Monte Carlo even if it was just an overnight stay. To be this close and not wander through the posh and famous casino would be a great disappointment.

Christina slept deeply that night and awoke refreshed and eager to explore. They had the weekend off and she promised to make the most of it with or without Evan D'Argent. She chose a casual and very comfortable ensemble for her luncheon date, expensive and chic, but in the soft beige tones that complimented her golden tan. She had room service bring her a light breakfast at nine a.m. and Christina had lounged on the spacious balcony overlooking the harbor. Below her she had studied the many types of sailing craft; magnificent yachts, large double sailing boats, small fishing tour boats. It all added to the ambience of this delightful coastal resort. She had noticed an enormous yacht that was anchored offshore, most probably too large to enter the small harbour and moor at the pier. A launch was dispatched on an as- needed basis to carry the passengers to and from the resort. Christina wondered if the sixty- five foot yacht was privately owned or was a commercial boat commissioned by the rich and famous. The telephone jangled at her elbow as she leafed through the fashion magazines. She spoke, "Hello, Christina speaking."

"Mademoiselle Corelli. This is the hotel concierge, Monsieur D'Argent is here in the lobby.

Will Mademoiselle be down soon?"

"Yes, in a few minutes. Thank you Monsieur."

"Au revoir, Mademoiselle."

She spoke little or no French other than what one uses during polite exchanges, and had no inclination to learn. In an international resort of this stature, many languages were spoken and the hotel staff was conversant in most. English appeared to be the accepted norm and she was grateful for this fact. Christina took one last turn in the mirror to ensure that her efforts made her appear perfect but casual and nodded to her image, satisfied that she looked her best, and left the suite. Little did she know that this day would change her life forever.

Chapter Twenty

A S SHE LEFT THE elevator Christina searched the lobby for Evan. Their eyes met simultaneously and she felt her heart beat faster. He was even more handsome than yesterday. Smiling shyly, she accepted his kiss on both cheeks, as was the European custom, and his warm smile. He said, "Good morning, Miss Corelli, you take my breath away."

"Please call me Christina, may I call you Evan?"

"Oui, Evan and Christina it is. Now, my lovely, I have a wonderful day planned if you will allow me to show you Cannes as it should be seen."

Christina nodded and they left the hotel. Evan had a way of encircling her waist so as to guide her through double doors, out onto streets, and dodge passers-by. It was intimate but not as lovers who stroll through parks with their arms entwined about one another. Christina actually liked the control, as it was meant to protect her rather than anything else. Evan had learned this trick many years before, when the girls had flocked about him in droves. He was twenty-nine, very continental and very experienced in seduction. Christina, although knowledgeable in the ways of the world, was not worldly as were Suzanne and Zoe, two of her agency's models. She was not totally innocent, but her adolescent voyage into motherhood had not prepared her for the Evans of the world. They had taken an immediate liking to one another, and Evan decided that slow and carefully was the way to treat this one.

She was very impressed when Evan stopped beside a small two-seater roadster with outside running boards, spoke wheels, and lots of chrome. When Christina got into the vehicle, she felt as though she was two inches off the ground, but the front bucket seat was extremely comfortable. Evan was a very fast driver, speed being an aphrodisiac to him. They sped away from the curb and darted in and out of oncoming traffic, through the cobblestone streets that hardly seemed wide enough to accommodate pedestrians, carts, bicycles, and cars. They left the port behind and began to climb, accessing switchback after switchback. Christina felt her breath coming in gasps and she began to feel faint. Evan had said nothing, hoping to reach the summit and overlook and share the view with Christina. They never made it. She slumped in the seat and her head lolled against the door. He could not pull the car over as the cliff road was far too narrow. He reached over and felt her forehead. She felt clammy. He did not panic but his alarm for her caused him to drive faster. He reached the summit in record time and pulled the car over onto the wide expanse of the overlook. He came to a screeching halt, killed the motor and reached for Christina.

"Christina, are you all right? Speak to me. It's Evan. What is it, *cherie?*" He rubbed her wrists and held her in his arms.

A few minutes passed by. Just as Evan was about to ask someone to come to his aid, she mumbled something and opened her eyes. "Evan, what happened?"

"I don't exactly know ... you were talking one minute then you fainted. Are you all right?" "I think so." She was beginning to feel rather foolish. She had never fainted in her life.

"Where are we?"

"I couldn't stop on the narrow road so I drove us up to the summit. We are above Cannes."

"Forgive me, Evan, but I think I know what caused me to faint. A few years ago we were driving from Rome to Milan and we all were involved in a horrific car accident. I received a concussion and spent an overnight in the hospital. It must have been the winding curves and switchbacks that triggered the panic attack. I must apologize."

"No, it is you who must forgive me. I drive too fast, more for the thrill than anything, and I should have thought better of it before I endangered your life. You have every right to be angry with me." He had grasped both of her hands in his and felt the coldness of her flesh. He bent to kiss her hands and then his eyes, filled with worry and distress, met hers. When she was emotional, Christina's emerald eyes darkened in color, the outer rim well defined, and they shimmered now with tears of relief.

"I'm fine, Evan, it wasn't your fault. I should have said something, but I didn't think that we would be out of Cannes so suddenly and climbing to these heights. I still have to go back down, don't I?"

"We will wait until you feel better. Come, let's walk to the retaining wall. I have my camera and I would like us to have our picture taken together. A memento of our first day together; it's just the beginning of a lifetime of days. We'll ask this lady to take our picture."

She smiled bravely as they approached the tourist. She gladly accepted the camera and Christina and Evan stood together looking into each other's eyes with the panorama of the Mediterranean Sea and the myriad of sea vessels and red tiled rooftops below. The flowers gave off a heady perfume and the trees offered shade to the onlookers. It was a moment captured in time, forever on film. The stranger asked, "Would you like a few more, Monsieur? It is no trouble." Evan smiled and agreed that a few more shots would take Christina's mind off her recent incident. She appeared to be fully recovered, her color returning to its natural golden state.

He accepted the camera and thanked the lady profusely. He rested his arm on Christina's shoulder casually, protectively, his head bent to hear her as they commented on the spectacular view spread before them. Evan, for a Frenchman, was very tall. His family averaged less than six feet, but Evan was six foot two and carried himself proudly; his posture was erect and perfect. His disjointed walk bordered upon the carefree, but it had been his signature feature since adolescence. Christina had worn flat sandals for the day and it was a pleasure to actually stand beside someone whose body moulded perfectly as they stood side by side. He curbed his desire to hold her in his arms and kiss her over and over again. She was the most delightful, stunning woman he had been with for a very long time. Lately his companions had been cheap, tawdry, classless, loud, overly everything ... make-up, low cut clothes, too high heels, too much skin exposed for public appearances. This one was perfect. She had been born beautiful and anything that was further applied only enhanced it without taking away or changing her look. Her hair and skin were vibrant, not washed out and pale as models who starved themselves to stay thin. Christina's height handled her weight and she was active enough to eat normally. Evan was very proud to be her escort. He had not missed the envy and admiration of the crowd milling about. She felt the pull of emotion as they talked, especially when their eyes met and his sudden smile transformed his face. Little did she realize that the effect she was having on Evan was being returned tenfold. He had never been so captivated by a woman in his life.

Perhaps the game he was playing would backfire. Seduce and conquer had always been his goal when it came to relationships, but this deepening emotion was new and rather painful. This one he wanted to protect, nurture, befriend, and love. Was this the birth of a long and lasting love? He had no idea ... Evan was entirely selfish. It came with his upbringing, the monumental wealth and prestige, the attention of the European best, and he had taken it all for granted. Christina was just another facet to add to his experience. He argued with himself that no, this one was different.

Christina was speaking, "Evan, I think we should go. It's almost lunchtime and you did say we had reservations at the pier. If you drive slowly down the mountain, then I think I'll be fine. Please, let's go."

As they drove down the mountainside she was not on the outer edge. Being in the passenger seat, she faced the oncoming traffic, which was few and far between. A tour bus was meandering its way below them as she studied the road. Evan had slowed the convertible to half his normal speed, and the ride down was soon over. Once again, they were in the hustle and bustle of the busy port. The restaurant Evan had chosen overlooked the pier and the inlet but afforded a quiet measure of privacy as they sat at a table for two against the stone parapet. Steps led down to the sea for the patrons to enjoy a walk after their meal. They lingered over wine as the luncheon wore well into the afternoon. Evan glanced at his watch and remarked, "Christina, it's almost past two and I wanted to take you to the market. Are you up to it?"

She accepted the challenge, rested and refreshed after the luncheon. If they lingered any longer she would feel the need for an afternoon nap. She gathered up her hat and handbag, putting on her sunglasses as Evan paid the waiter. Heads turned as usual as they left the restaurant, promising that they would come again and perhaps access the beach from the parapet. The pace of the day had slowed as the morning shopping activity and customers had diminished over the noon hour. Christina purchased a silk scarf and a few pieces of jewellery as gifts for the future, unable to resist the fine craftsmanship of the fine gold rings and bracelets. Italian gold was 24-carat, and a find in New York. Here it was prolific, as well as the choice. Evan bought her a fine gold cross and as they waited for it to be engraved she relaxed and surveyed the stalls and people of this delightful place. It would be wonderful if she could stay here forever. The thought surprised her, as everyone knew Christina loved her work, especially the cameras, lights, excitement, and anticipation before a show. Such was the pace of her life that this, in comparison, was as different as night from day.

She was reluctant to have the day end. With her purchases stored in the trunk of the roadster, Evan drove slowly back to the hotel. He kissed Christina on both cheeks saying, "Thank you, Christina, for a most enjoyable day. Perhaps dinner tonight would be in order?"

She did not hesitate. "Evan, except for this morning, this has been wonderful. No one approached me for my autograph, the only camera was your personal one, and I must say, I have never been in better hands. I've had a wonderful time. Yes, I accept."

"I have a surprise for you. Dress is optional, but you must bring a jacket, a sweater, or a wrap to ward off the evening breezes." With a promise in his eyes of better things to come, he left her in the lobby. She watched as his figure disappeared through the hotel doors. She was in a state of euphoria and reluctant to come back to earth. She literally swept through the doors of her suite and threw herself backward upon the spacious canopied bed. A great sigh of happiness escaped her and as she fantasized about Evan D'Argent and Christina Corelli, she fell asleep amidst her array of purchases and her hat. She slept deeply for two hours, until the phone on the nightstand awoke her. Still drowsy, she spoke into the receiver. "Hello, Christina speaking."

"Christina, it's Maggie. Where have you been? I tried your hotel a number of times at lunch, and tried searching the shops, but to no avail. I've been worried."

"Oh Maggie, I had the most marvellous time today. Evan D'Argent is the best thing that has happened to me in a very long time. I'm going to dinner with him tonight. He says it's a surprise."

"We've also been invited to dinner by Evan's personal valet. The whole crew, all of the models, Suzanne, and Zoe can't wait. I did some asking around about him. He is filthy rich, unmarried, and a womanizer. Please be careful, Christina. You are a baby compared to this one."

"Maggie, you worry about me too much, and I adore you for it, but we are just friends. He didn't even attempt to kiss me today. Perhaps tonight, but who cares? He is the handsomest man I have ever met and has the manners of a complete gentleman. I felt a little empty when he left me downstairs in the lobby, and it seems like days before eight tonight."

When Maggie heard this she felt a sinking sensation in her stomach. This Evan D'Argent was a womanizer of the worst kind: well bred, filthy rich, and handsome. Women had committed suicide over him ... well, only if you could believe the tabloids. However, they always had a basis in some of what they published. She promised herself that nothing would happen to Christina as she was so very dear to her, the younger sister she had never had. They chatted for a few more minutes until Maggie rang off, assured that she would see Christina that evening. Christina was puzzled as to where they were all going for dinner, but she imagined that Evan had most likely reserved an entire restaurant, and music, for the agency. It was exciting just to think about the evening before her.

Chapter Twenty-One

CHRISTINA WHILED AWAY THE ensuing hours before seven p.m. She drew a hot bath, filled it with her favourite bubble bath, called room service for lemon tea, and locked herself away for an hour, luxuriating in the aromas and sensations which surrounded her in the spacious tub. She relived her morning and early afternoon with Evan, rejected most of the information Maggie had imparted about his character, and decided that the best approach was to find out for herself. She was not as vulnerable as Maggie suspected, and her memories of Adam remained forever present in her heart. She tried to compare the two men. They were as opposite in coloring, personalities, clothing, and background as they could get. The only thing they had in common was their height. Adam was only slightly taller than Evan. She had placed the locket on the night table beside her journal next to the gold cross that Evan had purchased for her in the market.

Refreshed from her bath, Christina wrapped her long hair in a terry towel and clothed her body in the thick white terry robes supplied by the hotel. She placed her feet in the mule slippers which travelled everywhere with her and padded over to the writing desk. She opened her journal and was surprised that the date of the last entry was when she had received her last letter from Becka. She definitely had to write to Becka. Instead of doing just so, she thought it would be best to bring her journal up-to-date with the casual date with Evan and the promise of better things to come. She would write to Becka a day or so before she left Cannes to return to New York. When she returned to the States, Christina would telephone Becka and with the two-way conversation they could catch up very quickly. Becka had graduated from nursing school at the end of May and was working for her father, although she had hoped to be hired by the local hospital. Becka enjoyed the emergency department more than any of the other disciplines in nursing.

Christina had wired an enormous bouquet of flowers with a congratulatory note, a beautiful sterling silver nurse's watch, and a promise of more to come later. She had not corresponded with her parents since Christmas, and had no inclination to do so. Her Aunt Maria she called on a regular basis, and was always told how much they loved and missed her, but they understood that she was so famous that she didn't have the time to visit. Christina always felt better after touching base with her Toronto family. Sometimes Maria would give her little tidbits about her parents, but there really wasn't too much communication from out west. In a nutshell, her father was now a millionaire, Tonio was his right-hand man, and he and Becka were madly in love. Tonio's mother was so very proud of her son and she loved Becka as she would a daughter. She still continued working at the telephone exchange, having made her peace with Rosie the waitress and Gino's loose and reckless way of living. Teresa had no interest in male companionship since Gino had been killed, and she busied herself with her job and her home. She had included a note with Becka's last letter. It carried some hidden message hinting at some trouble in Angela and Frank's marriage, but Christina couldn't second guess anything in the cryptic letter. She would ask Becka when next they spoke on the telephone.

She carefully selected a two piece outfit, choosing a loose-fitting top of a sheer organza, a soft doeskin coloured-over blouse, with a solid halter top bra in a color slightly darker than the top. The slacks were cut to perfection, accenting her long legs and clinging to her thighs as she walked. To complement the ensemble, Christina recalled Evan's advice and chose a cashmere sweater of a matching shade, which she arranged across her back. She allowed the sleeves to come forward over each shoulder, folded in such a manner as to appear as a wool wrap. If necessary, she could put the sweater on over her thin blouse and still be dressed informally but not underdressed for the occasion. Her matching sandals peaked out from under the wide pant leg, revealing the gold braid that enhanced the leather thongs. She arranged her hair to match the look, tying it back with a round gold metallic clasp. Christina reached for the gold locket, then for the first time in many years she did not choose the locket, but substituted it for the gold cross. Her bracelets were many in number: gold filigree, gold hearts, all embellished and hammered in many designs. She placed gold hoop earrings in each lobe, stood back and inspected her image. It would do, according to her expectations. Christina used very little make-up when she was not working. A touch of green eye shadow, along with dark eyeliner, and a touch of color to her cheeks and her lips were about all that she required. The hot lights of the runway and the evening strobe lights during a show paled her complexion and washed her out, so her make-up artist had carte blanche when it came to making the most of her looks.

At five to eight, the telephone rang. A car had arrived to fetch Mademoiselle Corelli, if she was ready. She wondered where Evan was as she left the suite. An impeccably dressed man in a nautical uniform of a navy blazer, matching crown hat with gold emblem resembling a family crest, and white pants and shoes approached her as she entered the lobby. "Mademoiselle Corelli. I am Jean, the first mate. The limousine is at your service."

Unaccustomed to such service, Christina blushed as she became aware of the hotel guests admiring the tall, beautiful model and her escort. Jean opened the back door of the limousine for her and she slid onto a white leather seat that was butter-soft. He walked around the car, opened the door and slid behind the wheel. The glass partition was down and Christina asked, "Jean, where are we going? Where is Monsieur D'Argent? I didn't expect any of this."

"Patience, Mademoiselle, all will be revealed in a very short time."

The limousine came to a stop on the pier and Christina, upon alighting, was escorted to a large launch such as those which small tour groups rent for a day trip. An extended hand helped her into the launch as she joined the group already waiting. Many of her group was there, as well as Maggie, and all had the same question for her, "Where are we all going?"

Jean started the launch and over the roar of the motor explained that they would be boarding the large yacht that Christina had seen out in the harbour that morning. The name on the side of the small ship became visible as they drew near, The Elena. Surprised and very impressed, Maggie said, "I guess he really is filthy rich, as well as handsome,

Christina. Watch yourself or you'll be swept away, and the next thing I know we'll be looking for a model to fill your shoes."

"Don't be silly. I have no intention of falling in love with Evan, even if he is Europe's most eligible bachelor. He's not my type."

Zoe spoke. "Well if you don't want him, Christina, throw him my way. I'd marry him tomorrow."

They all laughed as the launch came aside the yacht. A boarding stairway was descending along the side of the boat and was held steady for the passengers to board. Once safely on deck, the launch had one more trip to the pier for the last load of guests. Evan helped her safely onto the deck; his arms held her firmly as she felt the yacht move beneath her feet. He laughed when she tried to steady herself, getting used to the roll of the ship. "Evan, I don't think I can walk around on the deck. Just let me sit for a few minutes." Evan guided her to a long table beside a buffet that was laden with everything a person could possibly crave. The fresh flowers on the table lent an air of festivity to the softly lit dining area. Glassware, and an array of liquor and wine bottles, was mirrored behind the bartender at the long gleaming bar. Pot lights set in the roof of the top deck shone down upon the guests as they admired the polished teak of the walls and ceiling. The floor was burnished walnut, darker than the walls but no less luxurious. Christina was totally captivated by her surroundings. Evan ordered a bottle of champagne, chilled to perfection, and they began the evening in earnest with a toast to love and what was yet to come.

Maggie and Jean, who was a splendid first mate, were drawn to one another at first sight. Christina was happy for her. Maggie had had a number of uneventful relationships, mostly with handsome young men wanting an in with the agency to further their careers. She had given up on finding any one who wanted to be with her for herself alone, without wealth, fame, or agency. Jean knew little or nothing about the fashion industry and cared even less. He no doubt found Maggie to be a very good looking, down-to-earth woman with a passion that just had to be unleashed by the right man. He opted to become just that man. They mingled with the guests, Christina having trouble remembering names, so she nodded politely and gave Evan the floor. He conversed with each guest in turn, put everyone at ease, and was the first to begin the dancing as the music played at just the right pitch to encourage conversation and not drown out words.

The food was incredible. The variety was decadent, to say the least; from Beluga caviar to freshly caught lobster, brilliantly red and shiny beside the freshly clarified butter. Salads of all kinds abounded for the discerning dieter, as well as sushi and fresh oysters. After the long luncheon with Evan earlier that day, Christina chose a few hors d'oeuvres topped with black Russian caviar and a tall fluted glass filled with sparkling champagne. The evening was thus far a definite success. Christina relaxed in Evan's company, still captivated by her surroundings. A funny thought crossed her mind, from Italy to Cranston, Paris to Cannes, and back again. It was almost a ditty as the words ran through her mind, over and over again until she had to share them with Evan. When he asked, *"Ques't ce que c'est* this Cranston?"

She merely said, "Another time, Evan. Come, let's dance."

Zoe and Suzanne were seated at the bar and had quite a congregation of young men at their beck and call. Zoe's need for attention stemmed from her Gypsy roots. She had a very passionate and fierce temperament and enjoyed life to the fullest. She thrived on attention no matter what the source. She soon latched onto a member of the crew, as attested to by his uniform, and they danced slowly, sensuously, their bodies moulded together. Zoe was not a tall model. She had just met the minimum requirements at five foot eight inches, but her startling black hair, olive complexion, and long, thick, dark eyelashes framing deep velvet brown eyes made the photographer job easy. She was a natural and knew it. After an hour or so they disappeared, most likely to take a turn about the deck.

Just before midnight Christina noticed through the haze of smoke and dim lights that the party noise level had increased as the liquor flowed freely. Couples were becoming more intimate, clinging to one another on the dance floor, whispering and kissing at the tables; the sound of seductive laughter drifted in through the open doorway to the outer deck. A few couples had drifted outside to escape the crowded room and seek privacy. A vivacious red-haired French girl known only as Colette was seated alone at a table along the far wall, staring out onto the deck. Her expression was definitely not one that indicated that she was enjoying herself. Her eyes were focused upon a couple silhouetted against the moonlight, the woman's back to the railing and the man hovering over her, unwilling to break the long embrace. Without warning, Colette butted her cigarette in an ashtray, knocking her glass over. She leapt from the table and made a dash for the open door, her hands clenched in fists and her face white with anger. Christina heard her scream, *"Cochon,* Motherfucker," and she was out on the deck. Evan and Christina watched in horror as they heard her curse, "American bitch," and Zoe disappeared over the railing. Armand yelled "Man overboard," as he attempted to control the pummelling fists and the hysterical Colette. A drunken woman was not a pretty sight, but a drunken woman in a jealous rage was a force to be reckoned with. Evan was out on the deck with Jean at his side. The yacht's powerful searchlights had been turned on and Christina could see Zoe far below her struggling in the water. Evan shouted, "Jean, the launch, it is near her on the port side. Come." They were in the launch in record time, the motor started smoothly about the same time as Zoe managed to swim and catch the lifesaver. Everyone was leaning over the railing, trying to get a glimpse of the drama before them. The conversation had died down to a mere murmur. Colette had passed out and was thrown over Armand's shoulder in disgust as he carried her into the lounge and literally tossed her down on the leather sofa. He left her there, passed out from the alcohol she had consumed, not caring whether she lived or died. His expression was one of total disgust.

Zoe was quickly plucked from the water and a heavy warm blanket was wrapped about her. She resembled a wet rat. Christina and Maggie were there to help her aboard and take her to the lounge. Big mistake. Zoe spotted Colette passed out on the sofa and her eyes blazed. "That's the bitch, isn't it? Let me at her. Maggie, Christina, let go of me."

The two women held Zoe firmly and felt the anger go out of her. She looked exhausted. Evan was by her side and Christina turned to him as she said, "It looks as though the party's at an end, Evan. I'm so sorry this had to happen. Zoe is none the worse from her swim, and I'm sure after a long day in bed she'll be just fine. It's been wonderful, Evan, thank you so much."

He answered, "Christina, I'm sorry too. I must stay and see to my guests or I would accompany you on the return launch. I will call you tomorrow." He bent his head and kissed her softly, moving his lips firmly but gently in a rhythm that sent tingling sensations coursing through her body. It was not passionate, but it was no less loving. She was shaken, by her response. Christina smiled, turned, and left the deck. She waved goodbye as Evan watched the boat pull away from the yacht. He sighed as he returned to organize the staff and entertain his remaining guests, awaiting the returning launch. The kiss had been successful. He had felt the electricity between them and he smiled inwardly. She was so damned incredible; she had no idea how much he wanted her. Perhaps that was just as well, as his passion and need would no doubt overwhelm and scare her away. He had sensed her inner naïve nature and respected her moral standards, to a point.

The hotel concierge was most concerned when he saw the bedraggled and still very wet Zoe being escorted by members of her agency into the lobby. They were whisked into the elevator before a crowd could gather, as the hotel's respect for the privacy of their guests was of the utmost importance.

Zoe was soon settled in a hot bubble bath with hot coffee at her elbow. The color had returned to her cheeks, and she began to find humour in the situation. That red-headed bitch had come at her like a charging rhino, and Zoe had had no time to defend herself. The water hadn't been as cold as she expected and the attention she received throughout the ordeal gave her an incredible rush.

Suzanne had surfaced and come to shore on the second launch. She had missed the entire incident. Suzanne had found entertainment elsewhere, such as in one of the staterooms with a little cocaine and a lot of sex. She was still high when she rushed in on Zoe in her bath. "Are you all right? My God, you could've drowned, Zoe. What the hell happened?"

"Not to worry. I'm an excellent swimmer, remember? It was just an attack by some jealous French bitch, but Armand was worth it. What a hunk. They don't grow them like that in America. These guys believe in foreplay, for hours and hours until I got so wound up I didn't know what I was doing. How about you?"

Suzanne smiled, sharing the secret. "I couldn't wait … you should see the staterooms on that tub. It was the ultimate luxury that money can buy. If Christina doesn't want Evan D'Argent then I'm in line. Just think, I'd never have to work again, shop till I drop, travel wherever my heart desires. Unbelievable."

Zoe replied, "In your dreams, Suzanne. I saw how he looked at Christina. You haven't a chance, but there's no harm in dreaming."

"That's it. You're fine, I'm fine. I'm going to bed. See you at noon for lunch." She left the bathroom as abruptly as she had entered.

Zoe was relaxed and now very tired. The bath had done its job, and she dried herself off haphazardly, threw on a nightie, and with a long sigh crawled between the satin sheets. She was asleep almost as soon as her head touched the pillow.

Meanwhile, Christina and Maggie were in a suite down the hall going over the evening's events. The incident with Zoe was dwarfed by the fact that Maggie actually confessed that she was falling in love with Jean. She cared not if he was married, single, or attached, she wanted him for herself. She said, "I would cross the Atlantic once a week to be in his arms. Does that sound silly, Christina? You probably wouldn't understand. You haven't been in love."

Christina paled as she accepted the words. The image of Adam, so close to her heart, swam before her eyes, and she attempted to compose herself, trying to appear nonchalant and happy for Maggie. She quipped, "How do you know I have never been in love, Maggie?"

"Well, I don't really know, do I? How could you? You're just a baby."

Christina yawned suddenly and stretched. "I know you'd like to talk about Jean all evening, but Maggie, I'm exhausted. The day has just been too long and eventful. Meet me for lunch, and put the do not disturb sign on my door on your way out."

Maggie arose reluctantly from the bed, said goodnight, and closed the door softly behind her. She floated down the hallway to her own suite, to dream the dreams of the newly-in-love. She felt the years fall away as she recalled the admiration in Jean's eyes and his protective arm about her waist as they mingled with other guests, the security in the circle of his arms. She was going to be twenty-eight years old in a matter of weeks and had seen the wrinkles beginning to form. She used all of the products available, but the laugh wrinkles were beginning to show, and a few creases at the corner of her eyes. Jean had been the soul of attention, and she had hopes of future days in his company.

Within minutes Maggie, too, was ready for bed. She chuckled when she recalled Zoe's wet form being pulled from the water. All Zoe could say, was "What will this do to my image, Maggie?"

She fell into a deep sleep, only to be awakened by a loud banging on her door. Maggie looked at the clock and saw that it was just past eight a.m. The phone jangled at her elbow. She quickly threw on a robe, picked up the receiver, told the person to hold on, and answered the door. John was there with a look of thunder on his face. "Get dressed. We have to talk to Christina."

"Tell me what's wrong, John. Has something happened to Ellen? It's not the baby, is it?" "No, they're fine."

Just then, she noticed the bundle of daily newspapers he had clutched under his arm. "What's with the papers, John?"

"Just hurry and get dressed. I'll wait." He called room service and ordered plenty of strong hot coffee, orange juice, and toast for three to be delivered to Christina's suite as soon as possible. "And keep the press away."

Maggie paled. "Press, what press?"

"That press, Maggie my dear. Have a look out the window."

From her second story balcony Maggie overlooked the parking lot and the front entrance of the old hotel. The parking lot was swarming with news people, cameras dangling from shoulder straps, all trying to get into the hotel lobby. They were being held back by a harried-looking doorman as a few more bellhops came to his aid. The press of the crowd was enormous, but the hotel concierge locked the front doors after announcing that the hotel was closed to the public. A loud roar echoed up from the entrance; the paparazzi refused to give up. This was the scent of a scandal with big names and famous faces, their bread and butter.

John and Maggie burst into Christina's room just as she was awakened by the noise from the street below. "What's going on? Maggie, what time is it?"

John spread the dailies out on the bed and the bold black headlines of the pulp trade leapt from the front page. A photo of Christina with Evan's arm around her as they leaned over the railing appeared before her and another of Zoe as she was being pulled from the water. The headlines were all alike: SUPERMODEL C.C. PART OF YACHT ORGY. Christina read another: SHIPPING MAGNATE D'ARGENT WITH A NEW CONQUEST AS YACHT PARTY TURNS UGLY'

Where did they get the pictures? Apparently, no one had noticed the photographer who had slipped into the last launch with his camera hidden under his wind breaker. As some of the guests were unacquainted with everyone, he was assumed to be a member of the party. His camera had taken a number of pictures, as was attested to inside the first page. There were pictures of couples dancing as one, a couple entering a stateroom, and a few patrons obviously doing cocaine, their backs to the camera, all in the guise of playing a game of billiards. It was a total disaster. The entire party was displayed for the world to see and feed their sick curiosity. The only picture of Christina was the one shown on the cover of most of the dailies. She was speechless. Finally she spoke, "What will this do to us? "

There was a firm knock on the outer door, and a male voice called out, "Room service, *Monsieurs et Madames.*"

"Entre," John replied. The waiter came in with a cart bearing their breakfast, and a very angry, very upset concierge in his wake.

"I must speak with you people, immediately. The reputation of this hotel is at stake. Never have we had such a scandal. The news people are all over the place. What is to be done? Should you wish to leave immediately we would be only too happy to oblige."

The man was obviously so distraught that John offered him a coffee and laced it with Cognac. He gratefully accepted the strong drink and attempted to calm himself. Christina remembered the private number Evan had given her in case she wished to reach him at all times. She said, "Hold on, I'm going to call Evan. He'll know how to handle this. I sure don't."

The phone rang three times and Christina heard Evan's voice, *"Allo. Ici Evan D'Argent."*

"Evan, it's Christina. We have a situation at the hotel. A cameraman was aboard the yacht last night and the headlines are not kind. Please, can you come? You must know how to handle these people. The concierge is almost hysterical, the front doors are locked, and the paparazzi have surrounded the hotel. We really need your help."

"I will be there as soon as the launch can bring me in. Don't talk to anyone. Stay in your suite. I will want to speak to the concierge as soon as I arrive. Tell him I will meet him in his office. Has he asked you all to leave? Yes, then I know how to handle this. I will see you soon, cherie, do not worry."

She relayed Evan's words as soon as she had replaced the receiver on its cradle. Monsieur le Concierge, Monsieur D'Argent is on his way. He will meet with you in your office upon his arrival. Please be patient. We will have the situation in hand. Until then, we will remain as guests of this hotel." Her anger and frustration rose as she finished the statement by reverting to Italian, *"Capice?"*

Without thinking he replied, *"Si, capice."*

"Stay away from the window, or some guy will probably attempt to climb the drainpipe up to the balcony. You don't want tomorrow's picture to be one of you peeking from behind a curtain. God knows what they'll make of that. The problem with these paper rags is that they make up what they don't know. By the time one gets around to the courts and suing them, the damage has already been done. How many people do you know that read a retraction or apologize over an incident that happened months prior? Time, momentum, and the public's sick need for scandal are all on their side. We have to find a way to get out of the limelight. I don't want this agency to be the news of the day."

"You're absolutely right. Here, give me some more of that brandy ... Christina, have some.

I don't care if it's before noon; we all need a little bolstering."

The concierge was summoned to his office within the hour. Evan had arrived and was escorted in through the back entrance, through the kitchen, and into the manager's office. Monsieur Cartier promptly left, promising to call them with any news. Another half hour passed. A knock on the door brought them to attention. Evan came into the room with a broad smile on his face. "Good morning my friends, problem solved."

"Hello to you too, Evan. What do you mean, problem solved? Just like that?" John said, snapping his fingers.

"Oui, just like that."

"You mean they're not going to throw us out?" Maggie asked. "No, that is very unlikely, Maggie."

"How can you be so sure?"

"I bought the hotel, so you are now my guests and you can stay as long as you wish. I have a suggestion. Leave behind most of your luggage and I'll invite Maggie and Christina, as well as you and your wife, to sail with us to Monte Carlo for a week or so, until this has died down."

John was the first to answer. "I cannot come, but thank you anyway. I have to remain here in Cannes to pack up our gear and the crew and get them on a plane back to New York. Our work is done here and we were just unwinding by attending your party. Besides, my wife isn't much of a sailor and she needs her rest. We are expecting our first child and I don't want anything to jeopardize her condition."

Maggie and Christina accepted. Maggie had always wished to visit the small kingdom of Monaco, and to be able to do so as a millionaire's guest in the company of her newly found love was an answer to all of her prayers. No one could reach them on the yacht once they set sail, and they could take as much time as necessary. The launch would go into the small fishing ports along the way and collect the dailies, just to see if the furor had died down as he had promised it would.

Christina felt swept up by the events. Everything seemed out of control. One minute she was sleeping, the next she was an infamous American supermodel, associated with a filthy rich shipping magnate of world renown. She decided to go with the flow.

Chapter Twenty-Two

JOHN, MAGGIE, AND CHRISTINA held a hurried meeting and agreed that the side excursion to Monte Carlo would not be a lengthy one, much to Maggie's disappointment. Christina had mixed feelings about the cruise. Evan was good company, but she just wanted to put the whole episode behind her and return to New York and her familiar world of work. Ellen was happy to be returning to the comfort of her own home, where she could rest and recuperate from the trip. It had certainly been interesting.

Evan sent the limousine around to the hotel to collect his guests at noon the next day. They had packed only what they required, leaving the rest of their luggage in one suite and cancelling the other. Maggie was walking on clouds. Jean was extra attentive as he helped her into the spacious back seat. Christina's smile suggested a conspiracy where Jean was concerned. The launch ride to the yacht anchored offshore was uneventful and pleasant. When they boarded the ship, Evan was there to greet them.

The yacht was spotless. All traces of last night's party had long been erased; it was spit and polished to perfection. Christina was still awed by the luxury of the interior. Lunch was waiting at the buffet and, once settled in their staterooms, the two women began to relax and enjoy their sudden mini-holiday. Evan was most attentive, while Jean attended to duties aboard. Once they were seriously on their way, he joined them for lunch. Christina refused the champagne for lunch, but did accept the demi-tasse of espresso. It was stimulating and delicious.

Evan took Christina on a grand tour of the lower deck and engine room. She was amazed at how large everything was, yet compact for storage. He had a games rooms which held a standard-size billiard table, and a long mirrored bar with attached brass and leather upholstered stools decorated the far wall. It featured a small roulette wheel, and a baccarat table was also evident. It was a personal floating casino, miniature but nonetheless very active and lucrative for the owner.

Maggie and Christina changed into beach wear with light cover-ups and enjoyed the hot afternoon sun on deck. An average-sized swimming pool was at their disposal, or Evan suggested a stop to anchor so they could swim in one of the rocky coves along their route. The water was so clear that one could see to great depths, and it was not as cold as they imagined. The swim ladder was easy to use and Christina was a strong swimmer. She swam for an hour and came aboard totally refreshed. Memories of the ugly tabloid headlines began to fade. Evan did not join them in their swim but promised he would do so the next day. They passed the coastal city of Nice, the yacht swinging closer to shore so that they could take pictures. Christina had refused an evening foray into the city, fearing that they might be recognized. Evan agreed, wanting to hoard his time with her alone.

He had become very attentive during the evening meal, and as soft music piped in throughout the lounge played, they swayed to the slow music. Moonlight poured through the upper deck windows, bathing them in rays of pale light. The mood became magical. Maggie and Jean disappeared outdoors for a stroll around the deck and to watch the play of moonlight on the wake. Evan spoke, "You are so lovely in the moonlight, *cherie*. I cannot tell you how happy I am that you are here with me."

"Evan, this is magic. I never imagined that a cruise could be so wonderful. The food, the weather, the sea, the company ... I can't thank you enough."

He leaned forward and kissed her lightly on the lips. She responded in kind, kissing him back. Perhaps it was the nearly empty bottle champagne, but she was already light headed. Another drink and she would be tipsy. He continued his advances until Christina found herself locked in an embrace that was no longer gentle, but passionate and aggressive, a man with a mission kissing an attractive and willing partner. She broke away gasping for air, unaccustomed to such ardour. He looked extremely serious as he said, "What is it, *cherie?* Have I done something to frighten you? I thought you wanted me to make love to you."

"Evan, please, it's not you," she replied, hastily arranging her clothes, "I just need a little time. I really don't know very much about you."

He laughed as he said, "What do you want to know?"

"Well, for starters, where do you make your home? Do you have brothers and sisters?

Have you ever been married, or are you married?"

His passion already cooling, Evan decided that conversation could be put to use as good foreplay. "My parents live in Paris and I live in Cherbourg, in the north where our shipping yards are located. My sister is married and lives in Paris for part of the year and travels with her husband during the winter months. I barely see her. I have no brothers, so I am the heir apparent when my parents are no longer living. I attended the University of Notre Dame in Paris, graduating with a law degree in commerce. To date, I enjoy my life to the fullest, which means surrounding myself with the world's best of everything, as well as a very beautiful woman. No, I have never been married, although I confess to a relationship or two in the past. I am unattached and totally attentive at the present."

She could not help but be relieved as she learned a few bare facts about this exciting man who was slowly breaking down her defences. She had not responded to anyone this deeply since her time with Adam. Christina realized that she would not fall in love with Evan, but the sexual pull was very strong. Perhaps a release was what she needed. After all, she couldn't be celibate all of her life. She suddenly changed the subject, realizing that this was dangerous thinking. In nineteen sixty-one, the decade of flower people and free love was evolving but the moral code of the present, especially in Canada and America, was not as liberal as it was in the European community. They believed that love was everything, the greatest emotion on earth, and when one was young why not enjoy the sensations of bodily contact and total abandonment in the bedrooms of Europe?

Evan had a way of always being close to her, a hand on her elbow to guide her through a doorway, an arm about her waist as they walked throughout the ship, a hip touching hers, his body pressed close to hers, moulding itself to her thighs. He was attentive, loving, and his adoration for her grew daily. Their first night on board, Evan had escorted her to her stateroom, kissed her long and hard at the door, opened it, and motioned for her to enter. He said goodnight and closed the door. For some reason Christina was very disappointed at this. Had she expected Evan to come into her stateroom and make mad passionate love to her all through the night? She had to be honest, and yes, she had expected just that. It was so unexpected that she was very let down. Little did she realize that Evan was building her need for him, slowly, expertly and most assuredly. She would succumb and meet his passion before another evening passed. He was that confident.

Maggie had a glow to her at breakfast the next morning that Christina could not fathom. She remarked, "You look absolutely beautiful, Maggie. Two days out to sea and you look as though you've dropped ten years. There is a sparkle in your eyes and a glow to your cheeks that I have never seen."

"Christina, I have never been so content. I know it won't last. Jean is married but separated from his wife, and they are devout Catholics and will never divorce. I guess I have to be content to spend this time with him and have the memories to last me the rest of my life. I could stay on this yacht forever. Yes, I did awake in his arms. It was wonderful. And the glow, that's from making love early this morning. I'm not saying you should act as I do, that is your decision to make, but whatever keeps you apart from the drooling male population that surrounds you on a daily basis must have been very traumatic."

Christina paled when Maggie mentioned her reluctance to commit to a partner. She changed the subject and was relieved when Evan appeared. They would send the launch into port to gather the newspapers and tabloids to see if they were no longer the news of the day. After breakfast, a lively game of shuffleboard followed and everyone was in high spirits by the time the launch returned. Much to their surprise, only a small article appeared in one edition on the second page. It attested to the disappearance of the "billionaire shipping magnate" and his "supermodel C.C." unknown at this time. It was a relief to them all.

After dinner that evening, Evan had become much more attentive. Christina no longer resisted his advances, and Maggie and Jean had retired early, unable to keep their hands off one another. Their apparent lust for one another enhanced the tension and electricity between Evan and Christina. She felt herself unable to resist. They were on a settee, which accommodated two people rather well, when Evan's hands began to wander. She could not stop the powerful rise of emotion as his hands began to stroke her breast and his lips left hers to wander down her neck and throat, to the cleavage between her breasts. She gasped as the passion coursed through her body, and her loins responded in kind. She pressed her body closer to his, and a silhouette would have become one. His passion aroused; Christina recognized the hardness of his phallus as he thrust against her clothing. She knew he was near the point of no return. His hands were removing her panties, and he grasped her buttocks and pulled her fully against his body. She felt the heat of his passion as he removed his shirt and undid her blouse. Her bare breasts, nipples erect, thrust upwards against his chest. She could not believe her response. Even her coupling with Adam had not triggered this response. That had been gentle, experimental, two young adolescents attempting to please one another. This was raw passion, and Christina's body was responding as never before. He suddenly stopped and whispered, "Come to my stateroom. I don't want to make love to you here. I promise you it will be so much better."

Unable to resist, she merely nodded, her colour high as she walked along beside him. It was a few steps down to the lower deck, and the first door to the right. Evan opened the door and carried her to the spacious bed along the far wall. Soft lights, indirect and subtle, painted a picture of total masculinity in the room's decor. It added to the seduction. He laid her gently upon the velvet spread, and his body covered hers. The warmth of his flesh was pleasant, comforting, and he began to move. She was naked without having taken anything off herself. Within a breath, Evan lay naked on top of her. Then, reality broke through. With no warning Christina pushed Evan away just as he had entered her. "Please Evan, I can't do this. Please, no." She covered her nakedness with the bedspread.

"What the hell are you talking about? You can't leave me like this. Look at me, for God's sake. What am I supposed to do with this great erection? What kind of icicle are you?"

He was so very angry, his anger fuelled by her turndown. This had never happened to him, not ever. What the hell was wrong with this woman? She was every inch a woman, but what had happened to her in the past to evoke such a sudden denial? He had not expected this to happen.

"I'm sorry, Evan … it's not you. You are a wonderful, passionate man and I wanted you to make love to me, but my mind won't accept it. I can't explain it."

"Has this happened to you before? Are you sure it's not me?"

"Yes, I'm sure, and no I haven't gotten this close to a man in a very long time."

She knew then that she had to tell someone or explode with the guilt and despair that was buried so deeply within her heart. He put on his trousers and padded to the small bar where he poured himself a large Cognac. He poured her one as well. He had to get over this hurdle. This woman was driving him mad. If he didn't have her soon he would be physically ill. His erection softened as the Cognac relaxed him. He took a few deep breaths and calmly approached the bed. "Come sit over here with me, and explain to me why you can't make love to me. I know you wanted me, as much as I need you."

Christina accepted the glass of brandy and settled herself curled up beside him. She looked into his eyes and saw the hurt of her rejection. "It was a long time ago, Evan, and I have never told anyone but my best friend Becka, and my parents. I was very much in love with a young man when I was just sixteen. We became very close, sharing our dreams for the future, even fantasizing about a life together. We were best friends and shared everything. One night, we could not resist and our bodies betrayed us both. It was over almost as soon as it had begun. I don't remember any build-up or foreplay, he was on me, we were both very naked and he was in me. I do remember that my first time was painful, but not unpleasant. We were both rather embarrassed by what we had done, and of course, the act being as spontaneous as it was, Adam had used no protection." She paused, sipped the drink and met his gaze. Evan was totally attentive. He did not interrupt or attempt to comfort her. He just sat quietly as she continued. "As a result I became pregnant, and Adam was unaware of my situation. He was enrolled in University to become a doctor and his career would have been ruined. I did not hear from him at Thanksgiving, and by the time Christmas rolled around my parents had put me a Catholic convent, a home for unwed mothers, and I gave birth to twin girls in the month of May." She began to cry.

She removed the locket from around her neck and opened it before passing it to him. The infant's faces stared back at him. Evan shook his head. He could not understand such a cruel culture. This experience had devastated this young woman and had marked her for life.

Evan murmured, "How cruel, how terribly cruel. Where are the babies now, Christina?"

"I don't know, Evan. They were adopted separately and the records are sealed. I will never know and it's killing me."

"Does the father know about his children?"

"No, and I don't think I will ever see him again. He is well into his studies and unaware of my career. Our paths have not crossed for five years."

"Do you have feelings for him, Christina?"

The last words Adam had said to her she recalled: I will love you all the days of my life, and she had vowed to do the same. "I haven't really thought about it for sometime, Evan." This was not true and she bit back another lie. She thought of Adam every day and wrote in her journal. The text was filled with her pain and heartache, and wishes for a future that appeared no less than futile.

Evan said, "I think I understand now why you are so reluctant to respond and allow your body to enjoy the act of love. Let me teach you, Christina, let me help you forget your pain. I have never felt so close to another person in my entire life. I cannot tell you how you have touched my life, and I cannot bear the thought of you not being by my side. I think I am falling in love with you, Christina, and believe me, I have never fallen in love with anyone before now."

"Evan, I really do appreciate your being understanding. All the act of love has brought to me is pain and heartache, a lifetime of regret and guilt. It's eating me alive and I throw myself into my work. Maggie and John do not share my secret. Please, Evan, do not disclose this to anyone. I don't think I could stand it."

"How do your parents feel about you?"

"You should ask instead, how do I respond to them? I have no feelings for my father, I am polite to him as always when we meet, but I treat a stranger with the same emotion. He was my adoring Papa, and I was his angel, until he rejected me and called me a slut and shut me away in that convent. For that I will never forgive him."

"And your mother?"

"My mother went along with his wishes, and has never spoken of the babies since they were born. They never got to see them, and I have never shown them the picture in the locket."

"How did you get the picture in the locket?"

"Another unwed girl snuck into the nursery and took the picture while the sister on duty was in the washroom. I will never be able to thank her enough, although I have to admit that the photograph still causes me great pain. But the love I have for those babies will carry me through the rest of my life. Does that surprise you, Evan, that I could love them having held them for only a short half hour? That bonding has to last me forever."

"Who brought you the babies? Don't they forbid you seeing them at all?"

"A young sister befriended me during my months at the home. She knew my parents had rejected me and locked their embarrassment away. She sensed my loneliness and her compassion and friendship and understanding helped me through my pregnancy. She broke all of the rules when she brought those tiny bundles to my bed. I have her address but I have not written to her since. It's just too painful."

She began to cry, exhausted from the terrible depth of emotion. Her stomach ached and her head hurt. Evan carried her to his bed and tucked her in. He kissed her softly on her forehead and stroked her long hair. "Sleep, my darling, I will rest elsewhere. We will not speak of this again. I want you to be happy, and if you are happy I will be also. Good night, *mon cherie*."

She whispered, "Goodnight, Evan, and thank you. You are a wonderful man."

He shook his head in sadness, all passion erased from his body. He knew then that he loved this woman, and if he could do anything at all to ease her pain, he would gladly do so. It would become his goal in life. Perhaps he could find the twins. He knew nothing of such procedures, but money could move mountains and he vowed he would try.

The following morning Evan was as attentive to Christina and his guests as usual. Anything that had passed between them was not mentioned. She was extremely grateful and their new relationship settled into growing friendship with sexual overtones. Maggie was radiant as usual, relishing this time in her life as a bonus. She was realistic enough to know that the ecstasy would not last, so she was determined to make as many memories as possible. Jean's eyes followed Maggie's figure wherever she was on board, adoring her every move. Maggie had remarked that for once, just once, all eyes weren't on Christina.

At lunch the crew and guests were on deck exchanging idle chatter about their experiences and their respective countries when a radio dispatch arrived. The radio operator gave it to Evan and stood silently waiting for orders. Evan quickly scanned the radiogram and his expression became serious. He looked around the table, his eyes coming to rest on Christina. He cleared his throat and said, "This is very serious news. May I ask that you all give Christina and I a moment of privacy?"

Without question the group left the table, retiring to the lounge. Christina asked, "What is it, Evan?"

"Here, you had better read this, Christina, it's addressed to you."

The radiogram was terse and to the point: Christina please come home. Angela, very ill.

Call me ... Becka.

"Oh my God, Evan. I'm halfway around the world." Christina worried that she wouldn't be able to travel to Cranston in less than four or five days. "When is it dated?"

Evan looked at the radiogram and saw that it originated from Cannes. So the office in New York had known where to reach her in an emergency but they had been at sea for two days. The date on the message was last night at 2200 hours. The desk clerk, now being the employ of his new owner, had been conscientious in his duties and had ordered the message to be sent the following morning when it was determined that Christina Corelli was a guest on The Elena.

Christina had paled considerably as Evan placed a reassuring hand upon her shoulder. She re-read the radiogram again, her hands shaking so hard she could hardly hold the paper still. She crushed the paper in her hand and the tears began. Evan said, "I will make all the arrangements. We will take the launch back to Nice and radio ahead for a small charter to fly you to Paris. I will accompany you and wait until you board your flight to New York. The airline will make connector reservations to Toronto and you can decide which domestic flight will be available to fly you out west. I have no idea where your destination lies but we will get you there in the fastest time possible, trust me."

"Oh, Evan, thank you. I'll get my things and tell Maggie. I'll only be a few minutes."

Evan was crestfallen. Their wonderful vacation was cut short by an emergency halfway around the world. Would he ever see her again? He could not think that far ahead. He had Armand bring the launch around. Maggie was beside Christina telling her not to worry, to take as much time as she needed, and to call her when she had some news.

They hugged and kissed one another in the French custom, and Christina boarded the launch. Armand gave the boat full throttle and they were up on plane, leaving a large wake behind them. They were only a matter of hours from Nice and a car would be waiting for them when they docked. Evan attempted to comfort Christina, but his futile attempts at conversation were met with sobs or a nod. He finally gave up and wrapped Christina in a heavy duffel coat, not to protect her from the wind or chill of the water, but from shock. She was doing her best to cope but, not having any information other than the fact that her mother was ill, was harder to handle than if she knew exactly the severity of her mother's illness. She kept saying over and over again, "What if I'm too late? What if she dies and I don't get a chance to say goodbye? God willing, she will recover and I'll spend more time with her."

Evan knew from their conversations that Christina's father was alive as well, and found the fact that she had not mentioned him in this crisis very disturbing. Something was not right. Within the circle of his own family the circle tightened in a crisis and the family drew on one another for strength; therefore, he thought this applied to all families. He had no idea that Christina was an only child. They had not had enough time to fill in their backgrounds. She was most secretive as to where she had been raised and had said little or nothing about her parents, but she spoke of the sender of the radiogram. This Becka person was as close or closer to Christina as a sister; that much he had gathered from listening to her speak of their school days together.

What followed the radiogram was a whirlwind of activity, travel plans, and transferring of luggage and Christina from one mode of travel to another. He followed through on his promise, and she was presently ready to board her flight to New York. He kissed her long and hard as he whispered, "I will never forget you, Christina Corelli. You are the love of my life ... always remember, I will be at your beck and call whenever you should need me. I love you. Go now, I will call you when I am in New York."

She kissed him back, gratefully, and sadly, but not returning his vow of love. She did not love Evan as much as she had tried. They did have a strong sexual connection but she recognized it for what it was. However, she valued his friendship and would never do anything to jeopardize or destroy what they had. She answered, "Thank you, Evan. I'll write. I'll be waiting for your call. You've been wonderful."

He had to be grateful for just that. Being wonderful wasn't as good · as being loved, but he was determined to change her way of thinking. The plane was on the runway, and he watched as it gathered speed and was soon airborne. Within minutes lost to sight. He didn't leave the tarmac until he could no longer see the plane. The limousine driver opened the door for him and, once he was inside, whisked them away from the runway. He gave orders to Armand to return to Nice where they would rejoin The Elena and go on to Monte Carlo.

Chapter Twenty-Three

C HRISTINA'S JOURNEY HAD BEGUN in earnest. She asked the stewardess if she could place a call to her home in Cranston, Alberta, but the weather had turned nasty and they were in for a rough flight. She opted for a telegram from the flight to New York, which she sent on to Becka: Becka, received message today, should arrive in Calgary two days from today...will call you when I arrive...will rent a car...you will be unable to reach me so I will have to contact you...Christina. Ten hours later her overseas flight landed in New York without incident. Christina retrieved her luggage and her flight bag. She was through customs and in a phone booth in record time. The agency had a few messages for her, one very urgent from her Aunt Maria. The secretary read it to her: Christina your father trying to reach you. Angela very ill. Come quickly...Aunt Maria

That last message had been hard to take. Christina was very distraught. She was booked on a connector flight to Toronto within the hour. The magic fingers of the reservations clerk had saved her at least six hours, putting her on standby and plugging her in after a last-minute cancellation. She smiled gratefully and made haste to board the flight. They had a slight delay on the runway, taxiing for a few minutes longer than usual, but all was well and the Captain's voice was reassuring on the intercom as he gave his passengers every assurance that the flight was on schedule and they expected no delays. She tried to relax; she had no time to call Becka from New York, and decided that to call from the plane now would only be frustrating and probably would not accomplish anything. She decided that she would call Becka when she landed in Calgary later that day. She had another flight to catch in Toronto and would have to stay overnight in Calgary, renting a car and leaving as early as possible the following morning. She was beginning to feel the strain of the overseas flight, jet lag, and the strain of not knowing what was happening. Christina began to reminisce about the happy times spent with her mother. Her father she kept in the background, able to control the images. She would deal with him after the crisis was past. In the meanwhile, she would sleep on the flight across Canada. Hopefully Becka would have her telegram and would be expecting her call.

All of her travel plans were glitch-free. As in all emergencies, the airline staff gave top priority to their passengers in crisis, and Christina, famous or not, was no exception. She was allowed to board first, was personally escorted to her seat, made as comfortable as possible, and the stewardess was at her beck and call. Dark shadows began to appear under her eyes as the worry, strain, and the hasty journey began to take their toll. Perhaps it was based on two factors: would she be in time … and not knowing the severity of her mother's illness. The hard core around her heart softened, and the tears that followed were an attempt to wash away the guilt her absence had created. A small part of the resentment would never go away, but she knew that her mother was not totally to blame for the loss of the twins. Angela had gone along with her husband's wishes, believing that Frank knew what was best for them all. She had not had a chance to be alone with Christina in many years, Frank saw to that. Whether he was jealous, or didn't want them to be as close as they had once been, the mother and daughter bond had definitely weakened. Aunt Maria had filled the void for many years, but when it came right down to it she was not Christina's mother.

Finally, she was in her hotel room. She threw her bag on the bed and picked up the phone. The call went through immediately, and Becka's voice was heard as she said, "Hello, Sanders residence, Becka speaking."

"Becka, it's me, Christina. How is she?"

"Christina. Where are you? Are you in Cranston? She's holding on, Christina, but she is very weak."

"I will be out of here in the morning. I've rented a car and will be in Cranston by noon. Shall I go straight home?" The word home felt strange to her ears. She had not used it many years.

"I've been staying with her during the day seeing to her every comfort, and your father is with her at night, along with a special nurse. It's her heart, Christina. She's lost the will to live."

Christina started to cry and was unable to speak for a minute until she could control her voice. "Becka, tell her I'm on my way. I've just got to get some sleep. I haven't slept for two days and I have jet lag. If I don't get some rest, I won't be able to drive tomorrow. Will she hold on until I arrive, do you think?"

"Yes, once I tell her that you are on your way. She's been asking for you daily, she has something that she has to tell you and I know she'll not go until she has seen you. It doesn't look good, Christina, I have to be honest with you and tell you not to get your hopes up. Her heart is worn out."

"But how can that be, Becka? She's not even forty years old."

"I'll fill you in on everything when you arrive, I promise. Good night, Christina, I'm going over there now to settle her for the night and I will tell her you called. See you at noon."

"Goodnight, Becka, thank you. Yes, see you at noon. I'm at the Outrider Inn in Calgary if you need to reach me. Bye."

Christina had a long, hot bath, washing the travel grime and the aches and pains that accompany long journeys, cramped muscles and a sore back. She crawled between the sheets and fell into an exhausted sleep. She awoke in the middle of the night bathed in sweat from a dream that found her reaching out to her mother as the clouds drifted around their figures. Angela was just out of reach and Christina cried out in despair, "Mama, mama, please wait ... I love you, Mama, forgive me." The only response from the silent figure was when Angela stopped and turned, and the sadness in her dark brown eyes gave insight into her troubled soul. She held the gaze for a long time and the two women were suspended in the swirling clouds. Christina's hands reached out as she said, "Mama, please wait. Don't leave me. Come back." But the figure disappeared amidst the clouds. Christina sat bolt upright in the strange hotel room, for a minute not recognizing her surroundings, which added to the panic of the nightmare. Did this dream mean that her mother had died? She glanced at the clock at her bedside. It was four a.m ... the time of day when the ebb of life is at its lowest. She fell back against the pillows and pulled the covers up to her neck. She lay staring up at the ceiling, counting the squares of the tile, not willing to think ahead. She did not return to sleep. At six a.m. Christina crawled out of bed, showered quickly, dried her hair, and was summoned by the desk clerk to tell her that her rental car was ready. She literally flew about the room, retrieving and packing her belongings, most of which fit in her flight bag. Her luggage was picked up by room service and stowed in the trunk. She paid her bill, thanked the desk clerk, and was on her way south, to face the worst, unable to dwell on the future.

Three hours later, Christina pointed the car through the iron gates of her parents' estate and sped up the driveway. Becka had been watching for her and opened the front door before Christina could ring the bell. They embraced quickly, Becka pulling away first. She motioned for Christina to follow her. The front study had been turned into a sunny, beautifully decorated bedroom and sitting room, so that Angela did not have to climb the stairs. Approaching footsteps were heard coming towards them, and Christina found herself face to face with her father. He said, "Angel, you came. Thank God. Your mother has been asking for you."

"Hello, father, yes, Becka told me." She met his eyes looking at him as she would a polite stranger. The years stood before them as a high brick wall, and Christina hadn't the time or the energy to scale the wall and break the stony silence. He had to be content with the fact that she had spoken to him at all. The room was not bright and sunny as it had been intended. A figure lay in the bed against the wall. A nurse was moving about the sick room, attending to the patient's comforts. The linen had been changed and Angela wore a fresh nightgown. The effort of her morning bath and ritual had tired her but she remained awake all the while, asking the nurse what time it was. How close it was to noon, and Christina's arrival. When the door opened, Christina had to wait until her eyes adjusted to the dimness. She walked over to the bed, not realizing that she was holding her breath. The figure in the bed was her mother, but the change was significant. This person no longer resembled the vibrant, vivacious, beautiful woman who had laughed and sang and danced and played with Christina through the years that she could remember. Instead lay a woman aged far beyond her years, not much larger in body than her Nona had been when Christina had stood at her bedside in Marino many years ago. "Mama, it's Christina. I came as soon as I heard. Mama, how are you?"

Angela's voice, though weak and breaking, held such happiness as she said, "Christina, it really is you. Thank you for coming. I must speak with you."

"Not now, Mama. You must rest. I'll be here when you wake up. I promise. I'll be right here by your side."

Becka motioned for the nurse to leave the room and the two of them left mother and daughter alone. Becka said, "Call me if you need me, I'll be right outside."

Frank made an attempt to enter the room, but Becka said a few words to him and he walked away. Christina heard a car start up and the squeal of tires as his car sped away from the house.

"Christina, come closer. Let me look at you." Christina did as she was asked. "You are even more beautiful than your pictures. Aunt Maria sends me all of them when she writes. I am so proud of you, my daughter."

"Please, Mama, don't tire yourself. Don't talk about me. I'm so sorry, Mama, I should have called or written more often."

"No, Christina. Don't apologize. You are famous and always traveling." At this Angela attempted to smile and Christina saw the two images of her grandmother and her mother merge. The heart condition had been passed on from the mother to the daughter. She read in her mother's eyes that it was only a matter of days before she would leave them forever. Christina allowed her tears to splash down and they landed upon the cold, skeleton fingers of her mother's hand as she grasped Christina's in her own. "I have to tell you something, my child. I do not want your father to hear this. It's about the babies, Christina. No, don't turn away. Please, it is very important." She waited until Christina settled down to listen. "When you left to go and live with your Aunt Maria, I believed that we were doing the best thing for you. We hoped that you would forget about the bambinos, and make a new life for yourself. Your father convinced me that we must do what we had to, to keep it from the community. Now, when I look back, I know we wronged you." She paused to gain strength, then continued. "It was the best thing for him, but when I thought about it, it was too late to reach you. Maria had no way of contacting you for many months. I know now that if anyone had asked me to give you up after I had held you in my arms, I would have died rather than say yes. And yet, we expected you to be strong and give up not one, but two babies. It was not right, Christina, it will never be right, what we did to you."

Again she paused, and Christina's face crumpled in grief, for her mother's despair and for her own heartache and pain. The tears were not cleansing. They were just there, uncontrollable and intermittent, the outpouring of her soul. "Mama, it's okay. I forgive you." But did she really? She said this as a matter of fact, in order to console a dying woman and give her peace.

"I tried to find them for you, Christina. I called and wrote many letters and hired people to trace the babies. The sisters of the convent kept the records sealed and it was no use." Her mother's voice broke and she could not continue. Christina became concerned as her mother began to cough, a paroxysmal fit that wracked her body and shook the bed. She called for Becka, who explained that her mother had contracted pneumonia from lying in bed for prolonged periods of time. She attached the oxygen and took Angela's pulse, checked on the I.V. drip, all the while under the wooden gaze of a daughter in total despair. As sleep claimed Angela, Becka ushered Christina from the room and they went into the kitchen, where Becka had prepared strong hot tea for them. Christina slid behind the table and sat in her usual place in the nook, a lifetime of habit, controlling her movements. She wrung her hands, until finally she wrapped them about the mug of tea, gleaning warmth and comfort from such a small source. Becka sat across from her long time playmate and friend, waiting until she decided to speak.

"Did my father drive away? I thought I heard a car pull away from the house. What's with him anyway? Did he think I would throw myself into his arms and ask for his forgiveness? Not in a million years, Becka, never in a million years."

"I have something as well to tell you, Christina. All this came about less than six months ago. Your mother heard about your father's ongoing affair with Sharon Nesbitt. He had promised to love her all the days of his life. She had believed he would mold her life to his, their thoughts, their activities, the love they shared for you. And she had been betrayed."

"Who told her? I want to know."

"This is hard for me, because I'm caught in the middle. It was her very good friend, Tonio's mother Teresa Marcellus. She was coming off evening shift about eight years ago, and had seen for herself the two of them embracing in the parking lot of the inn."

"Was this when my mother and I were in Italy?"

"Yes, it must have been. Teresa said that your father brought Sharon to the house and they made love in your mother's bed. Christina, she began to die from that very day. My father treated her for a deep depression but he could not bring her around. She shut Frank out completely, unable to look him in the eye. Teresa was the one who filled him in, and as she recalled his reaction, he just seemed to shrug it off. I'm sorry, Christina. It's all such a dreadful mess and your mother is the victim here."

"That bastard. All the while he was having an affair and my mother thought that he was just interested in the almighty dollar. And he called me a slut when I told them I was pregnant. I'll never forgive him, Becka, never! He doesn't deserve it. He's killed my mother and taken away my babies, I hope to God that he suffers a long and slow death when the time comes."

The depth of her hatred was not lost on Becka. Her nursing training and psychology courses came into play. "Christina, you can't let this eat you alive. He's suffering inside and I know that he carries your estrangement with him around on his shoulders. He knows he is to blame and has no idea how to say how sorry he is."

"How do you know that, Becka? Are you trying to whitewash what he has done?"

"No, Christina, but if you don't forgive him you will suffer as well. You have to move on with your life and leave it all behind."

"What do you think I've been doing? No one works harder at forgetting than I do." At this point she reached for the locket around her neck. She guided the chain over head and extended the open locket for Becka to see the pictures within it. Becka gasped as she saw the babies' photos, innocent and beautiful, their faces adorable and precious to any mother.

"Christina, I had no idea. I had no idea that you had seen them. They are perfect."

Christina studied Becka as she remarked upon the tiny photograph encircled within the locket. She thought how Becka didn't have any idea. Only Sister Rose shared this with her; she was compassionate and caring when she needed someone. But they were her flesh and blood. Where were they? No, Becka didn't have any idea. But she didn't say these things. Instead she said, "Perhaps someday, Becka, when you have a family of your own you will understand how this tore me apart. I was too young, too vulnerable, to be abandoned and left to cope with the loss of those children. I will never bear another child, I promise you."

They were interrupted by the appearance of the other nurse. The look on her face told it all. Angela was gone. She had waited and held on to the last, waiting for Christina to ask her forgiveness, and when Christina had said she forgave her, and kissed her on the forehead, it was the last time her mother would ever look upon her daughter. It was all too much for Christina. She refused to stay in the house a minute longer, and Becka invited her to stay with her at her parents' home. She worked for her father in his practice and was engaged to Tonio. They were planning a home of their own, but until then, Becka saved money by living at home. Dr. Sanders and Becka's mother were delighted to have Christina stay with them, but were saddened by the circumstances that had brought their guest to their home. Dr. Sanders administered a sedative and Christina lay back in total exhaustion. Becka said, "Christina, thank God you made it back in time to say goodbye."

"But I didn't say goodbye, Becka. I just told her I forgave her is all ... I didn't say goodbye

... I didn't tell her how much I loved her ... I thought I had more time."

"It's not for us to say. She was very weak, and when I sent the message I prayed that it would reach you in time. I told her that you were coming, and she rallied from her bad spell."

She continued, "Get some rest, Christina, sleep as long as you like. Tonio and I will tell your father and we'll make the arrangements. Your mother wished to be cremated and that you spread her ashes in the family vineyard in Marino. She asked me to pass that on to you."

At the mention of her father, Christina's tears stopped and her heart hardened. "Tell Tonio he'll no doubt find my father in the arms of Sharon Nesbitt. He probably couldn't wait to find comfort there."

Actually, her father had broken off the affair when Angela had taken ill, unable to live with the guilt that he may have triggered her first heart attack. Grief and despair and long suffering are often too hard to bear, and Frank was faced with the reality that his wife would die of a broken heart. Instead of seeking solace in the arms of his long affair of the heart, he sought out Tonio and Teresa. Tonio had become the son Frank had always wanted and the two had bonded firmly. Tonio was no longer wild and crazy; instead he had grown into a sensible, responsible young man, almost a cookie-cutter version of Frank. Teresa was grateful for the guidance and care given to her son, but with trepidation. She could not dispel the wrongful affair that was now one of the causes of Angela's illness. She, too, carried a burden of guilt. Teresa had struggled with the knowledge of the affair for many years, until she could no longer deceive her friend. She thought that if the information came from a friend rather than a nasty jealous acquaintance, that Angela could handle it much better. It hadn't mattered where the knowledge came from; the hurt was just too painful for Angela. She turned to no one, and no longer confided in Teresa as she once had. There was just too much water under the bridge, and forgiveness was not forthcoming. Each had fought with their own demons, and no one was willing to forgive or forget, Christina most of all.

Chapter Twenty-Four

ANGELA PASSED AWAY ON Tuesday. Funeral arrangements were completed for Saturday at two o'clock with high Mass and a memorial service. Her mother had wished to be cremated, and her ashes returned to Italy. A small reception was planned at the family estate where friends could call and pay their respects. The days following her death, as well as those before the funeral, were very trying for them all. Christina stayed apart from her father as much as possible; she stayed with Becka during the interim, making daily appearances to her parents' home only to visit with relatives and keep the household running. Flowers were everywhere and Christina had to send some of them to the local hospital and nursing home as there were just too many. Her Aunt Maria and Uncle Guido arrived from Toronto on Friday in time for the evening prayers. Her mother's body would be in an open casket for the family to bid a last farewell, but would not be present for the memorial service. She had not wanted everyone staring at her out of curiosity as she lay in state. A collage of family photographs and her mother's favourite poem had been put together and would act as a focal point for the mourners to reflect upon Angela's life. The evening prayer session was harder on Christina than she could ever have imagined. She was becoming emotionally drained from everything; her estrangement and distance from her father was becoming increasingly more difficult. He had tried to reach out to her, but Christina always arranged it so that they were never alone in the same room. No one appeared to notice them dealing with their own grief, except of course, Teresa Marcellus. She had seen to much of the personal arrangements, knowing what Angela would have wanted. For this Christina was grateful, but she harboured a growing resentment towards Teresa. After all, she had been the one to tell her mother the truth. Her aunt had pleaded with her to stay at the house, but Christina was fearful that the press would get hold of the story and hound them and invade their privacy. The Italian family closed the circle, her uncle Tony and Joe, her aunts Sophia and Isabella, and their children, as well as Guido and Maria. Dr. Sanders and Becka's mother came to pay their respects and Becka had attended prayers with Christina. Although the days before Saturday appeared to drag, they actually flew by.

Two o'clock arrived and Christina had her head covered with a wide-brimmed black hat and soft veil, making the need for sunglasses unnecessary. She was unaware that she looked extremely chic in her black designer dress, the jacket cut to perfection. She wore semi sheer black nylons and sensible heels. A touch of color to her lips ordinarily would have gone unnoticed but her complexion had paled considerably and the slightest color was a deep contrast. She removed the lip-gloss and decided that the veil would cover her well enough to conceal the red puffy eyes and drawn face. She had not slept these many nights, only fitfully, a few hours at a time at the most. Becka was worried about her, but with her strength and wisdom and her professional training she was a support and comfort for which Christina would be eternally grateful.

Father Perinni gave a wonderful eulogy, praising Angela as a devoted wife and mother, and a strong force in the women's church group, her energy for raising funds unparalleled. Christina was proud of her mother's contributions. She had chosen to be a stay-at-home mother, her family and home her life's work. How many women could say the same? Many were bent on a career, while trying to juggle home, husband, children and career, and only wound up exhausted, frustrated or alone. As they came out of the church, Christina's worst fears were realized. From the dimly lit interior of the chapel, the cameras blinded them, as well as the rays from the direct sunlight. Christina cringed and lowered her head. The hat was a shield, but because she was so tall, and carried herself professionally, they had no trouble recognizing her. She dodged them as best she could; her Uncle Guido pushed aside the microphones which were instantly in her face. The men of the family rallied around, and she found herself in the back of the car, being whisked away as fast as possible. The gates to the estate were plugged with onlookers, curiosity seekers, and the inevitable paparazzi. Christina needed the time at home to be part of the immediate family reception. She had to thank everyone on behalf of her mother, as much as she would have liked to leave it all to her father. The security guards that her uncle Joe had hired did their job, and only people who were sincerely there to pay their respects were allowed through the gates.

Christina removed her hat and ran her fingers through her hair. It was a relief to get out from under the veil. She gratefully accepted a proffered strong, hot coffee and laced it with Cognac. It had done the trick on another occasion and would serve her well today. Her father was at the head of the reception line and Christina placed herself between aunts and uncles. When the line thinned, they all retired outside to the buffet under the canvas canopy in the back yard, away from prying eyes. A scuffle at the end of the sloped lawn ensued and broke up the conversation. A photographer had fallen out of a large cottonwood tree that grew along the creek about three hundred feet from the back door. Security removed him immediately and the group actually found some relief in the diversion. As the liquor took hold, Christina began to relax. They had said goodbye to her mother, and the formality of closure could begin.

A voice at her elbow interrupted her thoughts, "Christina, hello, do you remember me?" Christina broke into a welcome smile. The woman who had spoken was Ellen Darby, her old theatre and dance instructor. "Miss Darby ... of course I recognize you. It's so good to see you. Tell me, do you still teach tall gangly young girls the arts of poise and decorum?"

"Yes, I do, but you have always been my best pupil. I remember telling your mother that you would someday be breathtakingly beautiful, and when I look at you now, I can only say that the pictures don't do you justice. You are by far much more beautiful than even I thought."

Unaccustomed to such sincere, open admiration, Christina blushed as she answered, "Do you believe that before my very first runway show, I said to myself, 'Now what did Miss Darby tell me about performing before a crowd ... I would take a deep breath, say a little prayer, and go out there thinking that they were all my best friends and we were at a party. It always worked."

They spoke for a few minutes more, then Christina was called away.

Becka was leaving with Tonio. Christina said, "Tonio, I haven't had a chance to thank you for everything you have done. It's been wonderful to see you again, but the circumstances could have been better." She hugged him and kissed him on the cheek, her eyes bright with tears. Tonio became very emotional as well.

"You take care of yourself, Christina, and always remember that Becka and I will be here for you, no matter what. We are friends for life no matter how removed we are from one another." His arm was placed protectively about Becka and Christina suddenly was jealous of the love they so obviously shared. She looked forward to their wedding.

"Becka, I'll see you later. I should leave tonight, if I can. I called John at the agency and he's up to his neck in work. Maggie hasn't returned from Monte Carlo, and I have to hold up my end of the business or we'll all be broke."

Becka and Tonio left with Teresa in tow. The group of mourners was thinning as people paid their respects murmuring, "It was a wonderful ceremony, and a tribute to your mother's life ... we will miss her always."

Father Perinni blessed them as he said, "My prayers are with you in your time of grief. If you wish, I will say a special mass from time to time."

"That would be comforting, Father," Christina replied. She retreated to the washroom for a few minutes alone, to splash cold water on her face, and arrange her hair. She stayed in the bathroom longer than usual, and when she came out the living room was empty save for one person ... her father. He was at the bar, pouring himself a stiff drink.

He said, "Oh, there you are. Can I talk to you, Christina? It won't take long."

She stiffened when he spoke. She had tried to avoid this confrontation because it would turn into just that ... it could never be just conversation between them. Christina walked over to join him at the bar. He poured her a drink and said, "I know you have been deliberately avoiding me, Christina, and I think I know why. I wish you would find it in your heart to let the past be the past and we can go on as before, without this excess baggage. I am so proud of you my daughter, you have no idea."

Whether it the term "baggage" or the act of forgiveness, whatever it was did the job. Christina's eyes blazed with sudden fury. "Baggage ... baggage ... you turn your back on your own flesh and blood, and you refer to your grandchildren as baggage. You conceited bastard ... you chose this community over us and rejected me, as well as my babies. You belong here in this little community, with your big frog, little puddle image. You added to the pain you caused my mother by rejecting her as well. I know all about the affair with Mrs. Nesbitt. Your macho, man of the hour image destroyed and broke Mama's heart." Her voice faltered and her breast was heaving from the tirade of pent-up emotions that had lain buried for five long years.

"And what about you? You turned your back on your mother. She pined away month after month, crying over the magazine photographs your Aunt Maria sent with news of your whereabouts. Don't you think that added to her pain?"

"Don't you dare lay that on me. Your Mr. Bigshot attitude kept her self-esteem at a low, and if it wasn't for her charity work, mother would have had nothing to do but dwell in the shadow of the great Frank Corelli ... pillar of the community. You can fool most anyone, father, but you don't fool me. Mother went along with your decision to send me to that convent and to give away my babies, but I'm telling you now, that if I ever find them ... and I will do everything in my power to find them ... you will never see them. They will never know who their grandfather was."

She was crying now, but they were tears of rage and frustration. His face was ashen, and he gulped down the drink. He tried to speak, "Christina, I'm so sorry ... everything you've said is true. I know that now."

"Keep your 'sorry' to yourself. I don't want to hear anymore. One thing you can do for Mama is take her ashes to Italy and scatter them on the hillside in the olive grove. It is the one that receives the last rays of golden sunlight every day. That is what she wanted. You can also face the relatives that are there. Comfort them in their loss and for God's sake try to live up to the memory of my mother, and be a husband for a change. Mama read me your letters when we were still in Italy. One she kept next to her heart and read it over and over to me. Do you remember when you promised, 'Mi amore, I will love you all the days of my life?' Well father, a man said that to me one day also and look where it got me. I should have known better than to believe him, especially when my own father could not be trusted to do the same. Good-bye, father.

Believe it or not, I do not wish you bad fortune ... it will find you. I never want to see you again."

With her words echoing in the spacious living room, Frank sat down heavily on the bar stool, the empty glass and the half-filled bottle of Cognac forgotten. He covered his face with his hands and his shoulders began to shake as Frank Corelli began to shed the tears of many years of loss, and the final loss of his one true love, his wife and companion. To lose her now when they had so much to live for didn't seem fair. Perhaps it was true ... that people are punished in ways unforeseen for their sins on earth. His only child was lost to him forever; she had not called him 'Papa' once and now she never wanted to see him again. He reached for a cigarette but his hands were shaking so badly that he couldn't control the lighter. He refilled the glass and walked out to the backyard to get some air. Frank Corelli had aged ten years in the past few days. He had to take stock of his life and decide whether it was too late to reform his ways. He was forty-five years old and alone, his surroundings that his accumulated wealth had amassed were just ... stuff. Without family and friends he had nothing, and the reality was killing him. Later on that evening, Frank Corelli threw his grief-stricken body onto the bed where his wife had lain for many months. The smell of her soap and scent of her hair was still on the pillow. He cried as though his heart would break. He had never felt so lost and alone. Frank had struck bottom.

Christina returned to Becka's still furious from her encounter with her father. "Maybe this will cheer you up. Tonio and I are going to be married."

Christina's smile transformed her face. Her happiness for her two best friends shone in her eyes. "I couldn't be happier. You're finally going to get your wish. Becka, I'm so happy for you. Have you set the date?"

"We thought a Christmas wedding would be different. I've waited so long for Tonio that if I have to wait a year, until next June, I don't know what I'll do."

"Will my father be invited to the wedding? I know Tonio works for him and looks upon him as a father, but after what I just went through, it will be a cold day in hell before I ever think of him in a good light. He's become a cold-hearted, money hungry, selfish, grasping bastard, with little or no love for anyone but himself."

Becka was a little embarrassed and unwilling to join in the tirade against Frank. After all, he had been the one to rescue Tonio from his petty life of pool hall infamy and larceny. He had taken him under his wing, taught him the trucking business from end to end, and the two had bonded as father and son. She cleared her throat, "It's still months away, Christina, and you may feel differently by then. We'll wait and see. I can't imagine you not being at my wedding. We promised one another years and years ago that our weddings would not be complete without each other."

"A lot depends upon my schedule, but I will tell Maggie and John that Christmas is very important and I will need some time off. John and Ellen's baby is due to arrive about that time, and Maggie will want to be with them. It's looking a little tight, but the agency is flexible in conducting shoots and runway shows. Our ad campaigns can be shot during any season, they just use the right backdrop and dress in seasonal garb." Her reassurance put Becka at ease.

As Christina packed they chatted about her travels, Becka very intrigued about her experiences in Europe. Suddenly, she remembered something. "Christina, I almost forgot ... and I would kick myself for not telling you."

"What is it, for Heaven's sake? You look so serious."

"It's kind of serious. Before I left the University, I bumped into Adam. I think that he was waiting for me, as I didn't see much of him in the three years I was in training. He made a point of stopping me in the hallway and walked along with me."

"So what did he look like?"

"He asked how I was, just to be polite, I figure. Then he changed the subject. How is Christina? Did I see you at all? She's getting to be quite famous. He stopped for a minute then stammered, 'Becka, she's even more beautiful than I remember.' He had such a forlorn, lost look about him that it took all I had not to sympathize with him until I remembered the twins. I asked, 'So, Dr. Carmichael, what's your point?' He said, 'My point is, will you tell her for me that nothing's changed. If she still cares for me she'll remember my promise.' At that point, I began to get angry. Hey, it's only been five long years. Where do you get off thinking time only moves for you? Get in line, Doctor. You'd be surprised at Christina's popularity. Incidentally, the pictures don't do her justice. She's breathtaking in person."

Christina had absorbed every word, as she reacted to Becka's story. "You said everything exactly right. Did he say anything else?"

"Just that he was going to transfer to McGill University in Montreal to complete his residency and go on into plastic surgery. He is a brilliant doctor, I'll give you that. So do you still have feelings for him, Christina, or you can tell me to mind my own business?"

"Becka, you've always been my confidante. It's as much your business as it is mine. Yes, I do have feelings for him. I can't help it. I've tried to find the same emotion with other men, but they are flat and boring. It's always been Adam."

Becka was more than a little upset after hearing this. She said, "You know you could have any man on the planet, why stick with one who dumped you?"

"It wasn't like that. He had no idea that I was pregnant and because of that terrible winter storm at Thanksgiving I didn't have the opportunity to tell him. Time went by and I couldn't hide the pregnancy until Christmas. My parents saw to everything, and I couldn't write and tell him in a letter. It was just too painful."

Becka's face softened. She hugged Christina, kissed her on the cheek, turned and picked up one of the suitcases, and they left the room together. Becka stood in the driveway as Christina's rental pulled away. She had no idea when they would see each other again. She hoped that Christina could find the love and happiness that she shared with Tonio. She deserved it.

Chapter Twenty-Five

C HRISTINA RETURNED TO NEW york about the same time as Maggie. Maggie's head was full of dreams that would never happen. She looked younger and softer, but saddened because her affair with Jean had come to an abrupt end. He had unleashed the passion long hidden within Maggie and had surprised even herself. However, it was time to move on.

"How was Evan after I left?"

Maggie replied, "I've never seen anyone so miserable. Oh, he tried to put on a brave front for us, but he drank twice as much as usual, gambled heavily at the Casino, and was not the gayest host I've ever seen. We all tried to take his mind off you, but your picture is everywhere. You, my dear, are inescapable. Did you know that? He did send his love and said he would call you soon.

How did everything go at home? You look exhausted. I know it was a trying time for you, but you must put it all behind you and remember the best of your mother. She must have been a wonderful person to have raised such a daughter."

"Thanks, Maggie, for the effort. But I just don't want to talk about it. My family and I haven't been close for a long time. My Aunt Maria and Uncle Guido were there and it was nice to see the relatives together again, no matter the sadness of the occasion. I didn't get to say too much to my mother. Her wishes are that her ashes be taken back to her hometown in Italy and spread upon the hillside facing the late afternoon sun. I believe my father owes her that much."

Maggie could tell by the bitterness in Christina's voice that all had not gone well. She knew so little of Christina's past; it had always been a subject that Christina skirted or refused to talk about. Something had caused that sadness that dwelt within her lovely model, the camera had caught it on a number of occasions and it had led to the mystery of Christina Corelli. They changed the subject as Maggie's secretary announced John's arrival. The trio prepared themselves for a heavy workload, and the apprenticeship of Christina began almost immediately.

She found in the months ahead that work was a release for her depression and loneliness. Her line of designs was accepted for the fall and winter showings. Christina was a fast learner and had brought her end of the company on the same level as John and Maggie's performance. They were a force to be reckoned with in the fashion industry.

Christina was finding that Zoe and Suzanne, their most seasoned and experienced models, were not exactly at their best. Zoe would arrive late for a shoot, eyes bleary, shadows under her eyes, her sparkle very dim. Suzanne had been very uncooperative with the show's runway coach. They had had a number of confrontations on presentation and behaviour, and the coach had recommended she be replaced. She was twenty-five, and in model years that was getting up there. The make-up sessions were taking longer and the cameraman had started using her best side in the shoots. Suzanne laughed away their accusations, acting as if she was indispensable. After they had spent millions of dollars in promoting her career, and she was almost as well known as Christina, why throw it all away on a coach who had a grudge against her?

Christina agreed to let it slide for the time being. She owed nothing to Zoe or Suzanne; they had treated her very coldly when she first entered the model pool. Jealousy had loomed its ugly head from the start, and Christina had chosen to overlook the fact but she knew how ruthless they could be. Her own twenty-first birthday passed with little or no fanfare. Somehow Evan had known, and his flowers, cards, and champagne had been gratefully received. She had accepted the telegram from her father with mixed feelings, and the card from Becka was beautiful, the message of hope and future happiness for Christina very uplifting. She had promised to write later. The wedding preparations were progressing well and the wedding was set for December twenty-first, allowing all of the guests to return home in time to celebrate their own Christmas holidays with family and friends. She was ecstatic. Christina smiled as she read the few lines within the card. She pictured Tonio and Becka together and decided that they would probably be married all the days of their lives. Realizing what had just passed through her mind, sudden tears brought the memory of Adam to mind. She longed for further news of him. He seemed to be lost in the world of medicine, as though it had literally swallowed him up. She had never been on familiar terms with his parents, having only met them only upon a few occasions. Becka was her only link to him, and she was entangled in wedding plans and a future with Tonio. Christina's memories of her summer with Adam she cherished, and would lose herself in remembering every word and gesture. She recalled how his reddish blonde hair framed his face, and the lock of hair that rested on his forehead giving him a boyish appeal. His grey eyes held a light for her that made her heart skip a beat. She had seen them become steely cold and piercing in anger, but never directed at her. She had even gone so far as to imagine him holding the babies, a family portrait she kept in her heart. Always the memories became too painful and she would shake her head, brush away the tears, compose herself, and return to the present. Work was her release. A visit from Evan would be welcome at any time. She missed his warmth and friendliness. Christina felt the need to be cherished and Evan was the answer to her loneliness. She decided that she would call him.

Chapter Twenty-Six

I T TOOK AWHILE FOR the overseas call, and her French was not as good as her Italian, but Christina finally heard Evan's voice as he said, "Oui, c'est Monsieur D'Argent."

"Evan, it's Christina. How are you?"

"Christina, what a pleasure. I didn't expect to hear from you so soon."

"Everything's fine, Evan, I just wanted to thank you properly for your hospitality and the cruise. I am so sorry that I had to leave so abruptly."

"I understand perfectly. It must have been hard for you to lose your mother. Tell me, how are you Christina, really?"

"Actually, Evan, I could use a friend. Do you think you could come to New York? I know that you are a very busy man, but I still have some time off before we launch the fall line and things are a little slow. John is working on new contracts but nothing is pending. Is it asking you too much to drop everything and fly over?"

"For you, nothing is too much. I will need some time to make the necessary arrangements at the shipping yard, but I should be in New York for dinner tomorrow night. How does that sound?"

"That would be wonderful, Evan, I'll see you then. Goodbye."

She didn't hear the last part of his farewell, "Au revoir, my darling." A little aghast at her impetuous act, she blushed as she replaced the telephone receiver on its' cradle. Had she actually been that forward? Oh, well, he hadn't been at all surprised, and he did sound pleased.

Christina decided to meet with Maggie and go over the day's itinerary, this being her first day back from her emergency leave of absence.

"Good morning, Maggie."

Maggie was on the telephone and gestured to Christina to take a seat. Her conversation was involved, a controversy over a clause in a contract. She was on the phone for a few more minutes finally hanging up on the note, "Handle it, that's what you get the big bucks for."

Christina was mildly surprised at the tone. Maggie was usually almost too polite; firm, but always polite. "What's wrong Maggie? You don't seem yourself this morning."

"I miss Jean, if you really want to know the truth. Their lives are so different from ours. All New Yorkers think about is work, work, work, and the almighty dollar. Evan and Jean work, but at a different pace. All of Europe strolls while we run as fast as our legs will carry us. I don't believe that we get any more accomplished than they do, look at their lifestyle. I just miss him, that's all."

"I did do something just now that I hope I won't regret, Maggie. I called Evan and asked if he could come to New York to spend some time with me."

"I don't believe it. You called him? That's not like you. You must be lonesome too. Or is this none of my business?"

"Not at all. I think it's time I found someone to share my life. Maybe I could fall in love with Evan. I won't know that until we spend some time together."

"Maybe you're right. I just know that when I first set eyes on Jean, he was the one for me. I actually think I would give all of this up to live a much different life in France. Simpler, deeper, more meaningful, but …" she continued, "It's never going to happen. He's married and I own a partnership in one of the largest couturier houses and model agencies on the East Coast."

"Are you trying to convince me, or yourself?"

"Don't go there, Christina. You'll just make me more miserable than I already am, and I know you don't want to do that."

"Maybe Jean will come over with Evan. He is his administrative assistant and personal valet, is he not?"

"Do you think so, Christina? We aren't that busy just now and I could show Jean our way of life. That is, after he's seen the inside of my apartment."

Had she overstepped the lines of decorum? Christina was reluctant to engage in details of the sexual encounters of others, perhaps because she was so inexperienced in that aspect of her life. She hoped to rectify that soon. Why save it? She was looking forward to Evan's arrival more than she knew.

Christina and Maggie decided to go shopping for a change. The clothes they designed and featured were one of a kind, not ready to wear, and Christina was in need of a lift in spirits. She said little to nothing about her mother's funeral, fearful that she would blurt out the encounter with her father, and the depth of anger that threatened to consume her. She was determined to bury it and put it away with everything else that was too painful to deal with. For a change, Christina was looking forward to the future, and all thoughts of Adam would remain just that … nothing more than thoughts.

Evan called from the airport. Jean was along with him, they would be staying at the Hilton. "The car will call for you at eight p.m. Our reservations are for eight-thirty. I look forward to seeing you again, *cherie*."

She did not miss the term of endearment, and surprisingly her heart skipped a beat. Perhaps this wasn't such a bad idea after all. She called Maggie, and was bombarded by a very excited partner on the other end of the line. Jean had called. He was with Evan. They were all going out to dinner. "Yes, Maggie, that's why I'm calling. Thank goodness we went shopping today. I can't wait to try out my new sequined, low cut, spaghetti-strapped, gown on Monsieur D'Argent."

"Me too, but if I have my way Jean and I won't remain dressed for long." She laughed into the receiver, and Christina caught the sexual overtones and the change in depth of Maggie's voice. "I'll meet you at eight-thirty in the restaurant, or better still, in the limousine when Jean picks me up. I can hardly wait, I'm so excited." She giggled like a schoolgirl and Christina smiled to herself as they said goodbye.

Her gown did justice to her beautiful, strong, lithe young body. The tan was incredible against the iridescent white sequined gown. The bodice was cut low enough to show a measure of cleavage but left something to the imagination. She felt the weight of the dress as it moved from her hips down her long thighs and flared out from the front slit just below her ankles. The white satin pumps were perfect with the gown. Christina gave a last minute inspection to her hair, caught up in a loose mass of curls off the nape of her neck and tied securely with a diamond clasp.

Her heavily lashed eyes were enhanced with subtle eyeliner to afford an almond shape to the corners of her eyes, and the eyebrows were touched up with the liner. Mascara combed and separated the lashes, and they curled upward naturally. She noticed that her color was high, most likely due to the anticipated excitement of the evening, and she needed no artificial blush to complete her make-up. She had no idea just how much she was looking forward to seeing Evan once more.

Jean had taken the liberty of picking up Maggie on his way over to Christina's high rise. They were chatting away when Christina entered the limousine assisted by the doorman from her apartment building. Jean expertly drove them through evening traffic as though he had been driving in New York all of his life. Compared to France's taxi drivers, New York was a piece of cake. At least they had traffic lights that worked and didn't have to dodge a Gendarme directing traffic.

Evan moved from his seat at the bar as he watched his party enter the Hilton. He had reserved the private dining room for them, and was certain that nothing had been overlooked, from the smallest detail up to the last item on the menu. His eyes changed when he saw her. She was a vision in sparkling white, as though she had just stepped out of a magazine. His heart warmed at the sight of her. He thought how she was every inch a woman, every inch his heart's desire.

He acknowledged Maggie's presence with a warm greeting before focusing upon Christina. "It is good to see you again, *cherie*. You take my breath away."

Slightly embarrassed by his open admiration, Christina said, "I must apologize again for leaving you on the yacht. It is good to see you too, and I hope I can make it up to you." There, that sounded much better, she thought.

"I'll admit I was devastated. Jean had to save me from squandering a fortune at the gaming tables in Monte Carlo, and from drinking the tiny kingdom dry of champagne. I did miss you very much, but now that we are together, let's not talk about it anymore."

"You are so right, Evan, thank you."

They followed the maître d' to their table. Fresh flowers were subtly arranged and placed so that their fragrance and color complemented the snow white linen and sparkling glassware of the carefully set table for four. Evan had decided that their first evening should be spent in the company of others. He had no wish to hurry their relationship along, as much as he desired her. Christina Corelli had to be courted, and convinced that making love with Evan D'Argent would be the most pleasant and exhilarating experience in her life. He would see to it. Sitting beside her, their hands and shoulders occasionally touching, sent waves of electricity through her body and she found herself admiring how his dark hair curled, the unruly lock falling onto his forehead, his eyes warm and wanting as they met. She was impressed by his table manners; he was the perfect gentleman, motioning for the waiter to keep their glasses filled and the courses coming at the right moment. Maggie was in a world of her own. Christina could see that Jean's presence was nothing short of magical to Maggie. She couldn't take her eyes off him. Jean was the debonair Frenchman, seemingly unaware of the adoration, but playing it for all it was worth. He really had deep feelings for Maggie, and didn't accept her willingness as a perk of his employment. If he wasn't married, he would have pursued and formed a strong future with this vibrant woman.

The music was perfect; subtle, slow, sensuous, and Christina found herself becoming excited as she moved as one within the circle of Evan's arms. She forgot Maggie and Jean and hardly noticed when they left the dining room. Soon, it was just the two of them. Evan's plan was to create a private world of their own, where they could discover and enjoy all of their senses as one. The moonlight could be enjoyed from the top floor balcony in all its intensity, not paled by the lights and signs of midtown New York.

They left the dining room at midnight, Christina light-headed from the expensive champagne, Evan guiding her along the corridor to the elevator. She did not protest. Christina had decided soon into the perfect evening that Evan would be the man to teach her what was so exciting about making love, or pure sex, if one preferred the word. She was aroused and looking forward to being alone and making love with this exciting man at her elbow. In the elevator, as they descended to his suite, Evan bent and kissed her fingers, one by one, and moved up her arm. His lips were soft and gentle, his eyes finally making contact. His lips were on hers before she realized that he was no longer kissing her hand. His lips moved to the nape of her neck, then down slowly to the cleavage afforded by her dress. A thin strap fell off her shoulder and she ignored it. The feelings coursing through her body were unfamiliar to her. Evan's breathing was becoming intense as his desire mounted. He stopped suddenly as the elevator rang, signalling their floor. His arm about his partner, they left the elevator and hurried along the corridor to the door of the suite. He deftly unlocked the door, picked her up in his arms, and swept through the open door. He kicked the door closed behind them and carried his prize to the massive satin-covered bed that was the focal point of the luxurious room. Christina had nestled her head under his chin, too shy to meet his gaze. Her body was filled with desire, and she had no intention of stopping the events about to unfold.

Gently, he placed her upon the bed and she felt the coolness of the satin against her bare back. He removed the straps and with kisses followed the descent of the dress. She found herself in her underwear, covered by the weight of his body. He was murmuring in French, endearments that sounded wonderful to her ears. She began to respond, moving with him, helping him remove her underclothes. He had deftly taken off his tie, shirt, and pants and his physique was a splendid male counterpart to her statuesque body. Their bodies matched perfectly. He was well schooled in the act of making of love, and it was all Christina could do to contain herself and not beg him to enter her as he caressed and stroked every erotic area of her body. She had never been at such a height emotionally before and was drunk with emotion. She cried out when he entered her, but not in pain. It was a welcome that they could finally begin the rhythm of love, he was hard and strong in his male prowess, his penis probing and thrusting deep within her, and she cried out in ecstasy. She found herself murmuring, "Evan, more, please."

His answer was, "Yes, my darling, as long as you wish." He had much stamina, as Christina was to learn. Evan had practiced his ritual and staying power until his partner was at the peak of her desire, the release came together and Christina's body and mind seemed to explode in the first orgasm of her life. Such ecstasy from the simple act of making love she had never, in her wildest dreams, imagined. They smiled at one another, Evan planting soft kisses upon her eyelids, her cheeks, and her breasts as he said, "You were wonderful, my darling. Absolutely wonderful! What more can I say ... except that I am falling in love with you."

At the mention of the word love, Christina felt herself withdrawing.

She was relaxed in the afterglow, unabashed and unashamed at her display of abandonment. He had taught her the true art of what her body had been designed for, and Evan was as delighted as she. "Don't say anymore, Evan, just hold me. Within a few minutes he was aroused once more and they repeated the first coupling, taking more time to enjoy the sensations their touching brought forth. Christina had never felt so fulfilled. Perhaps she and Evan did have a future together. If this was part of a healthy and loving relationship, Christina was convinced that if she had to let go of Adam, then so be it. They slept within one another's arms. Christina did not stir when, a few hours later, Evan removed his arm from under her, covered her nakedness with the satin sheet, and slipped out from under the covers. He found his gold cigarette case and removed and lit a cigarette as he moved to the window. He was shaken by his emotion for this woman. Evan was twenty-nine years old and had had many women. None of them had ever touched him this way. He surveyed the New York skyline from the ceiling-to-floor length skyscraper window. How many people out there had just enjoyed such an encounter as he? It was a strange thought, he decided. He drew upon the cigarette, inhaling deeply and exhaling slowly as his heart rate slowed and his breathing became normal. Just the thought of possessing this woman in his bed again had sent the testosterone raging through his loins. The hardness of his rising emotion he controlled, unwilling to awaken her from her sleep. He would save the desire and his strength for the morning. Evan decided that he would stay in New York just long enough so that when he had to leave, Christina would miss him with every fibre of her being. Her sexual need for him would be consuming, and he knew she was not a promiscuous woman who would turn to any man who would not be in her future. After a few weeks away from her, he would call her and suggest that she reciprocate and join him in France. They would renew their relationship and Evan hoped that she would not be able to leave him. He had already committed himself to Christina and only needed her assurance that they could make a life together. The very thought of them becoming a couple made him smile, as he finished his cigarette. He returned to the warmth of Christina carefully so as not to disturb her. She murmured his name as he lay beside her but it was the murmur of her subconscious. He was delighted that her dreams were of him.

She awoke to find him resting on his elbow admiring her as she slept. He smiled and kissed her gently and she met his lips, meeting the caress. He had ordered breakfast to be served within the hour, giving him enough time to arouse her, make love to her, and still have time to shower. Reluctantly, she left the bed after they had renewed their desire for one another in a coupling that left them exhausted and both delighted by the response produced. Christina was the first to leave the bed as she wrapped the sheet about her body and turned and smiled at him as she entered the bathroom. He wanted so much to join her, but the fact that she had covered her nakedness in preparation for her day meant much to him. He was accustomed to having his partner for the evening pad about in the hotel room or suite naked, and sharing breakfast at the table dressed in nothing. It was Evan's nature to find this distasteful. Once he had explored and conquered, he quickly lost interest in the woman's body. She had served the purpose as the vessel of his needs, and whether she padded about the room naked was of no interest to him. In fact he was often disgusted to find himself inwardly commenting upon the defects in nature's workmanship: cellulite, heavy thighs, long neck, bony shoulder blades, sagging breasts, all of this just so much flesh and bone. Not so with Christina; her actions by covering herself had only piqued his desire. He had no idea that her shyness stemmed from her inhibitions; he considered it to be a cut above the common, a touch of class.

A pot of hot strong coffee was available on the sideboard. It had a timer mechanism on the unit and the smell of fresh coffee had permeated the room at eight a.m.

Christina re-entered the room wrapped in a lush terry towel robe, her hair encased turban style in a smaller towel. Her skin was shiny and she wore no make-up, and Evan reflected on the fact that she had never looked so beautiful. "There's fresh coffee for you. I'm going to shower. Give me a few minutes and I should be done by the time breakfast arrives." He kissed her on the tip of her nose in passing.

Christina poured a cup of the hot coffee, wrapping her hands about the generous mug. It felt good to be here. She did not have to go into work for a few days, Maggie sensing that Christina needed some time off after her intense work schedule over the past few months. A knock at the door and the waiter's voice interrupted her reverie as she directed him to place the cart near the table. He was most polite, casting occasional admiring glances at the occupant. He had recognized her, and all of the hotel staff had tossed a coin to see who would get to deliver breakfast. Evan emerged from the bathroom in time to tip the man. They were alone again. Christina was ravenous. She said, "Evan, why am I so hungry? I never eat this much."

"Because, my darling, making love is rather a strenuous business and requires much energy, wouldn't you say?"

She smiled at this remark, nodding as she nibbled on a second piece of toast. "You have a point. Evan, thank you for a wonderful night, and thank you for not mentioning our last conversation about the twins. I don't know why I shared my secret, but at the time I felt so lost and forlorn, I needed someone to listen."

"Why are you telling me this now? I thought we would put it behind us."

"Not exactly. You see, I have never told anyone, not even Maggie and John. I can just imagine what the tabloids would do with the news if it was to get out."

"Cherie, you have my solemn promise. Your secret is safe with me. No matter what."

Christina breathed a sigh of relief. She trusted this man. He had taken her to heights that she had never so much as imagined. She was indebted to him for many things; his generosity, his kindness, his acceptance of her past, his devotion. They finished their breakfast, made plans for the day, and as Christina dressed, Evan called Jean to go over the day's itinerary. Jean answered promptly, but if it was possible to see through the telephone receiver he would have been discovered naked and in bed with an ecstatic Maggie Cole. She giggled at his shoulder as he covered the mouthpiece, admonishing her to be quiet. "*Oui,* it shall be done. Yes, yellow roses to be delivered to the table at the restaurant at noon. A carriage ride through the park, a limousine tour about the city … it shall be as you say. I will be at the front door of the Hilton at nine-thirty. *Au revoir.*"

Evan grinned as he hung up. Jean was not only his best friend, his aide and his confidante, but he knew more about his employer than anyone other than Evan's family. He chose to speak formally whenever they became employer and employee, and when Evan analyzed the situation, it did seem appropriate. When they were alone on the yacht, they shared a friendly nightcap, discussed the day's events, and acted as brothers. Evan respected Jean and relied upon his proposed solutions, oftentimes based upon Jean's own experiences. They did not trade stories of their sexual encounters. A gentleman never tells, and they stuck to that code.

Maggie stretched and lay back upon the luxurious, spacious bed. She had it especially designed to accommodate company. Jean was impressed with the opulence and wealth that surrounded him. She had exquisite taste in furnishings and in color. No wonder she was such a success in the fashion industry. He loved two women; first, his wife of eight years, and this natural, down to earth woman here beside him. Given a choice, he had no idea which he would select. They were as different as the night from day, and complemented his tastes in fantasy and actuality. No man should have to choose between them. He had discussed his feelings for Maggie and they decided that neither one could give up their current lives. Maggie had never been so fulfilled in her career with the Agency, and Jean was European to the core and could never leave France indefinitely. They opted for the time that they could spend together, a long distance relationship punctuated by sporadic phone calls and occasional encounters.

Maggie had to go into the office; Jean had to work as well. They did not bother with breakfast, as Maggie would have coffee at the agency and Jean would eat later when Christina and Evan were taking in the sights of New York.

True to his word, Jean was at the door of the hotel at the expected time. He had studied a map and tour guide brochure before coming to New York and had done rather well in threading the rented limo through traffic. The day was perfect. Evan and Christina rode the carriage through Central Park for a few hours while Jean caught up on much needed rest. Maggie had been insatiable, draining him emotionally and physically. She said she had to store up memories to last until they met again.

Chapter Twenty-Seven

E VAN STAYED FOR A week. During that time, Christina changed. She had lost her youthful innocence and her face had become that of a mature young woman with a radiance that was unmistakable. Evan became aware of the change when she came to the airport to see him off. "How can I leave you, my darling?" He had pleaded with her, "Come with me, Christina, be my love for always. I cannot leave you like this."

She was caught off guard. Evan had promised that there would be no commitments ... they had agreed. "Evan, please don't. You promised you would not do this."

"I know I did. But I didn't love you then as I do now."

She could see the misery in his eyes and was helpless to be able to change his expression. "Evan, I think very highly of you. I cherish your friendship, and I do love you, but I am not in love with you. It would be wrong for me to say that I was and to regret it later. It would be unfair and I couldn't do that to you. You have been wonderful to me, much more so than I deserve."

"Marry me, and I will share my world with you. Let me show you another side of life."

"If only I could. My life has only just begun. There is so much that I want to accomplish. I have just become a partner in the Agency and there is so much to learn. I am only twenty-one years old, Evan, and I feel that my life is just before me. How can I go to France and become your wife? I would resent it in no time at all. Do you understand?"

"Yes, I understand. I was only dreaming. But this does not mean goodbye. You will always be in my heart, Christina. You must promise to call me whenever you have need of me. If you are lonely, if you are heartsick, if you are in trouble, whatever, I am at your service. We are good friends and I regret that you do not love me. I was hoping to change all that, but I see it is not in the future. Goodbye, my love, I will call you."

"Thank you, Evan. Goodbye. She kissed him lightly on the lips and watched as he went through customs to the boarding gate. One last glimpse and he was gone. She felt detached, not whole, as though she had lost her best friend as indeed, she had. Christina squared her shoulders and left the airport, got into the waiting taxi, and gave the address of the Agency. There was still almost a full day of work and she needed to touch base with John and Maggie before they changed their minds and decided that she wasn't much of a partner. She would treasure the past week, but it had to be put in context, locked away in a special place in her heart. She probably would regret her decision to turn down Evan's proposal, but she knew in her heart that he could not replace the one love of her life. Even if Adam and she had no future together, the past was still too strong.

The Agency was abuzz with activity. Maggie looked relaxed, fit, and on top of the world. She was happy to see Christina. "Good morning, Christina. John and I have a meeting at eleven. I rather expected you to be in this morning. Jean said they would be leaving at ten. It's been a wonderful week, hasn't it?"

"Yes Maggie, it has been just that. A wonderful week, but it's time to get to work. I have so much to learn."

John entered the room. He had news of great proportion. "Sit down, ladies. Don't interrupt." He withdrew a sheaf of papers from his briefcase, and with much fanfare threw them upon the boardroom table. "That, my dears, is the fattest contract I have ever negotiated. I only have to run it by the two of you, get our lawyers to read it over, sign it, and we are set for the next ten years."

Maggie beamed. "What is it?" She saw the letterhead and gasped. It was the largest cosmetics company in the entire world. This branch of woman's cosmetics had reached monumental proportions with their new line. "Christina has been chosen as the model for their line. Exclusively, with no chance of being dropped, other than if she becomes ill or unable to perform as their spokes model. She will be featured on television, billboards, and magazines, everywhere cosmetics are sold. Ladies, this calls for champagne." He began to hum, "We're in the Money" as Christina and Maggie looked at one another in disbelief. They scanned the documents, and the amount of money offered in the contract was in the millions. "Now maybe I won't have to work so hard, and I can spend some time with my very pregnant wife."

"John, you can take the week off. This is incredible. Christina is already well-known, but this will put her on the 'Ten Most Beautiful Supermodels' list. A sobering thought though, Christina, this means that your privacy will be almost non-existent. The press will be all over you wherever you go. Scarves and sunglasses will become a permanent part of your wardrobe."

"I don't mind. I've had a small measure of happiness and work is what I chose to do. It couldn't have come at a better time. Evan and I parted company this morning and it has left a void within that I will fill with work. If I am busy, I will have little time to think. He proposed to me at the airport, but Maggie, the decision I made is mine alone and I believe that I can live with it. Perhaps the timing was not right, perhaps if I was older … I really don't know. I love Evan, but I am not in love with him. I cherish his friendship but I couldn't share my life with him. Neither of you has anything to worry about. I won't be dashing off to Europe at a moment's notice and leaving you both in the lurch. By the way, how much money are we worth to date?"

John answered, "We can't spend it fast enough. As equal partners, we are in the hundreds of millions."

Christina gasped. "I guessed at a few million at the most. But actually hundreds of millions

… if only my father knew."

She had not meant to make that last statement. It had just come out. Maggie saw her expression change and the tone of Christina's voice was bitter. She exchanged glances with her brother and they glossed over the remark, saying that John had to get the contract to the lawyers while Maggie would call the company president and confirm their commitment. It appeared as though they were about to board the gravy train. Maggie would retain control of the models, always on the lookout for fresh new talent, and John would exclusively handle Christina's appearances and photo shoots for the cosmetic firm. He dreamt out loud of cosmetics, fragrances, personal anecdotes, star billing for guest appearances. He loved his work.

It had been a very long day. Christina was happy to finally be alone as she threw her handbag onto the table in the entry hallway of her apartment. She rifled through the mail that her assistant had placed there, and selected a letter from Cranston. It was welcome news from Becka. Christina hung her coat up in the closet and flopped down onto the comfortable oversize sofa. She tore open the letter and read with amusement Becka's down to earth, droll humour as she brought Christina up to date on the wedding plans. As they had discussed when Christina had been home, the date was set. December twenty-first, an evening ceremony, a large buffet, head table festivities, followed by a dance to end the evening. Christina's gift to Tonio and Becka was a two-week vacation in Hawaii, an escape from the always bitter Canadian winter. Reluctantly, Christina had to answer Becka's letter almost immediately. She took pen in hand and shared the news of her new contract. With so many scheduled appearances, Christina had to express her concern that she may not make it to the wedding. If nothing else, she would attempt to attend the church ceremony, but that might be all the time she was allowed. In actuality, Christina realized that with this new claim to fame, some loose freelance photographer would follow her about and no doubt crash the wedding. In no way, shape or form would Christina allow this to happen. She had to stay in the background. This was Becka's day to shine and Christina would never forgive herself if she became the focal point of their very special day. By attending the mass, where no cameras were allowed during the ceremony, she could extend her congratulations and slip away before the lavish and very public reception began. She had to make this known to Becka beforehand, or she would not be attending.

She finished the letter, placed it on the table for posting in the morning and readied herself for bed. She slept dreamless; the day had been too long and exhausting. No thoughts or regrets of Evan, no fantasy dreams of Adam, no guilt trips about her past. She had only her future to look forward to and to focus upon her work. For this Christina would need all of her energy.

During the meeting the following morning the phone rang in the boardroom. John was angry at the interruption saying, "I told that damn secretary to hold all calls. This better be good."

"I'm sorry Mr. Cole, but the police are here to speak with you and Miss Cole. Shall I send them in?"

"I guess we have no choice. Send them in."

"What is it, John?" Maggie asked. He had no time to answer; he merely put his fingers to his lips to indicate that they remain silent. Two of New York's finest entered. Badges displayed, greetings aside, one detective sat at the table while the tallest remained standing. John shook hands and gestured for him to be seated. Reluctantly, he did just that.

"What can I do for you?" asked John.

"We have some rather bad news, I'm afraid. We found a body in a dumpster behind a posh apartment downtown and we believe it is that of one of your models. We need someone to come down to the precinct and identify it."

Maggie's face was ashen. Christina was in shock but she managed to ask, "What did she look like?"

The detective described Zoe to a "T". He said, "The body is that of a female, approximately twenty-five to thirty years of age with dark curly hair and brown eyes. She does resemble one of your models, a Zoe Carlson. However, we need confirmation and we will hold the body for autopsy. She was badly beaten and dumped around midnight last night, according to the Medical Examiner's preliminary report."

John said, "I'll come with you. Maggie, Christina, I'll call you as soon as I have any news. Don't let this get out. We'll meet as soon as I return. It's business as usual. We don't need the publicity, especially now. It could kill the deal with Distinctive Woman. Damn the luck."

Maggie left abruptly and returned almost immediately with two shot glasses and a bottle of whiskey. "We both need this, Christina." She poured a full shot for herself, downed it then refilled it while preparing a glass for Christina. They said nothing, allowing the whiskey to do its work. The hot burning liquid lay in Christina's stomach like fire, but she felt the warmth beginning to spread throughout her body. The shock of the news began to seep in, and they sat in silence for a good ten minutes. Maggie spoke first, "I knew she was into something. John said she had been coming late to her photo shoots and that she had been hard to deal with during the runway shows, and totally out of it. I think she was really into the alcohol, maybe something stronger. But

I don't think Zoe would do anything so stupid that would cause her to lose her life. How could we have missed it?"

"That's easy. We've all been so caught up in our own lives, making money, making more money, signing contracts, and traveling, we just lost sight of Zoe as an individual. If she was having trouble we should have listened to her and recognized the signs. We have no one to blame but ourselves, but Zoe, if it is her, has paid dearly for our mistakes. She couldn't handle the fame and wealth that came with her success. She said to me on one occasion, 'Chris, I sometimes have to pinch myself to see if I'm not dreaming. Is this really happening?' The flirtatious nature that we all believed was Zoe was just a front for her shyness and lack of confidence. I thought she had overcome this, but she must have turned to alcohol for courage. Why would anyone want to take the life of such a vivacious, kind, and beautiful person?"

John rang from the station. "Maggie, tell Christina that the body in the morgue, is Zoe. She must have suffered much before she died. The coroner thought that she died from a blow to the head, most likely from a tire iron after someone put the boots to her. It's not pretty. I'll be back in the office within the hour. Call our lawyers and have them meet me there. We will probably have to make a statement but timing is everything."

"I agree, John. I'll tell Christina."

Christina knew that the body in the morgue had to be that of Zoe's, just by the expression on Maggie's face and the tone of her voice. She poured herself another shot of whiskey and said absolutely nothing. What was there to say? Her friend and co-worker had met with a horrible death, and all they could worry about was the press and the impact upon the new contract. How cold they had all become. Christina shuddered, put the thought away, and decided to follow Maggie and John's lead. She was too new to this game and could not be blamed for any wrong decision making; she would leave it up to her seasoned partners.

They held the emergency strategy meeting and agreed to tell the truth to the press. The model was one of theirs, well known and famous, and she would be greatly missed by the Agency. They had no more clues than the New York Police Department as to who had killed her or why. It was an ongoing investigation and the Agency would attempt to find a new model to replace Zoe. That brought a frenzy of questions, such as,

"Do you have a model in mind?", "Will you do a nation-wide search?", "Will she have to be someone with experience?", callously forgetting that Zoe hadn't even been buried as yet, that her body lay forgotten in the police morgue. Christina was shocked by their coldness, their devious speculation as to why Zoe had met her untimely death. She had been murdered while still in the prime of her life; a beautiful, vivacious, young woman who loved life more than anyone Christina had ever known. Suddenly she began to cry. She excused herself from the meeting and escaped to the executive washroom. She entered a stall, sat down on the toilet seat, and cried her eyes out. She cried for various reasons, for Zoe, for her mother, for her estranged father, her go-nowhere relationship with Evan, her love for Adam … everything came crashing down upon her and she cried in the worst possible way, silent tears that streamed endlessly down her cheeks, causing rivulets of mascara. They, too, were almost washed clean as the flood of tears appeared unending. Exhausted from her emotional episode, Christina wiped her eyes with the available tissue, slowly got up, and left the stall. She surveyed her image in the mirror. She was pale, her eyes sad and distant, as she searched her soul. One thing she did come to realize was that she had not become as callous as she had first imagined. Whatever else her lifestyle did to her, she vowed never to become so unfeeling that she could come to resent the residents of New York's skid row, or the helpless and crippled that made up a percentage of her surroundings. She splashed cold water on her face, dried off with the available paper towel, and left the security of the washroom. She met Maggie in the hallway, and said, "Maggie, I'm going home. I've had it for today. Whatever else that we planned for the day will have to wait. I couldn't contribute anything creative or positive if my life depended on it."

"I agree, Christina. It's been a long day. John will make the necessary arrangements and call Zoe's family. There isn't much else we can do for her except see that she gets a decent burial."

They parted company. On her way home, Christina remembered when she had first met Zoe. Christina had been accepted soon into the tightly knit circle of the top models. Zoe had been especially kind to her, offering her advice regarding technique on presentation, tips that were invaluable to a new kid on the block. Fresh tears brightened her eyes, but she wiped them away. Where did Suzanne fit into all of this?

Where was she, anyway? John hadn't mentioned anything about Suzanne being away on a photo shoot. The two models had become inseparable, often working the same contract. They did a great deal of socializing together. Christina decided she would call Suzanne from home. She left the taxi outside of her apartment. The doorman smiled in friendly greeting. Christina nodded politely. The apartment afforded such a welcome measure of privacy that Christina went to her favourite seat in the high rise and stared out of the window. One very important thing she had learned thus far was that no matter how famous, how rich, or how protected she was, the world was still out there, waiting to strike. Christina had always felt that she was a world apart, living a fantasy, where the trials and tribulations of the world were for others, and not for the 'beautiful people.'

Zoe's death was a definite wake-up call. She would be less trusting with new acquaintances, less naive and more suspicious as to the aspirations and intentions of the people who surrounded her on a daily basis. Maggie and John were a given, but everyone else appeared to be out to use whatever means necessary to climb the ladder to its top rung. Christina intended to stay on top and climb ever higher.

Chapter Twenty-Eight

C HRISTINA WROTE A VERY long letter to Becka revealing her innermost thoughts. She was in better spirits after she had put everything down on paper. She was so looking forward to the wedding and promised to do her utmost to keep her departure from New York a secret. Maggie would say that she had left for an assignment in Miami, and that would send the paparazzi on a wild goose chase. In the meanwhile, she threw herself into her work, and the months began to fade, one into the other. Fall arrived; the leaves transformed the city into a glorious landscape, until a brisk wind drove the stinging sleet into their faces as the residents of New York braced for a chilling winter. The landscape became grey and bleak, overcast, wet and windy. A few weeks later in early November Christina arose to a white world of clean snow that swirled and danced across her windows, to rest upon the flat rooftops and find its way to the streets below, where traffic fought a losing battle trying to maintain the normal flow of vehicles, buses, and trucks. Everything slowed but New York was never at a standstill. The plows were out within record time, sand was spread upon the streets, and New York's pace picked up considerably by the noon hour. Becka's wedding was just six weeks away, the agency was making record profits, and John and Ellen's baby would arrive soon. Christina hoped that she would be away for the event. Newborn babies made her uncomfortable. She had mixed emotions about returning to Cranston. Her father would be at the wedding, accompanying Tonio's mother, and would be part of the head table. Christina decided she would play it by ear. For all practical purposes she wanted to attend the church ceremony. The rest of the festivities were not nearly as important.

The fall and winter shows had seen many of Christina's designs mixed within the line. She modeled none of her own. Maggie's thoughts on this strategy were that Christina would shine on her own without having to promote her own designs by using her supermodel status as leverage. Suzanne had withdrawn, entered into a chronic depression, and all attempts by management had failed to bring her to terms with Zoe's death. The police had listed Zoe as just another unsolved homicide. Christina had questioned Suzanne about her and Zoe's social life, as Suzanne's body language bespoke denial and a heavy burden of guilt. She would not open up to Christina, as the latter had hoped, and the incident was soon forgotten. Suzanne's career was on a tightrope. She could fall either way, and Christina did her best to buoy her spirits, attempting to rejuvenate the old Suzanne, the one with confidence, vivacity, and great presence. The cameras had always done her justice, now they were finding cracks in the facade. Suzanne, in Christina's eyes, was the second loneliest person in the world, Christina being the first.

The day before the wedding, the weather had socked in and closed two major airports in the New York area. Christina managed to secure a flight out of Connecticut. She was deep in thought as the airplane flew at twenty-five thousand feet, and the four hour flight was over before she realized that they were beginning their descent to the Calgary airport. A rental car was waiting for her, and she was in and out of customs in record time. The weather was much better in the Western region. Clear and cold, the air crisp and the snow piled where the snow plows had dumped it. It had been some time since Christina had been in Canada during the winter. She mused, "As things change, the more they stay the same."

She did not wish to stay at the local Inn fearing any publicity, so Becka had arranged that she stay in the guest room at the Sanders' residence. A few relatives would be occupying the Inn and the other spare bedroom in the Sanders' residence. A two and a half hour drive later found Christina on the outskirts of her hometown. Cranston lay peacefully on the crest of the hill; it had begun sprawling out from the epicenter. The growth was planned, and incorporated into the central downtown core so that everyone had the same commute to work, shopping and entertainment. She experienced a measure of pride, knowing that her relatives had been responsible for much of the prosperity of the community. She turned the car into the Sanders' driveway, parking out of the way so that deliveries could be made and other guests could arrive. She rang the doorbell and was quickly engulfed by a very excited, very euphoric Becka, who hugged her tightly as she said, "You made it. Christina, you're really here."

"Of course, silly, I told you I would be here, didn't I?"

Christina kissed her on each cheek and Becka motioned her into the living room. She proudly introduced her to the occupants, relatives who shook her hand, some of the women unable to disguise their open admiration for Christina. Her ensemble smacked of haute couture; the burgundy suit with gold embellishments had been hidden within the confines of a winter white cashmere swing coat with an attached scarf that unwound as a cape. Becka's father took Christina's coat and gloves as Mrs. Sanders offered her refreshments. Christina chose a cup of tea and ate sparingly of the lavish buffet. Traveling always took away her appetite. She worked the room, answering more than a few questions about her career. Christina tried to steer the conversation back to why they were all gathered together, to honor Becka and Tonio. Finally most of the guests got the hint, as they spoke of their own families, their work, and the coming nuptials.

Christina went along to the rehearsal as moral support for Becka. She couldn't tell who was the most nervous, Tonio or Becka, but it was clearly evident to all who surveyed the couple that they were very much in love, unable to conceal the need for one another. If Christina could swap places with Becka she would have done so, but only for a moment. She would not dwell upon her own disappointments; these few days belonged to Becka.

After rehearsal the wedding party and close friends retired to the local Inn for a nightcap. The regulars were in attendance, as well as a new band that had brought new customers into the bar. Becka found them a very large round table that would seat at least eight people. They managed to crowd up and the even dozen that made up the group settled down in their seats.

Tonio spoke, "I have to say that the group before me makes up our closest and dearest friends, many of you we have known since we attended grade school. To Christina Corelli, whom I met on the boat coming over from Italy. She was my first love and I was only six years old. I still love you, Christina, but you have been replaced." To the laughter, which accompanied his statement, everyone drank the toast, and Becka basked in the glow of Tonio's adoring embrace. She winked at Christina, and Christina in turn made a face. The group ordered a few more rounds until someone noted the time. With so much left to do, Becka kissed Tonio long and hard as she said, "I will see you tomorrow Mr. Marcellus ... church, five o'clock sharp ... be there."

He clicked his heels and hugged her tightly as he replied, "I wouldn't miss it for the world.

I may even be a little early." Becka left with Christina.

The two lifelong friends readied for bed, exchanging ideas, wondering who all would be at the church. Becka's parents were long time residents of the community, much loved and respected by many. The invitation to attend the ceremony had been posted in the local papers and within the church annals so that if anyone wished to come they would be made welcome. Christina was tired from her long trip across the country, Becka from seeing to last-minute preparations and making her guests feel welcome. They said goodnight, and Christina welcomed the privacy of the guest bedroom. Becka needed her rest; she had a very long day ahead of her.

The weather cooperated for the entire day of the wedding. By five o'clock, the church was packed. The word had gone out; this was a wedding that would do the community proud. The local newspaper photographer was in attendance doing his utmost to disrupt the movement of the crowd as they pressed into the confines of the church.

Assuredly, Christina helped Becka with last minute arrangements to her veil, hair, and make-up, and then left. She drove the rental car to the church parking lot and left it near the side door. She entered the church as the usher walked towards her. "Would you like to be seated with the family, Miss Corelli?"

"No, that won't be necessary. I would like to sit well back near the door, if that's all right." "Not a problem. Will this do?"

Christina was just three rows from the back, near the aisle. She could see the front of the altar as well as anyone; being as tall as she was, it had never been a problem. She waited patiently, as the hour grew near. At five to five it appeared as though no new guests would be arriving. The male members of the wedding party had taken their places to the right of the front row relatives, as the strains of the wedding march began. All heads turned as the flower girl preceded the bridesmaids, strewing fresh roses along the aisle. The color and pageantry of a traditional wedding captured the attention of all within. Becka appeared in a gown that was a signature of her very good taste. With seed pearls, hand-woven lace, and much satin, her dark curls escaped the confines of the short veil. Her color was high, and her eyes were intense with expectation and happiness. She was totally breathtaking. Christina was so proud of her. The ceremony began. Christina became aware of a last minute arrival. Someone slid onto the seat beside her. She did not glance away from the scene in front. Warmth began to spread along her right side as the person beside her was asked to move even closer by another occupant of the row. Christina was annoyed by the disturbance and turned to face the newcomer, "Please, you're being ..." She stopped in mid-sentence. Beside her, as close as they had ever sat in the front seat of his car, was Adam Carmichael. A more mature, much handsomer Adam, tall and strong, his grey eyes intent upon hers. She gasped, attempted to control the wave of emotion that swept through her ... but Adam spoke first.

"Hello, Christina." Just a hello, and the sound of his voice made her knees weak. She looked down at her hands; they were clasped tightly together with the hymn book clutched in her palms. Strangely enough, Christina became aware of an inner strength. So Adam was next to her, so what? Hadn't she dreamed of this moment over and over? Now that he was beside her, she had to say something.

"Hello, Adam, how are you?" Again her short, polite, words were meaningless, while she longed to release the years of unrequited love.

"Fine, just fine, and you?"

If it hadn't been so poignant, the whole conversation would have appeared ridiculous. His eyes weren't saying, "just fine," they were filled with longing, a desire to hold her in his arms and never let go. The ceremony was soon over, Becka and Tonio were Mr. and Mrs. Marcellus. Christina stood up at the same time as Adam. He bent and whispered in her ear, "Let's get out of here. I have to talk to you." She felt his hand on her arm, guiding her out of the church pew and out into the fresh air. As they emerged from the church double doors, a barrage of flash bulbs went off, temporarily blinding both Adam and Christina. His reaction was delayed. Christina acted instantaneously; she turned on her heel and made her way back into the church. The crowd opened a path before her and she found herself slowly making headway along the far wall of the church. She spied the side door, knowing full well her car was parked right outside, and without a backward glance she left the church, the guests, and the damnable paparazzi that had somehow discovered that she was inside the church hoping for a shot of her and a word or two to answer their questions. As she had stated, this was Becka's day to shine and she had no intention of allowing the day to turn into a feeding frenzy for the press. She drove to the Sanders', hastily scrawled a note to Becka asking her forgiveness, packed her bags, and within the next fifteen minutes was speeding along the highway, on her way to Calgary to catch a last minute flight to New York. As she left the Sanders' driveway she slowed for oncoming traffic, just missing Adam as he approached from the direction of the church. He had no idea what type of vehicle she was driving and his disappointment changed to anger as he realized that he had missed her. Why had she run? Was it away from the press, or was it from him? All the love and longing, his dedication to this wonderful woman, coursed through his body. Time had not dulled his love for her; it had merely put everything on hold until they could be together, this time forever. Now she was gone again. When he had entered the church, he was a man with a mission. Rumour had it that Christina Corelli would be attending the wedding ceremony of her best friend, and Adam was hell-bent on seeing her. His plans included a private place where they could talk, a meeting of the minds, his apology for everything, his explanation for not contacting her before everything fell apart. Now she was gone. Damn it all anyway. Five years had not changed her, except that she was lovelier than he remembered. The years had enhanced her beauty, maturity had defined it, and the outcome was indescribable. That he once possessed this woman, that he loved her still, more than ever, was as a dream, since she had disappeared once again. He was downcast, almost sullen as he cursed out loud, to fate, to no one in particular, to his dumb luck.

He would return to New York to begin his residency in the discipline of his choice ... plastic surgery and reconstructive surgery. He had graduated in the top five in his class, and had been snapped up by one of the most prestigious medical facilities in the U.S.A. other than the Mayo clinic. He was under the protective mantle of a very fine surgeon, Dr. Samuel Finestad, who was highly skilled and respected by the medical community. His practice was situated on Park Avenue and he catered to the wealthy. He had no sons, only a daughter, who was only interested in marrying money and spending it as fast as it came into the bank. Adam's future was secured. All he had to do was his part. He still had three years of study and practicum ahead of him, so what could he promise Christina?

The chance encounter left him visibly shaken. He knew that she had responded in kind. Their eyes had sent a message that their lips had left unspoken. The desire and longing in her eyes had matched his, but she had turned away first, murmuring something meaningless, all the while he wanted to crush her in his arms and repeat his vow to love her all the days of his life. He remembered that he had asked Becka to convey the message to Christina on Becka's last day at the training hospital. He wondered now if she had. He was so despondent that he decided that this was his last day in Cranston. The sooner he returned to New York, the sooner he would get his life back on track. With mixed emotions, he wondered if Christina was out of his reach. He had agonized over the magnitude of magazines whose covers she graced. He had kept the best ones in an album, unable to look at them again once they were placed between the hard covers of the glossy album. She was linked to a wealthy Frenchman not too long ago, but he believed that it was all the imagination of the tabloids. She was unmarried as yet, to his knowledge. Thank goodness for small blessings. Realizing that none of this was getting him anywhere, Adam emerged from his parent's home, suitcase in hand, his mother's tears apparent as he said goodbye, making him feel guilty for leaving so soon. He could not stay for Christmas. He would telephone. His father appeared to understand, the pride in his son shone in his eyes as he wished him well in his studies. "You'll do us proud, my boy. Until next time, don't forget to write if you have a few minutes. Mother and I are always looking to hear from you. Good luck."

"Thanks Dad, Mom. No more tears. I'll call as soon as I arrive in New York. I love you both." It was almost a relief for Adam to be alone in the car. It afforded him a few hours to reminisce, as well as to plan for the future. If at all possible, he would move heaven and earth if necessary, he would see Christina again. This time he would hold her in his arms and never let her go. He was two hours behind Christina, but the weather refused to cooperate and a ground blizzard developed. Adam had to pull into a truck stop in the nearest town, where he was stuck for six hours. He had no choice but to call and make new reservations for the following day.

Christina had watched the dark clouds forming to the south of her, but she was fortunate to be ahead of the storm. The encounter with Adam had left her visibly shaken, so much so that she could not clear her mind. The emotion that had coursed through her body when she felt his shoulder touch hers was nothing short of electric. What would have happened if the paparazzi had not interrupted their meeting? She probably would never know. She must call Becka and Tonio to apologize for running off the way she had, but she believed that Becka would have already guessed. She sincerely hoped this was so.

Chapter Twenty-Nine

Five Years Later

"I DON'T GIVE A DAMN what you say, Suzanne has got to go." John's anger filled the boardroom. "She doesn't show up for work, or if she does, she's so drunk she can't walk a straight line on the runway. The last show she damn near fell off the ramp. Who needs the hassle?"

Maggie said nothing, waiting for the tirade to end. She wasn't surprised by his words. They had hidden months of Suzanne's behaviour from him and it was only by chance that he had witnessed firsthand one of her worst days ever. Christina answered, "John, please. She's one of our best models; she has more experience than the entire group."

"You mean she used to be one of our best models. I can't afford to make excuses for her any longer. She has to go."

"Go where, John? This business is all she knows. If we let her go, the word will be out and no one will hire her."

"That's not our problem. I tell you, the woman is bad for business."

"We all agree on that, but what else can we do?"

Christina spoke. "I have an idea that might work, and it would ease the transition from the limelight to retirement. She has the most beautiful hands of anyone I have ever seen. Why don't we use them in one of the soap ads, or for skin products? She would be great, and no one would know if they belonged to a drunken model or a sober one. I'll talk to her about her drinking. Maybe she'll get help."

"I don't know ... what if she still turns up late for a shoot, or not at all?" This came from John, still angry at having to take the brunt of his client's anger, all the while threatening to cancel the contract.

"We could give it a try, John. We've always treated our models fairly, so why not give Suzanne a break? She's been with us for quite a few years and has brought much fame and wealth to this agency."

"You think I don't know that. How old is she? Twenty-nine is too old for a model. She's lucky her hands aren't wrinkled as well."

"That wasn't exactly kind, John. Will you say that about me in a few years? I just turned twenty-six." Christina glared at him. John could be so damn stubborn at times. Maggie wasn't too interested in the proceedings. Lately she had left many of the important decisions to John, while she simply appeared to be putting one foot in front of the other. Her interest had certainly lagged over the past year. Christina wondered if it had anything to do with her break-up with Jean. Since Evan had stopped coming to New York, Jean no longer telephoned or dropped a note in the mail to Maggie. She really had no social life to speak of. "Will you give it a try? I'll talk to her immediately. If not, then you can be the one to fire her. I just don't have the heart. Nothing like kicking a person when they're already down," she murmured.

"What do you say, Maggie?"

"If Christina says we can use her, then she's right, we owe Suzanne a chance to make a living at least. It won't pay anywhere near what she's making on the runway, but it should be enough for her to keep her apartment and live modestly. She'll get royalties from the television ads when they run on the network, as well as a signing bonus with the client. It will have to do. Talk to her and we'll have the lawyers draw up a new contract. Her old one is finished."

Christina left the boardroom, bent on a mission to save her friend and colleague. Suzanne was in her dressing room, attempting to repair the ravages of a hangover and lack of sleep, which left a sorry looking sight in the mirror. She was definitely hell bent upon self destruction.

"Come in, Christina. To what do I owe the honour?" Suzanne's sarcasm was only thinly disguised.

"I have a proposal for you, Suzanne, if you have the time to listen."

"What are you proposing, Christina, that I take a long walk and never come back? I've heard the rumours. Everyone says I'm too old for this business. Is that it?"

Christina took the opportunity afforded her by Suzanne. "You have heard the rumours, and in most cases they are correct ... but please listen, Suzanne."

"Listen, listen to what? Goodbye Suzanne, you old hag, your services are no longer required. We have hired a newer, younger, less experienced model, but she will soon learn the ropes." She began to cry. Christina heard the anguish in her voice, and attempted to console Suzanne. "Don't patronize me, Christina, leave me some pride."

"Suzanne, if you don't shut up and listen to me, then I will walk out that door, and John will have the dubious honour of firing you on the spot. If that is what you want, then say so, and I'm gone."

"I'm sorry, Christina. Sit down. I'm listening."

"It's true, John was all for letting you go as soon as possible, but Suzanne, look at your hands. They are perfect. Have you ever really noticed?"

"What have my hands got to do with losing my job?"

"We have a few clients who sell their products using just the hands-on camera. Lotions, perfumes, chocolates, hands that hold the product but the person belonging to the hands is never seen."

Suzanne looked at her hands as though she was seeing them for the first time. "I always thought of them as just hands."

"Put them against mine. Come on. Then you'll see what I mean."

Christina's hands were tiny; her fingers not meant to play a piano, while Suzanne's were long, beautifully shaped, enhanced by well manicured nails. "I've always taken care of them," she murmured.

"We'll work out the details as soon as possible, as your old contract is no longer valid. The pay won't be as much but I'll do my best to make it worth your while." Without hesitation she added, "And Suzanne, you've got to do something about your drinking. John will fire you on the spot if he so much as suspects that you've had a drink while working. I won't be able to get you out of hot water if you don't stop. Do we understand one another?"

"Yes, Christina, I hear you. I can't thank you enough. If I lost this job, I really don't have anywhere else to go."

"Will you do me another favour?" "Anything, Christina."

"I have always admired your inherent knack of being able to put together and match the most mismatched outfits that work. People fall in love with, and will spend literally their last dollar on, an ensemble that for all rhyme or reason shouldn't go together. For example, that lime green and orange beach outfit that sold our client thousands after you put it on during one of your tantrums. Our coordinator almost had a stroke when you walked out onto the runway. I can still hear the applause." She continued, "I would really appreciate it if you would work with her. The fashion industry has gone absolutely wild over the psychedelic colors, miniskirts, hot pants, and high vinyl boots. The scene is becoming chaotic. Frankly, how anyone can be seen in public wearing the latest fad fashions is beyond me."

Suzanne had brightened considerably. She was good at what Christina had just described. Her aim was to stand out in a crowd and still look chic, and she knew exactly how to accomplish this. "I would love to."

Christina said, "I'll call you as soon as your contracts are ready. If you want a few days off, that would be fine with the Agency. Pull yourself together, Suzanne, and I'll call you within the week."

Christina left the dressing room, glad that they had been able to salvage part of what had been an illustrious, although brief, career. When Christina gave the entire concept some thought, she arrived at the conclusion that Suzanne hadn't been on top of things since Zoe had died. The crime had never been solved and it weighed heavily upon Suzanne more so than anyone else in the Agency. She met Maggie in the hallway, nodded and said, "It's done. She's agreed to our terms. Thanks, Maggie, for backing me up. You've always been fair in making the most difficult decisions. Perhaps I should question my own immortality?"

"Christina, you're at the top. The camera loves you. You take care of yourself, that's the difference."

"If you mean that I have no social life, then I take care of myself."

"Whose fault is that? I know for a fact that you could have any number of handsome men calling on you. All you have to do is thaw a little."

"Someone gave me the tag of being the 'ice queen' and I'm afraid I'm stuck with it." "Evan wanted to marry you, silly."

"Yes, Evan wanted to marry me. He also wanted to hide me away in the family chateau somewhere in the French vineyards away from my friends, my work, and my life."

"So you gave up all of that wealth and prestige for the Agency. I hope someday you don't regret choosing us."

"I don't think that will happen, Maggie. Why John, Ellen, and John Jr., as well as you, are my family. I don't know what I'd do without you. By being a part of this company, if I can no longer model, then I will expend all of my energies making money."

"Will money make you happy, Christina, really happy?"

"I gave up all hope of happiness a long time ago, Maggie … before I met you or John. It's in the past and it has to stay there."

Maggie had never been Christina's confidante and she was surprised by the sudden display of emotion. She put her hand on Christina's shoulder as if to say, she understood and she respected her privacy. It was a spontaneous gesture, one which Christina appreciated.

A week later, Christina was awakened by a loud ringing at her bedside. She noticed the clock, which read midnight … who could be calling at this hour?

"Hello." She could barely recognize the voice at the end of the line. It was halting, each word a hoarse whisper.

"Christina, it's Suzanne. You've got to help me. Someone is trying to break into my apartment. I've tried calling the police but they keep putting me on hold. I don't know what to do. I think someone is trying to kill me."

She was awake, the adrenaline coursing through her veins. This was no joke. The voice was Suzanne's; desperate, filled with fear, almost incoherent. "I'll be right over, Suzanne. I'll call the police from here. Hold on."

She put her long coat on over her dressing gown, slipped into a pair of shoes, and grabbed her purse and keys. She stopped to speak to the doorman. "Murphy, call the police, have them come to Fifty second street and Broadway, apartment 3B. My friend Suzanne is in trouble. I'm going over there now."

Murphy's face held a look of disbelief until he noticed that Christina was still in her nightgown, the hem of which peeked out from under her long trench coat. "I'll call right away, Miss."

"Thank you, Murphy. Taxi …" She was in the car and closing the door as it sped away from the curb. The driver was able to make excellent time what with the little traffic at this time of night. He attempted to make conversation but Christina was having none of it. All she could say was, "Please, can you go any faster? A friend of mine is in trouble, and I must get to her as soon as possible."

"Sure, lady, I get it." With these words, he stepped on the accelerator and Christina was in for the ride of her life. They reached the apartment in record time. The street appeared deserted, except for a few parked cars and a man walking his dog. She threw a twenty dollar bill at the driver through the window and didn't answer when he said, "Shall I wait? Hey lady, shall I wait for you?"

Christina was inside the apartment building, punching desperately at the elevator buttons. It arrived quickly, no one being about at this hour. She left the elevator on the fifty-fourth floor and raced down the hall. The door to apartment 3B was slightly ajar, and she poked her head in. Christina froze in horror, as she was just in time to see Suzanne being hurled out of the window and heard her screams. She placed a hand over her mouth but not before the two heavyset figures at the window heard her gasp. "Hey, Bruno, grab the broad."

The last Christina heard was a voice in her ear as a strong arm grabbed her from behind and crushed her windpipe. The streetlight caught the glint of the steel knife he held in his right hand and she felt its coldness beside her left ear and at her throat. She tried to struggle and as the knife slashed the skin, she went limp. The man wielding the knife thought he had cut her throat by the amount of blood that was streaming from her neck as she lay on the carpet. "Let's get the hell out of here. That goddamned Suzanne broad made a big splat on the pavement and someone must have called the cops by now." As he finished the sentence, they heard the far off wail of police sirens, and without a backward glance, Bruno stepped over Christina's unconscious body, clucking his tongue against his teeth as he surveyed his work. "Such a shame. Nice-looking dame."

"Yeah, yeah, forget her. We did what we set out to do. Gustaf paid us good money to off the other dame, too bad this one had to get it too."

They were gone. They escaped up the back stairs to the roof, across to the adjoining building, and made their way down the stairs and out to the street a block away, just about the time the police cars arrived. A newspaper reporter, who hung around the precinct waiting for a story to break, followed the sirens. He stood outside the apartment while detectives blocked off the entrance. Two more detectives went up the stairs, having checked for any open windows. The only one was the one on the fifty-fourth floor, apartment 3B. The curtains were billowing out of the open window.

Christina was lying in a pool of blood, her breathing already quite shallow when they entered the apartment. Detective Halloran felt her jugular for a sign of life. "This one's still breathing. Call an ambulance." He applied pressure on Christina's wound to stop the flow of blood. It appeared to be working. Help arrived quickly; the ambulance had been dispatched upon the heels of the squad car. The photographer attempted to enter the building flashing his press card, but the area where Suzanne's body lay had been cordoned off, and the writing was definite: Police Line, Do Not Cross.

Detective Halloran was studying the face of the woman whose life was in his hands. He thought he recognized her. By God, he did. This was none other than Supermodel Christina Corelli. He had been a fan for many years. She sure had a nasty cut, from the base of her left ear, along the jaw line and down her throat. He wondered if he should call the agency where she worked. Not yet, in due time. First he had to make sure that she would be alright. The ambulance attendants took over for him, applying pressure to the wound as they placed her upon the gurney. She was covered and out of the apartment within minutes. The reporter attempted to take a few pictures as she was loaded into the ambulance but they blocked all his efforts. He asked her name, but was given nothing. Detective Halloran secured the crime scene, and decided to call John Cole. He knew John from years back, and really liked the guy. "John, yeah, this is Rick Halloran, NYPD, do you remember me?"

John was not quite awake and his reply was rather fuzzy. "Yes, I do. What's wrong, Rick?"

"We have some bad news I'm afraid. One of your models was thrown out of the window of her apartment. Her identification reads that she is Suzanne Ford. I'm afraid she's dead."

John answered something to the effect that he would take care of things in the morning and asked the number of the precinct.

"There's something else you should know, John. Another one of your models was also hurt in the break-in. She's on her way to City General as we speak."

"Who was it, Rick?" "Christina Corelli."

John began yelling into the receiver. "How is she? For God's sake man, don't keep me hanging here."

"Calm down and I'll tell you. Someone cut her up pretty bad with a very sharp knife, and I found her bleeding all over the carpet. She was still alive when the ambulance took her to the hospital. She'll be all right as far as I can tell, but hey, I'm no doctor."

John thanked him, and hung up. Ellen by this time was awake, her eyes wide with shock as she heard parts of the conversation. From what she could get out of John as he hastily threw on some pants, was that Suzanne was dead, and Christina was on her way to the hospital. She asked, "Shall I come with you, John?"

"No you have to stay with John Jr. I'll call you as soon as I have some news." With these words he was out the door. Ellen heard the car start and a squeal of tires as John backed out of the drive. Her face was white and pinched-looking as she splashed cold water on it. She made her way into the kitchen and put on a pot of coffee. It looked as though she was in for a long night.

When John arrived at the hospital, he ran into the waiting room and approached the front desk. He grabbed onto a nurse and took her aside. He asked, "Has an ambulance brought in a young woman within the last fifteen minutes? I have to see her."

"She's in emergency. The doctor is with her now. You can't go in there. We need some information about her. Can you help me?"

John said very quietly so that his voice would not carry, "Her real name is Christina Corelli, she is my most valuable model and I don't want the press to get hold of this. Can we admit her under another name? I'll pay anything. It's for her own good, I assure you."

"I think that can be arranged. I'll speak to the doctor. We don't like reporters swarming all over our hospital at the best of times. I'll see what I can do." She left John and returned momentarily. "We'll admit her under the name of Mary Reynolds and she will be in a private room, with a policeman outside the door. Detective Halloran told us someone left her for dead, so this becomes a police investigation. The other woman is in the police morgue, the coroner's wagon took her down there after the police photographer was through with the crime scene."

"How is Christina? I mean, Miss Reynolds?" "She's lost a good deal of blood from the slashing."

John cringed inwardly at the word slash. The agency couldn't afford to lose her. He was pacing nervously when the doctor came through the emergency doors. "Is there someone here to see about Mary Reynolds?"

"Yes, doctor, I am. My name is John Cole. How is she?"

"She's very weak, but she will pull through. She will require the services of a good plastic surgeon, I'm afraid. The damage is deep and extensive. We'll know more in a few days. I can assure you that we have the best in the business on staff here."

"Anything, doctor. We can afford the best, even if you have to fly the guy in. Do I make myself clear?"

"Perfectly, now if you'll excuse me, I have to see to my patient. We're taking her up to the top floor to the O.R. and later to a private room. You can see her in the morning."

"Thank you, Doctor. Remember, spare no expense, she gets the very best."

The doctor nodded as he walked away from John, who knew only that Christina's injuries were no longer life threatening, but would her career be over? God, what was happening to them? First Suzanne and now Christina. He had to get hold of Maggie. This would really shake her up but she had to be told in case some snoopy reporter put two and two together and associated Suzanne with Christina. Maggie had to be told so she would not be caught off guard. She would be devastated. He decided not to telephone but to go over to Maggie's apartment and tell her in person. Together they could plan their strategy. He did call Ellen. "Honey, it's me. It doesn't look good for Christina. She'll live, but the guy really did a number on her. She's slashed up pretty bad."

Ellen's concern became apparent as she said, "Stay with her as long as you have to John, we'll be fine. Try to get some rest."

"I'm going over to tell Maggie, so I won't be home for a few hours. I'll see you in the morning. Try not to worry."

The loud persistent knocking upon her apartment awoke Maggie from a deep dreamless sleep. She was disoriented for a moment or two. "Who is it?"

"Maggie, it's me, John. Open up. I have to talk to you."

She quickly put on a robe and made her way through the living room and to the front entrance. "John, what in the world? Do you realize what time it is? It's well after midnight."

"I know what time it is for Christ's sake, Maggie. Sit down. I have some bad news."

She did as he had instructed, keeping silent. Whatever had him so distraught had to do with Ellen or John Jr. What else could it possibly be?

"It's Christina. She got a call from that crazy Suzanne around midnight. She told Christina someone was trying to break into her apartment and kill her. Well, she was right. Just as Christina came into the open door of the apartment she saw two men push Suzanne out of the window. She cried out and they turned their attention to Christina. One of the men had a knife and as he grabbed her around the neck, he crushed her windpipe and slashed her throat just as she fainted. They left her for dead. Luckily, Christina had her doorman call the police before she left in the taxi. Suzanne is dead, and Christina is in the hospital. The staff surgeon placed a call to their plastic surgeon and Christina should be in the operating room about now." As he said this, he glanced down at his watch. It was one-thirty a.m. Maggie absorbed the news slowly, her face growing paler by the minute. "Did he cut her face, John?"

"The paramedic had placed a pressure bandage on the wound so I couldn't guess as to the extent of the damage. I couldn't see for gauze. The hospital couldn't tell me anything, they were busy working on her. She lost a lot of blood and was drifting in and out of consciousness. My old friend Detective Halloran was on the scene. We talked for a few minutes, and he is posting a guard at Christina's hospital room in case the killers find out that she is still alive and try to end her life. She can identify one of them."

"What about the press?"

"I had the hospital admit her under an assumed name and so far all appears to be quiet. There was one reporter who hangs around the precinct waiting for calls that he can chase down, but they kept him away from the scene. Suzanne was sprawled out on the sidewalk outside the entrance. It wasn't pretty."

"What name is the hospital using for Christina? I'd like to call."

"She's listed under the name of Mary Reynolds. But they won't be able to tell you much right now. We'll call in the morning. I don't think we have to call any of our clients until we have something definite to tell them. She may be just fine once she's stitched up, who knows?"

"But if it's her face, John, it means millions in losses for us. Our clients can and will cancel our contracts if Christina is unable to pose with their products. I need a drink."

"Pour me a stiff one, Maggie. We've got to stay calm."

Christina moaned as she tried to focus her eyes in the semi-darkness of the hospital room. She raised her hand to her throat and felt the wad of bandages. Panic rose and she tried to call out but her windpipe was badly bruised and she could only whisper hoarsely. "Nurse, nurse, can anybody hear me."

A figure approached her bed. "Now Miss Reynolds, don't try to talk. You are going to the O.R. in a short while. The doctor is waiting." She felt the prick of the needle in her arm as she tried to say, "Who is Miss Reynolds, I'm Chris ..." and her voice trailed off as the Pentothal began to work.

She was wheeled into the O.R. within moments and the team was ready. The best plastic surgeon in New York was in attendance. Nurse Conway said, "We are ready, doctor, if you wish to begin."

The anaesthetist had the patient breathing regularly as in a deep sleep, her vitals were stable and the team began. Nurse Conway was surprised as Dr. Adam Carmichael bent over the patient. His gasp echoed throughout the quietness of the operating theatre. "I thought this patient's name was Mary Reynolds, this is not Mary Reynolds, this is ..."

Before he could say Christina Corelli, Nurse Conway met his glance with knowing eyes, warning him not to say any more. "This patient was admitted under the name of Mary Reynolds for her own protection. The police insisted."

His expression changed and he became a medical machine trained in the art of precise, minute suturing that had become the envy of his colleagues. What was racing through his mind was anyone's guess. Knowing full well the ramifications of the outcome of this surgery, Adam used the finest silk, and one hundred stitches later he had closed the six inch gash that extended from her left ear, along the jaw line, and had just missed the jugular. He had to repair a few blood vessels as well as a nick in the jugular vein. He was sure that his patient would require further cosmetic surgery once the scar line had formed. He was determined that it would be as fine a line as possible. The suturing took upwards of an hour, and it was three a.m. before the team was finished. Christina had remained under the effects of the aesthetic, unaware that Adam had performed the surgery. He faced a sleepless night, wondering what to say to her in the morning when he came on duty. The extent of her injuries was severe, and he would not have a definitive answer for her or her agency until she had begun to heal and the bandages were taken off. He waited until she had been returned to her room, introduced himself to the policeman outside her door, and asked for details. The guard was not totally sure as the entire event, and his story, was sketchy. In essence, Adam found out that Christina had attempted to save a friend and had not only failed but had become a victim. It was all very bizarre. His emotions were all mixed up. When he had last seen Christina five years ago, she had literally run away from him. He had been caught up in his career and let the matter ride. Adam had buried his feelings deep within, or so he had thought. The surging well of emotion that had caused the beads of perspiration to accumulate on his forehead when he realized that his patient was Christina shocked him. She was as beautiful as ever, and more precious and vulnerable than he could ever imagine. How in God's name had he ever lost sight of their love? Why, he had even toyed with the idea of marrying his chief of staff's daughter, Joan Finestad. She paled in comparison to Christina, and all thoughts of a future with that broomstick, money grubbing Finestad went out the window. His only concern was for Christina and a possible future for them together as it was meant to be. He left the hospital and drove to his apartment. He lived within a short ten-minute drive of his workplace. Adam showered before he retired for a few hours' sleep. After years of catching twenty minutes here and an hour there, the old habit of his residency took over and he did sleep, albeit fitfully, awaking in a cold sweat with Christina's image stark before his eyes. He had dreamt that she lay dead in a pool of blood, lost to him forever.

He noted the time. Seven a.m. It was just enough time for a quick shower, shave and a quick breakfast. His housekeeper would be in at nine to tidy up and prepare his evening meal. He arrived fifteen minutes early and made his way up to the seventh floor to Christina's suite. She was conscious but under the influence of morphine for pain management. He couldn't risk a hysterical episode which might tear the stitches open.

He drew in a deep breath, his heart racing like a love struck schoolboy as he entered the room. She was resting, the bed slightly elevated, with her head turned towards the window. She felt his presence before he reached out and touched her shoulder.

"Christina, it's me, Adam."

Her quick intake of breath, was all he needed. She turned and faced him. He read the misery and terror in her eyes. "I'm going to be all right, Adam. Thank God you're here. How bad is it? I couldn't save Suzanne. She's dead."

"Don't worry about a thing. Yes, you have extensive damage to your neck, but the knife did no damage to your face. I won't know how much of a scar will form, but I used the finest silk available to form the suture line. We can only wait and see when the bandages come off."

His voice trailed off into the air, and he watched as her beautiful emerald eyes glistened with sudden tears. His hand on her shoulder remained as a steady pressure, an assurance that she was in expert hands. She tried to speak, but her throat hurt too much. She did, however, manage to say, "Thank you, Adam, thank you so much."

"Rest now, and I'll see you later on this afternoon. You'll feel better then, and your throat should begin to heal. You're lucky, very lucky to be alive. And so am I ... lucky that I didn't lose you. I love you, Christina Corelli, and last night when I realized that you might have been killed I knew I could never forget you. Now rest, I'll see you later."

She smiled crookedly through the bandages that swathed her left side, her forehead, and her throat. Her lips formed the words, "I love you too, Adam."

He couldn't believe that he had read her lips correctly. Yes, she had tried to say, "I love you too, Adam," he was sure of it. All the years that had separated them slipped away at that moment and he felt the power of their love surge, stronger than ever. He wasn't the same man when he left that hospital room. He was a man whose dreams were about to come true, at long last. The staff couldn't get over his good mood that permeated the workstation, the O.R., and the wards as Dr. Carmichael went about his routine. It was a very nice change. Oh, he remained professional, but with a difference in the inflection of his voice. He was not curt or short with a student nurse if she failed to have the proper instruments at his disposal, or the correct chart. He merely smiled and waited until everyone was ready. The few nurses that knew him well and had borne the brunt of his temper were the first to comment on the change. One nurse crudely remarked, "The boy wonder of plastic surgery must have gotten lucky last night."

When she awoke from a natural sleep, not one which was drug-induced, Maggie was in her room sitting quietly by her bedside, her face etched with new lines of worry. She opened her eyes and said, "Hello, Maggie."

"Christina, my God, are you really alright? I can't tell with all the bandages they have on you."

Because she both loved and respected this woman, Christina sought to put her at ease. "Of course, silly, I'm in the best of skilled hands. Maggie, I'm so sorry."

"Sorry, you're sorry. Christina, we might have lost you. Whatever possessed you to go over to Suzanne's in the first place?"

Her voice still hoarse from the trauma to her windpipe, Christina's answer was slow to come, delivered with much emotion, cracking, and halting as she retold the evening's events.

Maggie was horrified. How had Suzanne fallen so low? Drugs, alcohol, amphetamines, what else?

"I guess by the time we came around to offering her the other contract she was already in debt to her dealer and unable to pay. They had threatened her before, and hurt her, but she was unwilling to quit using and begged for more time. They must have realized that she was a bad debt and could lead the authorities to them. She was just too much of a risk."

Maggie shuddered. "It's all so horrible. The publicity has been linked with our company, but you are here as Mary Reynolds and the papers are seeking a mystery woman who had been injured or killed on the scene. So far only John, Ellen and I know about your accident, and the hospital and staff have been totally cooperative."

Maggie could not ask about the surgery. She preferred to remain in denial. Christina just had to be all right. Apparently, John had been assured that they had the services of the best plastic surgeon on the East Coast. She said, "I brought all the latest magazine issues for this month. Keep your mind busy and that creative spark alive; use the time to re-energize yourself. We need some very new ideas, or we'll be left in the dust. Not that I want you to overtire yourself, Christina. I just thought that the time in hospital would pass more quickly."

"I know what you mean. Yes, I'd like that. Have one of the secretaries bring me my portfolio and my sketching pad. I'll see what I can do."

Maggie had stayed an hour. She glanced at her watch and noticed that it was near noon. Just as she was about to leave, a tall, very handsome man wearing a white doctor's coat came into the room. She could not miss the light that sprang into Christina's eyes. She heard Christina say, "Maggie, I'd like you to meet my surgeon, Adam ... Dr. Carmichael."

"My pleasure, Miss Cole." Adam waited for Maggie's reply.

"My brother and I can't thank you enough for what you did for Christina. Well, I'd best be going." To Christina she turned and said, "Rest and I'll call in later this evening. Is there anything other than the portfolio that I can bring you?"

"No, thanks again, Maggie. I'll see you later." As Christina spoke, her eyes did not rest on Maggie's face, but were riveted upon the attending Dr. Carmichael. She had never seen such a look on Christina's face before. Where was that ever present sadness? She left the room to the two occupants, oblivious to her leaving.

Adam wanted to take Christina in his arms and hold her tightly, crush her to his chest, pour out all the years of not knowing, the yearning that was never far from his mind. His steely grey eyes were intense, as he could not break the eye contact. She lowered those long, dark silky lashes and the color in her visible cheek indicated that she was blushing.

He smiled, "Christina, I have to give you the facts. Within the next five days, the stitches will aid the process of healing. I will remove them at the end of the week. Until then, I don't want you looking into a mirror, or asking for one, when the dressing is changed. Can you promise me that?"

"I promise, Adam, but why?"

"The suture line will be reddish and discoloured. That will disappear with time and additional cosmetic surgery, but right now, you would become anxious and depressed at the sight. That guy really did a number on you."

"Will I be able to work again?"

"Yes, of course, but you will need some time off with no new photo shoots. Actually, it would be best if you stayed in the background, or better yet, took some time off. Is that possible?"

"Yes, it's possible. I own a third of the company. Actually, I was working on a new line to add to our holdings. I bought a perfume factory, and the chemists are attempting to come up with a new fragrance that will surpass Chanel No. 5, our competitors. If I can't do the promo, then the line will fail. How soon can I go back to work?"

"You're asking me to make a judgment call too soon after surgery. I don't want any heavy makeup applied until the wound has healed. Perhaps, if it is really necessary, they can shoot at an angle. Again, your face was not cut, but the scar line may whiten and pucker. It's too soon to tell."

Christina was crestfallen. What would she do with her time during her period of recovery other than sketch and design? Maybe that was all there was to occupy her time.

His manner changed. The professional air that he used with patients changed and he sat down beside her on the bed, took both of her hands into his, and looked deeply into her eyes. "Christina, will you spend your time with me? I didn't realize just how much I've missed you until I almost lost you. Please, my love, say yes."

"Yes, Adam, oh, yes my darling. I thought you'd never ask. A day doesn't go by that I don't think of you. For a time, I thought we had been just two kids in love, but I have carried you in my heart for ten years. I can't wait to get out of this hospital and be with you." A thought occurred to her and she foolishly blurted out, "You're not married, are you?"

He grinned at her embarrassment, "No my love, I am not married, I am not even engaged. I am married to my profession." He continued, "I have other patients to see, but I will be back as soon as I have some time. Would you care to share hospital food with me at supper this evening? If so, I will arrive with two trays at the stroke of five." He looked about to see if anyone happened to be peering in the door's small window, and bent and kissed her softly on the full lips that quivered in anticipation. The love they shared swelled and grew in that first kiss, his commitment strengthened by the love that shone in her eyes. He felt complete for the first time in many years. Now that he had found her, he would never leave her side. The promise was unspoken, his determination apparent in the set of his jaw, and the squared shoulders as he turned and left the room. Christina allowed a sigh of deep pleasure to escape, her throat now very sore and her voice raspy. She lay back on the lumpy hospital pillows and fell fast asleep, to dream the dreams of a fantastic future. They had found one another and nothing would part them again. The resolution was firmly etched in her heart.

By week's end, the bandages were ready to come off. Maggie and John waited outside Christina's hospital room, while Adam and his nurse carefully cut away the swath of gauze. Christina held her breath until the nurse jokingly said, "I believe you should take a few breaths, Miss Corelli, before you faint." Light-hearted laughter filled the room, breaking the tension.

She studied Adam's face. She decided that she knew him well enough to be able to read by his expression how badly the scars were that were left. He drew in a deep breath and said, "This is the last layer, and the sutures can be removed. Here we go …" he hesitated as he turned to the nurse. "Hand me those forceps and the scissors, please?"

She did as instructed. Christina changed her direction and watched the nurse's face, hoping to discern a hidden truth. She was surprised when they both smiled. The nurse said, "You did a fine job, Dr. Carmichael. The line isn't at all puckered."

He answered. "The discoloration is as I expected, but given a few more weeks we'll know for sure."

Christina could wait no longer. "Can I see, Adam, please?" she begged.

Wordlessly, he handed her the mirror as the last suture lay curled in the tray on her bedside table. She slowly lifted the mirror, as though it weighed a ton. Her eyelashes lifted and she summoned her courage as she glanced into the reflecting glass. With no makeup on, her lips still held a natural redness, and the eyes glistened with tears. He held the mirror so that she could better see the wound. Her intake of breath was all that broke the silence in the room. She put the mirror down on the blanket, covered her face with her hands, and her shoulders began to shake from sobs.

"Christina, what is it?"

"Oh, God, Adam you tried your best. But that ugly purple line all the way down my throat

… it's awful. Why didn't he kill me?"

The nurse took the suture tray from the room and left doctor and patient alone. Adam took her in his arms and calmed her fears. "It's only been five short days, Christina. You have to give it time. Trust me, you'll be as good as new, I promise."

She met his glance, "Are you absolutely sure, Adam? It looks so awful. Put the bandages back on, so no one has to look at me."

"Don't be silly. I want the air to get at the skin and hasten the healing process. The discolouration will slowly disappear as the days go by."

She fell back upon the pillows, too tired to argue with him. He bent to kiss her on the forehead, telling her to rest and he would see her later. She fell asleep, exhausted from the anxiety of the past few days. The wondering was over. She was a mess. How would she ever face Maggie and John? They had asked to see her when the bandages were removed but Adam said she must rest and he explained that she was better than he expected. His enthusiasm at the prospect of Christina's total recovery enlightened her anxious partners. They thanked him profusely, finally saying goodbye, and they left for their respective destinations, Adam to be swallowed up by the hospital, and brother and sister back to their high rise offices in downtown Manhattan. Work was the answer for them both, and their energy levels rose with the knowledge that with Christina on the road to recovery and they would not be ruined. They had other models, but no one compared to Christina. It had been a traumatic week, one they both intended to put behind them.

Detective Rick Halloran made a brief appearance, asking more questions of Christina. He asked if she could work with the police artist to compile a composite of the attacker, and she agreed. He was completely taken with her beauty, scar or no scar. When she lay with her head turned and her hair arranged covering the wound, one would never guess that she had almost been another victim of the crime that was ever-present in New York. She was not only gorgeous but she was also a very nice person. Not at all vain, or selfish, or self centered. He liked that.

Chapter Thirty

THE WEEKS FOLLOWING CHRISTINA'S release from hospital were spent in nothing short of a whirlwind of activities. All of her spare hours were taken up with Adam. During the day she was kept busy in the perfume laboratory of her new firm, testing the fragrances that the chemists concocted eagerly waiting for her approval as "the one." So far they had only managed to create either too heavy a scent or one that was cloying and lingering, overwhelming, and even nauseous. Christina kept hoping that they would discover the exact combination that she was seeking. A scent that was subtle and matched the woman wearing it, not sweet, or too flowery. It would have all of the subtleness of a field of summer flowers wafting on a light breeze, but induce a sensual response from the male sector. It was a perfume that lingered softly and did not cling to the wearer, which would emit a strong pervasive odour to her surroundings. Christina was excited about the possibility of using animal musk, but for many women it turned odorous. She had no idea that the combinations of smells could be so challenging. They appeared to have an unlimited budget but not an unlimited time frame. Christina had already chosen a name for the new perfume, the container design, and the advertising layout. All that was needed was the perfume. During this respite from modeling, Christina and Adam became as inseparable as their careers would allow. The phone rang at the bedside table. She picked it up and answered with a smile upon her lips, "Good morning."

"Christina, it's me, Adam. Are we on for dinner this evening? I have a few last-minute details to attend to, but I should be through by six p.m. Shall I come around to pick you up, say at seven?"

"Yes, my love, seven is fine, but if you are a little early, don't hesitate to come by. I can't stand it when we aren't together."

"I'll be there. I have to run. Love you." "You too."

She lay back upon the luxurious bed and touched the indent of the pillow next to hers. Adam had brought her home around eleven, and they had immediately gone to bed. The chilled champagne they drank later, after they had fulfilled themselves of one another. Evan had taught her the art of making love, but Adam had taught her how to love. She had existed in a state of euphoria since their first night together, and only came down to attend to her work day, living for the moment they would be together again. They didn't always end the evening with sex. Sometimes she just lay in the curve of his arm on the spacious chesterfield in his apartment, curled up in front of the fireplace, soft music playing as he told her of his dreams. She never interrupted him, content to listen to the deep tone of his voice. Sometimes the words were lost as she daydreamed of what was in store for them. His ideas were of his surgical career, new techniques, the implementation of new instruments, articles that he wrote for JAMA. He was every inch a doctor, a person born to medicine. She had fallen into her own career; her looks had taken her to great heights and staggering wealth. She was content to be able to share his time whenever possible. "Why is it that when we part, that I feel a loss, as though part of me has gone away and I find it difficult to come back to earth and function as Christina Corelli?"

"I feel the same way, Christina. I find that if I focus on the task at hand that I can actually not think of you until the task is finished. Then you are back in the forefront, making my blood quicken and my testosterone level soar. Do you have any idea how much I love you?

"No, tell me."

"I love you more than life itself. If this is all we ever have, then I would feel cheated. Our love must grow and last until we are no longer upon this earth."

"Why, Adam Carmichael, I had no idea you were such a romantic. I agree. Let's not make any plans. Let's just drift along in this wonderful state of happiness until we can no longer stand to be apart."

"Christina, when we were together that last night before I left for University and you gave yourself to me with total abandon, I was overwhelmed. No one had ever committed herself to me with such trust.

I meant it when I said that I would love you all the days of my life. Why did you not write to me?"

"Adam, please, let's not go there. We were just kids then, playing at love. Granted, I did love you then, but now that we have been together as mature adults, you cannot begin to measure the depth of my love for you. I knew then that you were the man for me, but I had no idea any man could make me feel this way." As she recalled the conversation and his question about the past, Christina shuddered. It was almost as if the voice of doom had whispered in her ear. She had wrestled with the truth ... should she tell him about the twins, or let it lie? He had caught her in contemplation a few times, asking if anything was wrong. Had he said something to offend her? It was a subject that she was to date unable to share with anyone. She had not written to Becka and Tonio for many, many months. It was as though their lives were truly moving in different directions, hers to greater fame and fortune, Becka and Tonio's remaining in Cranston, pursuing the dream of happiness and a comfortable life. They had two lovely children, Becka still nursed part-time at the hospital, and Tonio was almost totally in charge of her father's companies. Becka had hinted at a relationship growing between Tonio's mother, Teresa, and Christina's father, Frank. So, if anything came of it, her father will have found a new family and could become an integral part of the life they shared. Christina only wanted to be left alone. She had not, and would not, forgive him. If he married Teresa, she of all people would know exactly what she was getting for a partner. She had followed his indiscretions for many years, until, bursting with the knowledge, had confessed the truth to Angela and broke her mother's spirit. Perhaps Teresa and Frank deserved one another. She could care less. She was unwilling to share her secret of finding Adam again just yet, her journal was her confidante and she poured her heart out within the pages of the book that was almost finished. It was a journal that covered ten years. The twins would be nine years old in May. She always wondered what they would look like. When she was out with Adam she did not wear the locket, and he seemed to have forgotten that he had given it to Becka to pass on to her. Perhaps he thought that the locket had been lost or that she had not received it. Neither one of them had ever mentioned it. Christina didn't because she knew he would want to look inside the entwined hearts. On one side of the locket was the picture of her and Adam, and the other contained the sweet faces of their children. These thoughts always brought her down. The guilt lay heavy on her heart and she was helpless to do anything about it.

The scar tissue left after the fine suturing was barely discernible three months after the surgery. Adam remarked that her skin was very healthy, able to heal itself, and had an elasticity that most women would die for. They had taken the photographer into their confidence, and he, being Christina's personal photographer, had kept silent. The press had never been informed that she had been victimized. It was almost a miracle. Brian had used his skill with the camera, taken her best side, and used cosmetics and earrings to disguise the fine white scar line. Maggie and John had breathed a collective sigh of relief when the contract with Distinctive Woman remained ongoing.

Christina arrived for work refreshed from her shower, ready to face the day. She knocked lightly on Maggie's office door, opened it, and entered at the beckoning, "Come in." "Good morning, Maggie. I brought the ad campaign portfolio over for the perfume product. I need your expert opinion. Do you have some time either now or later?"

"Good morning, Christina. Of course I have time. John is away at the moment but we can fill him in later with our report. Come sit down." As Maggie watched Christina lay out the campaign on the large worktable at the far left of the room, she mentally formed an opinion of the new Christina. Was it the near brush with death that had changed her, or was it the new man in her life? Whatever it was, Christina walked with a bounce in her step. She was bright eyed and vivacious, her color high, her body language totally positive. The ever-present sadness that appeared when Christina thought no one was watching had all but disappeared, and her cameraman Brian wanted to meet the person or persons responsible for the change. They had all but given up on their livelihood when Christina had been injured, but this new Christina was better than the old one. Maggie picked up her ever-present mug of coffee and walked over to the table where Christina was enthusiastically poring over the concepts. Maggie was impressed. The name of the perfume was to be "C". The model would be Supermodel C.C. by Christina Corelli, in a fiery red crepe gown that showed just enough cleavage to be exciting but still within the bounds of good taste. Her hair fell over the left side of her face, and were brushed back and held with a gold clip on the right as the curls cascaded down her back. She was photographed in a slightly reclining pose, her arm propping up her head as she looked directly into the camera. Behind her was a magnificent amber glass bottle shaped in a capital "C," the C freestanding on a small black enamel base. The caption below the glossy merely said in bold black lettering, "'C' is me!" Maggie thought the whole concept was sensational and she promised to do her best in convincing John to go along with the idea, just so long as they could come up with the perfect perfume. It had to be one that every woman on the planet would feel comfortable wearing, from the most discerning in taste, to the woman on the street. It was a definite challenge. Christina was totally immersed in the project and loving every minute of it. Maggie had never envied Christina; despite the fact that nature had been kinder to her than to most women, she loved her unconditionally. They had come to believe that the three of them were more like family, as opposed to being corporate partners.

This project could net them millions. They were aware of the competition: Oscar de la Renta, Chanel, Gucci, all the big houses were launching new products and expanding their horizons. They had the expertise, they had the funds, they had the knowledge, and they were a serious contender in the global marketplace. With connections in Paris, Rome, and New York, they could do an all-out, no expense spared campaign that would drown out the competition.

They planned a blitz. The phone suddenly interrupted their meeting. "Christina, it's for you. It's the lab."

"Hello, Samuel, yes, yes I hear you. You think you have the perfect combination. I'll be right over. Listen, I'm going to drag Maggie along. Another woman's opinion in the big scale of things could go a long way." Samuel agreed and looked forward to meeting them within the hour.

"Maggie, cross your fingers. This may be it. The head chemist just called. Care to come along? This sounds like the breakthrough we've been waiting for. Everything else is in place and we could be in production by as early as next week." Maggie could not contain her excitement. She was out of breath by the time they reached the street. Christina hailed a taxi and they were on their way across town. "Now, if you don't like the fragrance, I want you to say so. Don't say you like it just to please me. I really mean it. I want your honest opinion as a businesswoman, and above all else as a woman who would feel comfortable wearing this." Maggie recognized the ring of conviction in Christina's voice, and promised sincerely that she would give her a completely unbiased opinion. Christina fidgeted throughout the taxi ride, but they were there within twenty minutes. They entered the large building together, accessed the elevator and were met by Samuel at the door. "You got here sooner than I expected, but don't worry, we are ready for you."

Upon the laboratory bench were a number of vials: clear liquid, amber, rose tinted, aquamarine. They were carefully labelled and upright in a chemistry rack. A few members of the laboratory staff stood quietly in the background as Maggie and Christina, led by Derek, approached the bench. He asked them to test each one closely, wafting the odour from the tip of the applicator and from the inner wrist area where it was to be applied. Maggie and Christina both selected the same vial, taking turns applying and sniffing. Maggie wrinkled up her nose at number one, as did Christina. They nodded negatively in unison, rejecting the first sample. Derek's face did not change. He remained as though detached from the proceedings. They cleansed the skin area that had contained the first sample. Christina applied number two, after wafting the applicator probe back and forth under her nose. Maggie reached for the wand. Their opinion took longer than the first sample. Maggie said, "This isn't half bad, Christina. What do you think?"

"You said it, half bad. Not quite good enough, I'm afraid. C'mon Derek, this wasn't worth the taxi ride across town."

"Ladies, try number three." He held his breath.

Maggie's eyes dilated in wonder when the new fragrance wafted from the open vial. Christina reached for the applicator in turn, and the new scent entered the room. Her eyes met Maggie's. "What do you think, Maggie? Hurry up, don't keep me in suspense."

"What do you think, Christina?" she countered.

Derek said, "Don't play games, ladies, I can't stand it."

Together they reached over and hugged him, Christina kissed him on both cheeks and said, "Derek, you're a genius. This is exactly what I wanted. You'll all get a bonus for this, I promise you."

Someone brought a bottle of champagne from the back room and they toasted to the new scent, months of hard work, and the success of "C." With Christina promoting it, Derek had remarked that she could sell pure vinegar, but with this new product, the sky was the limit. Christina had never felt so exhilarated. Her love life was fulfilling, more than she could ever have imagined, her fortune was growing by leaps, and now this, further success. It was her own initiative, her business venture, with Maggie and John as backers, and she had never been so happy. Perhaps the tragedy that always seemed to mark her life was behind her. They celebrated for another hour, then the staff took the rest of the day off and Maggie and Christina returned to their offices. What a day it had been. She couldn't wait to share her news with Adam at dinner that evening.

When Christina returned to her apartment, she showered and changed into a rough terry towel robe, soft slippers and wound her hair in a smaller towel to form a turban. She basked in the reality that they had and were about to launch a product that would, hopefully, be available in price and size to every woman on the planet who wished for it. Packaging would be dealt with by their manufacturing plant, and marketing would be handled by the advertising arm of Cole Agencies. She decided to count her blessings, reflecting on the present, not willing to dwell on the past. She hoped Adam would be pleased at her success. He had supported and admired her throughout the past and didn't mind at all being referred to as the new Mr. Corelli. He was a success in his own field and had the self-esteem and confidence to shrug the tabloids off as being parasites, seeking dirt and probing for secrets that were just not there. He had been asked if he had known Christina Corelli before they started dating. He had lied through his teeth, answering a definite, "No." Christina had given him a sideways glance at the time, but they had not discussed it further. Anything would do to keep the press away. She loved to read the legitimate reviews of the runway shows, but the constant harassment of the paparazzi had a negative effect on her mood. She would not display anger or surprise, always smiled falsely, said something noncommittal and polite, put on her sunglasses and turned away from the camera. Most of the shots never caught the glint of anger in the deep emerald eyes; the eyelashes remained half-lidded or completely downcast, avoiding the direct glare of the flashbulb. She had learned her craft well.

Chapter Thirty-One

A S SHE DRESSED FOR her dinner date with Adam, Christina's thoughts were filled with recent memories. When she recalled the events that had brought them together, it was almost as if fate had definitely had a hand in the meeting. Since that time they had celebrated Christmas, Boxing Day, and New Year's 1967 with the promise that their lives would go on forever in the current state of bliss. She had never been so happy. She was content to work at her career and lay in Adam's arms at night, secure in the knowledge that their love was growing every day, as she discovered the strength of character and iron will that lay beneath the surface of her love.

The black velvet gown, with the soft draping bodice held up by the fine spaghetti straps which criss-crossed in the back to form almost a spider web, leaving the low-cut back to stop in a "V" just below her natural waistline, was an excellent choice. The side slit allowed her freedom to walk, as the dress fit her hips comfortably and flowed to just above the floor. She donned a diamond necklace and earrings, diamond watch, and diamond ankle bracelet, which rested loosely just above the cut of her black patent leather sling pumps. The weather in New York in early February could change suddenly, as had been attested to just last week. They had spent the weekend cloistered within the confines of Adam's apartment, watching movies on television and listening to music in between times as their love making reached new heights, if that was at all possible. She smiled at her image in the full length mirror. She would knock them dead at Ciro's tonight. Adam had promised her an early show and late dinner, the opposite of what they normally did. Usually they had an early dinner, attended a live Broadway show, and retired after a nightcap. He said he had something important to discuss and they could linger over dinner. It must have something to do with his career. He had completed his residency and he anticipated that his mentor, Dr. Samuel Finestad, would bring him into the posh Park Avenue practice. She noted the time. Five minutes to seven and her doorbell rang. One last glance in the mirror, and she hurried to answer the door. His eyes told her that her efforts were well worth the time.

"You absolutely amaze me. Each time I think you are more breathtaking than the last time.

C'mere, woman."

His embrace was long and hard, as he was reluctant to release her. She finally pulled away, "You don't want to crush the image, do you?"

There was a soft kiss on her lips, eye contact that promised better things to come, and they finally broke apart. Christina put on her white mink cape to ward off winter's blast. Adam was aware of the admiration of the occupants of the elevator, and pride in his partner swelled. He had studied her from time to time during their evenings out in public, and he had never seen her work the crowd, preening falsely for the camera or pasting on a smile for the benefit of those who recognized her as the supermodel on the cover of this month's magazine.

They were right on time, arriving at Ciro's as the maître d' led them to their table. Christina preferred a table along a wall, as though to ward off anything or anybody that could sneak up behind them. This was a defence she had adopted since her assault. Adam didn't mind. He would be content to sit in the kitchen so long as they shared the table.

They ordered drinks before their meal arrived. The magic circle of their love kept them insulated from the conversation of the surrounding patrons, but the soft music and the wail of the blues singer penetrated the mood from time to time. Adam could not take his eyes off her. In many instances they did not have to speak, maintaining a comfortable silence as their eyes worked the room. The waiter approached with the cart. He did a fabulous flambé before their eyes, the platter before her contained delicious foods to tempt the most discerning of palates. She chose a few tiger prawns, asparagus tips in clarified butter, tomato aspic, as well as cracked crab. Christina's love of food leaned towards seafood and she always chose it from the well- planned menu. It was non-fattening, high in protein, and always delicious. Adam had long ago given up trying to convince her that a serving of filet mignon in tartar sauce was incredible. He chose the red wine and she the white.

As they lingered over the cherries jubilee dessert, which Adam insisted she taste, Adam reached into his suit pocket and withdrew and carefully concealed the black velvet box in the palm of his hand. He held the linen napkin in his hand and reached across the table to dab at a spot of red left on the corner of her mouth by the rich dessert. She laughed and finished the task, her eyelashes dropped to conceal the sudden glint of desire that shone in her eyes. He took her hand in his and said, "Christina, look at me." Which she did. He continued, "I have something for you. But first, I have something to ask you. Will you marry me, my darling? These last few months have convinced me that I could never live without you. I love you, Christina, more than you will ever know." He heard her sudden intake of breath and a long sigh escaped the perfect lips.

Her eyes shone as she said, "Oh Adam, I thought you'd never ask. Yes, of course I'll marry you. There has never been anyone but you."

He opened the velvet box to display the massive diamond solitaire in a 24-carat gold setting. It must have set him back at least by five thousand dollars, as heard in a comment by the woman who sat at the table at his left. Christina was speechless. Her eyes were riveted upon the ring and glistened with sudden tears as Adam slipped the ring upon her finger. Unknown to them, everyone in the restaurant had focused their attention on the couple, many envious as they recognized the depth of love these two people shared. The scene created a mood in the restaurant that lasted for many hours. Adam asked Christina to dance, and as they moved to the music, he could not believe his good fortune. Nothing in this world could be more perfect. They had a lifetime to share together and he vowed he would make the most of each and every day. He could not imagine anything that life could throw at them that they could not meet head on and overcome; or so he thought. Christina was content, Adam was all she had ever wanted and now he would be hers always. Little did she know that always did not mean forever. They left Ciro's around midnight, and the evening had turned cold. A mad dash to the waiting taxi, as well as the short drive to her apartment, was enough to cause Christina to shiver. She sat close to Adam stealing the warmth from his body, his arm resting comfortably around her shoulder. The taxi driver sensed the emotion in the back seat. He said, "It's a pretty nasty night out there, folks."

Adam answered, "We hardly noticed."

Christina flashed the ring under the cabbies nose as he stopped at a red light. He said, "That's some rock, lady. You must have this guy wrapped around your little finger."

They laughed at his remark, and Adam replied, "You might just have a point there."

Adam stayed the night. Christina decided that their lovemaking had surpassed anything they had experienced thus far. If their wedding night was as good as this, she would have to pinch herself to see if she were dreaming. No, there he was sleeping beside her like a baby; so vulnerable, and so loved. If only her mother were alive to share in her happiness. Christina thought of her father of all people. She silently formed the phrase in the darkened bedroom, "I told you so, Father, we belong together, Adam and I, and don't you ever forget it."

They made love in the early morning hours, oblivious to the new blanket of snow that covered the dirty slush of the previous night. New York looked clean and renewed in the early morning sunlight. A breakfast of bagels and cheese, orange juice and strong hot coffee and they left the apartment together. Adam used the underground garage to park his car, and Christina always taxied to work. He kissed her long and hard as he said, "Good bye, my love. Let's think about setting a date for the wedding."

She nodded and stood quietly watching as he started the sports, car gunned the motor, and waved as he sped by. She re-entered the apartment building and walked through the lobby to the front entrance, where the doorman hailed her a cab.

Maggie wasn't in her office as yet when Christina arrived. She immediately went to the "'C' is me" layout and began improving upon the campaign. She decided to try on a deep emerald green velvet gown, almost identical to the one she had worn the evening before. She was deciding upon another style when Maggie came through the door. "Good morning, Christina. What a sloppy day out there. That new snow is nice, but it's hell to get around in."

With a self satisfied smile on her lips, Christina turned to Maggie, her hand poised on the side of her face so that the ring would catch the light, Christina said, "Good morning to you, Maggie Cole. Notice anything different?"

"No, should I?" Christina wiggled her fingers and Maggie gasped as she said, "My God, Christina, is that what I think it is?"

"You're damned right it is, Maggie. I finally got the man I love and it feels like nothing else on earth."

"You look so happy, Christina. I'm jealous. If only Jean and I had been able to come to terms with our careers and the miles that separated us. I'm so happy for you. Will you allow me to throw an engagement party for you?"

Christina laughed, glad to share her happiness with Maggie, who didn't really have a jealous bone in her entire body. She had met Adam and had remarked, "What a hunk. And educated as well. A doctor, no less, we must have him over for dinner," she had said, imitating a proud Jewish mother announcing to the world that her daughter had snared a professional.

"Have you set the date?"

"I just got the ring last night, but Adam left me this morning urging me to do just that. We have to launch the perfume on Valentine's Day; it has to be in all the large department stores and boutique outlets on that day. Sometime soon after, I would imagine. It really doesn't matter. I belong to him, no matter if the ceremony hasn't been performed."

"It's nice to have the church's blessing, Christina. You are, after all, a Catholic and I know you are a religious person."

"Yes, I am, and you are right. Well, let's get to work. The sooner this perfume hits the street, the sooner I can make wedding plans. You will help me, won't you, Maggie?"

"Help you, I wish you'd let me take charge. Of all, that is, except your wedding dress. That's entirely up to you and our capable staff. Do you want a low-key wedding, or an all-out, shout-it-to-the-world celebration?"

"I'll have to discuss it with Adam. Our relatives live in the Canadian Rockies, except for my aunt and uncle in Toronto, and my relatives in Italy." Maggie looked at her suspiciously.

"I thought Adam said that he didn't know you before your accident."

"It's a long story Maggie, and I may share it with you someday, but not today."

Maggie realized that the subject was closed and they began their workday in earnest. Christina had almost let slip part of her secret. She would have to watch what she said in the future. As much as she trusted Maggie, the scar in her heart was hers alone to bear. She still did not wear the locket since she had begun dating Adam. It lay within the confines of her journal. In July Christina would be twenty-seven, a few years past a model's prime, but her beauty had not peaked, according to Brian. Usually one photo session was enough for him to capture a number of enticing, perfect poses; the light dancing on her honey-gold hair, her lips slightly moistened and full, and a glimpse of the fire that burned within the woman in the photograph. He said that she would be beautiful when she was old and in a rocking chair; it was eternal.

John entered the office. He took in the news of Christina's engagement with, "So you're going to be an old married lady soon? I couldn't be happier for you both. He seems like one helluvva nice guy, Christina. I will have something to say to him, though, before you tie the knot."

"And what might that be?" she asked.

"I have to warn him that if he ever beats you or hurts you in any way, he'll have me to reckon with."

"I'm sure he'll quake in his boots. But thank you, John, you're as close to a big brother as I'll ever have and I love you for it."

The moment passed and the three focused their attention on the task at hand. They worked diligently throughout the morning, stopped when Maggie's secretary Josy brought in coffee and rolls at ten, resumed work on the project within a half hour, and worked through lunch. John finally had the figures ready. He had checked with the manufacturing plant; the bottle design was workable, and thousands would be ready for next week. The new perfume would also be plentiful by the time they were ready to deliver. Everything was on target. They quit work at three, exhausted from the intense and emotionally charged day. Maggie relished a day such as they had just put in. She relaxed after each session as though she had just done a strenuous aerobic workout. It had been a wise decision on their part to have brought Christina into the firm. She was, to date, indispensable to the company. Her ideas to branch out and compete with the big corporate fish often left Maggie on very shaky ground, but their collective determination kept the company running smoothly; a well oiled piece of machinery that required little or no maintenance, running on sheer will and grim determination. She loved her life. She could not fathom any dire changes to the existing structure, even though Christina would be married soon. She had planned upon working for a few years yet, and Adam had his practice and the growth of his reputation before they decided upon a family. She mused how she was getting ahead of herself; they weren't even married yet. Anything could happen.

Chapter Thirty-Two

A FLURRY OF ACTIVITY FOLLOWED the announcement and launch of the new perfume line. Christina attended many of the openings and displays. She was re-energized from the overnight success. Adam couldn't have been more proud. He had not fully realized just how much the public adored her. His career, in kind, was on the fast track, perhaps from his association with Christina. Many of his new patients coming into the Finestad clinic were celebrities hoping to stay forever young, and were willing to pay for any treatment or surgery. At long last, Adam Carmichael and Christina Corelli were happier than they could ever imagine. Christina, now that the perfume was a runaway hit, began to plan their wedding. In the sixties it was considered upscale to be a June bride, so in order to please her fans, she went along with all the fanfare attached to the ceremony. Adam couldn't have cared less; all he had to do was to show up, and to make arrangements for his parents to attend. Maggie and her staff were delighted to do the rest, with the expertise of wedding salons, magazine editors, and photographers; the best were at their disposal. A few details were expertly leaked to the press and it seemed that all of New York was looking forward to what was fast becoming the wedding of the year.

After Valentine's Day, the weeks flew by in a whirlwind of activity. She still had a number of appearances to fill but these she did with a professionalism and presence that brought in the contracts. John and Maggie were working on a package of their cosmetics that would include: the "C" perfume and softer scent, lotions, and moisturizers to accompany the cosmetic line. The idea was to present the new Miss

America with a year's supply of their product. The advertising would be monumental. Actually, if the campaign worked, they hoped to initiate a model search, and the winner would be their spokesperson and new model. Christina had asked that she be released from the old cosmetic contract using the excuse that a fresh, younger looking model would capture the teenage interest. They appeared to have the most money to spend if one looked at the latest record and magazine sales. The Cole Agency became a corporate force to be admired and respected for their tenacity and innovation. The money rolled in.

* * * * *

IT HAD BEEN AN exhausting day, much more so than the usual, when Christina finally entered her apartment. She was past hungry, but she knew she had to eat something. Adam was coming over later to spend some time together. The apartment looked nice. Her housekeeper always kept fresh flowers in the dining room and entryway. She had changed the carpet to a neutral ivory, a change from the feminine rosy blush. The drapery was dark green moiré side panels with a deep valance that framed discretely laced white panels. Gold tassels tied back the heavy drapery, keeping the room light and airy. She had also changed the furniture to a much more comfortable deep cushioned sofa and chair, a patterned rug placed under the glass covered coffee table in front of the chesterfield. Adam had asked her why the change, and she had replied, "It's far too feminine for any man, don't you think?"

He had agreed. Adam's own apartment was a study in itself. Medical journals and patient studies littered his study, covered the massive desk, and spilled over into the living room. He was no housekeeper, usually just taking time for a quick bite of a TV dinner, a shower and change of clothes, and then go back to work. Discussing their new living arrangements, they had laughed at the very thought of Christina trying to cope in his world. She had re-decorated her suite with Adam in mind, using her creativity and expertise to shape a warm, comfortable, homey atmosphere where they could escape from the outside world. She had even hired a landscape artist to decorate their ample patio area with potted plants, wicker furniture, and urns. It was almost like having their own backyard but at fifty floors up from the street. She converted her guest bedroom into a study for Adam with shelves that reached from floor to ceiling and room for his great desk. He would bring his files and cabinets at the end of June when his 6-month lease was up. Everything was going along like clockwork.

She showered and changed into casual wear, her hair falling loosely around her face and upon her shoulders. She looked much younger than her twenty six years, especially without the eye shadow, eye liner and mascara which were her trademark. She planned a special buffet for them, cozy and intimate because she intended to have a very serious conversation with Adam after they had eaten.

He arrived at six, looking exhausted after a hectic day at the hospital. He had operated for six hours working on a cleft palate that needed to be corrected, and then had to patronize his wealthy socialite crowd of patients at the clinic. He did not realize that he was the "in" thing, and to be a patient of Dr. Adam Carmichael, even to just have a mole removed, put you in the inner circle. It was all too gauche and small for him, but he went with the flow.

He showered, changed, and came into the kitchen smiling at the difference in Christina's appearance, especially in this domestic role. Her face was flushed from the heat of the oven, and she was busily chopping greens for the salad. He came up behind her and encircled her with his strong arms. He pulled her hair aside and planted soft, tender, kisses along the nape of her neck. She shivered in delight, admonishing him to stop or they would soon be forgetting about dinner for a very long time. He was hungry, but his emotions were overriding his appetite, becoming more intense as she turned and snuggled into his embrace, lifting her lips to meet his in a long, passionate kiss. His arms tightened around her and she moulded her body to his. "Can dinner wait, my love?"

"Of course it can, I can always reheat it." She left his embrace, held onto his hand, and slowly, sensually walked to the bedroom door. The expression on his face was intense, his eyes glinted with passion as he followed her closely behind. He held back at the doorway, scooped her up in his arms and carried her to the spacious bed. He lay her gently down as she removed her top and bottom to lie naked upon the coverlet. His arms were busy, removing his own clothes quickly, and within moments he covered her body with his, long, supple, and masculine. With a gentle strength, he began the ritual of love. She picked up his rhythm and they soon reached heights of ecstasy that they never ceased to enjoy.

He murmured her name over and over again as well as special words of endearment. She arched her body to meet his thrusts, overcome by the intensity of his love. She cried out as she reached climax and he released within the very core of her body. Their eyes locked as he withdrew from her. "Do you have any idea how much I love you, Christina?"

"I think I do," she teased. "Do you have any idea how happy I am at this moment? I never, in a million years, dreamed that we would ever find one another again. I hoped and prayed but it just seemed so hopeless."

"I know what you're saying. I threw myself into my studies and work, but everyday a memory; an image of you by the lake, or in the car, or in my arms would sneak through the medical jargon and I would be sad. Sad for what we had lost, and despairing for what could not be." He kissed her long and hard, then left the bed. "C'mon woman, I'm ravenous."

"Me too," she replied, throwing on a robe and slippers, her casual outfit left haphazardly on the chair beside the bed. He dressed and left the room.

She sighed as she studied her image in the full length mirror. Her skin was absolutely glowing; her eyes held a sparkle of their own, as though she had just shared a special secret with someone. The secret promised that she would be treasured for a lifetime. She shook her head, smiled at her image, and left the bedroom. She was determined to discuss the most important factor in her life and Adam was to become a part of it. After dinner would be the best time to broach the subject, she decided.

The dinner was easily served; she had kept it warm in chafing dishes and the salad crisp within the confines of the refrigerator. They made small talk, conversation being the last priority as they were both very hungry from their lovemaking.

Christina poured the steaming coffee into large mugs and they made themselves comfortable in the living room. Adam settled his lanky frame against the curve of the armrest and back of the sofa, while Christina nestled against him, his arm about her shoulders.

She sipped on the coffee as Adam said, "You're very quiet all of a sudden. Where's my usual chatterbox?"

This was the opening she had been waiting for. Inwardly she summoned her courage, and with her hand fingering the locket about her neck, she sat up and faced him, meeting his eyes as serious as she had ever been. "Adam, I have something to tell you. Only a very few people know about this and only because they were directly involved."

"Sounds serious, my love. Okay, as of now, you have my undivided attention." He kept a half-smile upon his lips and the love he bore for this incredible woman shone in his eyes.

"This is very difficult. You have no idea." "Just begin at the beginning."

"Do you remember the last night we were together the summer in 1956, and you left for University the next day?"

"Yes, of course, it was the night we made love."

"Yes, Adam, and when you didn't call or write to me or come home at Thanksgiving, I was devastated."

"I'm sorry, my darling. I had no idea. The weather was so bad I couldn't come for the weekend and I hoped to make it up to you during the Christmas break, but you had already left Cranston. Becka told me that you were in Toronto, helping out your aunt."

"Part of it is true. I was away, but not in Toronto. The truth is that out of our love, I became pregnant."

She paused, to gauge his reaction. His face changed and he became serious. His silence prompted her to continue. She opened the locket, and the picture of the twins suddenly filled his field of vision. His eyes riveted upon the photo as he took the locket from her hands. "What the hell are you saying?"

She looked from the locket, to his face, back to the locket. "These are our twin daughters Adam. Yours and mine."

"Where the hell are they? When were they born?"

She wasn't quite sure how to continue. His voice was cruel. His eyes glittered like steel. "They were born exactly ten years ago today in a home for unwed mothers run by the Sisters of St. Martha in Edmonton. My parents shipped me out before Christmas, and I stayed there until they were born. The reason for my absence, explained to all concerned, was that my Aunt needed me to help her through an illness and I would be staying in Toronto for a long time."

"Where are the twins? Who has them? Does your aunt have them?"

His tone of voice was that of a stranger. She moved away from the comfort of his arm and faced him, her lip quivering and her voice breaking. "As soon as they were born, they were taken away from me, and adopted a few days later."

"Godamn you, Christina. You gave away my kids. You gave away my parents grandchildren. What the hell kind of monster are you? Your own flesh and blood! How the hell could you do this?"

"Don't you swear at me, Adam. Where were you when I needed you? I was just a kid. What was I supposed to do? My reputation would be ruined, as well as my parents'. My father made all of the decisions, called me a slut, and I was on my way to Edmonton. They hardly called or wrote to me. My only connection with home was through Becka. It was she who gave me this locket, sending it to me with a daily journal that she bought as a Christmas gift. I had nothing; I had nowhere to run, and no one to turn to. You could have written to me, but you didn't. So don't blame me for what happened."

"I have to blame you. No one in their right mind gives away their kids. What the hell is wrong with you? Why haven't you tried to find them? It's been ten years."

Finally, her anger rose to the surface and she shouted, "Don't you think I've tried? The records are sealed. The adoptions were final. Those babies are lost to me forever, get that through your thick head."

His eyes pierced her heart. She watched as the loving light disappeared and was replaced with shock and dislike. "I will never forgive you for this, Christina. So help me, I will never understand what possessed you to give them without a fight. I don't want you in my life, I don't want to marry you. It would be a mistake with this looming between us for a lifetime. No thanks, my dear, we're finished. I know you thought you were doing the best thing for us by coming clean, but you just destroyed my trust and faith in you. Without that, we have no future together." His hand reached out for the engagement ring. Wordlessly, she slowly removed it from her finger, the tears blinding her as she extended it. He snatched it from her hand, turned on his heel from where he had been steadily pacing in front of her as she confessed her secret, grabbed his sweater, and without a backward glance, left the apartment.

She was stunned. Although, he was no longer present, she shrieked his name, "Adam, no, don't leave me. Don't leave me again. Please don't leave me," but the sound of her hoarse cries echoed upon the walls of her apartment. She collapsed in a heap upon the sofa, sobbing convulsively, unable to cope with the sudden loss. Her entire world had just walked out the door, and she couldn't deal with the repercussions. She had lived without the twins, bearing their loss on a daily basis, she had lived without her one true love on a daily basis, and just when she was about to become the happiest person on earth, it was all gone. The apartment grew dark, the only light shining from the spring moon and the adjacent windows of the surrounding buildings. She had lost track of time, her eyes red and swollen from crying, her arms and legs leaden from grief. It was ten-thirty. Three hours had passed since Adam had stormed from the apartment, and it seemed like a lifetime ago. The despair was as great, or greater, compared to when the twins had been ripped from her arms, and she could not get past the impact it was having upon her. She recalled over and over again the piercing grey eyes as they filled with loathing and dislike, changing Adam into a cold-hearted stranger. She had witnessed the sudden pain as he learned that he was a father, but that his children were forever lost to him. He had said that he would never forgive her, so that made two people. She had never forgiven herself for giving them up. Christina had developed the philosophy that what was done, was done, and could never be changed. She could not go back and do it all over again. This was how she had learned to cope. The phone jangled at her elbow, shocking her out of her reverie. She let it ring, not having the strength to answer it or to deal with whoever may be at the end of the line. Finally, the telephone stopped ringing. The silence filled the room. She began to sob, the hysteria rising in her throat. She cried out to emptiness, "Please don't leave me alone. Please God, I can't stand this! Help me through my despair."

Another hour passed. The telephone rang one more time. After eight rings, Christina reached over to answer, hopefully thinking it just might be Adam calling to say he was sorry. Her voice cracked as she said, "Hello."

Maggie's voice sounded alarmed. The tone of the hello frightened her. "Christina, it's Maggie. I've been trying to reach you. What's happened? You sound awful."

Hearing Maggie's voice opened the floodgates. She could hardly answer. "Maggie, I need you. Please help me." Was Maggie the answer to her plea for help?

Without question Maggie replied, "I'll be right there."

Christina replaced the receiver onto the cradle and sat in the dark, waiting what seemed like hours for Maggie's knock. Actually, it was only a quarter of an hour and Maggie called through the door. "Christina, open the door."

She padded across the carpet, her hair in disarray and her shoulders slumped, looking ten years older than her twenty-six years. Maggie took one look at her as she entered the suite, and Christina collapsed in her arms. Maggie helped her to the couch, putting on a lamp or two so that she could talk to Christina. Christina's eyes retracted from the light as she shielded them from the soft glow of the lamp. Maggie said nothing as she waited for Christina to begin. Instead, she noted the dishes still on the dining room table, the half-filled coffee mug on the side table, the room in a cluttered state. Christina looked terrible. There was no other word to describe her. The sparkle in her eyes had been substituted for sadness so profound that it wrenched Maggie's heart. What had happened to cause this unhappiness?

Slowly, haltingly, Christina began to speak, her voice growing stronger as she walked Maggie through her life story, beginning with how she and Adam had met. When she reached the birth of the twins, she watched for Maggie's reaction.

Shock and dismay washed across her face in turn as she shook her head as the story unfolded. Finally, when she could no longer continue, Christina offered the journal to Maggie saying, "Read this. It explains it all. I can't go on, Maggie, I don't have the strength." Maggie poured them each a cup of freshly brewed coffee, made Christina lie down upon the chesterfield, covered her with an afghan, and sat at her feet, her eyes scanning the pages of ten years of Christina's life. Never in a million years would she have believed the heartache that was written within the pages of this journal. At last, she understood the reason for the sadness that was present in many of Christina's photographs. How she had lived with this showed strength of character that she, herself, knew took iron will and great courage. The fact that she had told no one, even to share the burden, was to be admired. If the paparazzi ever got hold of any of it, her career would suffer. Instead of being famous, she would become notorious, and a bad reputation would follow her throughout her lifetime, or as long as she remained in the limelight. Maggie had begun to think of Christina as her little sister, she had protected her from the evils of the world, had shielded her from the human parasites that clung to and finally destroyed a new fresh face, as so much fodder to feed their evil needs. Christina looked up to and trusted Maggie, knowing full well that she had landed in a very special place when John had discovered her that evening so many years ago. She loved them both and they had become her family. She did interrupt once while Maggie was reading to say, "Please don't tell John, Maggie. I'll be all right. I just need some time." Maggie didn't believe her as a fresh flow of tears threatened to consume her dear friend.

"Don't worry about a thing, Christina. I won't breathe a word, but honey, you won't get through this without help. I think you need to see someone."

"What do you mean, see someone? Do you mean a shrink?"

"Well, yes, Christina. At least find someone who can help you through this. I don't think you can handle another disappointment. Not of this magnitude, anyway."

"I don't want to see another medical person for a very long time, do you understand? Adam took back the engagement ring and the wedding is off. He looked at me with such loathing, as though I was something that had just crawled out from under a rock. Do you understand? He hates me."

"I doubt that very much. I have never seen two people more in love, or meant for one another, than you and Adam. I really mean that. You make one another feel wonderful and it shone in your eyes."

"What will we tell the press? Everyone has been pressing us for details for months now, and all were looking forward to covering the wedding."

"We'll work something out. I'll have to tell John that the wedding is off, and we'll come up with a statement that will just have to satisfy the public. In the meantime, you are not going to make any public appearances and you will say nothing to any reporters, not even the slightest innocent comment, or they will know that you are down and will use it to destroy you. Do you understand what I'm saying?"

Christina nodded, unable to speak. All she could focus upon was that her life was in total chaos, her career on a path of destruction, and she bowed to the wisdom of many years of dealing with reporters and the feeding frenzy of the tabloids. "Yes, Maggie, I promise."

The telephone rang again, and Christina's hand darted out to answer it. It was now close on to midnight, and Maggie thought that perhaps it would be Adam, calling to apologize. Instead, it was a wrong number. Her disappointment was all too evident. Maggie took the phone off the hook, settled Christina, and continued to read. A lifetime of ups and downs, highs and lows lived within the confines of the journal. Only a few days, weeks at the most were described as nondescript and uneventful. The meeting with John and Maggie, her rise to fame and fortune, all contained an underlying sadness as the sorrow of her adolescent years was lost and she became an adult far too soon in her young life. Maggie's eyes filled with tears as she read through the entries. When she reached the episodes of when Evan D'Argent had entered Christina's life, she detected a feeling that, perhaps, Christina had found a measure of happiness. A thought began to form in her mind. If she could reach Evan within the next few days, Maggie would use all of her powers to convince him that Christina needed him as she had never needed anyone before this.

It had been five years since they had all been together last, but Maggie knew that Evan regarded Christina as the love of his life, and she was certain he would come to her aid. What excuse Maggie would dream up had as yet to be determined. She had to act quickly, as she recognized the signs of a major nervous breakdown. If she ever met Adam Carmichael face to face, Maggie knew she could not be held responsible for her actions. So she had given up their children. She was just a kid herself at the time. And where had he been, the chosen one in the medical profession? The course of Christina's life had been taken from her hands, as her father had insisted upon the events that would prevail during the time she was carrying the twins. What an arrogant, small town, small minded bastard. He had also deprived them of being grandparents, they who could have provided a wealthy home and the best of everything. Instead, his reputation had been more important. His place in the community had brought little comfort to Christina's mother. She had attempted to find the babies but to no avail, and it had taken its toll upon her health. Her heart condition, which she had unknowingly inherited from Christina's grandmother, had worsened under the burden of guilt. All became clear now as to why Christina almost never mentioned her parents or her life before modeling. What a waste. Maggie's determination to see Christina through this sudden heartbreak grew as she read the journal. Christina fell into a deep exhaustive sleep, her breathing interrupted by a convulsive sob. Maggie covered her lovingly with the afghan and moved away from the foot of the sofa. She used the telephone in the bedroom, called John, and said she was going to spend the night at Christina's. They had a crisis to deal with in the morning and he had to leave all his appointments open. She did not know when she would be able to meet with him, but to trust her judgment as all would be revealed the next day. As usual, John bowed to her wisdom, and said, "Give her our love, Maggie. We'll talk tomorrow."

Chapter Thirty-Three

DURING THE COURSE OF the next two weeks, Maggie stood by helplessly as she watched Christina slowly disintegrate into a nervous wreck. Christina's depression worsened, she lost interest in her appearance, she picked at her food or pushed it away after the first bite, and her lack of interest in her surroundings was evident as she stared off into nothing while the television blared throughout the apartment. Maggie tried to coax her into eating and going out, but Christina just stared at her as though she had suggested they take a trip to Mars.

"Christina, you've got to get hold of yourself. I've never seen you so unhappy. John and Ellen are sick with worry. What can we do to help you?"

"Just leave me alone, that's all," Christina replied.

"No, I won't just leave you alone." Finally, Maggie's frustration peaked and she took hold of Christina's forearms, shook her until she knew she had the young woman's attention, and said, "Now, you listen to me, young lady. It's not the end of the world. You are not the only beautiful woman to get dumped by the man you love. So, I suggest you pull yourself together, and get on with your life. Many people are depending on you and care about you. Dr. Adam Carmichael isn't the only man on the planet, and even if he was, nothing says that you have to ruin your life and career for the likes of him. So you made a mistake. I repeat, you are not alone. Stop beating yourself up over this! The worst tragedy in your life is the loss of those babies, not Dr. Carmichael, and I promise you I will move heaven and earth to try to find them, if that's what you want."

She paused, hoping for a reaction. She felt Christina's shoulders strengthen as she pulled herself upright to her full height. Her eyes blazed with fury at Maggie's accusations. She said, "Who the hell are you to tell me how I should feel? None of this ever happened to you. How can you just stand there and tell me to get on with my life? What life? What future?"

"I can stand here and tell you what I think. You are like my little sister and I love you and care about you. Aren't we family?"

With the words hanging between them, Christina's anger began to subside and she looked at Maggie as though seeing her for the first time in the past weeks. "Oh, God, Maggie, I'm such a mess. I'm so sorry for putting you through this. Of course you're family. You, John, and Ellen are the most important people in the world to me. I don't know what I would do without you. I'm trying to get over this, but it just keeps on coming back into my mind over and over again."

"Honey, at least you're showing some emotion other than despair. Anger is good. Perhaps it is the strongest emotion next to love. Just don't let it consume you. What can I do to help? Would you like to go out to lunch?" Her look was hopeful.

"Not today. Maybe tomorrow. I have to do something about my appearance. My hair is awful, and my skin is sallow. I have to start somewhere."

"Come to the studio. We'll have lunch at the office. Everyone is so worried about you.

You can have a massage, a manicure, they'll do your hair, the works."

"I don't know if I can face anyone just yet. Do you think I can, Maggie?"

"I'll be right there with you, Christina, I promise." As she said this, Maggie began dialing the number of the agency as Christina left the room to change out of that same godforsaken bathrobe that had recently become her wardrobe. She spoke to someone at the other end of the telephone, rapidly firing instructions and admonishing anyone who dared to think of reacting other than positively to Christina's appearance when they arrived. Maggie's secretary promised that she would alert everyone but said, "I really don't think anyone has anything but Christina's best interests at heart. We've all been so worried about her and no one has told us much. Everyone will be glad to see her."

Maggie broke the connection, glad for the caring support of her staff. They were a great bunch, and rather than kick a person when one was down and hurting, they were there to lend their advice and expertise to bring the downcast member up and running to take up their position as a positive element of the team.

Maggie decided to make one more call. She leafed through her address book, found the number, and rapidly dialled. As she tapped her toe upon the rug, a sign of impatience, she thought over what she would say. The operator came on the line and Maggie placed the call to Cherbourg, France for Monsieur Evan D'Argent at three possible numbers where he could be reached. She heard Christina moving about in the bedroom so she knew she had little time left to talk to Evan. Surprisingly, the operator was able to reach him on the first attempt. She breathed a sigh of relief as she heard him say, *"Oui, c'est Monsieur D'Argent."*

"Evan, it's Maggie Cole. I haven't much time so listen carefully. I have some rather disturbing news. Christina needs you. She doesn't know it yet, but trust me, she needs someone, and I think you just might be the answer. She is on the verge of a nervous breakdown and I am at the point where I don't know what else to do to help her. She has refused professional help, and won't come out of the apartment."

"What the hell happened, Maggie?" Evan all but shouted.

"She suffered a great emotional loss, and we can't seem to shake her out of her depression" "How long has this being going on and why haven't you called me before this? I'm really very angry with you, Maggie. You know how much I care for Christina."

"Yes, I do, Evan and that's why I think you're the only person that can help her now." As she said these words, Christina entered the room.

"Who is the only person who can help? Who are you talking to, Maggie?"

Maggie changed the tone of her voice as she said, "Thank you so much, I look forward to seeing you as soon as you arrive, yes, and bring the invoices with you ... that will be fine ... thank you again." She replaced the receiver upon the cradle and turned with a smile to face Christina.

"No one important. I just remembered I had a call to make and I was just killing time while I waited for you to get dressed." The lie rolled easily off her lips; she was determined to get Christina back on her feet and through this emotional turmoil before it ruined them all.

She had been carrying a double load for the past few weeks and it was beginning to show on her. Maggie was a work horse but she was only one person. She had shifted much of the load to John and he, too, was feeling the strain of overwork.

"Do I look all right, Maggie?"

Maggie lied again. The truth of the matter was that Christina was a mere shadow of her former self. The sparkle had gone from her beautiful emerald eyes, her hair was lacklustre, and her skin no longer glowed. The lack of fresh air and sunshine, good food, and social contact had taken its toll. "Of course, you look fine, and you'll look even better when Damian the master of make-over is through with you. Trust me, let us take care of you, Christina. We've missed you so much."

Sudden tears brightened Christina's eyes as she attempted a grateful smile. "I'll try, Maggie, truly I will. It's just so hard to be interested in work when my whole world has fallen apart."

Maggie's "Dutch Aunt" voice returned. "Now, let's not go there. You think you hit bottom. Well, if that is the case then the only direction to go now is up, and that's what we're going to do."

They left the apartment, and the doorman beamed at the sight of his favourite tenant. Maggie shushed him with a gesture to her lips behind Christina's back as they approached the brass doors of the building. He was most polite, very professional, and Christina's shoulders squared after she had overcome her first hurdle. The bright June sunshine hurt her eyes as they stood on the sidewalk waiting for a taxi. Christina felt the healing rays of the sun upon her face, and, for the first time in weeks, relaxed. The worried expression on her face began to fade and her eyes held an interest for her immediate surroundings. The noises, smells, and bustle of the city bombarded her senses and she became aware of a stirring within, perhaps the beginning of the healing process. It was too soon to tell.

They were whisked away from the curb by the competent taxi driver, who over his shoulder asked casually, "Where to, ladies?"

Maggie gave him the name and address of the agency, and made small talk. All the while, she studied Christina out of the corner of her eye. She had settled back into the seat and was looking out the window, but was she seeing New York, or was she staring into space? Maggie couldn't tell. Thank goodness it was just a ten minute ride to the studio.

When they came through the office doors, everyone was at their work post, and each looked up in turn, smiled and greeted Christina as though she had never been absent. Maggie could see Christina relax as the warmth and concern of the staff lifted her spirits. She was warmed by their sincerity, a fact Christina recognized at once. She felt a measure of guilt that she had put them through a trying time. Damian and his staff literally kidnapped her. Maggie's pleasure was all too apparent, and she left Christina in his capable hands. She spoke quietly to him, "Thank you, Damian. I know one session won't do it all, she needs sleep and has to regain at least ten pounds, but this is a start. I give you a wreck, give us back Christina Corelli."

"I'll do my best, Ms. Cole. She looks like she's been to hell and back, if you'll pardon my expression."

Maggie said, "I couldn't agree with you more." This said, she left the salon for her office, which was just down the hall. John was there waiting.

"What's happened, Maggie? Was that Christina I just saw with you? Tell me it was."

"Yes, John, it was. I've also done something else. I called Evan. He's on his way. He is taking the Concorde and should be here later on tonight. I didn't have much time to fill him in, but he certainly reacted the way I'd hoped. That man worships the ground Christina walks on. He's rich, he's handsome, he's also a very nice man, and for the life of me I can't understand why she should beat herself up over the good doctor."

John said, "It's not for us to say." He paused, cleared his throat then asked, "Did you persuade her to see a shrink?"

"No, I didn't. I actually think that she has worked through many of her problems, and with our support and Evan's I believe that this is the first step on her road to recovery. Can we do without her, John? I believe it would be the best therapy if Evan were to take her away, to France, to Monte Carlo, anywhere so long as it is far away from all this grief."

"It will be tough, Maggie, trying to fill the gap that her absence will create. Why don't we hire someone, a seasoned executive that can handle the other companies that Christina has, and we'll focus upon the modeling and advertising end? Isn't that what we do best? We've got to persuade the company that holds her contracts that she needs some time away from the camera. I don't know how much time I can buy us, but I'll do my best. Is she up to posing for a few random shots that we could use in her absence?"

Maggie said, "John, she's a shadow of her former self. Damian is, as we speak, using all of his expertise hoping his magic will restore her to her former beauty, but it will take a lot more than a three hour session to accomplish. She's lost her spark, as well as her zest for living that shines from inside. The look the camera loves. The sadness has completely taken over and I'm banking upon Evan to bury it or erase it altogether. Keep your fingers crossed, John."

Christina emerged from the studio, refreshed, a new hairdo. The facial mask treatment had sloughed off much of the layer of old skin and her complexion did look partially rejuvenated. Damian's master craft of make-up and pizzazz played up the green of her eyes, and her hair shone with a new light. It was up to the rest of them now, Evan, Maggie and John. "I feel so much better, Maggie. I've missed everyone so very much. Thank you for dragging me out of that apartment. For the first time in two weeks I'm actually hungry. In fact, I'm famished. Let's go to lunch?"

Maggie's happy smile was answer enough and the two left the office, John noticing a new lift to Christina's step as they walked down the corridor. He breathed a long sigh of relief. He had stayed in the background, worrying and working desperately while he watched their future go down the tubes. Oh they wouldn't be bankrupt, not by a long shot, if Christina was suddenly no longer in the picture. However, he had worked long and hard and their studio was a huge conglomerate and he had no intention of seeing it reduced to just another run-of-the-mill Agency. He prayed Maggie was right, that Evan was the answer. When they had met seven or so years ago in Cannes, he had liked the man. For one so rich and important, Evan was unprepossessing, completely affable, and very much the gracious host. John had been at ease in his presence from the very first. He had no idea if Christina held any deep feelings for Evan, but he did know that she admired, liked, and respected the man. He had been surprised when they had ended their relationship. Christina said that she had not been ready to give up her career, and as they were separated by a vast ocean they could not come to any reasonable conclusion as to sharing a future. Evan had been hurt; although the reasons for his rejection were true, he felt that they could overcome anything. They had remained good friends, no bitterness between them; only regret.

Evan landed at LaGuardia Airport and the limo took him to the Hilton where he had reserved the V.I.P. suite, which consisted of at least half of the top floor of the very famous hotel. His first call was to Maggie to let her know that he had arrived. They spoke for the next half hour, Maggie filling him in on Christina's condition. She was surprised to learn that Evan knew about the twins. He cursed Adam's name when he learned how he had abandoned Christina and blamed her for their adoption. Maggie was greatly relieved that Evan had picked up the ball and was now, more determined than ever, to make Christina forget that Adam Carmichael ever existed. Should he wait until morning before contacting her? They agreed that would be best.

Christina's excursion into the real world and the lift that it gave her spirits was not long- lasting. She had pretended to be happy, for Maggie's sake, but in truth she was as abject as ever. She had enjoyed lunch, the pleasure of Maggie's company, and the ambience of the restaurant. That too, was short lived. When she let herself into her apartment at six p.m. she changed into her old bathrobe, made a fresh pot of strong, black coffee, and resumed her seat on the sofa, overlooking the city skyscrapers and the newly green foliage of the park. She began to pace about, noting that the cleaning lady had been in during her absence and the apartment smelled fresh and new, aired and dusted. It did feel good. For the first time in many days, she did not break into tears. Instead she began to analyze her situation. Was this the beginning of the rest of her life? If so, it was far too bleak a prospect. She did owe much to Maggie and John, and the staff whom she supported. She had felt their concern and love today for the first time; something had pierced the wall of depression that had overtaken her. The coffee stimulated her and she put on some soft music, nothing that would remind her of Adam. The song they shared since she was sixteen was the one sung by Nat King Cole that had the words, "When I fall in love, it will be forever," the lyrics beautiful and poignant, "Or I'll never fall in love."

Was this true? Was Adam the only man in the world for her? Surely not! For if this was true, she faced a very lonely future. Oh, Christina Corelli would always be surrounded by rich and famous people; acquaintances, people she had met during her photo shoots or through her companies. But they were not friends, they were casual acquaintances, save for her partners. Would she never feel a man's body resting upon hers, covering her and warming her soul as they made love? Would there never be another connection such as the one she felt with Adam? She shook her head, dispelling the grey prospect from her mind, attempting to focus upon her immediate future. She glanced at the clock, it was near seven and she had not eaten. She felt the stirring of hunger and decided a sandwich would suffice. As she was preparing her meagre supper, the doorbell sounded. Not expecting anyone, she was momentarily confused, asking herself who could be calling at this hour.

She padded her way to the door, bread knife in hand and half a sandwich in the other. She opened the door and her eyes widened in disbelief and shock.

"Christina, it's so good to see you again!"

"Evan, what on earth are you doing here? My God, I must look a sight. Come in."

"Actually, you do look a sight. But, nevertheless it's a sight for sore eyes. I've missed you so much."

It happened so quickly. Seeing him standing there, impeccably dressed as usual, handsome as ever, a little older but the same unruly lock of hair falling on his forehead, his head bent to meet her eyes, brought a flood of tears to her eyes. The surprise and emotion was so intense she felt weak. His arms reached out to encircle her and she grabbed hold of Evan as though he would disappear into thin air. He felt her thinness through the heavy terry robe and stroked the once beautiful hair, unable to believe that she had suffered so. His emotions ran high, anger at the man who had done this to her, concern for her future, and love returning in waves as he held her to his heart. Her sobs subsided and she finally let go, but held onto his hand as she led him into the living room. She was embarrassed at the sight of him seeing her in such a state. She tried to push her hair from her face, but Evan did this for her. He said, "My love, what has happened to you? Why are you so unhappy? I am here. Nothing will hurt you ever again, I promise, if you will only let me help you."

His loving arms about her offered her hope and salvation from all the troubles of the world. Christina responded with the desperation of a drowning woman. Her tears turned to those of joy, and the light returned to her eyes. Her smile was like sunshine breaking through weeks of darkened skies and grey clouds. Evan held her tightly, comforting her as one would a heartbroken child. Finally, she looked up into his eyes and asked, "For whatever brought you here to me at this time, I will always be eternally grateful."

"Actually, Maggie's phone call did it. She didn't think I should see you until tomorrow, but I just couldn't wait. I hope you don't mind."

"Mind, Evan, I can't tell you how good it is to see you. The fact that you are here tells me that you must still care a little for me ... is that true?"

"Christina, I told you when we parted that I would love you always, that you would hold a special place in my heart, and if you were ever in need of me, that I would be at your side ... and here I am."

She lifted her lips to his and kissed him softly upon the mouth, closing her eyes and hugging him tightly. He responded in kind, but kept his passion in check. She was in no shape for an emotional upheaval or passionate lovemaking, as much as his body ached for fulfillment. He could not get enough of her. Her appearance had changed but it only brought forth a strong protective urge to shield her from further pain. He looked up at the ceiling and whispered thanks to Maggie, as Christina tucked her head under his chin and rested against his chest. She had not felt this secure in many, many years, and the memory of her father flashed before her. Fleeting, but it brought back the happy times when he had carried her as a small child in his arms, delighting in her eagerness for life.

Chapter Thirty-Four

CHRISTINA HAD NOT REALIZED that her depression had jeopardized her health. Her hair had become lacklustre, her eyes dull and shadowed, her body thin but no longer toned. The truth hit her one day, quite unexpectedly, and it happened when she left the apartment clinging to Evan's arm. She glanced sideways at her image in the plate glass mirror in the condo foyer and despite the fact she was wearing dark glasses and a headscarf she hardly recognized herself. Even her posture and stride had changed. Her first thought was, that if Evan hadn't come when he did, she would have totally lost her self esteem as well as her health. She gave a grateful tug on his arm and moved closer to his strong lean body. He felt the pressure and squeezed her hand in reassurance as he smiled, meeting her eyes. "Do not worry so, my darling. I will have the old Christina back very soon, more vibrant and beautiful than ever."

She entered the limo, the door held open respectfully by the doorman, whom she had grown to cherish. He said, "Take care of yourself, Miss Corelli, I will miss you. Hurry back to us, won't you?"

"Thank you, Henry. I shall miss you also. Please be here when I return."

Evan waited patiently while the two exchanged promises, while his own thoughts were very different. If he had his way, Christina would be returning to New York as a visitor, and he would endeavour to teach her how to love the European way of life so much so that she would not want to leave it or him, not ever. He had never loved anyone as he now loved Christina.

She allowed Evan to take complete charge of luggage, plane and car reservations, passport desk, transportation, and customs, all of it.

Maggie had cried when they hugged and said their goodbyes. Christina was taken aback. She had never expected such a rush of emotion from the always-in-control Maggie Cole. John often referred to her as his rock.

Within the space of just hours they were on the transcontinental flight, first class and very comfortable. At last, Christina escaped the gossip mongering press and she gladly removed her headscarf and dark glasses. Carelessly she ran her fingers through her chestnut curls, using her long graceful fingers as a crude comb. She rummaged about in her spacious handbag, withdrawing a compact, and opened it to scrutinize her general appearance. She dabbed some make-up under her eyes, an attempt to camouflage the dark shadows which had taken up permanent residence under the emerald eyes. Evan sat quietly, his eyes alight with adoration. In many ways they were so comfortable in one another's presence that there really was no need for constant or idle conversation.

He did say, "Christina, we will fly to Paris, where my driver will pick us up at the airport. I know that you are still very exhausted so I have arranged for us to stay in the South of France in a modest villa overlooking the sea. Jean will bring the yacht into port and we can use it at our convenience. When you are feeling better I would very much like you to meet my family and my dearest friends, but only if you agree. I will not push you."

She smiled, grateful that he was leaving the establishment of the pace of their relationship entirely to her satisfaction. "You really are incredible, Evan D'Argent. Do you know how much this all means to me? I honestly believe you've saved my life." Impulsively she pulled his head downward and touched his lips with hers, ever so gently, softly as a butterfly's wings. He was extremely pleased.

The flight attendant interrupted to ask whether they wished anything from the bar, or perhaps an appetizer. They begged off, thanking her with a "Maybe later, miss." The flight was long, but comfortable, and they managed to sleep in snatches. Evan slept first, then Christina, taking turns.

Actually, Evan feigned sleep and waited until her eyes closed, and he felt her soft warm breath upon his neck. He loved to watch her sleep. She looked almost childlike, innocent and so very appealing.

Their arrival in Paris was routine, everything seen to by Jean, Evan's very capable manservant. He was glad to see them and discretely asked how Maggie was, everything from her health to her possible love life. Christina could see that he hung on to every word but with his usual decorum did not wish to impose his personal feelings upon his employer's guest.

They were whisked through traffic, down the Champs Elysee Avenue the Bois du Bologne, passing statues, fountains and very crazy taxi drivers, horns honking in protest and brakes squealing as they fought their way down the busy thoroughfare. Christina tried to crane her neck in order to see the wonderful old gothic buildings that had stood for centuries and wished that she had lived through the era of Louis the XV, Marie Antoinette, and the Napoleonic regime. What stayed in her mind were visions of the glamorous, heavily beaded, brocaded ball gowns, wigs, pompadours; the age of elegance that no longer existed in present day garb. It must have been a monumental task for anyone having to clean, press, and care for these magnificent gowns. Even with the modern conveniences that were at everyone's fingertips, steam irons, modern dry cleaning plants, it would still require a great deal of skill and expertise to maintain the quality of the beaded pearls, lace and brocade.

"A penny for your thoughts, my love."

"Oh, Evan, I'm sorry, I didn't realize that I was so lost in thought. I could not help but daydream of the past and how it must have been." She marvelled at such wealth and magnificence. "It must have been a sight to behold." Christina shared her thoughts with Evan.

"The Louvre holds the finest paintings in the international community and we will definitely be spending a few afternoons there. You can study the full body portraits of the wealthy Mesdames of the past until you have satisfied your curiosity."

"I can hardly wait."

Evan was quick to note that she had come alive. The downcast shadow and expression had all but disappeared and he looked up as his lips moved in silent thanks to the powers that be for giving his beloved an outlet for her spirit. He couldn't have wished for a better response, that his wonderful city of lights could work its magic so quickly.

"It's so beautiful, Evan. When I was in Italy, we were so very busy with the runway shows, packing up and moving, that I really didn't have any time to treat myself to a side trip to Paris. Now that we are here I can't wait until you show me your favourite sights."

Her words came in quick sentences, leaving her almost breathless with excitement. She was as inquisitive and excitable as a child and he found his heart swell with love and gratitude that she was here with him, and not with Doctor Carmichael. If the subject ever arose and his name was mentioned, it certainly would not be his doing. His goal was to make her forget her heartbreak and to heal her wounds, pouring out his love and concern until she was fully recovered and her Adam occupied a very small place in her heart, one that he intended to keep locked away forever.

Their hotel suite was the best that Paris could offer. She was a little tired from the traveling, but a long, hot bath, filled with aromatic salts, refreshed her and Christina emerged from the bathroom snugly wrapped in a luxurious white terrycloth robe and her hair encased in a matching towel. To Evan she looked adorable, almost childlike, with no makeup to mar her natural beauty. It was apparent that he was her most avid fan, completely captivated by her every move and word.

"Evan, all of a sudden I'm famished. Would you call room service and order us something quick and delicious?"

"Of course, leave the selection to me. It will be here before you are finished dressing. If you are not too tired, I thought we could go out this evening for a wonderful dinner and entertainment. The supper clubs are many and varied and we can stay as long as we wish to, but only until you are tired. It is still early, and if you wish, after the hotel maid has finished unpacking, we can stroll down the street from the hotel and take in the sights. A breath of fresh air is probably what we need. I'll have Jean follow us in the limo so that if we have ventured too far we won't have to walk back."

Christina attended to her dressing, choosing a casual street ensemble and a pair of Gucci sandals that were very elegant but also practical. She tied her hair back, but then allowed it to flow loosely around her face when she caught sight of the fine purple line along the left side of her jaw line and neck. It was a reminder of the tragedy and heartbreak that was still very fresh in her mind, and her breath caught as she squared her shoulders, trying to assume a brave front so as not to upset Evan. He had been her lifeline and she was not about to cut her only tie with a future that promised peace and happiness.

Apparently her appearance was to his liking, as Evan's face lit up when she emerged from the dressing room. He had changed from his three-piece suit to casual dress slacks, a black turtleneck under his dark blazer and his loafer shoes polished to perfection. They were an eye catching couple, turning heads as they emerged from the elevator and strode into the hotel foyer.

Evan had been correct. The fresh air and spring warmth of the Paris sun became a balm to her spirits and she soon became absorbed in the front windows of the many shops selling everything: perfume, jewellery, shoes, leather goods, finely tailored suits and dresses. These shops did not resemble the usual stores in New York, only some of them along Fifth Avenue had copied the elegance and ambience of these shops. They entered a shop at random, something having caught Christina's eye. Evan would have purchased the entire inventory if she wanted, but she settled for an exquisite gold necklace that held a small diamond cross, the chain was so delicate and intricate that she worried that it would become knotted and tangled before she could wear it. Evan laughed at her and the clerk beamed as he watched the gentleman carefully pull back her hair and lock the clasp at the nape of her neck. He watched as Evan's face changed and he felt the power of this man's love as he turned her to face him so that he could admire the necklace. It was a touching moment. They left the shop accompanied by a smiling clerk as he held the shop door open, thanking them for their patronage and wishing them a good day.

"Everyone is so polite and civilized," Christina could not help but remark. Was the necklace that expensive, or is this the normal way that customers are treated?"

"You are right on both counts. You will find the pace in France is not as frenzied as in New York, as many people walk to and fro as they shop. It is very difficult to find a parking place and the squares offer a place for people to rest and visit between shops. Almost every restaurant and bistro contains sidewalk seating so that the French can people-watch, a most enjoyable pastime."

The afternoon slipped by almost as quickly as it had begun, and

Christina was reluctant to return to the hotel although she was somewhat tired. Evan left her for a few hours and she decided to put her feet up, read a few pages of her novel she had been reading on the plane, but soon the book slipped from her fingers and she was fast asleep. A soft knock on the door a few hours later broke her sleep, and she arose feeling refreshed and energized. It was the porter with a fresh basket of flowers, from which he promptly removed the old ones, replacing them with the new. The room filled with the aroma of the red and yellow roses. As he was leaving the suite, Evan entered, they exchanged pleasantries, and he tipped the porter and came over to where she was standing. Impulsively, he took her into his arms, bent his head and kissed her upturned lips. The kiss was spontaneous, warm, loving, and undemanding, with a promise of deep passion. Christina was the first to break the embrace, her eyes filled with surprise and happiness as they met Evan's. He smiled and made a pretence of changing the subject, but the kiss was there between them, almost a living and breathing entity.

Slightly breathless, Christina motioned Evan to the sofa, poured them each an espresso and joined him. Evan spoke first, "I have made reservations through the hotel concierge for two tickets to the 'Moulin Rouge' this evening. If you are familiar with the Can-Can you haven't seen anything until you see it up close and personal. We can have our dinner around eight and the floor show begins at nine."

He waited for her reply. Almost shyly, her glance met his as the memory of the kiss lay between them. "Evan, you have yet to disappoint me in anything. Do you have any idea how much this all means to me? I can't begin to thank you."

"There's no need. I have everything I need when you are in my company. You have no idea."

The evening approached and was soon upon them. Christina's eyes glowed as they entered the elegant interior of the famous Moulin Rouge. The lights were dim, the room smoky, and the stage well lit with coloured spotlights. The anticipation for the emergence of the Can-Can dancers grew. Never in her wildest dreams had Christina witnessed the exuberance, the sheer energy of the dance. She could well understand how the artist Tolousse Latrec had become enraptured night after night as he sketched and captured the performers' images on the café tablecloths.

Shortly after ten p.m. Evan suggested that they return to the hotel as they would be leaving Paris in the morning. They had not time to visit the Louvre. Though Evan promised that it would be the first thing on their agenda, he had made other arrangements that were more important and required his attention. That was all he would say, leaving her to cajole, tease, and attempt to pry the information out of him as they were en route to the hotel.

She had not given a thought as to Evan's living arrangements. Christina had noticed that the suite contained two bedrooms, but had given the situation little thought. Even though it had now come to mind, she decided to leave the choice up to Evan. If he chose to share her bed, she would not object; the thought of a warm and loving person keeping her safe and close was not unwelcome. In her own way she loved Evan; supposedly not with the great passion she felt for Adam, but she did love him dearly. A fact that they both had realized was that they had taken an instant liking to one another and their relationship, erratic as it had been, had been based upon this strong feeling. There are many forms of love, and this was one to which she was fast becoming accustomed; being nurtured, doted upon, almost idolized, her every whim attended to, leaving her nothing but the enjoyment that such pleasures bring.

Evan escorted her to the elevator, always holding her elbow and steering her expertly to their destination. As they approached the suite Evan made polite conversation, reassuring her that he appeared to have no further agenda on his mind. With a small sigh of pleasure she threw her wrap on the table and reclined on the sofa. Evan watched her every move, relishing in the thought that he was successfully rehabilitating this wonderful, beautiful woman, watching her come alive and enjoy the world around them. He fixed them a mild nightcap poured from the shaker of martinis that had been prepared for them. Their hands touched as he gave her the glass, their eyes met, and Christina felt the warmth of his love rekindle her long dead passion. New York, Adam Carmichael, the fashion industry, the modeling career all faded taking their rightful place in the shadows of the moment. She carefully placed her glass upon the bar counter and willingly walked straight into Evan's arms. Wordlessly, he held her for a long time, and when he searched her eyes for a sign, she put her fingers against his lips, stopping all questions. With a coy smile, Christina put her arm through his and led Evan to her bedroom. With a groan, he picked her up and carried her through the doorway, kissing her with a force fuelled by his sudden passion, and laid her gently upon the satin bedspread. The four-poster bed was enormous but they needed little room, as he rested his body along the length of hers postured upon the bed. He noticed the light in her eyes, the soft smile of pleasure upon her lips as she succumbed to his caresses. How he had imagined this moment, and the fact that it had been so natural and so spontaneous, he failed to question. Evan said, "Christina, *cherie*, are you sure?"

She sighed and said, "Yes, my darling, I am sure."

Thus began the happiest, most enduringly loving an evening that Evan had ever spent with any woman. This was beyond his wildest dreams, Christina had responded kiss for kiss, exchanging caresses to match his as they joined together in suspended time, their bodies locking in and moving in the rhythm of love. All the wealth, power, prestige, and fame were nothing compared to what he enjoyed in her complete surrender. If she did not love him as she did "the good doctor," then he would be most willing to accept what had just occurred. When she had fallen into a contented sleep he left the bed and moved over to the window, coming down from the high they had reached in their passion, as he watched the activity in the street below. He did not linger at the window, but returned to bed, moulding his body against her soft one, warming to her warmth, relishing in the touch of her body. He had never been this happy.

Chapter Thirty-Five

CHRISTINA SLEPT THROUGH HER morning wake-up call that the hotel service provided and was only awakened by the opening of the hall door. Evan had left the suite at a very early hour, and had returned with a breakfast fit for a queen in Paris. Hot croissants, espresso topped with rich whipped cream, with buttered toasts and wild berry jam if she so desired.

"Good morning, sleepy head."

"And just where have you been this morning? I expected to awake to find a handsome man with deep blue eyes and curly black hair beside me. Instead I find an empty pillow?"

"Now don't get excited princess. I just stepped out to buy you a true Parisian breakfast. We have many miles to go today and I don't want us to start out on empty stomachs," he replied.

"I thought we were going to that glamorous villa you rented on the coast?" Christina was all ears awaiting his reply.

"No, mademoiselle, a change of plans. I have rented a sports car that will whisk us away from the crowded streets of Paris to the vineyards of Bordeau. There we will surprise very dear friends of mine, friends which I wish to share my good fortune, and finally introduce you to them. I hope you won't mind. Later, we will stay at the villa for as long as you wish, until of course I have to check in at the shipbuilding yards." As he leaned over the breakfast nook to get another croissant, Christina leaned forward and impulsively kissed him. "What was that for? Or dare I ask?"

"Thank you for last night. It was magical. And I mean that from the bottom of my heart. You are more dear to me than you realize, and probably more than I realized until we made love."

She was at once embarrassed at her words, not believing that she had actually taken the initiative in their relationship, but she knew he expected open honesty and the truth. The blush that coloured her cheeks only managed to make her all the more appealing and it was all Evan could do to control his urges. His sudden intake of breath all but gave him away, but he composed himself as he said, "Come, my love, there is no need. You are the light of my life; you must know that. Anything I can do to make your life more bearable and finally achieve happiness I will gladly do."

She changed the subject. "I wonder if I should call Maggie. She would be excited to learn that Jean inquired after her, don't you think?"

"Perhaps she would, but I don't believe that we have the time. You could call her when we reach our destination to let her know that you arrived in one piece and that all is well."

The maid arrived at that moment and Christina showed her where the luggage was and what needed to be packed. She, in turn, proceeded to dress for the trip and pack away her personal care products. They were ready within the hour. Evan paid the hotel clerk, thanked them for the wonderful service, and promised to stay at the hotel on his next stop in Paris.

Outside the hotel the valet brought around a deep sea blue sports car with an interior of white leather upholstery. It was built low to the ground and Christina had to step down into the lush contoured seat. She surveyed the car's interior and was dismayed by the number of dials and switches on the dashboard. Evan grinned at her as he said, "Hang on to your hat, it's a four hour drive and I'm raring to go."

The drive took them through cultivated rolling hills, past farm houses, small villages and towns, narrow roads, stopping for sheep and goats blocking the roadway. They stopped for a refreshing drink at an inn and continued on their way.

The powerful sportscar ate up the miles as Christina reclined against the leather seats, her face upturned to the sun with the wind tugging at her head scarf as a few tendrils of hair escaped and were blown across her face. "How much further?" she asked.

He glanced at his watch, and replied, "Another hour and we should be there."

Evan was true to his word as he slowed the car and turned right through ornate iron gates that were the entry to an impressive estate. The driveway wound past the extensive vineyards, their rows of carefully cultivated grapevines appeared to go on for miles across the rolling countryside. They passed the winery and storage area and entered the curved driveway that ended at the marble landing, leading up to the entrance of an old and very expensive stone chateau. Its massive double doors were ornately carved with the family emblem as a welcome sign beckoning to all visitors. Evan left the car, walked around to the passenger's side, and Christina joined him in the driveway just as two adults emerged from the chateau, followed by an exuberant young girl who called out, "Uncle Evan, Uncle Evan, bonjour." She bounded down the steps and, with a resounding squeal of laughter, leapt into his arms.

He caught and hugged her as he said, *"Ah, mon petit choux, comment allez vous?" "C'est bon."* She hugged him in return, then she turned about and spoke to Christina, *"Je m'appelle Nicole, Mademoiselle."*

Evan switched to speaking English as he was now joined by his very dear friends Jacques and Carliss Freemont, the imp in his arms their daughter Nicole. "I hope you don't mind our surprise visit *mes amis,* but I wanted so very much for you to meet my dearest friend, Mademoiselle Christina Corelli." Evan returned Nicole to the ground and she stood smiling shyly up at Christina.

Christina smiled and exchanged greetings, leaving Nicole to the last. She bent down so as to be at the child's level and as their eyes met, a shock went through Christina so heart wrenching that it was extremely disconcerting. She looked into the deepest emerald eyes of the child before her, eyes that seemed strangely familiar as she said, "I am pleased to make your acquaintance, Nicole. I think we will be very good friends, non?"

"Look Mama, Papa, Uncle Evan, her eyes are as green as mine, don't you think?"

Nicole's mother spoke, "Nicole, you must not be so informal. We have only just met Mademoiselle Corelli, but I have to say, you are right."

Christina made the effort to break the ice as she said, "Evan has told me much about you, and it is finally a pleasure to be here on your magnificent estate. Everything is so incredible, I can't wait to see it all."

"And so you shall, but first, let us go inside and get you settled." Jacques helped Evan with the luggage as the party of five ascended the staircase and entered the chateau. He spoke to the housekeeper and a butler, and they escorted the guests to an upstairs guest suite to freshen up.

Evan called down the staircase, "We will join you shortly."

Christina had recovered from her meeting with Nicole and remarked, "What a charming girl. She is an incredibly beautiful child, and her spirit shines so brightly. I couldn't take my eyes off her."

Evan answered, "She is an only child, and I'll admit, a little spoiled, but because she is adopted. They treat her with enough love and tenderness for ten children, and I can't see anything wrong with that. A child needs all the love one has to give, don't you agree?"

They were shown into a guest room to die for. The decor was warm and welcoming, the colors vibrant in dark green against warm oak paneling, and high ceilings composed of intricately carved wooden tiles that enhanced the warmth of the room, creating a floor to wall to ceiling entity that was at once inviting and cozy. Christina did notice that this effect was created by the patrons sparing no expense. Everything was not only decadently pricey but was in the greatest taste. She must express her admiration to Carliss Freemont, hoping that she had been the decorator. Christina admired quality and hoped to learn from Carliss how to cultivate her fine taste.

Christina freshened herself with a splash of cold water on her face, an application of a rich moisturizer, a touch of makeup on the scar, and no rouge. The fresh open air of the convertible had brought color to her cheeks that no amount of makeup could copy. The warm sun had begun to tan her olive skin. Although she had left New York such a short time ago, the restoration of Christina Corelli was well on its way. She would be well and whole very soon.

During the course of their stay with the Freemonts, Christina and Nicole became close. Christina had previously had little contact with children, but this one tugged at her heartstrings. She was inquisitive, precocious, and rather worldly for a ten year old, and they chatted together for hours on end while Carliss saw to the daily routine of the chateau.

They were having breakfast in the garden overlooking the vast estate while the morning sunshine bathed them in gold. Nicole said, *"Maman* tells me that you are a famous model from America." Before Christina could reply she rambled on, "And she says that you are very rich but that you have no husband or children of your own?"

"I guess what she says is true. But I was born in Canada in a small town in the West. Do you believe that?"

The impish smile remained on her face as she answered, "I thought you were born in New York."

"Well, not too many people believe that I was just a normal, happy young girl with a wonderful family of aunts and uncles, cousins, and friends just like any other. I also had a dog named Rocko. Would you like to hear about him?" Nicole hung on her every word, the adoration for Christina all too apparent on her face as Christina related the story of how Rocko had saved her from drowning in the Big Pond.

Evan and Christina had been guests of the Freemonts for two wonderful fun-filled weeks, but the time had come for them to take their leave. Nicole cried, begging them to stay on, but Evan had to return to Cherbourg and oversee a major ship building project outlined in a telegram sent by his father. Reluctantly, they said their goodbyes, Christina hugging Nicole until she thought the girl would cry out. "Goodbye, my darling, I will never forget you. We will try to come and visit you another time."

Nicole sobbed, "Please don't go, Christina. I will miss you terribly. Someday I will be a famous model like you. I promise."

Christina smiled, gave her another parting kiss and turned to Evan. They thanked Jacques and Carliss profusely, Evan inviting them to join them on the yacht for a wonderful, carefree cruise along the Mediterranean. They just had to say the word, and Jean would be by to collect them.

They all knew that it would not be before the harvest, as then they had to tend to the wine- making process. The vineyards were a full time occupation, and many stages of wine production were crucial and Jacques could not trust this to anyone. However, Carliss promised that she would persuade him to take advantage of their invitation.

Chapter Thirty-Six

E VAN MADE ARRANGEMENTS WITH the car rental agency to have the sports car picked up in Cherbourg, where he had his own selection of cars at his disposal. They drove for many hours, stopping to refresh themselves at roadside inns, and purchased a bottle of wine, some bread and cheese, and stopped beside a cool stream to enjoy a hurried picnic. Evan noted that the past two weeks had done wonders for Christina; she was relaxed, unrestrained, her laughter came readily to her lips, and she no longer brooded. The sheen had returned to her chestnut hair, the spark of interest in her surroundings was all too evident in her eyes, and her beautiful glowing complexion was now restored. The subject of New York, Maggie and John Cole, or her past life did not come up, and Evan would not broach any of these subjects. He described his boyhood home as best he could, but when they approached the gates of the estate, the sight of the massive stone chateau, carefully sculptured gardens, and stone parapets overlooking the harbour took Christina's breath away. This was a far cry from her small town of Cranston, and a totally different scene from the hustle and bustle and craziness of New York City. She was enthralled. They had stopped for a short while at the shipyards where Evan was swallowed up by a busy crew of engineers, architects, carpenters, tradesmen, and the like, and by the presence of a very distinguished looking gentleman with white hair that appeared silver in the late afternoon sun, and his clothes tailored to his frame spoke of impeccable taste and wealth. She thought, that had to be Evan's father. There was a strong family resemblance in their stature, their build, and their good looks. Evan was slightly taller than his father. Perhaps he had inherited this from his mother's side of the family. She amused herself by imagining what his mother would look like, and as they approached the front entrance to the chateau they were met by an immaculately dressed woman carrying a basket of freshly cut flowers. She removed her gloves and gave the basket to her companion as she was encircled in a bone crushing hug and a resounding double kiss by her son.

"Evan, it's so good to see you. We have been wondering just what you have been up to."

"Forgive me, mother, but I have been to New York, and have brought back this lovely young woman to meet you. Mother, this is Christina Corelli from America. She needed a vacation and I was just the right person to provide her with one. I hope you don't mind. I should have warned you that I was bringing a guest."

This wonderful, elegant woman extended her hands and clasped Christina's in her own as she said, "Nonsense, Evan, you know your friends are always welcome here. We have more room than we can possibly imagine and it is always nice to have new and refreshing people to fill our lives. Your father is always so busy at the shipyards, and I can only do so much gardening. I cannot tell you how happy this makes me. Please, come inside. You must be hungry. I'll have Teresa bring tea and a light lunch. We don't actually have our dinner until eight this evening, so this should tide you over until then."

They entered the chateau and the vastness and richness enveloped them. The high ceilings with windows that reached a height of twenty feet allowed the afternoon sun to bathe the room with warmth. Christina was so overwhelmed by the wealth and beauty of this place that she actually felt like whispering, not wanting to break the spell the chateau had cast upon her. Evan studied her face as she surveyed her surroundings. He remarked, "A little large for the average family, don't you think?"

"Large, Evan, it's a castle isn't it?"

"Well, I don't have any siblings, Christina, so I got to ramble about this place at will when I was a child. See that huge staircase railing? I could slide down that thing faster than anyone could race down the stairs. I'll bet I could still do it."

His mother intervened at this conjecture. "Now, Evan, remember you're no longer a boy. Don't get carried away." They followed her into a large informal eating area, just off the massive kitchen filled with gleaming copper pots and pans, a center island that was as large as any bar Christina had seen, and numerous kitchen appliances.

A maid arrived with tea and a platter of sandwiches, bite size delicacies which the French referred to as hors d'oeuvres. Christina was not a big eater and tried to choose what appeared to be the most appetizing. She had to put on the weight she had lost, but it would have to be gradually. Evan remarked, "Come join us, mother. These are absolutely delicious."

Evan's mother first name was Marie, not uncommon but it suited her. She said, "You can't go on referring to me as Madam D'Argent, please, call me Marie."

"And you must call me Christina." Evan beamed as he noticed that his mother had taken an interest in Christina and was making an all-out effort to extend their warmest hospitality to this beautiful, unassuming young woman whom, evidently, had captured her son's heart. She had been on him to find someone to share his life with, but he had continued to play the jet-setting field, partying and socializing with the rich and overindulged friends of his generation. One thing that set Evan apart from this crowd was the fact that he had been educated in Paris and had worked in the shipyards as a young lad, learning the basics of construction from the ground up. His father had insisted, and as Evan was an only child he should know as much about his inheritance as possible. Together they had worked to expand the shipyards and they now were known as one of the largest and best shipbuilders in Europe, if not in the world. Evan loved to work, which kept him out of the usual scrapes with the law that his set encountered. She was so overwhelmingly proud of her son and it was with trepidations that she now studied this young woman who appeared to have been schooled in manners, the art of conversation, all of the social graces. If she could make her son happy, then she approved with all her heart. Evan was speaking to Christina, sharing his long-range plans for the future, which always brought a light to his eyes. She watched the two of them together and realized that they were best friends sharing a mutual admiration for one another. Was there more to this relationship than she was seeing? Evan apparently adored Christina, but was the adoration returned? She was not convinced, but she had just met the girl and time would tell.

"Penny for your thoughts, *Maman*," Evan smiled. "We should go up to our rooms and get settled. I don't know how long we will be here.

It depends upon what has to be done at the shipyards. Until, we'll just make ourselves at home, won't we, Christina?"

"Thank you so much for the lunch, Marie. It was exactly what we needed. If it's all right, I would like to take a bath and perhaps rest for a few hours. It's been a very long day."

"I look forward to dinner this evening. Welcome to our home, Christina."

Out of respect for Evan's parents, Christina convinced Evan that they should occupy separate rooms. He reluctantly agreed.

Thus began a new way of life for Christina. She felt as though she had been uprooted and dropped down into fairyland, another planet where life was so much different than she could ever have imagined. When she had travelled to Italy for her Nona's funeral, she had been too overcome with grief and concern to experience much else. They had merely touched down in Rome, been whisked away to her grandparents village, and then back to Canada. During the runway shows in Milan, she had been too encompassed within her own world of fashion and design to be able to actually become engrossed in the European way of life. Who better than Evan to show her the best of everything?

Chapter Thirty-Seven

New York City

F OR DR. ADAM CARMICHAEL, life became a round of work and sleep. He had been so hurt and angry over Christina's leaving that he had thrown himself into his work with a fury. He had increased his patient workload and had cemented his relationships with his senior partner, Dr. Finestad, the ageing female population of the upper class, and the elite of the city's richest families.

In particular, one female had set her sights on the ever-growing popularity of Dr. Carmichael. Joan Finestad was not a romanticist. She prided herself on being a person who dealt in reality and circumstance, with both feet planted on the ground. She intended to marry well, someone to chaperone her to the charity dinners, the gala parties, the Broadway shows and the Country Club. Other than that, his time would be his own. She did not completely exclude the intimate side of marriage; it would suffice as an outlet for her unbridled passion and needs. His needs would not be tantamount to hers. Dr. Carmichael was the perfect candidate. He had become a workaholic, and would not be around to encumber her during times when he was not needed as an escort. She would be free to do as she wished, something which she had become accustomed to all of her life. She came from an independent, career driven set of parents, and the mould had not been broken. Joan had been groomed to become the perfect high-society wife, even looking to forgiving extra-marital affairs of the heart, if they should occur. They were to be viewed as mere dalliances, and to be discarded and forgotten when the passion had cooled.

Adam had been attacked and waylaid by the press, who asked a multitude of questions: What caused your break-up with Christina Corelli? Was there another man in her life? Was it the rich European ship builder? Did you cheat on her before the wedding? Where is she, Dr. Carmichael? Is her career on hold? You must tell us something, her fans are devastated at her disappearance!

To all of this he had merely answered through tight lips, "No comment, not now or ever, now leave me the Hell alone."

They had finally decided after a few weeks of harassment that he had meant what he said, there would be no further news of one of New York's finest. Miss Corelli had indeed disappeared. Her office would offer no information regarding her expected return, if or when it would occur. They had moved on to the next scandal.

As he left the elevator one day, his briefcase in hand, he met Joan in the hallway. She was an amazing woman. Never had he met anyone who was so goddammed organized, always cool under duress, a woman with a mission, unflappable and determined. She wasn't as becoming as Christina, but in her own right, with ice-blond hair and blue-eyes, tall and willowy figure, and dressed in designer clothes to turn any man's head. He had decided to give up on women for the time being, but was nonetheless flattered when she included him in their family dinner parties, where he rubbed elbows with the movers and shakers within the medical community. Many a dinner party guest appeared in his office within weeks seeking his expertise and advice, wanting all that cosmetic surgery had to offer in order to prevent the ravages of time.

He was only too happy to oblige. He felt he should thank Joan. "Wait just a minute, Joan." "Yes, Dr. Carmichael?"

"I want to thank you for all you have done for me in such a short time. If you hadn't included me and introduced me into your high society, I would not be so successful. I guess what I'm trying to say is, will you have dinner with me, let's say this Friday?"

Her smile was unexpected and completely changed her countenance. He was taken by surprise, as she was always so aloof and collected. This was an insight into a new Joan Finestad.

"I'd be happy to have dinner with you, Adam. But you don't really have to thank me. Your work speaks for itself. Everyone you have worked on has nothing but the highest praise, claiming that you are able to take at least ten years from their appearance."

"I'll call you when I have made the reservations." He turned on his heel and continued on down the hallway towards the plush and very spacious office space that only Fifth Avenue could offer. So he had come to a crossroads. He would no longer pine away for Christina and what might have been. He shook his head sadly when he realized what could have been. They had been so close to a perfect match. Adam knew he would always love her all the days of his life, but he had to move on and his life demanded a companion. He would deal with his innermost feelings sometime in the future, right now he was on the road to recovery and Joan Finestad was the perfect choice, not only to further his career but to merge his life with a long- respected New York family, one held in the highest esteem. What could be wrong with that? Did he have feelings for Joan? She appeared nice enough, what harm could come of getting to know her? With these thoughts filtering through his brain, he entered the waiting room, the scent of very expensive perfume wafting and mingling amongst the patients seated about the main area. His receptionist greeted him, "Good afternoon, Dr. Carmichael, shall I fill your rooms, or would you like a few minutes before seeing your first patient?"

"Is Dr. Finestad in, Jessie?" "Yes, shall I ring him?"

"Please do, I just need a few minutes to discuss a case. I won't be long."

She nodded politely, smiled at no one in particular, and raised the telephone to her ear. She spoke quietly, waited then nodded once more, broke the connection and busied herself with the appointment book on the desk before her.

The waiting room emptied, filled again then re-emptied. The afternoon had literally flown, and Adam glanced at his watch. It read six o'clock. He stretched and reclined in his leather armchair, turning to look out at the Park. Summer was in full bloom, the trees forming a lush green blanket at the foot of the skyscrapers. Their foliage was always a welcome sight after one experienced the long, wet, cold New York winter. He remembered his promise of the dinner date and scanned the phone book, not wanting to alert his receptionist or nurse as to his new partner. He chose the finest: Ciro's. It was the place to be seen, to see, and to enjoy the club atmosphere after the impeccable service provided during the course of an evening meal. The Ritz was another fine choice, but Ciro's was more for the "in" crowd, with many celebrities arriving and leaving during any given evening.

Reservations were confirmed for eight o'clock and Evan dialled Joan's private line. She answered in her business tone but quickly changed to a more friendly chatter when she recognized the caller. "I look forward to Friday night, Adam. I can hardly wait. See you then."

John and Maggie Cole were enjoying a last minute drink before they would return to their respective apartments. John, to his wife Ellen and their children, and Maggie to her upscale apartment on the West Side, empty as usual. "I miss Christina so very much, John. Has she really been gone two months? We've hardly heard from her."

John's reply was meant to soothe, "I know exactly how you feel. I miss her too. But, we know that she had to leave us in order to find herself. She has been through a terrible ordeal. The press was relentless in their pursuit of information even to making up some of the dreadful headlines. It must have been a double blow after her wedding was cancelled. I can't begin to imagine what she suffered."

"If only she would give us an idea as to when we can expect her to return."

"Maybe we should consider hiring someone to act as an administrator. We have become so big, with so many extra departments other than the modeling agency end of our company, that we can't do it alone. Christina's leaving has created a large void in our operations."

"I'll have to give it some thought, John. Do you have anyone in mind? I surely don't."

"I think we should advertise the position in the Fashion News World, looking to hire someone with a graduate degree and from high end society. It will not be an easy task, but we can't go on as we have, trying to fill the gap left by Christina. Do you agree?"

"Yes, yes, you're absolutely right." She finished the last of her drink, picked up her light coat and purse and said, "Goodnight brother dear, my love to Ellen and the kids. You are one lucky man."

"Goodnight, Maggie. See you tomorrow."

* * * * *

EXHAUSTED FROM HER DAY'S work, Maggie greeted her doorman not stopping to exchange pleasantries as was her usual custom. She decided a long, hot soaking bath would alleviate the tiredness and nagging headache that had become a part of the aftermath of a day at the office. Her condo was not too large, but airy and light with windows that extended from floor to ceiling. She could draw the drapes or allow the sunlight to stream in, but Maggie preferred the touch of moonlight, which bathed the rich furnishings in a soft, almost blue-white light. She found this most relaxing, especially after her bath. She curled up on the sofa, dressed in the ever familiar white terry robe and matching head wrap, and decided to write to Christina. As a full partner she should have a say in their decision to hire an administrator for the company, and she valued Christina's input. Also, she wished to discuss next year's spring and summer lines. The designs which Christina had been working on for the upcoming fall and winter had come to an abrupt halt and the other designers on staff had taken up the slack. As well, Maggie just wanted to hear from her. She missed her dreadfully.

* * * * *

ELLEN GREETED JOHN WARMLY and the children, both toddlers, ran to their father, both talking at once and the apartment became a haven. To be loved by his family was the best gift John could ever imagine. All else paled by comparison. He was, in his own right, a simple man, self made and determined, but he lacked the drive that was instilled in his sister Maggie. She was the driving force behind the company, his skills lay in the discovery of what had potential, and Maggie took it from there. With Christina so far removed from the picture, they had to meet on many more occasions and the added responsibility and workload were taking their toll. His smile was evident, but Ellen noticed the tired lines beginning to appear, a shaping of a furrowed brow.

She kissed him and murmured, "Dinner is almost ready. I fed the children but they will probably have dessert while we eat. It's still too early for their bedtime. I thought you would like to spend a little quiet time with them?"

"You always know what's best for me, don't you? I couldn't imagine my life without you in it, Ellen, believe me."

She didn't answer but busied herself with serving dinner, but her heart swelled when she heard the words. She had counted her lucky stars when she had met and fallen in love with John. He was no male model, but looks were not a substitute for character and good solid values. They were best friends as well as lovers for the duration.

As he ate the scrumptious meal before him, John shared his thoughts with Ellen. "Maggie and I reached a decision today that may have far reaching effects on the company. We have tentatively agreed to hire an administrator for the department. Since Christina has left us rather high and dry, the workload has increased for each of us and it's beginning to tell on Maggie. I can't remember when she took some time off just to enjoy a relaxing vacation somewhere out of the city."

Ellen asked, "What type of person are you looking for?"

"We require someone who has an excellent education, a person with Public Relations skills, one that will be able to get the last ounce of work out of our staff, especially when we have so many deadlines to meet."

"I'm sure you'll find the best person for the job. You are an excellent judge of character. After all, you married me, didn't you?" She laughed as he grabbed her in a tremendous bear hug and the children watched happily, secure in the knowledge that they were part of a very happy family.

The following morning, Maggie and John held a hurried meeting with the staff, revealing their intentions to hire a new supervisor. A few of the more loyal office staff were rather upset that their employers were seeking outside help. A few were of the thought that perhaps one of them could take over, and someone said as much. Maggie explained, "That is one area of thought, but we feel that there might cause a wave of envy for the one which we select, and that the remainder of you would not be willing to take any direction from one of your own. That's the only reason, believe me."

"We will give it a try and if it doesn't work then we will have to rethink the decision. How does that sound?" John asked.

A murmur of agreement followed his question and the meeting was ended.

The advertisement was drafted and sent to the New York Times' classified section and hopefully interviewing would begin the following week.

* * * * *

D R. ADAM CARMICHAEL AND Joan Finestad's first dinner date had been most enjoyable. Schooled in the art of conversation, the knack of being able to put people at ease, had definitely worked their charm upon the plastic surgeon. He found himself relaxing, surveying his surroundings for the first time in many months, taking an interest in other sights and sounds other than those which filled his daily routine. The day's weariness began to lift, and he studied the woman seated across from him. She was definitely a head turner; not so much from the male counterpart, but from other females. He noted the look of envy when she walked through the restaurant on her way to the powder room. Female heads stared, then bent to whisper behind their hands. He felt proud to be seen with such an attractive and compelling woman. Joan had remarked at one point in their conversation, that she believed in the philosophy that one could be neither too rich nor too thin. He had not totally agreed with her but now he did, though he may also add "too powerful" to her list.

During her absence he ordered a very decadent dessert for himself and a half portion for Joan. She drank white wine with her dinner and liberal amounts of sparkling water. He decided that he would cultivate their friendship and see just where it would lead. Thoughts of Christina ran fleetingly through his mind but he shook them away. She had to be dealt with, out of sight, out of mind. The old cliché fit the situation but was considered cruel by many.

Thus began a relationship that would raise many eyebrows in the high society of New York, as well as the medical community. Dr. Aaron Finestad was definitely glad that his junior partner was seriously seeking the company of his daughter Joan. Joan's mother was overjoyed. After all, it was the culmination of her careful rearing of her child, the ultimate goal for her happiness, that her daughter marry well and maintain the respect of the inner circle.

The whirlwind romance was recorded in all the papers. The Society Page contained weekly pictures of the couple dining at the finest restaurants and coming and going to Broadway shows, the opera, and many charity dinners. They literally fed upon the couples' actions, and in many cases the headlines speculated upon if and when they would announce their engagement.

Maggie had read the Society Page with interest and was torn as to whether she could contact Christina with the latest gossip. She decided against the idea until of course they did, in fact, reveal their upcoming nuptials. Why open freshly healed wounds? She had received a rather lengthy letter from Christina supporting the hiring of the new staff member, her plans to design the spring collection, and her newly found happiness with Evan. Maggie had been relieved when she read the letter. Christina was getting on with her life. Too bad Maggie wasn't. She could not forget her beloved Jean, the man who had come into her life so unexpectedly. They would never be able to marry, but both knew that they had met their soul mate. Any time spent together would have to last a lifetime. Maggie sighed and returned to the mound of work upon her desk. She rang her secretary, asked that Miss Winslowe be sent to her office, and waited patiently for their new employee to enter. Kate Winslowe had been chosen from an impressive list of candidates. She was a Vassar graduate and a product of an established old family and old money. Most importantly, she had class and connections, and a hardness about her that was required in dealing with disciplinary situations and hard decision-making. So far, during the past six weeks she had shone, and John and Maggie were happy to have her on board.

Under Kate's direction, the pace of the company had accelerated dramatically. The race was on for the launch of the fall collection and the staff was working at full capacity. Maggie and John concentrated upon filling the positions of models, their most outstanding as well as those added to the entourage. They had each fallen into their comfortable niche and profits were soaring. All this was reported to Christina with the third-quarter figures and although she was becoming much richer, she felt a little out of sorts, almost neglected and only slightly missed.

It was time she confided in a letter to Becka. Evan was out, having decided to go into the village for a few hours. She surveyed her surroundings; the villa Evan had leased for them was situated on the Italian Amalfi Coast, overlooking the deep blue Mediterranean. The climate was comfortable year-round; balmy, extremely healthy. She marvelled at the view from the stone ramparts, the niches in the stone containing stone planters filled with vibrant, colourful flowers, their aroma filling the interior of the villa when the direction of the wind wafted from the sea.

She had become somewhat bored with her daily routine. Although Evan attempted to fulfill her day, he was often away in Cherbourg, leaving her to her own amusements. When Maggie had requested that she design the spring and summer collections, Evan had ordered that a spare room in the villa be converted to a drafting and design facility where Christina could work undisturbed as the creative mood dictated.

She gazed out upon the sea, actually unseeing the beauty before her. Her thoughts were in Cranston.

Dear Becka,

As usual, it is time that I shared my thoughts and feelings once again with you. You are my living diary and I could never imagine not sharing my life with you, although we are separated by thousands of miles and many months.

I have purchased a few gifts for the children, a locket for Andrea and a child size watch for Mario. The gift shops here are filled with wonderful treasures but, not being familiar with your children's likes and dislikes, I chose these as they would last much longer than the usual fad toys that are on the market everywhere in the world. I thought it best to leave that up to you and Tonio.

Unbeknownst to Maggie and John, I have been receiving copies of the New York Times delivered to the villa by special courier. It seems that Adam has moved on, and just today there was a photo of him and his new fiancée, with a column devoted to each of them as to the upcoming nuptials. He is to marry Joan Finestad, his senior partner's daughter. She is completely opposite from me in looks and upbringing. Should I take that as a good sign? I don't know how I feel about it all. Very sad when I think of what might have been. You know as well as I do that I will love him always, but life goes on. Evan has persisted in asking me to marry him, and with the knowledge of Adam's intentions, perhaps it is time I gave him a positive answer. I should tell him soon, and I will hide the issue of this paper from him. I would not allow him to think that I married him out of spite or a rebound. I really do love him, but not with the passion and abandon that Adam and I shared. This is more settled, more sustaining, more mature. It probably is just what I need. I send you all my love and I shall write as soon as I have reached a decision regarding my relationship with Evan. All my best to Tonio and give the children many kisses and hugs from Aunt Christina.

As ever, Christina

She re-read the letter and partway through felt the rush of tears. She brushed them away in an attempt to clear her vision, but gave up the effort. Were the tears for remorse, for envy, for a lost love, for what might have been? Would she finally relinquish the idea that there would be a future for her and Adam, as well as the search for their twins? She heard the car door close and Evan's footsteps approaching the patio and his figure appeared silhouetted against the blue sky.

She quickly collected herself, bowed her head to hide the tears and pretended to be engrossed in the half-finished design in front of her. He came up behind and gathered her in his arms, planting welcoming kisses on the nape of her neck. She shivered in delight, a half smile formed, and she turned and rose, moulding her figure against his. Their silhouette became as one. In surprise he held her for a very long time. Finally, she withdrew and gazed up into his eyes.

"Evan, I have been thinking long and hard about our relationship and I think you deserve an answer. You have been the most thoughtful, sincere and loving partner any woman could ask for ..."

He interrupted, "If you are going to refuse my offer of marriage, then don't say it. If you don't wish to be married, then we can continue on as we have. I have never been so happy, *mon cherie.*"

"No, Evan, let me finish. I just want to say that I return your love, and I accept your marriage proposal if you will have me."

For a moment Evan decided that his ears were playing tricks on him. "What are you saying? Christina, are you agreeing to be my wife? Never in my wildest dreams did I expect a yes, and to think that I was beginning to lose hope. Oh, my love, this is the most wonderful day of my life. Are you absolutely sure?"

"Yes, Evan, I am absolutely sure." He kissed her long and hard, held her at arm's length, and looked deeply into her eyes, seeking reassurance that he had not misread her answer. Yes, there was love shining in her emerald eyes, yes, there was adoration as well, mirroring the deep abiding love, which never waned as he searched her face.

Chapter Thirty-Eight

NOW THAT THE DECISION had been made that they should marry, Evan became a changed man. He could not contain his happiness. It was tentatively agreed upon that a late fall wedding at the Chateau in Cherbourg would be the ideal location. Christina intended to keep the ceremony and festivities low-key, as she had not totally recovered from the last tabloid attack. They both realized that because of her fame and his family's reputation, the wedding ceremony would have to be celebrated with the utmost security in place.

"I hate to break the news my love, but we must give up the villa and return to Cherbourg.

Maman is awaiting our return with so many plans that she must consult with you."

"I will miss this place, Evan. It has brought me such peace and comfort over the past few months, but you are right. We must leave. As much as I would like your mother to attend to all of the wedding arrangements, I should be there to order the gown and bridesmaid's outfits, as well as go over the guest list. I don't have many people to add as only a few will be attending. It is such a great distance to travel and some may not be able to get away from their work. We must have Jacques and Carliss Freemont, as I would like to have Nicole as my flower girl. She has become so dear to me, that it would be a huge disappointment to me if they were left out, don't you agree?"

"I was thinking of asking Jacques to be my best man, and I thought Carliss could be your maid of honour? That is, if your friends from Canada can't attend?"

On these points they were in complete agreement. Christina had little to do with the closing of the villa as Evan hired a crew to pack up her design equipment and their personal belongings were seen to by their housekeeper, and within a week they were on their way to Cherbourg. Christina decided that she would stop in Paris for a few days to choose her dress, as it was to be a Christian Dior design and she would have to be measured and fitted. Evan, rather than stand idly by while this was being attended to, called in the family jet and left Paris with Christina comfortably settled in the Ritz. The time would pass quickly, hopefully unencumbered by plans gone awry. With his mother's expertise in planning large social functions, and Christina's taste in dress and decor he was certain that all would go well and his dream would be realized. Christina Corelli would become Christina D'Argent. He would spend the rest of his life making her happy.

Christina's fame preceded her and she was greeted with open arms by the entire staff of the Dior empire. Christian himself devoted an entire afternoon, discussing choices of material: silk or satin, lace or seed pearls, tulle or net? The choices appeared to be endless. Christina asked to see past designs, had drafted a few of her own, and all were either discussed and commented upon or discarded. After many hours of deliberation, the perfect dress was chosen, a Dior design with a few Corelli changes, and the entire staff agreed that it would be a dress to end all dresses, a gown that would set the fashion world on fire. The staff was sworn to secrecy and Christina promised that as soon as she had heard from her intended wedding party, she would give them the go ahead to design the dresses for her attendants. The color and choice she would leave to the expertise of the Dior team, insisting that fall colors be chosen.

Her days were so busy that she no longer dwelt upon the fact that her beloved Adam would be married a week before her own wedding. She had read Maggie's letter with interest, the part about the addition of the intrepid Kate Winslowe hurt just a little. They were moving on, their lives going forward in opposite direction from her own, but she knew this was for the best. She had not intended for her absence to create any hardship for the conglomerate, but nevertheless she was still torn with feelings of having been cut loose. Maggie had insisted that she continue designing for them, her new approach to the line had been infused with a definite European flair and were literally flying out of the high end Fifth Avenue shops. They could not keep up with the demand. Christina's heart soared as she basked in the praise that was eagerly imparted in Maggie's letters. The fashion industry had done a complete turn-about from the late fifties. Coiffed and manicured, girdled and fitted-to-perfection ensembles, hats and gloves, stoles and furs had been replaced by psychedelic colors, higher skirt lengths, and very thin models who did not have to wear girdles and under wired bras. In fact, many of the models had thrown away their bras and dieted away any excess weight that would normally be encased in elastic and stays. Hair styles also fell by the wayside with beehive, backcombed, and hair spray as well as short cap cuts, whichever suited the model. Everyone was interested in creating a style of their own that would be their signature to fame. An English model had emerged upon the runway, lovingly referred to as "Twiggy". She wore miniskirts, knee high leather boots, her hair piled high upon her head, and her large eyes framed in false eyelashes and green or blue eye shadow. Every teeny-bopper on the planet attempted to look like her. The fashion industry was faced with a dilemma. What sector of the industry's consumers had the most cash to spend? Should they adopt the younger line, only to leave the haute couture too stagnant in their old designs?

Maggie and John decided that the younger set was just as important as the established one and made an all out effort to launch two lines of clothing to see what the impact would be. Never in their wildest dreams could they have imagined the overnight success in their new endeavour. Profits soared and demand was overwhelming. From New York to California, to Palm Springs, Florida and into Canada the new trend was like a tidal wave of color, change, fad, and craziness that set the stage for future projects.

During this frenzy of activity, Maggie, John, and Ellen received the news of Christina's upcoming wedding. As Maggie read the letter she could not help but feel sad. With the course of her life changing so rapidly Maggie, realized that Christina would not be returning to them at any time soon. She was relieved that Christina felt that she could find happiness with Evan but she had witnessed firsthand the devastation and near emotional destruction of Christina when she had broken her plans with Adam Carmichael. Maggie had read of his upcoming nuptials but still withheld the information from Christina, not wishing to put a damper on her future happiness. Reluctantly she discussed the possibility of their attending the ceremony in France with John and Ellen, but because of the turn of events within the industry, one of them must remain in New York to oversee the changes. John agreed that he would be the one and he would use Kate as his assistant during Maggie's absence.

Maggie placed an overseas call to Christina in Cherbourg. She was overjoyed to hear her voice. "We've missed you so very much, Christina, but John and I both agree that if this is what you want then we are only too happy for you both. John can't get away, but I will be there with bells on. Shall I make reservations in Cherbourg?"

"Maggie, this Chateau is like a castle. Evan's parents have insisted that all of my overseas closest friends must stay with them. An entire wing of their home is dedicated to guests and has been for years. Just come when you can, call us when you get to the airport, and the chauffeur will collect you. I can't wait to see you again, it seems I've been gone for years and it's only been months."

Maggie felt a rush of tears as she confirmed and agreed upon everything Christina was saying. "Is there anything you would like me to bring you from New York?"

"No, Maggie. Just yourself. You have no idea how happy this makes me. I will keep you posted on the plans, but Marie and Andre D'Argent have set the date with the parish priest for November the seventh. The church they selected is the very one in which they were married and I could not have been happier with her choice. It is absolutely magnificent."

"Shall I ask you about your dress, or is that a sight that is reserved for the day of the wedding?"

"I will only tell you that the House of Dior in Paris has exceeded all my expectations. I would have had our company design team in on it, but I could not travel for fittings to New York. I did incorporate some of my suggestions into the design and I'm sure you will love it. That's all I'm going to tell you. I hate to say goodbye Maggie, but I really must go. Bye for now. I love you."

"Goodbye Christina, I love you too. I can't wait."

Christina became sadly quiet when the conversation was over. She hadn't really thought about how much she missed her old life while being caught up in the plans for her wedding. She wondered why Maggie had not mentioned Adam and Joan's wedding, but all things considered, she was probably trying to spare Christina any heartache the news might bring. It was very disheartening to see it in print, the fashion headlines seemed to jump out of the page with the news of a marriage made in high society. The picture of Adam was not a very good one; he looked tired, thinner than she remembered from last winter. Joan was depicted as the proverbial ice queen, not a hair out of place, the jewels encasing her neck and wrist costing a small fortune, and which she wore as one would wear an old watch, accustomed to the best as always.

Marie's voice broke her reverie. "Is everything all right, Christina? Is the news bad?"

"No, thank you, Marie. Actually, it was the best news. Maggie will be attending the wedding, but I'm afraid that John and Ellen will be staying in New York. They cannot both be away for the week as someone has to be there to run the company. It is a little disappointing but I do understand. I don't think that my friends from Canada will be attending. It is just too far to travel and their children are quite young. Work commitments and family have to come first, but I promised Becka that I would send them a copy of the film of the whole week for them to watch. It's the next best thing to their being here."

"What a wonderful idea, Christina." She had grown extremely fond of this unencumbered, beautiful young woman who would soon become a loving member of their family. Marie had never seen her son so happy. She had fretted over his jet-set image, flitting from one debutante to another, traveling throughout Europe, Cannes in the summer, Switzerland in the winter, and who knows wherever else they roamed. He had taken a desultory interest in the shipyards.

Although he had been educated and groomed to take over when Andre decided to retire, his interest barely masked his boredom. She had witnessed a complete turnaround since his relationship with Christina had begun and her heart soared with the knowledge that he was finally on the right track.

Chapter Thirty-Nine

THE ENSUING FEW WEEKS were filled with a flurry of activity involving reservations, decorations, caterers, billeting for the wedding guests, invitations, selective menus, and all the special preparations which are related to a wedding which was to excel all weddings. Evan was from old European money, a family which could be traced back to the seventeenth century as foretold by the wonderful portraits which graced the halls of the family chateau. Money had never been a hardship, old money was used to amass new money, and the prosperity was evident everywhere in the style of living to which he had always been accustomed. Although Christina was rich in her own right, having invested her profits wisely, she was somewhat surprised by many of the proposed festivities to which Marie had her heart set on. Christina, knowing full well that the guest list would be comprised of the D'Argent side of the family, did not exclude any of the names on the list, which Marie put forth.

She was more than a little sad when she thought of how far away her friends and family were. New York, Western Canada, Toronto. About the only thing which gave her comfort was the fact that she had relatives in Italy, and invitations were gladly sent as she wished they could all attend. Her grandparents were no longer alive, but her aunts and uncles were her greatest fans, always bragging to anyone who cared to listen about their wonderful, famous model Christina Corelli and how beautiful she was.

Evan appeared in the sunroom where Christina was reviewing the guest list. "Good morning, my darling, what has you so lost in thought?"

"Evan, good morning. It's really nothing. I just thought it would be so wonderful if all my nearest and dearest could attend our wedding. But that would be impossible, I know that."

"What do you know? Nothing is impossible when it comes to your wishes, you must know that."

"How could Becka and Tonio and the children travel this far, just to celebrate our wedding? How could my Aunt and Uncle in Toronto leave the bakery unattended for a week or so to come? How must Maggie and John, Ellen and the children leave New York at will? They have commitments as well as the rest of us."

"Have you anyone else in mind? Let's see the list. I know it's probably none of my business, but you have not included your father, Frank on this list."

"Of course, it's your business. My father is not welcome. He destroyed my life when he ordered me to give up the twins. He had an affair with a woman for many years, and when my mother learned the truth from Tonio's mother, she took to her bed and died of a broken heart. I can't forgive him for any of it, and although he has since found happiness with Tonio's mother Teresa, they really aren't welcome. Can you understand how I feel?"

Evan could see the rising emotion in her face, the color heightened by anger and frustration and deep hurt that festered within. He took her in his arms and held her gently as he murmured, "Yes, of course I understand. If you do not wish them to even know of your wedding, then so be it."

"But your mother intends to make this the most extravagant and highly publicized wedding of the year. A late fall wedding, the colors all turned in their glory before the onset of winter, the guests as high up the social ladder as they can possibly get, the glitter and glamour that is characterized by the finest taste that money can buy."

"Well Christina, you have to realize that I am my mother's only child and she intends to give me away in style. She really loves you, if you must know, and is very proud to be able call you daughter."

"That makes me very happy, Evan. My deepest regret is that my mother is not alive to celebrate our happiness."

"I'm positive that you will feel her presence during the ceremony and celebrations."

"She lives in my heart, along with my grandparents." With these last words they parted company. Christina decided to take a walk throughout the magnificent gardens before the noon day lunch, and Evan was off to the shipyards.

* * * * *

No one worked harder than Marie on the preparations for the upcoming nuptials. The day of the wedding was fast approaching, just a week away and everything appeared to be in readiness. The list was checked and double-checked. Last minute suggestions were incorporated. Christina, at one point, detected a note of secrecy, having interrupted a very whispered conversation amongst Evan and his parents. They had nodded in unison and stopped talking when they became aware of her presence in the room. She shrugged it off, thinking she was imagining things, but why was Evan wearing such a self-satisfied look and his mother beaming at her, unsuspecting as always?

Christina was looking forward to seeing Jacques, Carliss, and Nicole Freemont. They had replied early on that they would be attending and Christina had persuaded Carliss to be her maid of honor and Nicole her flower girl. They had sent their measurements to the Dior House in Paris and their dresses were being designed and sewn.

Guests began arriving on Friday, the day before the wedding. The chateau swarmed with caterers, decorators, delivery people, valets, maids, and musicians setting up for the reception. The weather was completely co-operative. The mornings had been slightly cool, but the late fall sunshine warmed the grounds and emanated a golden light, bathing their surroundings in beauty.

Christina's special entourage of designers had arrived from Paris, and she was cloistered with them for many hours, seemingly unaware of the frenzy surrounding them all. Marie and Andre, always the gracious hosts, greeted their guests and had them settled within the hour of their arrival. A special pre-nuptial supper party was to be held in the great dining room at eight o'clock that evening and a very special surprise was planned for Christina. Everyone was sworn to secrecy.

Christina spent the day happily engrossed in the final fitting of her gown. It was so simply designed that the cut and drape of the heavy taffeta and the hint of sheen in the material caught the light as she turned to catch the view in the mirror of the gathered train that was not too encumbering in length as to cause her problems in walking to the altar. It lent an air of elegance that was the Dior signature. The bodice was cut and draped in a straight line across her bust and embroidered white roses with centers of seed pearls adorned the front of the dress, trailing down to her waist and culminating in a sweep to the hemline of the dress. Tiny spaghetti straps held the dress in place but left her gracefully curved neckline bare. Marie had presented Christina with a diamond necklace that had been in the family for many generations and had been worn by many a bride, herself included. Christina could not even begin to guess at the monumental cost of this gift.

Christina had designed her veil with great care. A tiara had been purchased to which the veil could be attached. She had the same simple roses embroidered in a scattered pattern and the veil cascaded fully down the length of her hair to her waist. The way it had been fashioned enabled the wearer to style her hair at will, wearing it up or down.

She decided to wear it up, fashioned in a style that left the mass of curls clasped at the back of her head to cascade freely in tiny ringlets and waves that could not escape the ornate veil. Diamond earrings would grace her lobes, and she would finish the ensemble with long white gloves, the fingers exposed so that Evan could place the wedding ring upon her finger.

As the wedding party was to be driven to the massive stone church in open carriages, the Dior team had suggested that the female members of the party wear long matching capes of soft velvet, hooded for comfort in case they encountered a brief shower, strong gusty winds, whatever Mother Nature could send that would disarrange the carefully coiffed, perfumed and perfectly groomed entourage during the two mile carriage ride to the church. The time chosen for the wedding was two o'clock, just after the guests had partaken of a light lunch, leaving time for them to dress for the ceremony.

Christina spent a few minutes in contemplation. Adam's face flashed before her, but she was determined to put the past behind. She reclined upon the luxurious, spacious four poster bed, her thoughts far away. Before long her eyes closed, and with a small sigh she fell fast asleep.

The next thing she knew, her maid was gently calling her name to awaken her from her deep sleep. The rest had refreshed her, and glancing at her watch she instantly became alert. She had an hour before the dinner party. She looked out upon the garden from the second story window. Everything looked fantastic. White flowers adorned wooden trellises, pink and yellow roses were everywhere. Satin ribbons were attached to chairs and adorned the tables set for the late afternoon reception. She decided a quick shower was in order and turned away from the window.

Marie had approached Evan to collect Christina from the upstairs floor at exactly eight o'clock. She assured him that all of the guests had arrived, gave him a meaningful look, and said everyone would be seated awaiting their arrival. He smiled, his pleasure all too apparent. "Thank you, *Maman*. I love you dearly."

At precisely eight p.m. Christina tucked her hand under Evan's arm and he escorted her to the top of the staircase. She heard the murmur of many people; the dining hall seated fifty. The scent of fresh roses wafted up the stairs, and her whole body became electrified with excitement. This was the beginning of a new life for Christina.

They descended the stairs and a butler led them into the dining room. The room was lit by candles. As the light flickered upon crystal stemware, it reflected off the extravagant bejewelled woman. Christina's eyes became accustomed to the diminished light as Evan led her to the head of the table where he seated her beside his mother. He, in turn, took his place beside his father who was at the head of the table. Before she could sit down, she heard a familiar voice, "Hello, Christina, we've missed you."

"Maggie, is it really you? John, Ellen and the children? But how in the world did you all manage to get away?"

Evan said, "Keep searching the table, my love. Everyone is here. Everyone whom you mentioned that couldn't attend because of their commitments."

There, seated comfortably, were her relatives from Italy, her Aunt Maria and Uncle Guido, Vince, Vito from Toronto. From the opposite side of the table Christina gasped when she saw Becka's smiling face. "Oh my God. Becka! And Tonio and the children. I must be dreaming. Evan, how did you arrange all of this?"

"Let's just say I made them all an offer they couldn't refuse, isn't that right?"

The laughter echoed throughout the great dining room, and everyone began to relax. The waiters, upon a cue from Marie, entered the room carrying large platters of scrumptious smelling food, offering and serving portions to everyone in turn. The flow of perfectly chilled champagne began, a gift from the Freemont winery, and the chatter became louder. After everyone had finished their meal, Andre stood and cleared his throat to gain their attention. All conversation stopped and the waiters refilled the champagne glasses.

"Friends, it is with great pleasure that I welcome you to our home to join with us in wishing my son, Evan, and his beautiful bride-to-be, Christina, as much joy and happiness as my beloved Marie and I have had throughout our lives. Evan has chosen the perfect match and we, in the short time we have known her, have come to love her as our own." He lifted his glass and said, "A toast, to Evan and Christina." Everyone lifted their glasses, clinking the delicate crystal to meet with their counterparts across the table.

Christina's eyes filled with tears of happiness. She wanted to pinch herself to see if she was dreaming. No, there was Becka, there was her Aunt Maria ... Vince, everyone. How could tomorrow bring her more happiness than this moment?

Marie said, "Another surprise, Christina. Nicole will be your main flower girl, but she will be behind Becka's children, one ring bearer and one tiny flower girl. Carliss will be your bridesmaid, and Becka will be your maid of honor. Tonio has agreed to act as an usher, and Jacques will be Evan's best man. All of the tuxedos have been fitted and the dresses have been completed. I hope you are happy with the arrangement."

Christina embraced Marie, tears of delight blurring her vision as she said, "You are so very, very wonderful. This means more to me than you can ever imagine. I have not been this happy for a very long time. Thank you both." She had focused on Andre, as he sat overseeing the festivities. It was indeed, a banquet to remember.

After dinner, Christina was surrounded by the entourage from Italy basking in the attention. They marvelled at the wealth and magnificence, the luxuriousness of their rooms in the chateau. Their every comfort had been seen to. *"Bella, bella,* Christina. You are so lucky. He is a fine man, this Evan D'Argent."

The hours flew by and Christina realized that she should get a good night's sleep before the wedding preparations, which would begin in mid-morning. She bade everyone a fond goodnight, and the revellers continued on well onto midnight. By then, all had imbibed much champagne and the talk and laughter began to ebb as the children had been put to bed, and the light string orchestra played softly in the background. One by one they filtered out of the room, wondering if they would be able to sleep with the anticipation of the great day to follow.

* * * * *

CHRISTINA WAS ALMOST ASLEEP when she heard a soft tapping upon her door. She arose from the bed, put on her dressing gown, and padded her way to the sound. A voice whispered, "Christina, it's Becka ... are you awake?"

"Of course I am silly. Don't stand out there all night."

"I just had to have a heart-to-heart with you." The two lifelong friends hugged and then seated themselves comfortably upon the massive bed, just as they had done for as long as they could remember. "Now, tell me the truth, how did you manage to land in the lap of luxury? Do you realize just how far you've come? I, for one, can't believe your good fortune."

"Neither can I, to tell the truth. Evan is good for me. He has my best interests at heart and he has said that although I may never love him as I loved Adam, he will settle for just being in my company for the rest of his life. Actually, what I didn't realize until we met once again in New York is that I do love him. And I truly believe that this love will grow until we are old and grey."

"That's what I wanted to hear. I couldn't bear it if you were substituting love for wealth and luxury. I know you are not a shallow person, but you have been through so very much, Chris, it just wouldn't seem right for you to forsake all and give up on yourself."

"I would never do that, Becka. Adam will always hold a special place in my heart, but he chose to walk away from what we could have shared. I guess the fact that I gave away his children was too much for any man to forgive. I couldn't believe that he would just turn on me. It was devastating. For many days I waited for him to come back and say he was sorry, but he never did. So, having made that choice, when Evan returned to me, I did the same. Perhaps it was a drastic measure to turn away from my life in New York, my career, and my ambitions, but Becka, I have made a large fortune and it is time to enjoy it all. I will still endeavour to find my children, but it seems such an impossible task. Going to the adoption agency is like approaching a stone wall with no way around. I keep hoping that Evan will be able to use his money and influence and find out further information that will keep my hope alive. The trail is so very, very cold. It's as if the earth opened and swallowed them up."

Sudden tears filled Becka's eyes as she could relate to Christina's lost babies, now that she was a mother herself. "I could never in a million years imagine my children taken from me. Andrea and Mario are as precious as life itself. I know how you feel."

The two women hugged and as Christina found herself yawning; the gesture being infectious, Becka yawned as well. They laughed together and Becka said, "Well this is the last evening that you will be Christina Corelli, but you are moving on to bigger and better things, I can see that now. I'll go now, good night Christina, sweet dreams."

"'Nite, Becka, thank you."

Christina lay back upon the satin pillows, her thoughts filled with some regret but she shrugged these off, and began to dream of the following day. It would be a new life, a different country, a whole strange and wonderful setting that she had found thus far, very pleasant, comforting and loving. She could not help but find happiness surrounded by so much love.

It was a beautiful morning in late fall, the early morning sun slanted in golden rays, touching and painting the garden with wonderful warm rays. The evening had brought a slight touch of frost, but this soon disappeared and once the fog had burned off, there was not a cloud in the sky. Happy the bride, the sun shines on ... her thoughts were positive, her heart filled with anticipation. Her reverie was broken by the sound of voices drifting up the staircase to the room overlooking the garden. She had opened the window, throwing the casements wide to catch the sun's rays. The wedding was scheduled for 2:00 p.m and there was much to do. An army of attendants was about to arrive, so she decided to dress casually in order to come down for breakfast. Everyone was there; her new family, her relatives, her dearest friends, but not Evan. Thinking something was wrong, she asked, "Marie, where is Evan?"

"Cherie, you must not fret. It is bad luck for the groom to see the bride on their wedding day, is that not so?"

"Of course, you're absolutely right."

Marie gestured for Christina to come sit beside her at the massive table as she imparted the day's plans. There were hairdressers, make-up artists, Dior staff here to dress the wedding party, last minute fittings, the florist and his entourage. It was all so exciting Christina felt her spirits soar; all this for a little girl from Cranston, Canada. It was a fairytale with the heartache and tribulations behind her. If only they would live happily ever after. It certainly would not be from a lack of trying.

The morning passed by in a flurry of activity. Christina was dressed to perfection. The room was quiet. Becka and Carliss stood beside her, the three of them reflected in the vast mirror. What a wonderful sight. The deep aubergine color of their dresses contrasted effectively beside the dazzling white of Christina's gown. They helped her to place her veil upon her head, the tiara all but lost in the gathered tulle. Becka looked out of the window and turned as she said, "The carriages are here, everyone has left for the church. The rest of the wedding party is waiting for us. I would say it's time, wouldn't you?"

Carliss said, "Yes, we only have twenty minutes to get to the church so we'd better be going." She planted a soft kiss on Christina's cheek. "Good luck, my dear. Evan is a wonderful man, and you deserve one another. I couldn't be happier for you both."

"Thank you, Carliss." Becka merely nodded in agreement, her smile saying it all. The three beautiful women descended the staircase where an attendant was waiting to help them on with the matching capes. The florist was at the church where they would receive their bouquets.

Christina knew that she would be in the limelight for the next many hours, drew a deep breath, and said, "Let's do it."

The carriages had been decorated for the occasion, white satin ribbon and red roses adorned the one carrying the bride and her bridesmaids, the dark burgundy Brougham drawn by two white horses. The carriage ahead of them contained Marie and Andre, and Nicole, Andrea and Mario. Sally, as the flower girl, looked adorable in her soft lilac satin and lace dress, her hair adorned with ribbons and flowers. Mario looked every inch a gentleman in a miniature tuxedo the color of doves. The white rose in his breast pocket was the final touch, lending him a festive air.

The twenty minute ride seemed to take forever. Christina thought her heart would burst with excitement. All thoughts of her past life were erased from her mind. She could hardly contain herself.

They arrived at the front of the massive stone church with great regalia. The photographers began their work as the carriages began unloading their precious cargo. Christina was able to ignore the flashbulbs having become accustomed to the paparazzi following her every move in New York. With bated breath she entered the church, the foyer darkened within, with only sunlight beaming through the stained glass windows. Her eyes grew accustomed to the changing light and she was escorted to a small room off the foyer. The florist waited within, as well as the tiny members of her wedding party. Christina had not given much thought as to who would accompany her down the aisle to give her away, as the task usually left up to her father ... but this would not be. She had chosen her Uncle Guido and he had happily accepted the task.

The clear, sweet tones of the soloist poured forth, filling the church with magnificent sound. When she had finished the last verse of Ave Maria, the pianist began to play the Wedding March.

Sally, armed with her basket of rose petals, walked beside Mario, who was carrying the velvet pillow bearing the rings. She strewed the petals lightly along the aisle, and as Nicole followed behind their footsteps she crushed the petals and released the scent of natural perfume wafting throughout the church. Carliss, as the bridesmaid followed Nicole, then Becka as maid of honour, walked in step to the march. All heads were now turned upon the procession passing by them.

Christina, her arm entwined in her Uncle Guido's smiled shyly as they made their way to the altar and approached Evan, his heart almost bursting as he stood beside his best man, Jacques.

A sigh escaped the guests as they gazed at the beautiful spectacle unfolding before them. The bride was unequalled in her carriage, her gown, her demeanour, and her shy smile, capturing the hearts of her guests. Her emerald eyes appeared to be larger than life as she focused upon Evan waiting in anticipation. Their eyes locked and she never once looked away.

A few of the professional photographers which had been hired for the occasion were allowed to take a few pictures just before the formal ceremony, but not during the actual exchanging of vows, this being a very religious part of the ritual. Pictures would be demeaning to the rite of marriage.

Respecting their privacy, they began to click and posture when the minister pronounced that they be husband and wife.

A great burst of sound emanated from the crowd, a though they had let out a collective sigh. It was a moment frozen in time; the color, the grandeur of the church, the scent of the flowers, the sparkle of fine jewellery. This was a wedding that would live in the hearts of thousands.

After Evan and Christina had signed the register, they found themselves outside the church, being kissed and hugged repeatedly, as they made their way down the path to the limousine. The carriages were filled with the wedding party and would return to the chateau for the formal garden party. Flashbulbs lit the air around them, brighter than the afternoon sunlight and the limo afforded an escape from the tirade. In the backseat Evan said, "Well, my darling Mrs. D'Argent, we actually did it. I can't tell you how happy I am."

"Evan, my darling, I meant every one of my vows. I will make certain that we are always this happy every day of our lives. I promise."

His answer was a long and passionate kiss that would have gone on forever, if Jean hadn't interrupted by saying, "We're almost there, you two. Save it for this evening." Evan and Christina both laughed at his admonishment.

Thus began their new life together. Christina felt that she had been plucked from the hustle and bustle of New York, and put gently down in fairyland. She did realize that this was her new reality, but had no regrets. Nothing could top this.

Within the walls of the large chateau there was created, without Evan and Christina's knowledge, a separate and totally refurbished suite of rooms that rivalled even the most lavish hotel in Europe. It was built for them and presented to them during the wedding banquet. Andre and Marie were especially pleased by the loving response of their new daughter-in-law.

As the evening wore on, Christina became rather tired. The day had been so full of emotion, tears of happiness at seeing all of her closest friends and relatives. She threaded her way through the crowd of tables and dancers, and at last was at Evan's side. She whispered into his ear that she would meet him upstairs within the hour, confessing her fatigue.

He, too, was feeling the day's emotion and the thought of further hours of celebration was not at all welcoming.

Christina made her way discretely up the staircase, down the corridor and entered the beautiful suite of rooms that was to be her new home. She decided that a hot bath would refresh her and she would be in a much more romantic mood when Evan joined her.

She had just finished bathing and had dressed in the erotic nightgown which had been a wedding gift the House of Dior. It was absolutely stunning, clinging in all the right places, flowing luxuriously to the floor, the silken material like velvet touching her skin. She smiled at the vision in the mirror, envisioning Evan beside her.

Just then the door opened and he stood in awe of the vision before him. They had been living together for some time but he had never seen her look this beautiful. Her hair shone with a new lustre, and the light in her eyes as she met his was full of love and longing. As his eyes moved downwards, his breath caught in his throat. He crossed the room in long strides and encircled her in his arms. No words were necessary. They were husband and wife, about to begin a new life, and he could control himself no longer. He lifted her gently up in his arms, strode to the large four-poster bed, and placed her upon the satin coverlet strewn with fresh rose petals.

She moaned and said his name, over and over. Within minutes their lovemaking reached a crescendo of emotion, both experiencing new heights of passion, secure within the knowledge that they were now joined together in mind, body and spirit.

Evan was the first to speak as he relaxed beside the long length of her lithe body. "Christina, I don't have the words to tell you how happy I am ... this whole day has been absolutely wonderful, and now that we are alone, this is the best of all. I promise to love you all the days of my life."

For just a split second Christina reacted to those words. Someone else had said the exact same thing to her many years before and she grimaced at the old broken promise. Evan was too lost in his own happiness to see the reaction and she quickly recovered as she replied, "Evan, you needn't promise your love, I feel it every day when we are together. Your every thought and move is always for my concern. When we enter a room, you hold the door open, when we meet people, you are the one to introduce me with such pride in your voice, when we go out in public, you take care that I am never jostled by the crowds ... I could go on much longer, but know this ... I have no doubts whatsoever of your love for me, and I only hope that I am worthy of it."

Their conversation took on a less intensely emotional turn and finally both yawned, kissed goodnight and snuggled in for a well-deserved sleep. During the night Christina awoke for no apparent reason and could not settle down. She slipped quietly out of bed, draped a robe about her and padded over to the window seat. As the moonlight bathed her in its soft blue light, Christina looked out over the grounds. Her thoughts were reminiscent of the course of her life. She could not believe that she had come this far. It was thousands of miles from her childhood beginnings, her beloved New York, her wonderful friends and family. Now, her new family was Andre, Marie, and Evan. It was as though she was living in a dream and was almost afraid to wake up in case it would all disappear.

She missed the warmth of the coverlet and hurried over to the bed to join Evan. As she snuggled against him she felt him stir but did not awaken. Soon sleep overcame her and it seemed as though her head had just touched the pillow when she heard Evan say, "Good morning, Mrs. D'Argent," and he kissed her long and hard.

Breathless from the kiss, she moved away from him, "Good morning, Mr. D'Argent. Hello to you too."

Because they were already comfortable in their day to day relationship, Evan plodded over to the bathroom and within minutes she heard the shower running. A knock on the door, Christina's reply to enter, brought the aroma of breakfast into the room. Julie, Marie's maid, smiled shyly as she said, "Madame sends her greetings to you both, and hopes that you enjoy your breakfast. The guests are having breakfast in the dining room but Madame thought you might enjoy a little more privacy before coming down to wish them goodbye. Some have already left for the airport, but you said your farewells last evening. Bon appetite, Madame."

"*Merci*, Julie. Tell Madame Marie we will be down shortly."

Evan appeared, towelling his hair. "Something smells delicious. I'm famished." As he surveyed the lavish tray of hot croissants, a bowl of caviar, French puff pastry, crisp bacon and eggs Benedict, he began filling his plate. Christina was just as hungry, the aroma of food had spiked her appetite and she joined him.

Christina said, "I have to hurry down to say goodbye to Becka, Tonio and the children. I have some gifts to give them. My Aunt Maria and Uncle Mario have already left to return to Toronto, but Maggie and John are still here. I'll tell them you will join us."

Christina heard the murmur of conversation emanating from the large dining hall as she descended the staircase. She was spotted by her aunt. "Good morning, Christina, come join us."

Happily, she chose a chair that faced almost all of her remaining guests, aligned beside Andre and Marie. No one spoke for a minute then everyone began to speak at once. "What an absolutely lovely wedding. The whole day was so perfect. We hate to leave this wonderful place." Someone lifted a coffee and they drank a toast to the beginning of Christina's new life. Again someone spoke, "Don't forget to visit us very soon. We will miss you terribly." This from Becka.

Maggie lifted her cup, "To my wonderful partner, Christina, whom I love as my own sister. I wish her all the happiness in the world, but we must keep in touch. She is the lifeblood of our company."

Christina blushed at the accolades given to her and basked in the warmth of their well wishes. "How can I say goodbye to you all? You are so very important to me. I wish we could move you all here to France, or else pick up this chateau and drop it the middle of upstate New York."

Everyone agreed to the fairytale proposal as they were joined by a beaming Evan. "Don't worry, we will be visiting you all in the very near future, or at least we are just a phone call away."

The next few hours rushed by. The limousine whisked a party of relatives away, and returned within the hour to claim another load. By noon everyone had left, and the D'Argent family was alone. Christina was saddened by their departure, but her spirits lifted at the happiness shining in Evan's eyes. They had no plans for the remainder of the day as they were not leaving for their honeymoon until the next day. Evan retired to the library with his father to go over some new plans for a large cargo ship they were to build. Marie and Christina wiled away the hours planning a new rose garden, an extension of Marie's well established one.

Evan and Christina made love that evening but it did not hold the passion of the previous night. They had established an already comfortable relationship and found nothing wrong in returning to it. Sometime during the night the wail of the fire engines' sirens awakened them. The phone rang repeatedly from the downstairs hall and a loud knocking on the door brought Evan to a rude awakening. "Evan, it's the shipyard. It's on fire. You must hurry. Your father has already left for the docks."

Evan was out the door within minutes, the concern written on his face. "I'll call you as soon as I can Christina, stay here."

She nodded and placed her arm around Marie, the two women drawing comfort from each other. "We can do nothing, Marie, Evan will call us."

"When Andre spoke to someone on the telephone, he mentioned that there was a large explosion in the chemical storage area. It is apart from the construction building but the whole shipyard could be in danger if the fire is allowed to spread." Marie shuddered.

Christina suggested that they go downstairs and have a large brandy followed by hot tea.

They could do nothing else but worry throughout the ensuing hours.

Within a few hours, the silence was broken by the jangle of the telephone. It was Evan. He was sending a car to pick them up and take them to the hospital. Andre had been badly burned trying to save an employee trapped within the burning building. The firemen had arrived in time to pull them both out, but his father was suffering from smoke inhalation as well. Marie's heart beat rapidly as the color drained from her face. Christina caught her as she collapsed.

With Julie's help the two women placed Marie in the limousine and Christina joined her. They were soon at the hospital entrance. Marie had calmed down enough and had regained some of her strength. Nevertheless, Christina held her arm as they entered the emergency department. Christina seated the distraught Marie in a chair and approached the desk. The nurse immediately called the doctor who was attending the burn victims. Evan suddenly appeared, his face blackened by the soot and smoke, his eyes full of shock and horror. "Christina, *Maman*, it's okay, he's alive. He has burns on his arms and face, but the worst is the smoke damage to his lungs. Come with me. Don't be frightened by the oxygen mask. It's helping him to breathe. The doctors have given him something for the pain."

Marie's heart was in her mouth as she clung to her son's arm. "Andre, oh Andre, my dear.

Can you hear me?"

Andre opened his eyes and was grateful to see his beloved Marie. "Don't worry *mon cherie*, I'll be all right. But I have to stay in the hospital for a few days. At least until they say my burns are healing. We managed to save all but the chemical storage building. Everyone is safe."

Marie began to cry. The tears ran unchecked as she touched her lips to her husband's hand.

He said through the mask, "There, there my love, no tears."

Marie, Evan and Christina spoke with the doctor regarding Andre's condition. He assured them that his burns appeared to be superficial but would require dressing changes, and they were going to monitor his lungs. "You should all go home and get some rest. It's been a long night. I'll call you later on today after he has rested and had some X-rays taken. Please, go home."

"Thank you, Doctor. Yes, we'll leave, but we'll be back here early on. Goodbye, and thank you again." Evan took hold of his mother's arm and Christina took hold of the other as they left the hospital. "Are you all right?" he asked

"Yes, Evan. Now that I have seen and spoken to him, I'm much better, thank you. I am very tired. A few hours' sleep will do me much good."

After they had made Marie comfortable in her room, Christina and Evan returned to their own quarters. "Evan, we can't go on our honeymoon tomorrow after all that's happened. You are needed at the shipyards, and Marie and I have to attend to your father. I insist we postpone our trip."

"You are the best. It may be sometime before we get back on line at the dock, maybe even months. Does that bother you?"

"No, Evan, we can't travel through Christmas and I don't relish the thought of going to Greece, Spain, and Portugal in the middle of the winter. I love to ski but I would rather soak up the sun. We can surely wait until the time is right." Christina showed no disappointment whatsoever, her concern was for her new family.

The following morning Evan had already left for the factory before Christina finally stirred. Her first thoughts were for Marie and Andre. She dressed hurriedly and was delighted to see that Marie was in the spacious kitchen. "Good morning, Marie. Did you sleep well?"

"I managed a few hours but I was too worried about Andre. It was so very hard to leave him in the hospital. We've been separated only one other time during our marriage. I know that the doctors were optimistic about his burns but I worry about his lungs." Marie looked tired and worn.

"We'll leave as soon as you are ready and we can get an update on his condition. I'm sure you'll feel much better after we get some news. Evan has left for the factory and will probably be gone all day, so we have one another for company."

"It is so wonderful of you to postpone your honeymoon. I can't thank you enough." Marie said.

"Don't even worry about it. You are my family and we couldn't possibly think of leaving you during this tragedy. Evan and I have a lifetime ahead of us and will probably take more than one honeymoon trip," Christina replied. "Let's get started."

Jean had the limousine parked in the driveway, his services at their disposal. They were soon on their way and reached their destination within a short while. Marie and Christina approached the Emergency Department desk clerk and were directed to Andre's room.

"Good morning, my dear," Marie said. A warm smile greeted her, and Marie was surprised that the burns to Andre's face were superficial and not even bandaged. He did look a fright though.

"Shall I leave you two alone?" asked Christina.

"No, please stay. Did Evan have any news this morning about the extent of the damage?" Andre waited for her reply.

"I'm sorry, Andre, but I didn't speak to him, as he was up at dawn and left to survey the aftermath. I expect he'll call later to update us. We'll keep you posted. From what I gathered last night when we spoke, the fire appeared to have started in the chemical building … Evan mentioned a loud explosion, and he believes it was contained to that building alone."

Andre's look of relief was evident as he settled back down onto the pillows.

They chatted for a half hour more, until Andre appeared to be tiring. He was beginning to show signs of being short of breath and the nurse suggested that he rest. They could return in the afternoon or evening and they would have more on his condition. The women agreed and reluctantly said their goodbyes.

Jean was there to collect them and they were home within the hour.

Marie said, "I think I will have that sleep that I missed last night. I feel so much better now. Thank you, Christina."

"I'll see you when you awaken," she replied.

Christina spent the latter part of the morning in her new surroundings. Although the D'Argents had full maid and housekeeping services, Christina felt it was her duty to sort out her drafting desk and organize the area set aside for her work. The task didn't take up too much time and, when done, she decided a turn about the grounds would do her a world of good. She could collect her thoughts and reminisce upon the past few wonderful days, storing in her heart all of the memories of her wedding celebration and her dear friends.

By lunchtime Christina realized she was very hungry, having skipped breakfast because of their hasty visit to the hospital. Surprisingly, Marie was there in the kitchen, preparing something for them. Apparently, Evan had called shortly before and was going to the hospital to check upon his father and would be home soon after for lunch. Christina was glad that he had called his mother.

Lunch was ready when Evan arrived. "Hello, *Maman*, Christina. I'm home." "We're in the kitchen, Evan. Come join us."

Marie asked, "Did you see your father? He looked much better this morning when we were there."

"Yes and the doctor says we can take him home tomorrow morning. He will have to take it easy until the lungs are healed but with fresh air and sunshine and *Maman's* cooking he will be his old self in no time," Evan began, filling his plate as he spoke.

They engaged in small talk during the meal and reluctantly Christina had to say goodbye as Evan had to return to the factory. The work crews had to be organized and he did not want to take the boat building crew away from their work, so he had to hire a construction crew from the city. Everything was falling into place and they could all breathe a sigh of relief, for one thing that no one had been killed or badly injured. That was of the greatest importance.

Chapter Forty

AS EXPECTED, ANDRE MADE a full recovery over the next few weeks and the family returned to normal. Christina and Marie were preparing for Christmas and Evan and his father were very busy at the factory. Christina was enthralled by the Christmas celebrations, as she had never been a part of a European holiday season. Instead of Santa Claus, they referred to the big guy as Father Christmas or *Pere Noel*. The Christmas Eve festivities combined eating and drinking, carolling, visiting neighbours and hosting a large party for their servants and their families. Evan dressed up as Father Christmas much to Christina's delight. She was sad when the week was over but Evan was grateful that their lives could return to a normal routine.

The New Year's Eve party was formal and very elegant. The women wore their finest jewellery, dressed in the latest fashions from Paris, drank champagne and gossiped the night away. Christina basked in the admiration and respect that was given her as a member of the D'Argent family. For once in her life, she was not Christina Corelli, international model and darling of the fashion world. She thought about it later, and she confessed to Evan that it felt good not to be photographed everywhere she went, the cameras flashing so close to her face as if to frighten her. Besides, she joked, she didn't want anyone to address her husband as 'Mr. Corelli.'

Christina began working on the Spring Collection for their fashion house, the designs practically flying off the drafting board. She had so many ideas, but would leave the selection of color, material and embellishment to the team in New York. The weeks passed and before long it was nearing the end of March.

Evan asked her, "Christina, how do you feel about going on our honeymoon? I thought we could leave right away."

She looked thoughtfully at him and replied, "That sounds wonderful. The weather will be perfect in April, the trees will be in leaf and the flowers will be in bloom, that is depending on where you intend to take me."

"Just pack what you need, the absolute minimum as I intend to outfit you for whatever climate we encounter. I didn't cancel our plans, just put them on hold and everything can be arranged within a matter of hours. If you really want to know, I'll tell you but don't you think that the element of surprise adds to the enjoyment?"

"Evan, as usual you always have the best answer. Yes, I can be ready whenever you say, and no, I don't want to know. Surprise me!" she replied.

Andre and Marie bid them goodbye, good luck, and safe journey their voices still ringing in their ears as they drove down the long access from the Chateau.

"Oh my God, Evan. A world cruise! How long will it take? Two months? But that will take us into summer and I have to be in New York before then?" Christina said.

"Well, we can always leave the ship for a few days until you have had your fill of New York and then continue on. By then we will have cruised the Carribean and will be ready to dock in Miami. We can take a flight to New York...then fly back to Europe if that suits you.

But our honeymoon won't be over. We have to tour the Greek Islands, and revisit our Amalfi Coast. There is more after that but that's enough information for now." Christina nodded in reply.

There appeared to be a change in plans at the last minute but Evan and Christina had nothing but time and they decided to cruise the Mediterranean on the family yacht. Their first stop was in Cannes, where they had met and Evan had fallen in love at first sight. Christina was enchanted with Monte Carlo as Evan new she would be. After Monte Carlo they left the ship and flew to the Italian Lake District...Lake Como. The Hotel D'Este was famous because of its location, excellent hospitality, and impeccable service; all their needs were catered to at their slightest whim. Celebrities from all over the world came and went at their discretion and they were never hounded by the press. Evan and Christina were delighted to have made many new and famous friends throughout their month-long stay.

As the month of June approached, Christina was anxious to hear from New York and begged Evan to take a break so that she could catch up on the spring collection and then could carry on with the fall and winter ones. Time was of the essence. As they surveyed the magnificent grounds of the hotel against the backdrop of the deep blue waters of Lake Como, the spell of their surroundings promised to linger in their hearts and memories for a lifetime.

Christina called Maggie, telling her to expect them at the end of May. They would call her from the airport. Maggie was ecstatic. It seemed so long since they had seen Christina. When they broke the connection, Christina said to Evan, "Something in Maggie's voice, Evan, she didn't sound herself. Maybe it's all the stress she's been under. I hope nothing is wrong that can't be fixed."

"Don't worry so, Christina. Maggie and John have been at that business for a long time.

You'll find out soon enough. Now, relax my love, we're still on our honeymoon." "You're absolutely right, as usual," she replied.

They drove to Rome and caught a flight to New York the next day. It was difficult to leave the captivating Lake region but Christina's heart wasn't really in it any longer. She was much more anxious to catch up on what was happening in New York.

The long flight was exhausting, as Christina was unable to sleep while traveling. She could only catch a few minutes of rest and that wasn't enough to restore her. At long last they reached La Guardia airport and hastily disembarked. Maggie had sent a car to collect them and with luggage on board they were soon within the streets of Manhattan. Evan decided to stay behind once they had registered at the Hilton and Christina returned to the waiting car and her much anticipated meeting with John and Maggie.

"Miss Corelli to see you, Maggie." The voice from the intercom brought the welcome of Christina's arrival.

"Don't keep her waiting a minute longer, Caroline," Maggie answered. "My God, it's good to see you. You look absolutely wonderful. Marriage does agree with you, I must say."

"Why don't you try it sometime?" Christina smiled as they hugged one another. "Easy to say when you've found the right man," Maggie said.

Christina folded her coat over an empty chair and placed her purse on top. She sat across from Maggie who was ensconced behind her massive desk, her papers and files well organized in neat piles, some to be worked upon, others to be filed.

"You know, Maggie, you belong behind a desk. Some people are overwhelmed by it all, but you thrive on it. Do you understand what I'm saying?"

"I guess I do, but sometimes, just sometimes mind you, I wish for greener pastures, a calmer less stressful life, but it seems I get drawn back into the picture very easily. John says I have ink for blood, and commerce for a heart. I'm glad you're here. We have scheduled a meeting with Kate Winslowe, it's about time you met her. We think she's doing a good job, but we would appreciate your opinion."

"That's why I'm here, among other things. I brought the fall and winter designs along. I drafted them before we went on our honeymoon. As you know, Evan and his father were faced with a long re-construction of the shipyard's chemical building after the fire. It was not extensive but the fire itself was extremely intense and many people could have been injured. We were very fortunate. As you know, there's not much to do during the winter months, no gardening, no outdoor activities, so I took the opportunity to work."

She opened the large portfolio, which Maggie proffered, and they laid the large illustrations out upon the spacious table designed just for this purpose. Christina didn't color her drawings, she left the selection of material, texture, and color to the manufacturing team and they were never far from the mark.

The two women were engrossed in their work when John and a very tall, striking woman in her early thirties entered the office. John immediately crossed the room, "Christina, it's good to see you again. You look wonderful."

Christina returned the greeting with, "Good to see you as well, John. Ellen is taking good care of you."

She glanced towards the stranger prompting John to introduce them. "Kate Winslowe, I would like you to meet the other third of our partnership. This is Christina Corelli."

"I would have known you anywhere. After all, you are the signature model and the marketing face of this company. My pleasure." Kate studied the impression she hoped she had made upon this incredibly beautiful and very important figure. "Shall we get down to business?" Kate asked, as she passed copies of the agenda. They discussed the financial report, the new marketing strategies, and the ongoing visions of the seasons. By the look of it all, not too much had changed since Christina's departure a year and a half ago, and she was largely disappointed in it all. She had fully expected something fresh and new, as Maggie had fully sold her on the intrepid and highly talented Kate Winslowe. Perhaps when Christina knew her better she would change her view, but she had always trusted her first instincts and something was just not in sync. She decided to take the role of observer, and her impressions became almost a certainty when she watched Kate in action. She was very smooth, polished, her attitude compromising, and her convictions easily changed and moulded to John and Maggie's. Christina decided that Kate was a willing and sincere employee in the presence of her bosses, but what was under that ice queen exterior? Why was it that when she smiled, it didn't reach her eyes? She thought it was cold, very cold. Christina decided that she had better focus upon the meeting at hand and put aside her first impressions. John was not an expert upon women's clothing, as he had been the search-and-discover aspect of their modeling agency, while Maggie controlled the commerce side of the corporation. Christina was their inspiration and marketing figure, and had been greatly missed. It appeared that Kate was now in charge of the models, and for the time being they had almost none in their repertoire. Kate had convinced administration that it would be cheaper to hire freelance models, or sub-contract them from other modeling agencies. Somehow this didn't sit right with Christina, but as she had been absent for such a long time and felt responsible for having abandoned her role within the company, she said nothing. The meeting lasted for a few hours, they broke for lunch and decided to resume later on that afternoon without Kate. She had presented her monthly report, taken the suggestions on memo from the meeting, and promised to work on them straightaway.

The three long-time friends turned their attention to the new designs. John suggested that it just might be time to look to the off the rack sales competition, instead of the runway seasonal line. When they had furnished the models the business had been most lucrative, but now that they were in the design and manufacturing business they had to look to other markets.

Maggie and Christina agreed that it could be a lucrative prospect and drafted a proposal to be presented to the large department stores within the Greater New York area with hopes of expansion to the west coast. Many of Christina's designs were not too outlandish or outspoken to demand a one-of-a-kind for a client, but were casual. Some were for daytime wear to appeal to the growing female workforce and a wonderful array of evening wear that was perhaps too expensive for most, but a must have for the New York elite.

Late that afternoon they decided to call it quits. John and Maggie couldn't believe the ground they had covered and how much had been accomplished. "We haven't done this much positive work in months. Christina, you're a breath of fresh air. I guess I had forgotten just how serious and committed you are to this company." Maggie hugged her as she uttered the words.

Christina's eyes welled with tears. This kind of praise from her mentor was wonderful. John looked upon them with great pride before leaving the board room. They had agreed to meet for dinner and drinks later on that evening. Christina suggested the hotel dining room where she and Evan were staying. It was convenient, as well as a popular restaurant catering to an international clientele, the food much to their liking.

Christina brought Evan up to speed concerning their meeting. He was pleased about the reservations for dinner. They had coffee brought to them by room service, Christina relaxed and Evan read the New York Times. These two had no need for constant conversation, they were comfortable in one another's company, each preoccupied with their own thoughts.

The four met in the lobby and entered the bar situated at the far end of the spacious dining room. Gleaming white tablecloths, waiters in black and white formal wear, soft spoken clientele seated comfortably, their needs catered to quickly by the service personnel. The high ceilings were hung with crystal chandeliers placed strategically so as to shed soft light upon the patrons below, providing a relaxing and soothing atmosphere.

Dinner was wonderful. They talked about the wedding and how much they had enjoyed themselves and thanked Evan for making the necessary arrangements. They agreed that he was a hard man to refuse once he had made a request. They drank a toast to Evan. Christina felt a rush of pride for her husband. His continental upbringing and jet-set ways allowed him to fit into any society within minutes as others felt his ease and relaxed as well.

They parted company a few hours later, Christina promising to come into the office to tie up any loose ends before she had to resume her honeymoon. Evan was busily preparing the itinerary for the next leg of their journey, so he would be occupied for a few days.

As they were preparing for bed, Christina said, "Evan, do you always trust your instincts?" "Instincts concerning what, my love?" he asked.

"Just instincts. I guess I mean about people you have just met."

"Mostly, I do, but I like to reserve judgment until I have seen what they can accomplish.

Why, is something troubling you?"

"I don't know. This afternoon when we met with our new Administrative Officer Kate Winslowe, I watched her interaction with Maggie and John. She is a master at manipulation. Her proposals were turned around to make them appear as though we had presented them, and of course John and Maggie promptly agreed with everything in the long term. I honestly don't think that she carries out their proposals but interjects her own and gives a false report at their monthly meeting. I know that sounds serious but that's the impression I came away with, today."

"You're right. It is serious. Have you tried talking to Maggie about it?" he asked

"No, we didn't have time, but I still have a few days left and I could ask her about it at lunch tomorrow when it's just her and I."

He crossed the room and kissed her goodnight. They were soon settled comfortably, both agreeing that what they needed most was a restful night's sleep and decided that a respite from lovemaking could wait, just for tonight.

Christina and Maggie had a very productive session the following morning, both focusing upon the work at hand knowing full well that they had to accomplish a monumental amount of subjects before Christina's departure.

Maggie took Christina to her favourite place for lunch. It was a small, usually crowded diner just around the corner from the Cole Corporation offices. The noise and other conversations blended together and if any one cared to eavesdrop on someone their words were be lost in the crowd. It was possible, though, to have a serious conversation between two people and Christina decided to seize the opportunity.

"Maggie, I have something to ask you and I'm not sure just how to approach the subject." "Just blurt it out, Christina. We have no secrets."

"Okay, here goes. First of all, have the police made any arrests after my attack and Suzanne's murder? I still have the odd nightmare about it. Did they find out why she was killed? It couldn't have been just a random killing. When she called me, her voice was so distressed and she was terrified that someone was going to harm her. She begged me to come and get her as she had no means or money to flee the apartment. If I had only been a half hour earlier she would be alive today. What does it all mean? Do you have any idea?"

Maggie waited a few moments before replying, collecting her thoughts. She did not want to disappoint Christina but she didn't want to arouse her suspicions regarding Suzanne's real reason for her demise. "Christina, the detective in charge, a Mr. Rick Halloran of the NYPD, has been forthcoming with as much information as he is allowed to release without jeopardizing the investigation. It seems Suzanne was making extra money on the side by buying drugs for a crime organization and she reneged upon a transaction. It seems that she and her boyfriend set up a buy wherein he would supply the drugs and she would make the buy. As it turns, they thought they could get away with keeping both the drugs and the money, but as you know it didn't work out. Suzanne's boyfriend's body turned up on the East River a few days after she was murdered. The police are trying to get information on the crime organization by working undercover, so we are not allowed to discuss this with anyone. This is within the strictest confidence."

"I understand, Maggie, but it's been months."

"I guess this all takes time and with all of the murders taking place in New York, we can't expect them to solve this overnight. Apparently, the organization is suspected to be large and far-reaching. Trust Suzanne to get herself involved so deeply, and in doing so give her life. I haven't heard from Detective Halloran for quite some time but I have been told not to contact him, as he will keep us informed. We have to trust them on this, Christina. That's about all I can say about it."

"I'm glad no one asked me to pick out a suspect from a line-up because I couldn't do it. The man grabbed me from behind as I got into the apartment and saw Suzanne getting pushed towards the window. When I tried to scream my attacker slashed my face and I passed out. That's what most likely saved my life."

"Let's not talk about this any longer. When I think how close we came to losing you, I shudder at the thought. Have you and Evan any plans after you return to France, long-range ones, I mean?" Maggie asked.

"No, not really. He's totally committed to the shipyard. Apparently, he has plans to build a racing boat and when the summer season begins he likes to take it easy and says he is going to enter a few of the regattas, just to see how good he is at the sport. It doesn't sound too dangerous; at least I hope it isn't. He won't tell me what the next leg of our journey is, as he's still working on it. We'll probably be gone most June and July, but I'd like to get back to Cherbourg to help Marie with our new rose gardens. She enters most of the flower shows and has even developed a hybrid tea rose that bears her name. I couldn't ask for a better mother-in- law. In fact, although she is as different from my mother as night from day, she is always there if I need any advice or guidance. She is very supportive when I am at the drafting table and gives me all the privacy I could possibly want. There is one thing, though, that I know is troubling her ... that is, she hopes Evan and I will have a few children. She loves the sound of children's laughter within the chateau. I haven't confided to her about the twins and I don't think I will. The fact that I relinquished them at birth still haunts me and I just don't want to take the chance that she will react the way Adam did. I couldn't bear it."

Christina's face had paled somewhat during her recollections of troubled times and Maggie could only sit and sympathize with her. She prayed Christina's life would continue on an upward course. Evan was exactly what she needed. Maggie asked, "Forgive me for asking you this Christina, and you needn't answer if you feel it too intrusive, but did you marry Evan on the rebound or as a needed sanctuary from Adam's rejection?" She reached across the table and took hold of Christina's hand in comfort.

Christina looked long and hard into Maggie's searching eyes, and replied, "At first, I was thankful for his presence. He took my situation in hand, brought me away from everything that was traumatic, introduced me to a new way of life, as well as his friends and family, and then finally we reached a decision to live together in our villa on the Amalfi Coast. I can forget my troubles and concentrate on my work. No one means more to me now than Evan. I have learned that there are more kinds of love than just the highs and lows of unbridled passion. He is caring of my emotions and my needs, he comforts me when I am hurt, he protects me from the paparazzi, everything. Sometimes, I think that I can never make it all up to him. But I truly believe that this kind of love is completely enduring. Do you understand what I'm saying?"

"Of course I do, and I am so very happy for you. Many times I think of Jean and the affair we had during the summer when we were in the south of France. Those are the happiest times of my life, but I realized that even if he had left his wife, where would we live? I couldn't live in France, and he couldn't adapt to New York. So that would leave us both homesick and miserable. Perhaps it just wasn't meant to be." Maggie sighed and she had a long-lost look in her eyes.

Christina squeezed her hand and said, "You really made the only choice opened for you. I don't think I could have been quite so forthright, even if the truth was staring me in the face. But then, we're very different from one another. Jean will ask about you when we return, I'm sure about it. He always does. He spends more time with us at the chateau than he does with his estranged wife, and has no one new in his life. Any time you care to visit us is just fine with me."

"That's a great comfort Christina, thank you."

The two women left the diner and returned to their workplace. The afternoon flew by, and Christina returned to the hotel by five p.m. Evan was relaxing by the pool, refreshed from his swim. His smile was a welcome sight to Christina as she realized that she had finished a heartrending and trying day. She had not broached the subject of Kate Winslowe; somehow she had been sidetracked with the topic of Suzanne.

Chapter Forty-One

Five Years Later

"WELL, WELL, THE PRINCESS has returned. How long has it been this time? Five or six weeks, give or take a few days?" Evan was not only angry but he had been drinking again.

Christina was much too tired to argue and said, "Not now, Evan, the flight was noisy, rough, and exhausting. I don't want to fight with you."

"Shall I ask you how your trip to New York was this time around?"

"Please, Evan, I've only just arrived and I can't deal with your belligerent attitude."

"So now I'm belligerent," he poured another drink straight up from the decanter at the sideboard.

"I've barely had time to say hello to Marie and Andre, and I begged off from visiting because I really am very tired."

"Christina, we can't go on this way. When you are here, all I see you do is sit at that drafting table and sketch away, design after design. We haven't been out on the yacht for many months; we haven't entertained, or been entertained. I go to the shipyards in the morning, come home to you willing to discuss your designs, which I am no longer interested in, have dinner, a few drinks, and then to bed, and the cycle begins all over again. For Christ's sake, I'm only thirty five years old and I feel like my father."

"All right, you asked for it. For your information, New York gives me the boost I need to be able to suffer through your elite friends' boring conversations during luncheons, evening dinners, and after-theatre parties. I don't care who's getting divorced, I don't care who's having an affair, and I really don't give a damn about politics. My so-called women friends love to have lunch with me on the off chance that they will be photographed by some rag magazine lunching with me, and then they will make up some nonsense headlines that will sell their smut. Yes, I have made a name for myself here on the continent, but that's due to all of my hard work. The least you could do is recognize my creative talents."

"If that's how you feel, perhaps you should make a choice. You can't go on living half of the year in New York, with four trips a year six weeks at a stretch, and still feel that we have a loving and fruitful life thousands of miles away from your previous home."

Christina's face drained of all color but her eyes blazed with anger. "And what about your latest weekend toy? That goddamned power boat that you roar up and down the coast in is a joke. You say you have racing in your blood but it's more than that. I believe you have become an adrenaline junkie and that you love living on the edge."

As she accused him of his latest hobby taking up their weekend time together, she recalled the day he had taken her out into the harbour. He had told her to hang on because she was about to get the ride of her life. Within minutes the powerful speedboat was up on plane and they were skimming the water, barely touching it as the boat sped out into the bay, leaving a large wake behind. The wind whipped her hair in her face and the spray lashed her face, hurting her eyes. She clung to the seat in terror, while he had laughed at the look on her face. She held out for a few minutes until, in a state of frenzied terror, she begged him repeatedly to slow down. Finally, face jubilant from the power rush, he decided to slow the boat, cutting the throttle back until they were no longer up on plane and were cruising at a normal speed. He had laughed at her terror, saying, "Is that better my love, or shall we try it again?"

"Please, no Evan. I love the yacht, but this boat is just not my idea of enjoyment. I'd much rather leave the racing up to you. Perhaps one day, I'll come and watch the competitions, I just don't know."

"Well," he replied, "that's up to you, now isn't it? Why can't you take pleasure in whatever makes me happy? It's always about you, that's the problem."

"Please, Evan, just take me back to the dock."

His face had looked like chiselled stone as they made their way back to the marina slip. That was the first and last time she had ever set foot inside the speedboat, even though she knew he had been terribly disappointed. She could not enjoy herself when she was terrified, that was final.

Her thoughts were interrupted as he slammed out of the suite, saying that he had better things to do than argue with her, especially as he had early morning plans and wouldn't see her again for a few days. She attempted to ask him what they involved, but he was gone. Christina sat down on the sofa, a long sigh escaped her, and she put her head in her hands as the tears welled in her eyes and spilled over. She could not reach Evan. He had lost interest in her and she had been replaced by a powerboat. For a few years now, she had the distinct feeling that all she had become was an accessory, poised and beautiful on his arm as he paraded her throughout Europe. People flocked around them, drawn to the limelight that surrounded them. She had always been introduced as Mrs. Evan D'Argent, and never as Christina Corelli, but her picture was on magazine covers, her perfume and cosmetic products used as commercials on European television, and it became a thorn in his side. She decided that a hot bath and a good night's sleep would be the best remedy for calm after their tirade. She would discuss their situation in the morning. She waited for him to return to the suite to join her in bed, but he must have decided to occupy one of the many guest rooms within the chateau. How had they strayed so far from their loving relationship? Evan had become her best friend as well as the love of her life, and now they could barely occupy the same room without harsh words being exchanged or Evan pouring drink after drink from the decanter. When had he taken to drinking alone? It was almost as though he expected to gain courage from the bottle. She shrugged off her thoughts as she waited for sleep to overcome her.

Christina awoke around eight in the morning, ready to meet the day. Her jet lag was over, and she quickly dressed to join Marie and Andre in the breakfast room downstairs. "Good morning, Marie, Andre, it's so good to see you. You look well."

"Good morning, Christina, welcome home. We've missed you very much. When you left in mid-May we expected you home sooner, but if the fashion world has become as competitive as you say, then you must spend the time necessary to handle all of the tasks. It's already the end of June and the rose garden is doing well. We can take a walk after breakfast, if you wish."

Andre said very little. It was Friday and he was preoccupied with work. His health had improved since the fire and it just remained a bad memory. They enjoyed their breakfast, chatting about past events, social and otherwise. Christina loved them dearly, and they had become the closely knit family that she had longed for over the years. "Where is Evan? Has he come down for breakfast yet?" Christina asked.

Marie and Andre exchanged looks before Andre cleared his throat and replied, "Evan left very early this morning, Christina. He and Jean are taking the powerboat to Monte Carlo for the international speedboat races set for July first and second this weekend. They needed a day to travel."

Christina said, "I had no idea. Evan did say that he had plans over the next few days but didn't elaborate." The thought struck her that if she wanted to save her marriage perhaps it would be a good idea to become a spectator at the races and join him between competitions. "How can I get there to watch the races, Andre?"

"Why don't you surprise Evan and use the helicopter? I can make the arrangements early and you should be out of here by noon."

"I can't thank you enough, Andre. I'll go and pack a suitcase and be ready whenever you say. In the meantime, I would love to take a stroll around the grounds. I've really missed this place. As much as I love the hustle and bustle of New York, the solitude and serenity of the chateau estate rejuvenates me within hours of my return and my exhaustion and stress fade away."

Andre excused himself, gave Marie a loving kiss on the cheek, and said, "I'll call you as soon as the arrangements have been made, Christina." To his wife of nearly forty years, he said, "*Au revoir* Marie, until this evening. I shouldn't be late."

Andre was as good as his promise and the helicopter collected Christina shortly after twelve noon. She didn't even have to drive to the airport, as the chopper landed on the helipad near the guest house on the estate. Within hours, she was safely put down in Monte Carlo and placed a phone call to the Marina, where Evan and Jean were staying. Jean collected her. She was glad to see him, and inquired as to the day's racing agenda. Evan hadn't come with him, as he was extremely busy with his maintenance crew going over the boat engine. Everything had to be perfect. Jean said that Evan had been practicing for this race for a few months now, and had every chance of winning. Christina could hear the pride in Jean's voice as he spoke of his employer's latest venture.

Christina loved Monte Carlo. Evan and she had spent many wonderful vacations here, staying in the casino hotel or on the yacht when they were moored within the harbour marina. It was a playground for the rich and famous, and as they could be described as a very rich and famous couple, they fit right in with the rest of the crowd.

The first race was set for Saturday morning at ten a.m. Christina knew Jean would not spill the beans and tell Evan that she was here; it was to be a surprise. Also, she didn't want to change his focus from the condition of the boat and the upcoming race. She spent some time in the casino, but her luck wasn't there and she, not being an intense gambler, took her losses and left. She had a light evening dinner on the patio of the restaurant overlooking the harbour. It would have been a good start for the couple to begin to repair their broken relationship, as the magic of the sunset, and subsequent moonlight reflecting upon the water, created a soothing and romantic scene that was a perfect setting for a couple in trouble. Christina sipped her champagne and collected her thoughts. She hoped that Evan would win the race and his mood would be so high that the sight of her would only add to his happiness. He wasn't a totally unforgiving man, and she wished fervently that they could put aside the angry words and ugly scene after her return from the U.S.A.

Christina was up early the following morning. She looked out from the window of the upper floor of her room and was surprised by the activity in the harbour. The race course had been flagged by buoys and bumper pads coloured bright yellow and deep red. The crowds were beginning to gather by nine a.m. as the most avid fans wanted to get the best seats. She could have witnessed the race from the upper terrace of the hotel but she decided the best way to get totally involved was to sit side by side with the spectators. She met Jean in the lobby after breakfast and he said, "I didn't tell Evan that you were here, and I managed to get you the best seats that I could from a spectator point of view. They cost an arm and a leg, but seeing as this is one of the most popular races of the season, I could not allow you to watch from a poor angle. Shall we go over to the seats now? I will stay with you during the race as Evan won't need me for anything and he told me to go and enjoy myself."

Christina was thankful for the company. Jean was able to tell her how the course was set and that two speedboats at a time would race in what were described as heats. The fastest boat would then be able to race the winner of the previous heat and it would go on until the final heat on Sunday, when the winner would be declared. The luxurious yachts that had been moored in the slips had to be taken far enough out to sea so as not to hinder the racers. A shuttle boat collected them from their yachts and deposited them upon the docks. Everyone was in a festive mood, anticipating the excitement and placing side bets on the prospective winners. Christina found herself caught up in the excitement. Before she knew it the first race was on. Jean explained that Evan would not race until around one o'clock, but he thought she would enjoy the morning races just to get into the excitement of the day. Christina agreed, and sure enough she found herself rooting for the deep green and white speedboat, the owner of which was quite renowned in the world of racing. Happy that she had picked a winner for the first race, she began anticipating the next heat.

They took a short break for lunch and Jean left her for a few minutes to check with Evan. When he returned to their seats, he looked extremely happy as he described Evan's mood. "The boss says to be ready to celebrate, he has every intention of winning the race, and I believe him. He is in an exceptional mood and the boat appears to be in top condition. Cross your fingers for luck, Christina, this means a great deal to him."

She promptly crossed the fingers of both hands, looked skyward and said a prayer. Jean was pleased. "The race is about to start," he said.

She looked out across the harbour and saw Evan's boat in place beside his competitor's. The start gun sounded and the roar of the engines was almost deafening. The two boats were side by side for about a half mile when Evan's boat began to pull away. As they rounded the buoy the boat responded to his hand and he was able to maintain the small lead. Jean sat, silently pulling for his boss. Christina watched in wonder as she witnessed the skill which Evan had acquired during his practice sessions. The striping on the side of the boat appeared blood red in the afternoon sunlight. There wasn't a cloud in the sky ... it couldn't have been a more perfect day. The roar of the crowd was exhilarating, egging on the competitor to catch up. He immediately gave his boat full throttle and it leapt forward, the bow lifting up high in the water. Evan had not expected him to catch up as quickly and he, in turn, gave his boat full throttle. The two boats were side by side, neither giving an inch. Christina held her breath as they sped toward the docks. Suddenly, there was a loud noise heard above the voices of the crowd and they all watched in horror as the boats side-swiped one another. Evan's boat veered toward the dock while the other, being on the open water side, veered to the right while he attempted to take control. Evan was not so lucky. Christina grabbed Jean's hand and held on tightly. Evan struggled to gain control, but the boat had been up on plane and his steering was compromised. An ear-splitting crashing sound of metal and wood was heard and Christina watched the scene as though everything was in slow motion. Evan's boat became a great ball of smoke and flames as the boat collided into the dock. Evan was nowhere to be seen. The boat was reduced to rubble as most of the wreckage settled upon the water. Within seconds, sirens sounded and emergency crews were on the way to the dock. Christina's voice could be heard screaming, "Evan, oh my God, Evan. Please God, not Evan." Jean caught her as she fainted, oblivious to all but the vivid picture of the flames and acrid smell of fuel burning on the surface of the water.

Jean heard the collective sigh of shock and horror of the crowd, but he was oblivious to their reactions, as his first concern was for Christina. He scooped up her limp body, hurried down the steps of the gallery, and raced towards the nearest emergency vehicle. Two ambulance attendants were on site and placed her upon a stretcher. They took her vital signs and asked Jean some pertinent questions. He said, "She is Monsieur D'Argent's wife. She is in extreme shock and traumatized so badly that she fainted."

Jean realized that there was nothing he could do for Evan and decided that the best course of action was to ride along with Christina and see that she received the best possible care. He would insist that they keep her overnight in hospital. In the meanwhile, once she was resting comfortably, he would check with the harbour authorities about the cleanup of the accident, as well as having to make the heart-rending telephone to Evan's parents.

Christina moaned softly while they transferred her from the stretcher to a bed in the hospital. Nurses and an attending doctor examined her for any injuries but fully agreed that she was in deep shock, and they immediately administered an intravenous line and hooked her up to a monitor.

The information necessary to admit her for observation was provided for by Jean, and once done he took his leave, knowing Christina was in good hands. He had no idea what he was going to say to her when she finally awoke.

After meeting with the accident investigation team Jean was informed that there was nothing left of Evan's body and what was scattered over many meters should be left to nature. The wreckage of the burnt-out hull had already been towed away from the docks, and preparations were underway to repair the damaged dock. A loudspeaker informed the crowd that in respect for Monsieur D'Argent the rest of the day's races had to be postponed but would resume the next day. They were thanked for their concern and patience.

Jean decided that he should be in a quiet place to make the necessary phone call. The reality of what had just happened finally hit him and he felt his knees wobble. He sat down on a bench and gazed out upon the water. A sudden splitting headache threatened to overwhelm him but he steeled himself, took in a few very deep breaths, and attempted to calm himself. Awhile later, Jean arose from the bench and made his way to his hotel room. Once inside, he made his way over to the bed and settled down. He reached for the phone and dialed the senior D'Argent's number.

Madame D'Argent answered. *"Allo, c'est Madame D'Argent"*

"Madame, this is Jean. Please, Madame, is Monsieur D'Argent at home as well?"

"Oui, Jean. What is it?"

"Please, you must sit down. I have some very bad news and I just don't know how to tell you."

"What is it, just tell us. Is Evan all right? Has something happened to Christina?"

"There was a terrible accident at the boat races here in Monte Carlo. Evan was involved with another racer, they collided and Evan's boat exploded upon impact. He is dead, Madame."

"Mon Dieu," Madame D'Argent placed her hand over her heart and the tears began and she was unable to speak.

Andre took the phone away from his distraught wife and asked, "What has happened?"

"I'm so sorry Monsieur, Evan was in a terrible boating accident. His boat collided with another and exploded. He was killed instantly."

For a fraction of a minute, Andre could not speak. Finally, he said, "Jean, shall we come to Monte Carlo?"

"No, Monsieur, there is no need. I have to know your wishes, as well as Christina's. She is in hospital overnight because she was here and witnessed the accident. She was in shock and traumatized. I will see her tonight and discuss arrangements. Again, I am so sorry for your loss. Evan was much more than my employer; he was my confidante, my friend and as much as ever my family, as you all." Jean's voice began to break from grief as he attempted to quell the emotion the phone call had caused. By telling them of the accident, reality hit him and he had no choice but to accept the inevitable. His best friend was no longer with them. Jean squared his shoulders, realizing that he must be strong for the loving survivors. He said, *"Au revoir,* I will call you this evening. *Oui,* at eight o'clock, *oui, Monsieur.* Until then."

Jean would tell them later that there was nothing left to salvage of Evan's remains. They would probably be able to hold a family memorial service at the chateau but he would leave it up to them. His immediate concern was for Christina. He had no idea how she would handle the next few days. He glanced at his watch and saw that late afternoon was upon them. He decided to consult with the harbour authority and the police to find out if they had a financial obligation to the Monte Carlo Marina for the repairs.

Because Evan had become such a good friend to the Monaco Royal family, and their son-in- law was much involved with racing, the costs would be absorbed and Jean could leave at will. They were completely sympathetic to his loss and extended their heartfelt condolences to Evan's family. As hospital visiting hours approached at six p.m., Jean indulged in a light lunch, but found that once the food had arrived he had no appetite. His stomach felt as though it was full of rocks. His eyes welled with tears as the scene of the accident played over and over again in his mind. Finally, he could sit no longer and decided he would walk the distance to the hospital to clear his head. He had to rehearse what he would say to Christina, but first he would consult with her doctor before seeing her. She would most likely be heavily sedated and he didn't want to pressure her as to any arrangements, but she must assuredly be informed of the state of Evan's remains.

Jean was surprised to see Christina propped up in her bed, seemingly staring off into nothing, but she managed a weak smile as he entered her room.

"Jean, how are you? I've been waiting for you. Do you have any news?"

"I'm sorry, Christina, I don't know what you mean? You know that Evan was killed instantly, you saw what I saw."

"Yes, I know that, but what happened to his body?"

Here was the question before him that Jean had been dreading. "Be brave, Christina. I'm afraid that there was nothing left to recover. Evan was blown to bits, literally, and the port authority informed me that there was no evidence left of him."

She said, "Oh no, Jean. What will I tell his parents? Have you called them, or should I?" "Everything was done to spare them the worst details. I called them early this afternoon and Andre asked if they should come to Monaco, but I told them it was not necessary and that I would have to consult with you. All I can say, if I may suggest, is that arrangements be made from France by his parents with your consent to have a cairn constructed on the premises, perhaps beside the family mausoleum. Evan and your friends will have to be contacted, so I suggest we travel as soon as you are released. Do you have any idea when that will be?"

Christina replied, "The doctor said he would give me something to help me sleep but other than the shock, I'm all right. He suggested an overnight stay and that I could leave early in the morning. I think you're right. The sooner we get away from this place the better. I keep seeing the flames and black smoke and hearing the impact over and over in my mind."

Jean reached for her hands and held them tightly as he said, "I do, too. We must be strong. The next few days are going to be difficult. Evan was their only child, and it will be devastating for them to accept the truth. We know he isn't coming back but they didn't witness what we did."

"Jean, stay with me until I fall asleep. The nurse gave me my sedative just before you came in, and I don't want to be alone. Please."

"Of course, I will stay as long as you wish. I will collect your belongings from the hotel and call for you tomorrow. The helicopter will be on standby and we can leave as soon as you are ready."

The two friends grew silent, each completely engrossed in their own thoughts. Within a few minutes, Christina nodded, lay back upon her pillows and was asleep. He released her hands and tucked them under the coverlet. Jean bent over and kissed her softly on her forehead then tiptoed out of the room. He stopped at the receiving desk to inform them of the travel arrangements. The nurse made note of it upon her chart so that the attending doctor could sign her release. He bade her goodnight and left the building. He had one more call to make, and this tragic day would finally be over.

Andre answered the telephone on the first ring. As Jean proceeded to tell him that Christina was recovering in hospital, his hand began to shake and he had to grasp the receiver with both hands. He asked, "How is Madame?" The reply was that she was resting and had been given a sedative by the family physician. She had become hysterical during the past few hours and nothing he had done or said had calmed her. Jean told him that they had time to inform everyone of the accident, and they could hold a memorial service either as soon as possible or when most of the initial shock had worn off and acceptance had settled in. Andre agreed that a week or so would probably be best, as many would have a good distance to travel. They bid one another good night as Jean said they would probably arrive on the estate helipad before lunch.

True to his promise, the attending doctor had signed Christina's release and she was dressed and ready to go when Jean arrived at 8:00 a.m. She was pale and drawn, but her walk was steady and her shoulders squared as though she had steeled herself to meet the day. She avoided the accident scene as they drove past on their way to the helipad. Once in the air Christina did not encourage conversation. Her replies were non-committal, a simple yes or no or a nod. Jean became preoccupied with his own thoughts and the hours flew by. As expected they landed on the estate shortly before noon and disembarked to be greeted by Andre and Marie. Christina was so glad to see them both that she ran to them and they embraced; all three together to form a triangle of grief. The tears ran unchecked as they clung to one another.

Finally, still clinging to one another, their bodies pressed against each other, they walked slowly towards the chateau. Andre said, "Lunch has been prepared for us. We can talk in the dining room and the maid will unpack your belongings."

Christina agreed. She noted that Marie had said nothing, her face was white and pinched- looking and new lines had appeared on her face. Christina's heart went out to her. She loved these two people as much as she had loved her own grandmother and mother.

It seemed as though they had sat at the table for hours trying to decide on the memorial preparations. Christina wanted a memorial service to be held in the Church of the Lost Mariners and then a small ceremony with mourners gathered around the newly erected cairn, which would bear an inscription to celebrate Evan's short life. Only then did Marie understand that there was to be no body, no cremation, just a heart-rending farewell. Did Marie and Andre wish a picture of Evan etched in bronze to be embedded on the face of the cairn? The funeral arrangements appeared to have been settled and the date was set for a week hence.

Christina excused herself, begging exhaustion, and Marie retired to her room as well. Andre and Jean left to arrange the details of the upcoming funeral. When they returned, Jean also retired to his quarters. As soon as he was alone he placed a call to New York. "Operator, I must speak personally with Ms. Maggie Cole of the Cole Modeling Agency in New York. I don't have the number. Yes, I will wait. *Merci.*"

"Cole Modeling Agency, how may I help you? I'm sorry but Ms. Cole is in a very important meeting and has instructed that I hold all of her calls."

"Operator, tell her it is an emergency and I must speak with her immediately."

"Mademoiselle, my caller insists that this call is of the utmost urgency. Please put your party on the line."

"Just hold on, and I'll ring you through. Ms. Cole, there is an urgent overseas call for you from Jean. Will you take the call?"

"Yes, of course I will, just put it through to my office. I'll be right in." To the members of the meeting she said, "Excuse me, go on without me and I'll catch up later. I must take this call."

"Hello, is that you, Jean? It's so nice to hear your voice. How are you?"

"Maggie, please, just listen. Christina needs you desperately." He explained in as few words as possible what had happened and heard the shock in Maggie's voice as she exclaimed, "Oh no Jean, tell me it isn't true. Of course I'll come. I'll be on the next flight out and I'll call you from the airport when I arrive. Yes, I promise, and Jean, tell her I'm on my way. Perhaps it will give her some comfort. I'll see you soon. Goodbye, Jean."

Maggie replaced the receiver in the cradle, her hands shaking considerably. Poor, poor Christina! To lose her husband was tragedy enough but to have witnessed the event was hellish. She remembered the meeting, called and excused herself, but asked to speak to her brother John. He knew something bad had occurred when he heard Maggie's voice. She just said, "John, Christina's husband Evan has been killed. I'm going home to pack a bag and then on to the airport. Look after things while I'm gone. I may be gone for a week or so."

"Don't worry, Maggie, give my condolences to Christina and Evan's family. Now go."

Christina felt as though her head had just hit the pillow, but truth be known she had slept through the rest of the day and had only just woken to find that the room was in darkness. She glanced at the bedside clock and realized that it was past nine. Out of habit she reached across the expanse of bed to touch Evan. All that greeted her was an empty pillow and undisturbed bedcovers. Reality brought sudden tears, which she brushed away. Christina arose from the bed, put on a robe, and made her way to the window seat. She had always drawn comfort from this serene place and collected her thoughts. The first searing reminder was of the quarrel they had had the night before Evan had left. She hadn't even had the memory of his comforting arms about her but had slept fitfully, not getting much sleep as she recalled over and over the angry exchange of words. He had looked at her with such coldness, no warmth or humour in his eyes, as though she was an unwanted stranger in his presence. Was all of this anger her fault alone? How had they reached this low in their once loving relationship? Well, there would be no one to discuss it with now. Should she beat herself up forever, wondering if he had truly meant that she had to make a choice, between him and her work in New York? Finding no answers, Christina decided to go downstairs and make herself a fresh cup of tea. No one was about within the confines of the great kitchen and she found that a welcome respite. She had to deal with her own grief before she could reach out and help his parents. They had one another; she had no one. A note left on the table caught her eye. It had been hastily written by Jean telling her of Maggie's decision to be at her side. Christina was overwhelmed with relief. She would draw strength from Maggie; thank God she was coming.

She drank her tea, felt the warmth spread throughout her body, and decided that she would return to her bed. Sleep might overcome her, and it would be a welcome relief from the images that kept flashing when she least expected them. She felt the horror of it all would never leave her.

As expected, Maggie arrived the following afternoon. Her flight had been routine, no delays, no unexpected turbulence, and she had managed to catch a few hours sleep. Jean greeted her at the airport and she refused to sit in the back of the limo. He looked as though he hadn't slept in days and as she loved this man like she had loved no other, she would do her best to comfort him. Jean had no close friends other than Evan and although he had remained strong for Christina's sake, he looked as though he was about to fall apart. He clung to her and held her tightly as she murmured, "Jean, please don't cry. I'm here for you." His response was to hold her even tighter until she felt as though he was about to squeeze the life out of her.

"Maggie, *mon cherie*, my love. Thank you for coming. You are the best thing that ever happened to me and I draw comfort from you. Christina will be overjoyed to see you. She slept well last night after I told her that you would be coming. Thank you so much."

They were soon driving on the estate grounds and Maggie saw the workmen gathered near the entrance of the family mausoleum. She asked, "What are they doing, especially now when all of this has just happened?"

"Andre and Marie are having a cairn built in Evan's honour," his voice faltered for a minute and Maggie waited for him to continue. "There are no remains to be buried or cremated. He was blown to bits."

"How horrible. How can his parents say goodbye?"

Jean filled her in as to the funeral arrangements and Maggie agreed that they would be appropriate. They fell silent as they drew up to the entrance of the chateau. Maggie was in Christina's arms almost before she had left the limo. They hugged and cried, Christina's devastation appalling to Maggie. Wordlessly, she held her tightly and they made their way into the chateau. Maggie greeted Marie and Andre politely but excused herself so that she could be alone to comfort Christina. They understood.

Throughout the day, the telephone range incessantly, calls from friends, relatives, offering condolences, sharing their grief at the D'Argent family loss. Andre had come from a large family, consisting of three brothers and two sisters. Most of them worked at the shipyards, and some had to make travel arrangements but all would be attending. Jean asked Christina if there was anyone else that she cared to have attend. She was reminded of Carliss and Jacques Freemont and asked Jean if he could call. He agreed immediately. Was there anyone else? Christina thought about all of the women she had lunched with, and her opinion of them hadn't changed. They would only come as eager spectators and she doubted their sincerity. One thing which worried her was the paparazzi. Could Jean arrange for very tight security at the estate gates and ensure that no one be admitted who wasn't a close friend of the family. The ceremony at the church would probably be overrun with the press but the final laying of flowers at the foot of the cairn was to be strictly private. He had no qualms about her wishes and set about making the necessary calls.

Maggie decided that it might be a good idea to talk shop, even though Christina had just returned from New York. Christina hadn't broached the subject of Kate Winslowe, but in order to clear her mind she decided that this would be an appropriate time to discuss her instincts.

"Maggie, how has Kate Winslowe worked out? Has she met all of your expectations?"

"Why do you ask? I guess she has. Her reports are always on time, she seems confident that all the photo shoots are going well, she has surrounded herself with competent staff. What else can I say?"

"I ask because something just doesn't ring true with her. While I was in New York, I noticed her patronizing manner towards you and John, but on one occasion I happened to be walking past her office door, which was slightly ajar and I couldn't help overhearing her. She was on the phone with someone and I wouldn't have wanted to be the other person at the end of the line."

"What did she say?"

"Well, if went something like this, 'You'll damn well do as I tell you. You will keep the appointment or else. Do you understand? It's for seven o'clock in the gold room at the Hilton. I don't care how you feel. Be there or you'll regret it for the rest of your life. You're getting well-paid for this, so don't blow it.'"

"That certainly doesn't sound like Kate," Maggie answered.

"I know. I didn't think so either. No one in our office treats anyone with such disdain. I certainly would like to know to whom she was speaking. It couldn't have been one of our advertising companies. Do you think it was one of the models?"

"It could be, but I can't imagine which one. They are all so very well bred. Kate insists that they are well educated in the high society mannerisms, always well dressed, well voiced in current events ... although I can't imagine why that is important. All we ever look for in a successful model is her looks, her decorum, her enthusiasm and we did the rest to promote her."

"How many models do we have on payroll?"

"That's just it," Maggie replied. "I don't know. What Kate had proposed soon after you left the agency was that we hire models on a contract to contract basis. Freelance girls who fit the image she set forth. John didn't agree with her proposal but we decided it would save us a great deal financially and agreed to give it a try. Apparently, it went off without a hitch, according to Kate's reports anyway."

"Something is just not right. I can't put my finger on it, but trust me Maggie, I don't like her manner, I don't like her attitude, and I resent anyone telling me that I should just go with the flow. To tell you the truth, she treated me as though I was just a passing problem that was easily dealt with so long as I was on the scene, and would be promptly forgotten when I left. Does that sound strange to you?"

"Yes, it does, actually. But if you think we should watch her more closely, then I'll put John onto it. He is an excellent judge of character and his suspicions may mirror yours. I had no idea you felt so strongly. Why didn't you mention this when we were working together last week?"

"We had so much to do in so short a time. We had the designs to choose for the ready to wear market and I had to go out to the West Coast to launch the new perfume and meet with the Los Angeles merchants on Rodeo Drive. It just stayed in the back of my mind."

"I understand. I'll discuss it with John when I return to New York."

The room grew quiet for a few minutes. Christina cleared her throat and said, "Maggie, I have something else to tell you. I didn't mention it to Andre or Marie because they have enough on their plate right now."

"Go ahead, I'm listening."

"The evening I returned from my New York trip, I was exhausted from the flight as well as having a bad case of jet lag. All I wanted to do was have a hot bath and a good night's sleep. Instead, I came upstairs to find Evan in a foul mood. He had been drinking heavily and I think that with each drink his case against my working away from home on a regular basis got stronger.

He was exceptionally angry over the fact that I had been away six weeks and I didn't get a chance to tell him of the last-minute trip to the West Coast. Instead, he gave me an ultimatum, saying I had to choose him or New York. I was appalled at the idea of giving up my independence as well as my creative endeavours just to please him. It was so unfair. Four trips to New York a year don't end up as desertion, in my estimation. Just because we had missed a few social affairs, and the fact that I wasn't there to bolster his image, apparently upset him to no end. I pleaded with him not to discuss this until we had both calmed down and I had recovered from my trip. Instead, he slammed out of the suite, and he didn't come to bed later on. He must have slept in one of the many guest rooms in the other wing. I awakened early enough, hoping to catch him before he left for the shipyards, but he had left with Jean, towing that insufferable powerboat on their way to Monte Carlo. When I decided that we couldn't leave this a day longer, I decided I would join him and within hours I, too, was in Monaco. I found Jean at his hotel and asked him not to tell Evan that I was there, that it was supposed to be a surprise. Needless to say, you know the rest. Evan had no idea I was a spectator and witness to his death, he had no idea that I was there to make a choice concerning our relationship." She shrugged her shoulders and continued, "Well that's been taken out of my hands, hasn't it?"

Maggie saw the brave front that Christina was attempting to put on, and tried to placate her. "Don't beat yourself up over this. It was a wonderful gesture, and it would have been a terrific surprise. Especially if he had won the race. You have to put it behind you, Christina. The next few days are going to be extremely hard on you emotionally. We'll get through them, I promise."

"Maggie, you have no idea what it means to me to have you here. I feel better already for having confessed to the argument. What's done is done, I guess."

"Let's go downstairs and see what has to be done, shall we?"

The two women left the suite, both feeling better now that they had their heart to heart talk. Maggie was concerned for the actions of Kate Winslowe, which must be pursued in the near future, and Christina for the support of her beloved friend.

The service the following morning at the Church of the Lost Mariner was incredible. The pastor was well schooled in services in which the departed had met their demise suddenly and tragically, as well as having no remains to place in consecrated ground. He had known the D'Argent family all of his life and Evan had been a bright and shining star in his parish. Father Beauchamp's eulogy was comforting and heart-wrenching as he tried to bring solace to the family. When the service was over, he accompanied the family to the estate where members and friends could lay roses at the base of the cairn. Father Beauchamp presided, welcoming all mourners, blessing them in turn. The weather had cooperated by being overcast and gloomy, although it was the beginning of summer. It seemed to reflect the sad mood of the people gathered about to pay their last respects. The security people had done a fantastic job at the church as well as at the estate gates. No sudden flashbulbs exploded in Christina's face and no hot shot photographer was discovered up one of the giant elm trees, endeavouring to invade their privacy. Andre and Marie were exhausted within a few hours and Christina urged them both to seek some rest; she would greet the families and guests within the great room and see that all were taken care of. Marie smiled wanly and thanked her, grateful for the respite. She promised she would be available within a few hours to continue to circulate throughout the chateau greeting and thanking everyone. Christina noticed a welcome couple approaching across the expanse of the great room.

"We're so sorry, Christina. We can't begin to express our sorrow at your loss," this from Carliss and Jacques Freemont.

Christina welcomed them and said, "It's so good of you to come. Evan loved you both so very much." She looked about and asked, "Where is Nicole?"

Carliss and Jacques exchanged glances and hesitated before Carliss spoke. "Maybe it's not the time to tell you this, Christina."

"Tell me what? Where is she? Has something happened to her?"

"Well, we were going to tell you that she is away at private school, but the truth is, she has run away."

"Run away! To where, exactly? She's only a child. What will happen to her?" Christina was shocked. "How long has she been gone?"

Carliss answered, "She left with our hired hand a few days after her fifteenth birthday in May, about six weeks ago. We called Evan to ask if she had come here to find you, but he told us you were away in America. He promised to do all he could to find her, but I guess we'll never know if he had begun the search. Did he say anything to you?"

"No, we had less than an evening together when I returned from my business trip, and he left early with Jean for Monte Carlo. I'm so sorry for you both. If she ever contacts me, rest assured I will do everything in my power to keep her safe and will let you know immediately of her whereabouts and intentions. My heart goes out to you." Christina could say this with all sincerity, as she knew full well what it felt like to lose not only one child, but two.

They talked on for a few minutes then Christina excused herself to cross the room and welcome more well wishers.

Later on that evening, Maggie and Christina were alone. Maggie opened the conversation by saying, "I really regret that I didn't have more time to spend with Jean, Christina, but he was so busy that I couldn't catch up with him. I think he was holding his emotions in check by keeping on top of things and I'll just bet he's having a difficult time coping with Evan's loss."

"They were more like brothers than employee and employer. Jean took care of and arranged all of Evan's social life down to the last detail, and he loved doing it. I can well imagine what he must be feeling," she said. "How long are you going to be staying, Maggie?" I'd like to be able to show you around the estate, and maybe within a few days we can go into the city and do some shopping. I don't need anything, but you just might want a different continental style outfit to wow them at the office."

This was Christina's first attempt at light-hearted conversation, and Maggie warmed to the suggestion. "Whenever you are ready. Today will most likely be the hardest, and as the days turn into weeks and months, your heart will not be so heavy with grief. Time dulls and heals the worst pain. That sounds so cliché, Christina, but it really is true. You know that from having lost your grandmother and mother. The pain seemed unbearable but now you can remember the wonderful times with joy and love. I'll stay on until the weekend, and then I must return to New York. John is holding down the fort with Kate and they don't see eye to eye on anything. I can well imagine the chaos I'll be faced with upon my return. Don't worry, Christina, we're just a phone call away."

"I know that, Maggie, and I appreciate all that you have done. Let's get this day behind us before I make any plans. If I find myself overwhelmed with sad memories, I'll just sit at the drafting table and concentrate upon the fall line. Work is my panacea, and has been my escape from the harshness of reality." Maggie nodded her approval and they parted company for a few hours, Christina to see to the guests, and Maggie to seek out Jean.

The week passed by quickly, the days spent catching up with late mourners who came by to pay their respects, as well as the many telephone calls. Marie appeared to have caught up on her rest and was coping much better. Andre was putting everything behind him as he closeted himself within his study and worked upon new drafting plans for the order of luxurious yachts as well as a large cargo ship that was in the works.

Chapter Forty-Two

C HRISTINA HAD GIVEN MAGGIE much to think about on the return flight to New York. She found herself analyzing the Kate Winslowe situation from Christina's point of view. Maggie and John had hired her based upon face value and her excellent resume. She hadn't checked the references and she doubted whether John had as well. A few incidents came to mind that had gone unnoticed beforehand, but she now realized that they should have been dealt with at the time. Kate had been rather short with them with the proposal of contracting out the models instead having them work from the Cole Agency, which could then take a percentage of their work. As well, the models were still available to work for their own fashion line and do the runway work as required. She had seemed unwilling to discuss the situation, and it had become a done deal whether or not John and Maggie agreed. Thinking about it at this point, Maggie wondered just how much of a grip this employee had upon the company. Now to discover that she had been overheard being particularly rude to one of the models created a problem that had to be clarified. She had every intention of discussing this with John as soon as she had returned to work. That put aside, Maggie turned her mind to Jean. She recalled how wonderful he had looked when she had arrived, saddened, but wonderful to her eyes. They had spent a few hours together but his heart wasn't in anything too emotional, as he had been struggling with Evan's loss. One good memory had just occurred a few hours ago. Jean had driven her to the airport, accompanied by Christina. The two women said their goodbyes with Jean looking on. He had kissed Maggie on each cheek as was the custom, and upon impulse she had clasped his face with her hands and kissed him long and passionately on the mouth, almost taking his breath away. She had whispered after the kiss, "I have been longing to do that for the past week. That will have to last until our next meeting, Jean."

His face had broken into a wide smile as he said farewell and returned to the limousine.

Christina had chided her saying, "That was a pretty definite kiss, wouldn't you say? You were about to draw a crowd, or so you hadn't noticed. It was a lovely thing to do. I believe it not only cheered Jean, but it reinforced just how you felt about him. He adores you and probably always will."

Maggie settled back into the first class seat with the collection of memories of the past week no longer haunting and weighing heavily upon her. She slept well on into the flight and was disturbed only once by the stewardess, inquiring if she intended to awaken for a light lunch that was about to be served. Maggie opened her eyes momentarily, declined the offer and promptly returned to her nap.

Her arrival in New York was routine. She collected her one suitcase at the baggage terminal and was whisked away in a yellow cab. She decided that it was too early to go into the office and decided that jet lag would hamper her ability to put in a good day's work. She entered her comfortable apartment, threw her handbag onto the table in the foyer, hung her raincoat on the rack and slipped out of her high heels. Why women wore the damned things in the first place … so they made their legs more appealing and their clothes decidedly more eye- catching, but they would never be considered comfortable in her opinion. Maggie glanced at her watch and reached for the telephone. John would be home by now with Ellen and the children.

"Hi, Ellen, it's Maggie. I'm home. Yes, Christina is coping rather well, but Evan's parents are totally devastated. I'll tell you all about it at a later date. Is John home? I need to speak with him."

"Hi, Maggie. Good to hear your voice. What's up?"

"John, let's go into the office a half hour early tomorrow. I have to meet with you alone, without Kate being present. Christina brought a few things to light and we should talk them through before they became a problem. I don't think it's anything we can't handle. Shall we say half past eight? Thanks John, see you then. It's good to be home." She rang off, mulling over what she would tell him about Kate's activities, but decided it was best not to worry until they discussed it in the morning. She took a hot shower, refreshed but suddenly tired from her journey. Sleep claimed her almost as soon as her head had touched the pillow.

John was already at the office when she arrived five minutes late at eight thirty-five. He kissed her hello and they sat down in the board room in complete seclusion. Maggie got right down to business. She described in detail what Christina had told her about Kate's overheard conversation. "Have you had any incidences of this nature that you shrugged off, or decided that they were of little or no importance? Tell me about the current situation regarding our models."

John looked long and hard at his sister. He said, "You know, now that I think about it, I have heard not only Kate being short with some of them, but when I approached a small group, they stopped talking until I had passed by. No one comes to me with any problems, large or small, as they always did in the past. Also, these new girls appear to be much older than our policy for fresh, young faces to market our products. I don't know where I'm going with this, Maggie, I guess I'm just thinking out loud."

"Do you still maintain control over the models?"

"No, I don't. Kate has taken over completely after she manipulated us into accepting her proposal of outsourcing our photo shoots. I hardly know any of the girls, and there don't seem to be any regulars. Actually, Maggie, come to think of it, not many of them would pass my standards. Yes, they all seem very poised, polite, and well groomed, as models should be, but they are hardened. I haven't studied the photo shoots as I used to because Kate administers all of it and doesn't keep me in the loop. Because we have other interests, the ready to wear, the perfume manufacturing, and the cosmetics line I guess I really didn't mind when she took over the agency."

Maggie spoke, "I believe we had better do some investigating without her becoming suspicious, but so what if she does get suspicious? We own the business, she is just an employee, don't you agree?"

"You're absolutely right. I've always trusted Christina's judgment about people. I remember all too clearly when many years ago I discovered her coming out of the theatre and when I handed her my business card, she just laughed it off, thinking I was some kind of pervert. She was wrong, of course, but at the time I admired her for not being innocently accepting. Lord knows I could have been there to exploit her. Well, that's about it, Maggie. Shall we wrap this up?"

They left the board room just in time to greet the day staff, Maggie's secretary, Kate just entering her office, and the daily hum of the office began in earnest. Maggie was engrossed in the pile of mail that had accumulated during her absence when the phone rang. Her secretary said, "Ms. Cole, there are two gentlemen here to see you, on an urgent matter. Shall I send them in?"

"Did they say what it's about?"

"No, but I have to tell you that they are detectives from NYPD and are on their way in as we speak."

Maggie was putting the receiver down when they came into her office. One of the detectives closed the door, while the other showed her his I.D. badge. He said, "Ms. Cole, my name is Rick Halloran and this is my partner, Detective James Gray. We need to speak with you regarding one of your employees."

Maggie asked them to sit down and then, "Shall I call my brother in to this meeting? I'd like him to be here. He is also my business partner."

Rick Halloran nodded his approval and they waited in silence while John was summoned.

He arrived within minutes. "What's going on, Maggie? Why are these policemen here?"

"Just take a seat, John, and we'll get to the bottom of this. Gentlemen, you have our undivided attention. Wait, just one minute," and she opened the intercom to instruct her secretary to hold all calls.

Detective Halloran cleared his throat and began. "This concerns your employee Kate Winslowe." John and Maggie exchanged glances, this statement coming so soon after their meeting. "We believe that she is the head of a high-class prostitution ring and is operating out of your agency. We have had her under surveillance for the past six months following a complaint by a man who came forward to say that he had been a willing customer, but now one of the girls was blackmailing him. By the look on your faces, neither one of you had prior knowledge. We know this because the surveillance team had you under suspicion but heard nothing at all on the wiretaps. Kate Winslowe is the Madame, she arranges all of the meetings with the clients, from what type of evening, the duration of the meeting, where the escort takes the girls, everything. I have to tell you, these girls come at an extremely high price. Two thousand dollars for an evening is the minimum rate."

Maggie and John were appalled at the news. How had this been going on under their very noses without any suspicions being raised? Maggie asked, "Then we are not being accused of having taken part in this operation?"

"That's right."

"Then why are you here? Just arrest her and get her out of here before the press gets wind of this. We would be left in a fine state of affairs and I don't know if the company could recover financially."

"We can't arrest her until we have more evidence. She's very careful when they make the engagements. She uses words that could be construed as totally innocent, but the clients are from an elite group with a great deal of influence. We need her black book, that's the best evidence we can get to put her away for a long while."

John asked, "Do you have a plan? We'll cooperate in every way, you have our word."

"Here's the deal. We have checked all of our police force to see if we have a drop dead gorgeous policewoman who we can infiltrate into her operation as an undercover model." As he spoke, Detective Gray walked out of the office, and momentarily appeared with a beautiful young woman in plainclothes, high fashion no less. John was openly impressed. This was the calibre of talent he expected when he searched for a new model. She was about five foot nine inches, lithe, and of perfect posture. She was a dark brunette with snapping dark brown eyes, full lips and a jaw line and cheekbones that were a photographer's dream. "I'd like you both to meet Marla, Ms. Maggie Cole, and her brother John." They exchanged the usual amenities and the meeting continued in earnest. Maggie and John agreed that Marla should be introduced to Kate as having been their discovery, who they wanted to feature as a signature model of the business. Many of Christina's advertisers, although reluctant to substitute a girl in Christina's place, were becoming desperate in their search and had approached John just recently to step up the pace or have Christina return from France.

They believed that Kate would probably be a bit miffed about this, but she would have no choice in the matter. They could leave the rest up to Marla, as she was a well trained professional who had been working undercover successfully for quite some time. John asked her to do an about turn as he studied her stature. The tilt of her head and the lithe movement of her slim hips met with his approval. Maggie was also impressed. John said to no one in particular, "She's absolutely perfect. No one would suspect that she isn't what she appears to be, a model of high calibre. We should say that we discovered her on the West Coast, so that Kate wouldn't be able to find any background on her. We can make up a portfolio of an agency we use from time to time when Christina travels to Los Angeles."

The four exchanged handshakes and Rick said, "We thank you for your cooperation. We'll be in touch through Marla. Not a word to anyone. And by the way, we'll remove the wiretap from your phones. Marla will contact you from a pay phone or through the office during working hours. She must remain under your control, as well as Ms. Winslowe, is that understood?"

All agreed. The officers left and John, Maggie, and Marla put their heads together, Marla doing most of the talking and asking questions. Within an hour they had cemented a plan that appeared to be foolproof. Maggie asked whether Marla intended to carry through on a date as the other girls did. Marla clarified this by saying that not all of the girls prostituted themselves but some of them were hired as arm dressing for high society functions. Many of the clientele were politicians, judges, attorneys, staff attached to the Mayor's office. Marla's job was to record as many conversations with her dates as possible, and to plant a hidden camera in a few of the rooms that Kate rented on a regular basis. She had some of the hotel staff in her pocket and they found that she paid well for their cooperation. They decided it was now time to summon Kate to the office.

Marla studied her new boss with admiration when she entered the room. Maggie said, "Kate, this is Marla. She has just joined our agency as our signature model. I want you both to work closely together but in this case, John and I must be informed as to her assignments. This is very important."

Kate was a little surprised at the conditions, but when she saw Marla she realized this one would take the top price in her stable of prostitutes once she had been brought into the fold.

"I'm very pleased to meet you, Marla ... do you have a last name?"

"No, just Marla. That's part of my portfolio."

"Whatever. It sounds intriguing when you put it that way. I'm sure we'll get on well and work together successfully. If that's all, I really have a meeting I must get to. We'll talk later."

She was gone as quickly as she had arrived. Marla said, "She is a smart one. My work will be cut out for me, I can assure you, but she isn't the first that I've brought down and probably won't be the last."

Maggie introduced Marla to everyone in the outer office. She was aware of the admiring looks especially from the male counterpart. Marla was one of those women who knew she was stunning but took it for granted. That made her more appealing as none of her mannerisms were feigned; she was as natural as the person standing next to her. They had launched the investigation without a hitch. Now it was up to the police to do the work and Maggie and John had been instructed to carry on as usual, which they happily agreed to, knowing they would not be indicted or arrested as accomplices in the sting.

Six weeks passed. Maggie had tried to contact Christina but she was not available. Marie said that Christina had felt the need to leave the chateau for a while. She was on a journey reliving the memories that she and Evan had formed by visiting all of the places they had been together. Marie said that Christina would call from time to time but always from somewhere different. The last call had come from somewhere in Italy. She thought it was from Lake Como but couldn't be certain. Maggie left a message to have her call as soon as possible, or if Marie knew of her whereabouts to send a telegram. Marie agreed. Maggie asked as to her welfare and she replied that they were coping as well as could be expected. Andre had returned to work at the shipyards, but she missed Christina dreadfully. Christina had become the daughter that Marie had never had, and it was like losing two children. Maggie responded with compassion, thanked her again and hung up.

She didn't want to intrude upon Christina's grief, as she knew she was saying goodbye to her past. Maggie hoped that she could convince Christina to return to New York, to home if she could use the term, as well as to her family here, being John and Ellen and Maggie.

A few days later, Maggie and John received word from Detective Halloran to be prepared for a takedown. Marla now had all the evidence that was necessary for a major arrest of the prostitution ring and said that it would be unlikely that they could keep it out of the press. They would have to do some major damage control.

As luck would have it, Marie called to tell them that Christina was in Paris at the Hilton. Maggie called the telegraph office and the wire read: Christina Stop Urgent you come to New York Stop All hell is about to break loose Stop Don't bother calling, just come Stop Maggie.

Christina received the telegram as a total surprise. Whatever could have caused Maggie to send such an urgent message, especially so soon after Christina's loss? She packed and was at the airport within the hour having procured a last minute cancellation on the earliest flight to New York. She arrived the following morning and went straight to the office. Maggie was so glad to see her.

They remained cloistered within the office for an hour while Maggie brought Christina up to speed. Christina said, "I just knew something was wrong with Ms. High and Mighty Kate Winslowe. That conversation I overheard fits now, doesn't it? Will I get to meet Marla to thank her?"

Maggie said, "Detective Halloran approved of our calling you. You are as much involved as John and I as the victims. We have to draft a plan that will indicate that we are in no way implicated and that the prostitution was the brilliant idea of Kate, as well as hiding the operation under the auspices of our modeling agency. If they get her, the girls will be charged as well so we'll have to decide if we wish to continue with the Cole Modeling Agency or if we should scrap it and just carry on with our other endeavours." She paused for a moment then continued. "We can't have too many closed meetings without Kate or she will become suspicious. If you want to we can meet after hours with John at my place. You'll be staying with me until all this is resolved, I insist."

Christina was still overwhelmed by it all. Realizing the seriousness of the situation and what they stood to lose, she agreed to Maggie's suggestions until she could come up with some of her own that would pave the way to a solution that would not see them go down the proverbial toilet. As it stood they could lose their reputation, as well as millions of dollars. The after-hours meetings were a start and would not arouse any suspicions because they never had socialized with Ms. Winslowe during her time of employment. Christina left Maggie, saying she would be at the apartment and Maggie could call her there if anything arose during the remainder of the day.

Later that evening, Christina had settled in the spare bedroom and when John and Maggie came in, Christina called room service and had a lunch and coffee sent up.

They sat around the spacious dining room table with files spread out around them. John said, "Here's the financial sheet from the modeling shoots, expenses seem to have overcome profits over the past six months." Maggie and Christina read their copies and agreed.

Christina asked, "Where is the list of advertising companies we represented?" Maggie handed them to her. After a few minutes Christina said, "These are companies I have never heard of. Are they small companies or new ones? We used to represent large corporate advertising firms, and our models were very well paid, as well as our agency. What's happened to their business? They were the backbone of the agency."

As the evening wore on the facts and figures became steadily worse until the trio broke for a stiff drink. Normally Christina drank nothing but white wine, but welcomed the generous whiskey on rocks. Christina said, "Here's to reality and better times. They can't get much worse."

The expression on her partners' faces mirrored her own. "We can't do much to turn the company around until we weather the media storm that's about to break. Marla said she would do her best to keep the blame away from us. However, human nature being what it is, I doubt very much if she will be credible enough. I can just hear them, 'How can three very successful people be so blind to the fact that one employee duped them for so many months? What's the real scoop?'" Maggie and John agreed.

"Should we focus on where we'll go from there?"

"We could speculate. It wouldn't hurt. Any suggestions?"

They were interrupted by the sharp ringing of the telephone. Maggie answered, "Hello, yes, speaking." She silently mouthed Detective Halloran's name. "Yes, we are all here, please come up."

They waited patiently as Maggie said, "He didn't say anything, just that he had to speak to us."

"Come in, Detective. Would you like a drink?" John asked.

"No, nothing, thanks." He pulled up a chair and began to speak. "Well, it's all over. We had the suite that Kate rented bugged and our officers were staked out on 24-hour surveillance. When Marla entered the suite she was wired, and as she circulated the guests she picked up incriminating conversations on all counts. The men spoke of past girls, who of them was the most sexually talented and the price she brought. It was all very explicit. What we were waiting for was the icing on the cake, when one of the men said, "That Kate Winslowe sure has talent for picking out the best New York has to offer. Her girls have a clean bill of health, are schooled in all the amenities, are able to converse on many topics, and never have more than one drink. I always look forward to my stay in New York and Kate always keeps her promise even when I arrive unexpectedly." That's about when my men moved in. After we had arrested and charged them, we found a few highly important men in the crowd. It took a while to find a judge that wasn't reluctant to issue a warrant for us to search Kate's apartment. We surprised the hell out of her and she hadn't been tipped off about the arrest. We found her black book of clients and I have to tell you, there aren't too many important people left off the list. The shit is about to hit the fan. We have no obligation to protect anyone, no matter what their social status. Soliciting the services of a prostitute for sex, and the procurement for the purposes of the same, are felonies and what we have on them, especially Kate Winslowe is iron clad. Marla did a bang-up job for us. She didn't have to compromise herself in any situation, but wriggled out of a sexual encounter with the skill that would make any mother proud."

The three had sat silent throughout his report. When he had finished speaking, they breathed a collective sigh of relief however trying the ensuing weeks promised to be.

"Did anyone see the press about when the girls were being arrested?" Maggie asked.

"Well, there's always a snoop that follows police cars, and this was a big one. We did the silent alarm during the surrounding of the hotel, but a few reporters were at the front entrance when we came out. They didn't see Kate because she was not on the premises. No one had enough facts to call and warn her except the girls, and we made absolutely sure that they could not reach her."

"Do you mean that so far, there is no connection to us?" Christina asked.

"Not until someone puts two and two together and recognizes one of the girls from a magazine cover," he replied.

"Then we have some time. Not much, but we should at least draft a statement to use when the time arrives," Maggie said, as she began writing.

Christina asked, "Where is Marla? "

"She's down at headquarters making out her report. It will probably take her a few hours." "Could you give her a message from us? We would like to see her tomorrow at the agency to thank her. That is, if she has the time." John looked dreadful, wondering how he was going to explain all of this to Ellen.

"Can do. Well, folks, I'd better get back to the office. Don't take any calls other than from police headquarters. The commissioner will, no doubt, be issuing a statement to the press tomorrow. Until that hits the television airways, just go about your business as usual. That's my advice, for what it's worth."

"Thanks very much, Detective. Do you think we should hire counsel, just in case Kate attempts to implicate us?" Maggie's common sense always reigned supreme.

"That might not be a bad idea. Not a bad idea at all. At least you will know where you stand legally, although as I said, we have nothing on any of you. But it just might come down to Kate's word against yours. In this case the public would probably be sympathetic to the underdog, that being Winslowe." With these words, he turned and left the apartment, telling them all to get some rest, the days ahead would be trying.

A few minutes later, John left. After Detective Halloran had left they seemed at a loss for words. Everything had been said up to this point and, as expected, the shit had hit the proverbial fan. They decided that they should sleep on it and pick up the pace at the office in the morning. Maggie poured herself another stiff drink and offered one to Christina, who did not decline. They sat quietly, sipping on the strong whiskey, looking off into space. Christina finally broke the silence saying, "I've had one of the longest days of my life, Maggie, and I'm going to bed. I suggest you do the same. We'll need all our strength to face the reporters and gossip mongers in the morning."

Maggie said, "Good night then, Christina." "'Night, Maggie."

The following morning, after a rather fitful sleep Christina crawled out of bed, glanced at the clock and couldn't believe that it was only six a.m. No sense in trying to fall back asleep, so she stretched, rose from the bed, and padded off to the bathroom to shower and make ready for the day. Fifteen minutes later, she emerged from the bathroom and found that Maggie was also awake. They exchanged greetings, and Christina looked through her suitcases to find the perfect traveling suit that had the current fashion cut meant for executives but was crafted from the finest of materials. The deep navy color brought out the chestnut highlights of her hair, but she pulled it back in a severe style, which reflected her mood. She pulled the collar of the snow- white blouse out upon the blazer so that it framed her face. Satisfied that she looked her business best, she called room service, most likely awakening the kitchen staff, but they answered cheerily, promising a delicious breakfast for two. Christina had gotten used to the continental breakfast, with lots of hot coffee and a Danish. That was her only food vice, and as for Maggie, she ordered the usual large American breakfast with toast, eggs, bacon, the works.

When Maggie was done in the bathroom, breakfast had arrived. She said, "I don't think I can eat anything, Christina."

"Don't be silly. Are you going to let this delicious food go to waste or are you going to let your nerves get the better of you? At least have some toast. You've got to have something in your stomach or by lunch you'll be a bundle of nerves." Christina poured a second cup of coffee for herself and proffered the toast.

Maggie sipped on the strong hot coffee and nibbled on the toast. She, too, had selected her best business suit to face the trials of the day. The two made a perfect picture of the emerging women executives of the early seventies. Many women were becoming a force to be reckoned with in the corporate world, finally giving up the highest position of administrative secretary and becoming the executive directors of many corporations.

Before leaving the suite, Maggie placed a call to the law firm who represented their companies. They agreed to meet in the board room at eight-thirty sharp.

Neither of the two was prepared for what awaited them in the hotel lobby. They were both reeling from the flashbulbs that began popping off in their faces as soon as they emerged from the elevator. They clung together as they met the onrush of reporters, microphones shoved under their noses and rude questions coming from all directions. Maggie whispered, "Say nothing, or just 'no comment,' and keep pushing your way through. John sent the limo, and it's just outside waiting. Hurry Christina, keep pushing."

Christina put her hands out in front of her and began forcing her way through the crowd. She put her head down so that the camera couldn't catch the expression on her face or the look in her eyes. All she said was, "No comment, no comment, no comment."

"Are you both involved in the prostitution ring, or does Kate Winslowe run the show, as the police say? How much are the girls paid for an evening's work? How long have you been running a high class operation under our noses? Is this how you treat your models when they are over the hill and the camera doesn't like them anymore? "

They were both shocked at the accusations and insinuations being flung at them, but after what seemed an eternity they were in the limo, driving away from the curb as the flashbulbs still popped through the open window as Christina tried to close it. "Get us the hell away from this mob, and hurry," Maggie yelled at her driver.

He stepped on the gas, narrowly missing a dumb-assed reporter who had attempted to take a photo of them from in front of the car. He jumped aside as the car sped forward, dropping his camera in the path of the automobile. He shouted at them, "You rich bitches owe me a camera, you'll pay for this, I promise you."

As expected, more press was waiting for them at the office building. Maggie instructed the driver to use the underground parking garage and they would use the freight elevator to gain access to the upper floor, which housed their offices. They appeared to be alone and had eluded the press successfully. Maggie and Christina both breathed a sigh of relief once inside the elevator. They were in the office in moments but no one was at their desks, as they didn't begin work until nine. Five minutes later, at exactly eight-thirty, their lawyers arrived. Everyone was seated and they began the meeting in earnest. John looked as though he hadn't slept a wink and Maggie became concerned that he wouldn't handle the stress of the coming weeks at all well.

She was the stronger of the two and her decisions had always been accepted. Within a few hours everyone was made aware of the possible implications that could connect them to the operation. They asserted their ignorance of having any knowledge of what was apparently going on under their very noses, as hard as that was to believe. Christina was exonerated from the accusations as she had been living in France during the whole time. She was very annoyed at the suggestion that she was involved in any way but firmly defended her partners as well. Finally in complete frustration she threw her hands in the air and said, "For crying out loud have you no respect for any of us? Who the hell do you think pays you a fat retainer every month? You're supposed to be looking for an explanation which will clear us of all suspicions and an explanation that will make us appear cleaner than the driven snow. Also, have a heart, I just said a final goodbye to my husband a few months ago and I ask you to respect my grief. All I can say as a final word, is get the hell out there and earn your keep. We have nothing to hide as we are completely innocent of all charges."

The tirade had lasted a few minutes but it left Christina exhausted. She was right. The past few months had been extremely hard on her and this had just been the last straw. Maggie said, "Good for you, Christina. That last bit about them earning their keep was the clincher."

"John, you don't look well. Are you okay?"

"Yes, I'm fine. Ellen and I talked long into the night and I really didn't get much sleep. Now that we have that meeting over with, I feel the need for another shot of whiskey." He approached the sideboard cabinet and poured out three drinks, just as he had the previous evening. He lifted his glass and said to Christina and Maggie, "To better times, may they be just ahead."

They answered, "To better times."

That evening all the publishers in New York had gotten on the bandwagon. So many of the facts had been skewed and misconstrued. The photos of Maggie and Christina in the hotel lobby were splashed across the front pages, with a small insert of Kate Winslowe in the upper right hand corner. It was as if they were treating Kate as the victim and Maggie and Christina as the instigators, just as Rick Halloran had warned. The headlines read, "Who Has the Black Book, is it Maggie Cole, Christina Corelli or Kate Winslowe?"

"How dare they suggest any of this?"

Maggie spoke, "Don't get upset, Christina. It's just mob mentality. If we keep working as usual, staying on the beaten path so to speak, they'll get tired of hounding us. The police have only arrested Kate and we are as free as the birds."

"Yes, but some of them are saying that we have the financial where-with-all to stay out of jail, but Kate doesn't."

"We have to just give it time. Let's concentrate on our fall line until things die down."

Christina said to no one in particular, "Yes, but who will give a damn about our fall line? I see our sales falling and our orders being dropped because of the bad publicity. I know it seems senseless but you know how the buyers are. They would be accused of taking the side of two very famous "Madams" and selling their products to help support their covert activities. Some women would probably be unwilling to 'dress like a prostitute' by wearing the line."

True to Maggie's predictions much of the publicity had died down by late August, but their sales were definitely down and profits were in the red. They were still able to keep their personal wealth but they had to close the clothing manufacturing but kept the cosmetic and perfume line pliable. Maggie suggested that the public sympathy had turned towards Christina once the knowledge of her recent loss had come to light. They also accepted the fact that Christina had been living abroad when all of the incidents had occurred.

The monthly meeting opened as usual. The picture was glum but a glimmer of hope remained in the overseas sales the markets, which Christina had opened and kept supplied over the past few years. They had remained loyal, not too concerned that what happened in America could stay in America. Thank goodness for small favours.

Christina cleared her throat and said, "I have a suggestion that just might turn us around." She waited for a moment but continued as John and Maggie gave her their undivided attention, the financial reports lying forgotten in a heap in front of them. "I suggest that we re-invent the company in the following way. First of all, we must forever relinquish the Cole Modeling Agency and all contacts with the past. Second, I suggest we begin to manufacture a line of lingerie that will become the finest lingerie in the world. We will market this product aggressively along with the perfume and cosmetics. It will become our package and I feel that this will put us back on top. Also, if I may I would like the company to be known as "The House of Corelli" and that way it will have no connection to the Cole name." She paused momentarily and continued, "If I have to, I will use the enormous amount of money left to me by my husband and we will establish our own outlets to sell our products. In Paris we will open The House of Corelli as Chez Corelli, and in Spain it will be known as Casa Corelli. Whatever it takes. Also, it would do us no harm to purchase a place on Rodeo Drive in Los Angeles, far away from the madding crowd in New York. We will return to the New York market only when we are asked to, after we have established ourselves worldwide. How am I doing so far?"

"You're a genius, Christina. We'll let the Cole name take the fall, and establish ourselves in an entirely new venture. We know the markets and you know the designs. We may not sell a damn thing for at least six months until we get established, but I'm willing to give it a try if John is."

"I'm all in. It's a wonderful idea. I can seek out the locations that will best suit our needs and buy up the property. Christina, we trust you will put together a design team that is willing to work sixteen hours a day. Maggie, you still have connections, and you must badger them until they say yes. How soon can we have some designs in place? We need a portfolio to show our prospective buyer. If we market them in advance just as we did with our seasonal lines, we should have enough stock to launch by Valentine's Day next year. That will be our make or break day, but I believe the time is right. There are too many houses and too many lines that are undercutting the competition and the last few seasons the designs have been so far out there that no woman in her right mind would wear them, let alone spend thousands of dollars on a garment that looks like a gunny sack. We were right in getting into the ready to wear line when we did, but now this venture will be our grand entry into the fashion houses around the world."

"One more suggestion, if I may, we should look to the Asian market as well. Hong Kong and Singapore are emerging as cosmopolitan cities and the Asian women are looking for a change."

"Good idea, Christina. Well, let's get busy. Time's a wastin' so they say."

Maggie hadn't seen John this enthusiastic since his marriage to Ellen. He was bursting with newly found energy and initiative. They laughed at his receding back. Christina and Maggie reached across the expanse of the board room table and clasped hands. They looked deeply into one another's eyes and Maggie said, "Thank you, Christina. I have never doubted your sincerity. You have paid us back a thousand times over from when we first discovered you. I thank my lucky stars that you are here now."

"We're in this thing together, Maggie. Don't thank me yet. We have a lot to do in a very short time, but I know that we can pull this thing off. To hell with Kate Winslowe, to hell with the Cole Modeling Agency, we can bury it and forget it."

Chapter Forty-Three

WITHIN A MONTH CHRISTINA put together a team of designers and they created a portfolio that was destined to please the most discerning of buyers. At their month end meeting in September the financial figures had not changed, they were still in the red, but their spirits were lifted by the promising designs. They decided unanimously to send John on the marketing trail. He would have his work cut out for him as they intended to reach everyone from coast to coast. Maggie worked on his itinerary so that he would have something to follow. She included his key contacts and had her staff make all of his reservations, and all that was left was for John to leave.

Christina approached Maggie with the, news that she, too, must leave. Maggie asked, "Where are you going? We still have a mountain of work to do."

"I know that Maggie, but I have to return to France to settle Evan's estate and sign a whole lot of legal papers. I must see and speak with Marie and Andre to finalize my plans. There are a few close friends that I have to say goodbye to as well. I will be seeing Jean, if you have a message for him, I'll be glad to pass it on."

"I understand. How long will you be away? Remember, with John away, I'm it for the duration."

"I don't expect it should take more than a few weeks at most. The lawyers don't require notification months ahead as they do here and the papers should be ready to sign soon after I arrive. I'll telegram Evan's parents today and I'll be on the next overseas flight. The sooner I leave, the sooner I'll be back." As she spoke, Christina began gathering up her papers to leave with instructions to her secretary. "Will you look after all of my mail while I'm gone?" she asked. "I've left the design team in very capable hands, just check with my secretary if you have any questions. They have promised faithfully that they will continue to work at the pace we set last month. I have never seen people so excited about their new creations."

"You'd best get home and pack. I'll see you off if you like."

"Actually, that won't be necessary. We can say goodbye now, and I'll call you from Cherbourg when I arrive." Christina replied.

Maggie felt abandoned when the door closed behind Christina, but she knew that the time would pass by quickly with all that she had to do. John would check in on a daily basis and that would hopefully cheer her up.

Christina was on a late afternoon flight that same day. She had nothing to do on the long flight other than read and relax. Her hectic work schedule over the past few months had left her drained but still very enthusiastic. The sketches had received many accolades thus far, and the next step was to procure the orders and begin production. They already had the manufacturing ready to wear floor and it only required stocking. A thought suddenly occurred to her which seemed a little far-fetched but worrisome nonetheless. What if the name change House of Corelli meant to some people that it was a house of ill repute? The association with the Cole Modeling Agency had been put to rest and she fervently hoped that people were soon to forget and move on to the next scandal.

She put her thoughts to rest, snuggled back into the seat and soft cushion and was soon fast asleep. The stewardess awoke her a few hours later to announce that dinner was being served and required her choice. Airline food wasn't all that bad. At least it was served fresh and hot. She ordered coffee with the chicken cordon bleu. A trip to the cubbyhole washroom refreshed her and she noticed the admiring glances sent her way by the other passengers. It was always a surprise that this happened. Christina had always taken her looks for granted, but was not insensitive to open admiration. It was a boost to her self-esteem. She no longer fretted over the fine-lined scar that was easily concealed and only manifested itself in times of strife, when Christina's color became high. Adam had promised that it would fade and almost disappear, as he had used the finest silk to suture the six inch wound. Her reverie was broken by the arrival of her dinner. Christina had not eaten any lunch, and was surprised to find that she was famished. She felt much better after the meal and a few more cups of coffee. The airline was showing a late evening movie, and she appeared interested in the title. Everyone settled down, overhead seat lights were turned off, and the passengers settled in for the night.

She must have dozed off during the movie, because when Christina awoke it was to the sound of the Captain's voice announcing their arrival in Paris within the half hour. They were beginning their descent and he thanked everyone on board for flying with his airline. Christina was through customs within a short while; she always knew what to say, what to declare and how to conduct herself, having traveled so much in her short lifetime.

The telegram had reached Andre and Marie, and to her surprise there was Jean waiting beside the limousine for her to appear. She kissed him soundly on both cheeks. "It's so good to see you, Jean. I'll sit up front if that's all right?"

Jean responded with a wide smile and a hug. "Christina, you look wonderful. Madame and Monsieur have been waiting for your arrival ever since your telegram came."

"How have they been, Jean?" she asked.

"It has been a sad time for everyone. Madame lost interest in her rose garden after you left and has just been marking the days one by one. Monsieur Andre returned to the shipyards but his heart isn't in it. His brothers have been looking after most of the orders and only consult him when necessary. They have been strength for him to draw on."

"Jean, what about you? Evan treated you like a brother. You must miss him as much as I do."

"Yes, that is true. But life goes on, and I have promised I will stay with his parents as long as they need me. My wife and I are estranged but she will not allow us to divorce as she is a devout Catholic. I see a long and lonely life before me, Christina, and I must fill it with helping the people I love."

Christina realized that she was not the only one that was lonely even though she also was surrounded by people who loved her. Maggie, John and Ellen, and the children were her family as far as she was concerned, but she understood what he was talking about. He asked about Maggie and during the remainder of the drive to the chateau she told him about the scandal involving the modeling agency. He was horrified that a trusted employee could have taken advantage of them, causing them to lose their reputation and many millions of dollars. Christina then filled him in on the new prospects, and he became very interested. "This new venture sounds exciting. With everyone's combined business expertise you should have no trouble coming out of this situation. I can assure you that the French will be most receptive to your lingerie line. After all we are known as great lovers, are we not?"

Christina's laughter joined with Jean's as he skilfully turned the limo through the estates iron gates. Andre and Marie were outdoors awaiting their arrival. Christina left the limo in a bound and was encircled within their arms. Marie began to cry. Andre tried to keep his emotions in check but Christina could see that he was very moved at the sight of her. Her eyes welled up but she smiled through the tears. "It's wonderful to see you both. Are you well?" she asked.

"You too, Christina. Yes, we are well. Each day gets a little easier to bear. The chateau is so empty." This said, Marie turned and made her way to the entrance. Jean followed carrying Christina's luggage, as Andre walked alongside.

Marie had prepared a light meal and they gathered around the large dining table just off the spacious kitchen. Christina breathed in the delightful aroma of freshly baked croissants, hot coffee and hot apple pie. "I've almost forgotten how wonderful everything smells. This was always my favourite room."

With much trepidation, Marie asked, "Christina, are you here to stay?"

The room grew suddenly very quiet as all eyes turned to Christina. She waited a few moments to reply, wondering in her heart how she would break the news. "I am very sorry, Marie, Andre, but I can't stay. When I left after Evan's death, I visited all of the many places where we had been and loved and I guess it was my way of saying goodbye." She continued to tell them of the tragedy that had befallen her company in New York and what they were doing to recover from the scandal. Having changed the conversation from Evan to something entirely out of their realm appeared to have a calming effect. Andre said, "Whatever you do, Christina, we are sure you will be successful. We have always admired your creativity and drive. We will miss you, as you well know, but we are surrounded with family. Marie's family is small but I have three brothers, and their families have been extremely caring, including us in all family gatherings. We are especially blessed to be able to share in the lives of their children."

Christina was glad to hear this news. She had been very lonely until she had returned to New York. Maggie's no-nonsense, get-down-to-business attitude had helped her tremendously. Their latest endeavour had left her tired at the end of each day and she had welcomed sleep. Their conversation turned to lighter subjects and the meal was soon over. Christina felt her heart skip a beat as she ascended the stairs to the suite that had been her and Evan's home. Nothing had been changed and as the memories flooded back, especially the last time they had been together. She shook her head to dispel them.

When she had unpacked, Christina decided that she didn't want to prolong the business part of her visit. She met Andre in the library where he was studying a set of plans.

"May I interrupt you, Andre?" she asked as she entered the spacious room. "Yes, of course. This can wait. What is it, my dear?"

"I know that Evan made me his lone beneficiary and that is one of the reasons for my visit. I believe we should settle any outstanding matters as soon as possible. I don't mean to sound callous, but I don't know when I will be returning to France. May we meet with the lawyers tomorrow?"

"I'll call now and arrange the meeting. Do you have any special requests that perhaps we can discuss now?"

"Well, I would like my shares of the D'Argent Shipyards to remain in the company. You can have my dividends sent to New York after your annual meeting. I have more money than I will ever need, although we are spending much on this new venture."

"There is something which I have to tell you that came to light when we read Evan's will." Christina was surprised by his tone but waited in silence.

"When we searched Evan's personal records we found a letter and a key. There was a letter addressed to myself and Marie, and a card within an envelope containing a key with your name on it. The lawyers decided that it should be opened and that you be informed of the contents at a later date."

"Go on, Andre."

"Well, during your last trip to New York in May, Evan purchased a chateau on a large estate just a few miles from here. He knew that you had no wish to move from our home but he said that as soon as you set eyes on it you would fall in love with it as he had, and you would not be disappointed." He continued, "Here is the letter."

Christina's hand was shaking as she took the letter from Andre. She sat down across from him and began to read the first one:

My wonderful parents.

When you read this you will know that I am no longer alive. I have tried to be the son you have always wanted and I hope with all my heart that I lived up to your expectations. Do not be saddened by my death but promise that you will celebrate my life, that is my wish.

Andre handed her the other letter, which, in her haste to depart for Monte Carlo, she had missed seeing, as it had been left on the mantel just before Evan had left.

> *My beloved Christina,*
>
> *This key opens the front entrance to a chateau, which I purchased in your absence. This chateau is meant to be the beginning of our life and with the grace of God a home for the children you will bear. This is my dream. When you read this, call me or come to Monte Carlo and I will know what you have chosen.*
>
> *Your love always, Evan.*

She began to cry. Finally, the tears that she had withheld throughout the past months overwhelmed her and she could not control the tide of emotion. Andre stood beside her, his arm about her shaking shoulders as he attempted to comfort her. Christina continued to sob, the sound of her grief echoing within the room. At long last, she controlled herself, wiping the tears away and blowing her nose. Andre's face was ashen but he sat stoically at his desk waiting for her recover. "I'm sorry, Andre. I didn't mean for that to happen."

"Do not apologize, Christina. I understand fully. You have held that in too long. Come my dear, perhaps some fresh air will do us both the world of good. We'll ask Marie if she will join us in a walk upon the grounds." With these words he helped her up from the chair and followed her out of the library.

Marie donned a light sweater as they left the chateau. She said, "Christina, I hope you are not too disappointed in the rose garden. I have just rekindled my interest in it, but it remains far less glorious than in past seasons. Here is the one which you and I planned. The groundskeeper kept it as free from weeds as he could, but it does need some tender love and care. I do hope you will have time to attend to it in the months to come?" she asked with such hope in her eyes that Christina had to look away.

"I'm sorry Marie. I won't be staying in France. That is why I am here. I need to settle all my affairs and return to New York. The only thing that I can promise is to visit you at least once a year, I'm truly sorry, but my life is no longer here in France. It stopped when we lost Evan. I love you both so very dearly, but I can't bury myself here reliving the past. Life goes on, and I must go where I am needed and I can thrive. I hope you understand, please for my sake, understand."

Marie was silent as they continued their walk. She spoke of the times their grandnieces and nephews had spent during the past summer. Their laughter had warmed her heart and lessened her grief. Christina felt that she was avoiding the inevitable. She would try to stay as long as possible, but the situation in New York was critical and needed her attention for at least the next six months. She promised to return to France whenever she could and invited them to come to New York.

Andre spoke, "We are getting on in years Christina, and have no desire to travel long distances. As you may have noticed we hardly ever leave the estate except for short trips to Paris and Rome. Marie has never been a seasoned traveler and I must admit I agree with her. As much as we would like to see how you work and live, it would not be possible. We would be most happy if you would send us photographs. Could you do that for us?"

"I'll send you a whole album if that's what you want." She laughed, "Maybe when you see how wonderful it all is you will want to come and join me after all."

They were refreshed from the walk and quite hungry. Marie noticed that the time was drawing close to late afternoon. The meeting with the lawyers was scheduled for the early morning. They had no further plans for the remainder of the day, and Christina decided she would go and look at the chateau that had been destined to become her home. She asked Jean if he would drive her. He didn't appear at all surprised and she knew that he had been a part of Evan's plan when he had purchased the estate. They were there within a ten minute drive. It was much like Evan's childhood home, but this had more open areas; the smaller trees had been cut, leaving room for the magnificent hundred year old elms that spread their foliage as a mantle of shade to shield one from the hot midday sun. To the left of the grounds was a natural lake, not extremely large but a lake meant for the enjoyment of afternoon picnics, boating, and fishing. The driveway was long and straight, and as they emerged from the trees she was stunned at the sight of the splendid stone building before her eyes. Jean said, "It takes your breath away, doesn't it?"

"I can't believe that he bought this, Jean. It's absolutely beautiful. And he was right. I would have moved here right away." She dabbed at the sudden rush of tears. "To think that Evan loved me this much. It's so sad, Jean."

"Yes, Christina. I recall how excited he was when we first came to view the property. The people were returning to Italy and the chateau had just come on the market. He was especially enchanted by the location. It meant that he could keep a watchful eye upon his parents during their golden years but still maintain a special place for the two of you."

Christina knew then that Jean had no knowledge of the terrible fight that Evan and Christina had on their last night together, or that Evan had asked that she choose him or New York. Well, she still didn't know what her choice would have been, now that she had seen the chateau. Fate had made the choice for her and she said, "The chateau will have to be sold, Jean. My life is in New York, and I would not be happy here. Memories become cold after a long while, and I cannot live with just memories."

"I understand, Christina. Without Evan this place would be just a stone building with no heart."

"Take me back now, Jean. I've seen enough. We'll have the lawyers handle the sale as well as settling Evan's will. Then I must return to New York."

* * * * *

THE FOLLOWING WEEK WAS filled with meetings, signing of papers, visiting the cairn that was dedicated as Evan's final resting place, as well as attending a few social functions with the family. The day arrived when Christina was to leave. She had not told Evan's parents that she was going to visit a few friends before she finally left the country. She had placed a call to Carliss and Jacques Freemont. They were delighted to hear from her and looked forward to her visit. They would fill her in on all that had happened in her absence. Jean rented a car for Christina and she bid farewell to everyone. The sport scar afforded her the luxury of freedom, the wind in her hair, and the sun on her face as she drove expertly along the familiar route that would take her into the wine country of Bordeaux. It was a rather long drive, but Christina stopped at a roadside inn to refresh herself and have a light lunch. She was soon back on the road. She called to tell Carliss of her whereabouts and when to expect her. Carliss cautioned her to drive carefully and they would soon be together.

Christina's arrival was met with genuine fondness. The Freemonts were the first couple Evan had introduced her to when she had come to France, and they had liked one another instantly.

After they had exchanged hugs and kisses, Christina asked, "Where is Nicole?"

Carliss's smile disappeared. "I have no news of Nicole, Christina. Come inside, we'll get you settled, and I'll tell you all about it."

Christina read the consternation on their faces and said no more. "Carliss, has something happened to her?"

"Not exactly, Christina," she said, as she gestured for Christina to make herself comfortable in the spacious living room. "As I told you, last season we hired a young artist from Paris, who had been struggling to earn a living from his painting but found himself at a point when he could no longer afford not to work. We agreed that he could work through the summer, stay and help with the harvest, and then be on his way. During the summer, he became friendly with Nicole and when he wasn't working, they became inseparable. Jacques and I were not too happy but decided that if we forbid her to see so much of him she would choose to do the opposite and go against our wishes. He asked if he could paint her portrait. We agreed, thinking that it would give them something to do rather than become so enamoured with one another."

Jacques said, "We thought we were being so clever by allowing this and it backfired on us." "How so?"

"When we were about to begin a new season, we found a short note one morning left on the sideboard in the kitchen. In it, Nicole said that she loved Yves and that they were going away together, and not to try to find them. She said she would rather be poor but happy instead of rich and lonely. Imagine this from a young woman who had just turned fifteen. We tried to find them, we hired investigators but the trail was a dead end. There are so many thousands of struggling artists in Paris and surrounding area that we had nowhere to look. Talk about ungrateful, after the life we gave her."

His last remark was full of bitterness and pain. Carliss said, "We adopted Nicole and brought her here to France when she was just a few months old."

Christina asked, "Where did you take her from?"

"We arranged the adoption through the nuns in the mother house in Montreal. They were looking for a French couple with ample means who could care for a child exceptionally well. Nicole was the answer to our prayers, as you well know. You must remember how precocious she was, even at the tender age of ten."

"She was absolutely adorable. I remember when she said to me, 'Someday I will become a famous model, the same as you, Christina, you just wait and see.' I've never forgotten her."

Christina told them then of her plans to remain in New York and pick up the pieces of her life. They were sad to see her go and regretted her decision. They welcomed the fact that she invited them to visit whenever possible. She promised to drop whatever she was involved in to make their stay a memorable one. As an afterthought Christina asked, "Would you like me to assist you in your attempt to locate Nicole? Perhaps if she is going to become a model I could call the couture houses and make inquiries. Do you have a recent picture of her that I may keep?"

"Yes, of course. You can have this one. It was taken on the day of her last birthday in May."

Christina said, "Carliss, she's stunning. How tall is she? She looks so much older than her fifteen years. She must have matured rather early."

"Yes, it seemed that from the time she turned twelve until her thirteenth birthday, she blossomed into a beautiful young woman. We were so proud of her."

"If only she would call and let us know that she is all right. That would be a beginning at least," Jacques said.

"I don't know if this will help, but if I hear so much as a mention of a girl matching this description in our circles, I'll follow it up, I promise." Christina attempted to boost their spirits and raise their hopes. Their visit lasted well into the late evening but Christina begged weariness and the fact that she had a long drive the next day and wished an early start. They bid goodnight and retired to their rooms.

She was on her way early the following morning after a wonderful continental breakfast and friendly conversation. Christina reached Paris approximately six hours later. She left the car at the rental agency and hailed a cab to take her to the airport, where she boarded the plane within a few hours. She called Maggie from the plane to give her the flight number so that someone could meet her at the airport. All was well at that end, so Christina settled back to rest during her flight, which was to be her last return flight from Paris for a very long time.

Upon Christina's return to New York, the new ventures resumed at a very fast pace. John had successfully captured some very large orders for the new line of lingerie. He had received a warm welcome from the West Coast, especially from the high-end boutiques of Rodeo Drive. It appeared that Christina had made a lasting impression during her last trip. They were enchanted by the prospect of a whole new endeavour and their enthusiasm was infectious.

September, October, November, and the better part of December passed by in a flurry of work. The design team was extremely proud of their work and Christina didn't have the right words to thank them. They had conveyed on paper exactly what she had envisioned. All that remained to be done was to begin production and prepare for the official launch on Valentine's Day, 1972.

The next hurdle was to find the perfect signature model for the new line. The person they were seeking had to be sensual but not cheap, very appealing, one who could wear the apparel in such a manner that would make every man fantasize his wife in each ensemble. Christina knew that the model must differ from the norm; she must be pert, sassy, voluptuous and not too tall. Five foot seven was the cut off size. An ample bosom, tiny waist and curvy hips, as well as a pair of legs that, when extended, were in perfect proportion to the rest of her body. This all seemed such a tall order but everyone agreed to the concept.

Christina was still sharing Maggie's apartment for two reasons, one for convenience, and the other for companionship. Christina also had no time to spend looking for the perfect apartment during this very busy time. Perhaps after the launch, if all were successful, she would consider a change in residence.

Nothing untoward had happened on the day before Christmas. The office staff had a small party to celebrate the holiday well wishes, and an early departure from work went off without a hitch. No last minute decisions, no last minute crisis, everyone was in a festive mood and eager to spend time with their respective families.

Maggie and Christina were relaxing in front of the fireplace when the phone rang. Christina glanced at her watch saying, "It's just past eight, now who could be calling us on Christmas Eve?"

"Why don't you answer it and find out," Maggie said. "Hello, hello, is anyone there? Hello? Who is this?"

"Hello...is this Christina Corelli?" a female voice asked, sounding very frightened. "Yes, this is Christina. Who is this?"

"Christina, it is Nicole. I have no one else to turn to. I am in terrible trouble and I must ask you for help."

"Nicole, is it really you? Where are you? Yes, I'm listening, go on, what terrible trouble?" She mouthed the name Nicole Freemont to Maggie, who understood.

"Christina, I have been living in Paris with Yves, posing for him and his friends. All was well until we became very poor. He began to take his frustrations out on me until I could bear it no longer. I left him and got a job on a cruise ship that was coming to America. I lied about my age so that they would hire me. The thing is, I am not returning to France on the ship. I left the ship when we docked thinking that I could call you or find you and everything would be all right, but it wasn't."

"What happened, Nicole?"

"The ship's captain reported me to the port authority and they caught me just as I was about to leave the pier. Now they have me in custody and only allowed me one phone call. If I have no one to sponsor me in America I will be detained and deported."

"I'll be there as soon as I can. Let me speak to whoever is in charge, Nicole." The line was silent as Nicole gave the phone away. "Yes, this is Christina Corelli. I am a friend of the young lady's parents. I'll be right down there and I'm sure we can clear all this up. Do I need legal counsel? No, all right then, Pier One, ask for Inspector Duvall. Thank you. You may expect me within the hour. I'll sign whatever papers are necessary. What time do you close? This is, after all, Christmas Eve? Ten o'clock, that shouldn't be a problem. Goodbye."

Maggie decided to accompany Christina on her mission to retrieve Nicole from the port authorities when she heard the circumstances of the situation. The two women donned warm coats and rushed out into the street, where the doorman had a cab waiting at the curb. "To the docks, Pier One, port authority, and hurry, driver." Christina was extremely excited. So many thoughts were rushing through her mind, but the one thought was that Nicole sounded fine, just very frightened and alone. That could soon be rectified. She had every intention of taking control of Nicole and signing anything which would give her sole responsibility of Jacques and Carliss' daughter.

When they reached their destination, Maggie stayed behind to pay the cabbie, while Christina made her way into the offices of the port authority. Inside she found a much bedraggled, rather shabby-looking Nicole, whom she found difficult to recognize from the photograph her parents had given her. This Nicole was thin, her complexion pallid, her usually luxurious raven hair lacklustre and obviously neglected. Her smile, when she saw Christina, was radiant. "Christina, it is really you. I knew you would come. I didn't think you would remember me, it was so long ago when we first met."

"I told you then that I would always look out for you, Nicole. Now we must get you out of this mess before they arrest you for being in this country illegally."

She asked for Inspector Duvall and was greeted by a serious looking gentleman in a naval uniform. He gestured for Christina to be seated across from him. He had a sheaf of papers and documents in front of him. These were the necessary papers which had to be completed and signed before he could release Nicole into her care. She had to produce proper identification documents as well as have someone vouch for her character. Luckily Maggie had entered the building and spoke up. "Mr. Duvall, Christina Corelli is my friend and business partner. We have worked together for the past fifteen years and I would trust her with my life."

"That's good enough for this office, Ms. Cole. Thank you."

Within an hour, all the paper work had been complete, and Christina found herself thanking Inspector Duvall again while she encircled her arm around Nicole. She discovered the girl was shivering and cold. Christina removed her coat and placed it about her. Nicole smiled her thanks and snuggled into the warmth left by Christina. The trio left the shipyard offices and entered the waiting taxi. Maggie had instructed him to return within the hour and to wait until they came out onto the docks. Christina said, "You're wonderful, Maggie, as usual you think of everything."

The spacious apartment appeared as a large mansion to Nicole as compared to where she had been living. She was speechless turning about to inspect the interior of her new home. "It's beautiful, so warm and comfortable," she said.

"Come over by the fire and warm yourself and we can talk." Christina pulled up a second chair closer to the warmth and settled Nicole opposite.

Maggie left for a short time and returned with some hot tea and sandwiches. Nicole accepted the drink and food with relish. They were quiet as they exchanged looks, watching her devour three sandwiches and sip the scalding tea. Finally, the warmth began to spread throughout her body and she removed Christina's coat. Smiling she said, "I guess I was really hungry, *n'est ce pas?*"

"Yes, you sure were. Now, *Madamoiselle*, let's start from the beginning and don't you dare leave anything out. Do you know that I visited with your parents in late early September and they were worried to death about you? All they wanted was a word or two to let them know if you were all right, or if you needed any help. Was that too much to expect?"

"No, it's just that I didn't want them to come and take me back to the vineyard estate. It felt good to be on my own, but I guess that I am not as worldly as I thought. When things got rough, Yves began to leave me in that squalid loft and go out at night carousing with his artist friends. He expected me to pose in the nude for them for free. It made me feel dirty."

"You must be exhausted. It's Christmas tomorrow. Why don't I get you settled for the night and we'll talk some more in the morning. Come with me."

"Good night, Ms. Cole. You've been most kind. Thank you." "Good night, Nicole. Welcome to my home. Merry Christmas."

Christina had her settled in the large queen-size bed that had been her haven for the past six months. She didn't mind sharing. It would be nice to have a warm body next to hers for a change. She would telephone Carliss and Jacques in the morning. It would be late in the evening and a nice Christmas present for them to learn that Nicole was safe. Inspector Duvall had urged Christina to attempt to gain guardianship of Nicole after he had learned that she was not eighteen, as she had stated, but a minor of fifteen. If she could convince them that a temporary guardianship was the best way to handle the current situation then she would be only too happy to assume the responsibility. There was a bond between these two even though they had been apart for five years. Maggie had seen how Nicole looked at Christina, with such admiration and respect. Almost as though she was mesmerized by Christina and was obsessed in becoming just like her. When one thought it through, it wasn't such a bad idea. At least the kid would have a mentor who cared about her welfare.

Christina entered the living room and said, "She's out like a light. She fell asleep almost as soon as her head hit the pillow. I wish I could do that."

"We don't have any gifts for her for morning. What shall we do?"

"Let's go through our makeup and perfume and see what we can come up with, shall we?"

Maggie replied, "That's a good idea. I have a nice cashmere sweater that I haven't worn yet and it should fit her nicely. Kids like clothes to be on the roomy side, don't you agree?"

They found a few nice items that would please Nicole and quickly wrapped them and placed them under the Christmas tree. "How about a nightcap, Maggie? It's been a long and surprising night and I could use a brandy." Maggie nodded her consent and they sat sipping their drinks, watching the flames in the fireplace as they danced and shifted, casting a soft light upon their faces. Maggie looked ten years younger in the shifting shadows, as Christina relaxed, reclining on the plush rug. An hour passed when finally they agreed it was time to call it a night. "Merry Christmas, Maggie, have I told you how happy I am to be here with you?"

"My pleasure, Christina, I wouldn't have it any other way. 'Night."

Christina carefully climbed into bed so as not to awaken Nicole. Within minutes she was asleep. Nicole was the first to waken as she quietly slipped out from under the covers and made her way to the bathroom. Christina heard the water running and for a split second thought they had an intruder. However, she quickly remembered yesterday's ordeal and her new responsibilities. Maggie was also astir, padding about softly in the en suite kitchen. The aroma of freshly brewed coffee wafted throughout the apartment. Christina joined her in the living room, her hand cradling a large mug of the hot brew. "Merry Christmas, Maggie," and she nodded as Maggie returned the greeting.

"Our guest is awake. Shall I go and get her? We have some serious presents to open this morning."

"I'm here," said Nicole. "Merry Christmas. I'm delighted to be here, I had to pinch myself this morning to prove that I wasn't dreaming."

"Come over by the tree. We have a few surprises for you," urged Maggie. "But I have nothing for you," Nicole replied.

"Don't worry about it. Just come over and join us. There is fresh orange juice on the sideboard if you're hungry. But hurry, we have some presents to open," added Christina.

The next fifteen minutes or so were filled with the sound of tearing paper, squeals of laughter and happiness as the trio indulged in the exchange of gifts. "How wonderful," Nicole smiled, as she placed the soft cashmere wool sweater against her face. It's like angel hair," she exclaimed.

Maggie and Christina exchanged glances each with a pleased smile as they surveyed the mess in the living room. All the gifts were perfect. Nothing had to be returned. Nicole to another pile of gifts and asked, "Who are these gifts for, may I ask?"

"We are all going to my brother John's home to spend Christmas Day with him and his family. You will get to meet the other partner in our company and his wife and children."

Nicole was delighted. "But I have nothing to wear that would be suitable. My clothes are well worn and shabby. The newest outfit I had was my domestic uniform that they gave me on board ship."

"Don't worry, we'll scare up something that will be bound to please you," Christina promised. The apartment was soon tidied up, the kitchen put to rest as the time approached noon and they were to join John and Ellen. True to their word, Nicole looked quite presentable in her makeshift outfit. Christina had arranged her hair in a casual style that framed her oval face. She had studied Nicole as she helped prepare her for their outing. The hair was almost jet black, thick and full, with a few unruly tendrils escaping the confines of the combs as it cascaded down her back and around her shoulders. Her complexion was milk white with very little colour in her cheeks. She was too thin for her frame. Christina decided that she would take her to her doctor in a few days and have her examined thoroughly. She was probably undernourished and run down from lack of sleep and good nutrition. "We have one more task to complete before we leave the apartment."

"What is that?" asked Nicole.

"We have to make an overseas telephone call to your parents."

"No, please no, Christina. They will have you send me back and I don't want to go. Please, don't call." Nicole's voice was filled with fear and longing.

"No, I won't send you back. I have to convince them that they approve of a temporary guardianship for me, so that we can file for immigration status. If they don't grant me this, I believe that because of your age, you will have to return to your rightful parents. Now, I want you to speak with them and I want you to be on your best behaviour, do you understand?"

"Yes, I understand. There, it is ringing. *Maman, Papa*, it is Nicole? *Joyeux Noel*." "Jacques, it's Nicole. Come quickly. Nicole, where are you? Are you all right? We have been so worried. Are you coming home?"

"No, *Maman*, I am not coming home. I am here in New York with Christina Corelli and her friend Maggie Cole."

Christina took the phone from Nicole and spoke, "Carliss, its Christina. Nicole arrived here last evening. She telephoned from the port authority where they were holding her. She came to America aboard a cruise ship, hired on as a domestic. She jumped ship but was reported missing and they caught her." As Christina explained the situation, she was entirely committed to keeping Nicole safe and required the necessary papers to keep her in America. "Please think about this over the next few days, but I must caution you, we must act soon or she faces deportation. If that happens she has told me that she will not return to you, and I don't think that wandering the streets of Paris is exactly the best thing for her. I'll try to talk her around to coming home, but this is not the time. Please help us out."

Jacques had heard all of the conversation and said, "Christina, thank goodness she is with you. I will convince Carliss to let her stay with you and we will airmail the papers to you. When you think she is ready to see us, we will come to New York. And Christina, this is the best Christmas present we could ever have. Thank you. *Joyeux Noel.* Good bye."

Nicole sat throughout the conversation almost shaking with fear. Was Christina going to send her back? When she heard that she could stay, she jumped up from the sofa and threw herself into Christina's arms. "You're the best person in the whole wide world."

"Well, we'll just have to see about that now, won't we? I can be pretty tough at times." Maggie laughed and said, "That will be the day. But we do want you to pull your weight.

After all, we have your best interests at heart but we will not be taken advantage of, young lady. Do I make myself clear?"

"Yes, Ms. Cole. I will behave, I promise." Nicole's happiness lit up her face and her emerald glistened with tears.

"I'll call Ellen and tell her to expect one more for dinner, although I don't think it will matter. She usually has enough food for an army."

They donned their coats and waited outside hoping to spot a cruising cab. The doorman had the day off and they had to wait ten minutes. Nevertheless, they were successful in hailing a cab and were whisked away on the fifteen minute drive to Maggie's relatives.

John and Ellen had purchased a lavish home in Queens a few years ago, as their two children needed more space than a Manhattan apartment could afford. It had a swimming pool and a generous back yard, as well as each had a room of their own. The house was set back on a quiet street, lined with large shade trees and long front lawns. Everything was covered in snow; the trees were bare but the Christmas lights in the early evening would decorate the entire block, their welcoming colours beckoning passers-by and friends. Nicole was enchanted by them. Ellen's girl was just thirteen, but she was so interested in Nicole's life in France that she practically pestered her throughout the entire dinner. Christina hoped fervently that Nicole wouldn't tell her about the past eight months, where she had been living and what she had been doing. When it appeared as though this was about to happen, Christina quickly changed the subject and admonished Nicole with a stern look. Nicole got the message and began asking questions about the life of a thirteen year old in the Big Apple.

The day passed quickly. Everyone was totally relaxed, full of good cheer, delighted with their gifts and no one mentioned work. Around seven, Maggie, Christina and Nicole decided it was time to leave. John's son was disappointed, especially to see Nicole leave. He was totally stricken with puppy love; they were the same age but Christina could see that they were worlds apart. She hoped nothing would come of the infatuation.

Nicole said, "What a wonderful family you have, Maggie. I loved the entire day." She was now on first name basis with Maggie, as she had insisted she drop the Ms. Cole.

"I know that I'm getting on in years, the big 40 is looming, but Ms. Cole makes me sound ancient."

The next morning the three set out to shop the day away. Maggie and Christina braved the crowds of bargain hunters, crowds returning or exchanging gifts, and delighted in purchasing a whole new wardrobe for Nicole, who just tagged along, her eyes trying to see everything at once. The mall was a whole new experience for her and she couldn't get enough of it. By noon, they were ready for a break. They found a table in a very nice restaurant, deposited their purchases around their chairs and dropped down in exhaustion. Maggie ordered a tall rye, Christina a white wine, Nicole a large cola. The drinks came while they studied the menu. Nicole would settle for nothing less than a hamburger and large fries. She had dreamt about this, wondering what was so wonderful about a sandwich that made half the world crazy. Maggie ordered her usual clubhouse with a side salad and Christina did likewise. They watched laughingly when the waiter brought the burger. Nicole's eyes widened as she saw what he had placed before her. "How do I eat this? It's too big to cut into little pieces. Won't it fall apart?"

Christina told her that she must grasp it with both hands and lift it to her mouth, but not before she had dipped it in the ketchup."

"What is ketchup?" she asked.

"That red sauce in front of you. You will also need some for your fries. Nothing tastes as good unless you have it with ketchup."

For someone who had never had such a generous portion of food before her at one time, Nicole relished every bite of the famous meal and was done in record time. "That was totally awesome. Just the best." She finished up by sipping on her cola and finally paying attention to the conversation between Maggie and Christina.

Christina was saying, "I thought John looked a little tired yesterday, didn't you?"

"Yes, I noticed that too. We did put him on a busy agenda over the past four months. It's no picnic living out of a suitcase and eating restaurant food. He did an exceptional job and deserves a rest. When we get back to the office on Monday, let's tell him to take some time off or just take it a lot easier. We have some pretty tremendous talented staff now and it's time that John delegated much of his work. He can oversee the orders but we can handle the advertising and marketing from our end. That should lighten his load and he can spend more time at home with his family."

"Good idea. Now Nicole, do you want to go to school?"

"No, I do not want to go to school. I want to be just like you, and I can't learn that in school, Christina."

"But you must learn the language of business, some mathematics, the social graces." Maggie admonished.

Christina said, "All right. If you won't attend a girl's school then we will bring the school to you. While we are at the office, you will be there also, but you will have a tutor for at least four hours a day. That will allow us time to conduct our business and also spend time teaching you the serious end of our business. You will find out that it isn't all fame and glory, but ninety percent hard work. The rewards are the end product of our endeavours." Her voice was firm.

"Maggie, I must ask you this, in all honesty. Should Nicole and I find an apartment for ourselves or will you put up with us until her immigration status is settled?"

"Christina, I wouldn't have it any other way. You have no idea just what having you here with me over the past months has done for my spirits. Now that we have another resident in the apartment our lives will get ever more interesting."

"Would you object if we moved that massive queen-size bed out of the spare bedroom and substituted it for two separate beds? I think there is enough room. Also, the walk in closet is spacious enough to hold our two wardrobes. Nicole hasn't much in the line of clothes as yet, so we shouldn't be cramped for space."

That settled, the trio picked up their packages and resumed their shopping spree. A few hours they had to admit that they were all shopped out and the crowds were beginning to get to them. They returned home, tired and happy. Nicole exclaimed over and over again at the purchases. She felt like a princess, and memories of her life from the previous month began to fade. Yves was already a bad memory that she had put to rest on the working voyage to America. She believed in her heart that he had seduced her with the hopes that her rich parents would welcome him into their home. That not being the case, he had intended having Nicole ask them for money when they reached Paris, or they would never see her again. That hadn't worked out at all ... and he had spent many months ignoring her or verbally abusing her whenever he felt the need. She had been the one to run away, realizing that she had been the victim and could not stay with him any longer. She didn't have the strength of character to admit her mistake and beg her parents' forgiveness, so the only course was to follow her impulses and dreams. This she had done, so far successfully. Speaking with her parents on the telephone had been the first step to her rehabilitation and only time would tell if they would remain estranged.

Christina followed through with her promise to have Nicole undergo a complete physical. Her doctor's receptionist had called to set up an appointment to meet with him to discuss the results of the tests. For a moment Christina's heart raced, thinking that they were about to receive some very bad news, but the receptionist explained it was a routine thing with their office. Nicole and Christina were ready the next day and found themselves seated across a wide expanse of desk with neatly piled folders, one which was directly in front of him.

"I don't wish to alarm you, Ms. Corelli, but Nicole's tests are not all normal. She is moderately anaemic and in need of some vitamin supplements as well as the B factors. Within approximately a month we should see a marked improvement in her appearance. As you had noticed, her color is not exactly good and she is underweight."

"You don't think this condition will have any effects upon her at a later date, or will she recover totally if we follow the regimen?" Christina asked worriedly.

"I promise to do whatever Christina tells me to, and to take my medicine every day," said Nicole.

"You should be completely well by the end of January, and I will see you then to follow up on the blood tests. You should schedule this appointment on your way out. Thank you, Ms. Corelli. It's a pleasure to meet someone as famous as you."

"The pleasure is all mine, Doctor, believe me. Nicole is very precious to me and I would have great difficulty coping with anything worse than this condition."

They left the doctor's office, made the ensuing appointment, and Christina said, "Let's do a bit of shopping. I have to fill your prescriptions anyway, so why not take a cruise through the mall?"

"You read my mind, Christina." Nicole looked much relieved after the appointment had revealed that she could recover fully with lots of rest, good food, and the best of company.

They returned to the apartment laden with packages both large and small. Most of the items were intended to round out Nicole's wardrobe. Christina had suggested a number of items but had left the final decisions to Nicole. She actually had very good taste as to how to complete an ensemble and was very color-conscious.

Because of the doctor's appointment, Christina and Nicole had decided to play hooky for the rest of the day. They relaxed, read the latest fashion magazines, ate a very nourishing lunch, and wiled away the remainder of the day.

When Maggie came home, shortly after six, the apartment smelled absolutely delicious from the aromas wafting out of the kitchen. The suite was immaculate but the kitchen was a bustle of energy, the two of them happily engrossed in a recipe that must be so complicated that it required half of the cupboard supplies, as well as an array of pots and pans. As it stood, all they were making was spaghetti and meatballs, but the secret was in the sauce. Maggie's stress of the day slowly disappeared as she sipped on a glass of white wine and watched the activity in the kitchen.

Nicole set the dining room table, very festively, with candles, flowers, linen napkins, the works. At long last, dinner was served. The crisp salad was the entree and disposed of by the hungry trio shortly. Christina brought in the platter of meatballs and spaghetti and they dressed their portions with various cheeses. In no time, the linen napkins were stained with sauce, and Nicole's ice water needed replenishing, while Maggie and Christina enjoyed the last of the wine.

"That was absolutely delicious, you two. It sure beats a TV dinner and an empty apartment to come home to."

"You're very welcome, Maggie. We try our best." Nicole laughed as she accepted the compliment.

This evening was the beginning of a routine that they all grew to love. Nicole had settled in well with her tutor for the four hours daily set aside, but she became restless when it came time for lunch and the afternoons spent with Christina and Maggie, learning the ins and outs of the business.

The month literally flew by and Christina had noticed the wonderful transformation in Nicole's appearance. Her thick, richly coloured hair had assumed a life of its' own, the curls trailing down her back and around her shoulders the shine, predominant in no matter what light. Her color was renewed, radiant with blush in her cheeks and minus the dark shadows under her eyes. No longer was there a lacklustre look in her eyes, they now shone with the light of the richest emeralds. Christina paused for a moment one day and realized that this girl was totally stunning. Her beauty shone from within, and her youth and exuberance added a glow to her complexion. Her posture had improved, no longer the sag of shoulders as the weight of worry had been lifted when the papers had arrived from her adoptive parents and Christina was now her legal guardian. They had taken all of the documents to the law office and they were given the okay to relax. Nicole's immigration application was in the works.

The search for their signature model for the Valentine's Day launch of their lingerie line had thus far been unsuccessful. The advertisements had brought in the usual tall, willowy models, too thin for this line of apparel. John had called all of his former contacts hoping they would come up with the right one. They were not doing a runway show as it would appear too provocative for the television of the seventies, so the model would be photographed in a number of ensembles which were to appear in all of the well-known magazines. They appeared at an impasse.

As Nicole, Maggie, and Christina one afternoon were seen poring over some new designs, John entered the office. They were oblivious to his presence. Nicole arose from behind the drafting table to retrieve a sketch from across the room. John watched her closely as she walked across the room, picked up the paper, pivoted perfectly in a half turn and, head held high, returned to the task at hand. He studied her for a few more minutes, cleared his throat and said. "Ladies, your undivided attention please. Christina, Maggie stop what you're doing. Nicole stand up and walk slowly towards me, turn and walk back to Maggie and Christina."

They trio looked confused, but decided to humour him. Nicole did as he had instructed, with a little coaching as she was about to turn. "Don't drop your shoulders or your chin. Small steps, keep the hips straight in line, and place one foot directly in front of the other."

Nicole did as she was told. The women were amazed at the transformation. Their eyes widened as they realized what John had seen in Nicole. This signature model was under their noses all the while. "John, you're an absolute genius. Look at her, Maggie, she's perfect! She's not too tall, she has ample voluptuous assets, her legs are perfectly shaped, curved in the right places and not too heavy. Her color is perfect. I can already picture her in the red outfit with that long black hair framing her face and curling softly on her shoulders. Quick, let's get a photographer in here."

Nicole was completely taken aback. These people were professionals and they were talking about her as though she had left the room. The good thing about it all was that she could listen in. They were as excited as anyone could possibly be. She thought how it must be impossible that they must be considering her as the signature model for the House of Corelli Lingerie Line. But no, they sounded serious.

Their best photographer entered the office, wondering what all the commotion was about. "Hey guys, I'm here. What's all the fuss about?"

"Give us your unbiased opinion. We all think that our next supermodel is sitting right in front of you. Look at her as a prospect, from all angles. We value your expertise." John could hardly contain himself.

Christina and Maggie drew away from the drafting table to allow a clear view of Nicole. Domingo put the camera up to his face, and used the lens as a natural eye. He focused in upon Nicole's face, studying the jaw line, cheekbones, and natural shadows. The colors of his model had his hands shaking. The sheen of her hair, the blaze of her green eyes, the blush of her cheeks brought out the milk-white complexion. There were virtually no shadows to change the contour of her face. Her young age lent an air of innocence but there was a hint of fire and ice within this lovely creature. His camera clicked in a rapid series of shots, pose after pose, action photos, his voice mesmerizing her into obeying his direction. John's intake of breath was the only other sound in the room.

He said, "Christina, believe it or not she is as natural as a sunny day. I remember when I first laid eyes upon you under that marquee so many years ago. This is exactly the way I feel when I look at Nicole. It's something that happens only once in a lifetime and I know that this is the second time I have felt this way."

Maggie had never doubted John's instincts when it came to discovering beauty. She began to look at Nicole through his eyes, and she saw what he was describing. Christina was imagining Nicole in the Grecian white and gold, braid-trim, short baby doll nightie, her hair drawn back from her face with a cascade of raven curls all fastened by a gold lame braid which allowed the mass of curls to fall towards the nape of Nicole's neck. At an angle she looked like a Grecian princess, her profile chiselled against the deep blue background, with the moonlight bathing her features and highlighting her form. Christina opened her eyes, but the vision was still before her, only in her street clothes.

"Nicole, come with us to the wardrobe and make-up room. We'll put together a portfolio that will take the fashion industry by storm." To Domingo, Christina said, "She must not be compromised in any way. This girl is my charge and I cannot allow her to be exploited in any way. She is a minor and I am responsible for her. Every pose and outfit must be provocative, but not sexy, sensual but not seductive, pert, and very beautiful. If any of the pictures are not of high quality, and high class, I will personally discard them."

"I understand, Ms. Corelli. It would be a shame to produce anything that depicts even a hint of shabbiness or low class. Trust me." Domingo was eager to begin, but the ensembles had to be brought up from the lower floor, hair and makeup staff were summoned, and the transformation of Nicole Freemont was about to begin.

As Christina and Maggie looked on they were caught up in the excitement of the moment. Nicole was basking in all of the attention, but she remained detached, trying to take in all that was happening. The camera flashes didn't faze her at all, and she took her direction from Domingo almost as if they had been working together for many years. Christina saw in Nicole a great deal of herself when she had been pampered prior to her first photo shoot. It brought back many fond memories. Domingo had finally finished. He asked them all to be patient while he retired to his dark room to develop the photos. Nicole looked tired but very pleased with herself. This had been much easier than sitting still for hours on end while a group of drunken starving artists attempted to capture her innocence while in the nude. All that seemed a lifetime ago.

Christina, Maggie, and John put their heads together and began to brainstorm. How many ensembles were available and what colors should they have Nicole wear? Thus far, the deep red and the white were the only two they had used, but Christina was thinking ahead. The soft pastels would be best served by using a background model along with Nicole. She suggested that they use a black model, totally opposite from Nicole for some of the poses, as well as a platinum blonde as contrast. She was about to suggest this when Domingo re-entered the room.

"You won't believe these shots. I haven't been this happy since I first photographed a seventeen year old Christina Corelli. Nicole Freemont is your next top fashion model. This girl would look good in sackcloth and ashes. She would give new meaning to grunge. What else can I say? See for yourselves." Domingo laid out the shots in a long line upon the drafting table. All eyes focused upon the array of photographs. The colors were superb, the light perfect, and the model looked about to pop out of the photo and come to life. John couldn't constrain himself any longer as he let out a triumphant whoop.

"This will shake their booties," he said. "Every magazine in the fashion world will want a picture of Nicole, and it will be our discovery as usual." He made his way over to Nicole, who was looking at the photographs in wonder. She couldn't believe it was really her; she looked so grown up. She couldn't believe her eyes. John turned her about and gave her a great big bear hug.

"Congratulations, my little wonder girl, welcome to the world of high fashion and fame. I promise you the world, Nicole, as sure as I live and breathe."

It was hard for the occupants of the room to come down to earth but they managed to strike a note of seriousness. Christina said, "We must keep this under wraps until about a week before the Valentine's Day launch. The photographs will be delivered as promised to our advertisers. I only wish I could be there to see the expressions upon their faces."

"That's my pleasure, Christina. I can hardly contain myself. The media will eat this up, and I hope they will be eating crow along with our success. How soon we forget. They kick a guy when he's down, but when the first sign of success looms, they are ready to get on the bandwagon. We must proceed cautiously, release very few details of Nicole's background. She must remain a mystery find." John waited for approval, which came simultaneously.

The rest of the afternoon was used up during the drawing up of contracts so that Nicole would benefit richly from her upcoming success, but the money would be held in trust by Christina.

"Do you wish to call your parents, Nicole?" she asked.

"Not just yet. Let's wait and see how this plays out. Maybe I'll crash and burn. It's up to the media to make or break me. I won't talk to anyone on my own, or better yet, not at all. The PR department can create a profile for me, which I am sure will be adequate even for the most discerning reporters. Is that all right, Christina?"

"Yes, of course, my darling. We will not do anything to jeopardize your reputation. We have your best interests at heart and believe me when I say that they don't come any better than John and Maggie Cole. They are the best, the most honest and sincere people I know. Besides, they are as close as family."

"I have to pinch myself to prove that I'm not dreaming." Nicole's smile made her eyes shine. "To think that this is my dream come true."

"Let's go out to Sardi's for dinner tonight to celebrate. Maggie and I will put on our best bib and tucker and we'll play down your outfit until the launch. How does that sound?"

"I can't wait," Nicole said, her tears of happiness threatening to spill over and run unchecked down her cheeks.

"Let's get out of here. We've had enough excitement for one day," Maggie suggested, as all agreed. Domingo left with a satisfied smile upon his face. His camera had done its' magic. Maggie envisioned a renewed upturn in their finances; John was happily collecting his thoughts, pleased with his discovery. Christina vowed to channel the sudden inevitable rise to success so that it didn't change Nicole, harden her, and make her self-centered. The camera would pick up these characteristics and her future most definitely would be short and not so sweet.

The Valentine's Day launch was even more successful than their wildest dreams. Nicole Freemont became a household word overnight. The New York Times' review was the best of all. They described Nicole as fresh, exciting, stunningly beautiful with an innocence that was usually hard to capture on camera. Her ensembles and poses were anything but seductive, they were in good taste and the lingerie line was exquisite.

"We can't just rest on our laurels, there's a great deal of work to be done. The orders are coming in as fast as the mail can be delivered. I suggest we hire more seamstresses and put on an afternoon shift," John asked of his two colleagues.

Maggie answered, "That's a good idea. We'll up the pay a dollar an hour over our competitors, and maybe we can entice some of their workers to come over to us. I know that's not kosher, but that's free enterprise in my estimation."

Christina didn't usually get into the cutthroat aspect of the business, but she did not want any of their customers to be disappointed and not have the orders filled within a reasonable amount of time, so she agreed as well to the tactics proposed by John.

Because Nicole was immersed in her daily studies, calls from the entertainment sector to have Nicole come on their television shows had to be put on hold; at least until the end of June, when summer would be upon them. She asked Nicole's tutor if she wanted the summer off with pay, and whether she would resume work in September. The opportunity was too good to pass up and she readily agreed. Christina felt that Nicole needed some recreation time and the summer would be her reward. John and Ellen's kids had asked Nicole to their basketball and volleyball games at school, to the movies, and whatever events kids do at that age. Nicole had met others during these outings and, although she was the career Valentine girl, when she was hanging out she dressed the same as they did. She pulled her hair back into a ponytail, wore flat shoes, and used very little makeup. Andrea never introduced her as the Valentine girl, but just as her good friend Nicole. She was three years younger than Nicole but her admiration knew no bounds. She knew she could never be as famous as her friend, but Andrea also admired Nicole's drive for a proper education, which would enable her to be independent when her career was ended by age.

Easter was fast approaching and Christina thought that this would be a good time for them all to go to Miami, Florida for a week. They would fly commercial, keep a low profile if possible and take in the sights or just relax in the sun. Nicole was beside herself with excitement. They were destined to leave on Friday and they all worked very hard to complete their tasks before leaving the office in the charge of the team department heads. They had even talked Maggie into putting down her pen and retiring her telephone for the entire week.

The trip was incredible. The adults relaxed poolside with staff circulating with exotic drinks as they made new acquaintances. John and Ellen felt that they were on a second honeymoon, only the kids were along for company. Nicole was recognized a few times but the hotel assured them that their privacy would never be compromised and kept the paparazzi out. Maggie and Christina were out one afternoon on a shopping expedition when Christina was recognized. Someone from Evan's yachting club in France saw her from across the expanse of the outdoor restaurant where they were enjoying a light lunch. He crossed the floor and stopped in front of their table. *"Excuse moi, Madame D'Argent.* How nice to see you. You are well, I hope. Such a tragedy about Evan! We miss him very much at the club."

Christina vaguely remembered him and returned the comments, nodding when it was appropriate but adding nothing to the conversation. Whether he took the hint that his presence was disconcerting or not, he promptly left with the usual "au revoir".

Maggie could see that the incident had left Christina shaken. Oddly enough Christina rarely mentioned Evan at all these past six months. It was as if she either didn't care to remember or it was too poignant. She asked, "That obviously put a damper on our outing. Let's pack up and get back to that luxurious hotel and have an hour long spa treatment. I know I could use the pampering."

Christina welcomed the idea as she shrugged her shoulders to shake off the intrusion of the almost total stranger. "Let's go, Maggie."

Their last evening in Miami found the group of seven at dinner. The young people ordered what the young crowd ate, hamburgers and pizza, while the adults enjoyed steak and lobster with all the trimmings. They were in a festive mood but sad because their holiday would end when they boarded their flight in the early a.m. They were all very suntanned; even Nicole's milk white complexion had taken on a healthy glow. She never allowed herself to sunburn but maintained a healthy tan throughout the summer months when she was a child in France.

There was a large contingent of press, reporters, photographers and freelance journalists at the airport when they landed at La Guardia in New York. Andrea and her brother reacted with surprise, as they had never experienced such attention. Even though it wasn't meant for them, they were still a part of it all. To their chagrin, everyone answered "no comment", as well as "just a small family holiday outing, and it is back to work as usual the next day. Thank you all for coming".

They settled back into their routine as though they hadn't left the building for a week, but their telltale tans gave them away. The department heads met and delivered their reports. An extra shift had been hired and production was well ahead of schedule.

This state of near nirvana continued until a day before Nicole's birthday in May. The loud jangling of the telephone resounded throughout the apartment, waking Maggie and then Christina. Maggie answered with, "Who is calling at this hour? It's two o'clock in the morning. What the hell is so important that it couldn't wait?" She answered the phone. "You want to speak to Christina? All right, all right, hold on, I'll get her. Christina, telephone's for you. Overseas call, that's all they'd say."

Christina's heart missed a beat. She thought the news would concern Evan's parents. They were getting on in years and not as well as they had been. "Hello. Yes, operator, this is Christina D'Argent. Hello, who is calling?"

"Christina, it's Carliss and Jacques Freemont. Just what the hell are you playing at? We just saw an issue of the fashion magazine out of Paris and the pictures of Nicole were featured in an article done by an

American journalist? You've turned our daughter into a public 'baby doll'. Who gave you the right?"

"Actually, when you think about it, you gave me the right. Let me explain. Nicole came to me half starved, unhappy, and desperate. My heart went out to her and I have taken on the responsibility of raising a young woman experienced beyond her years from her ordeal in Paris. How dare you accuse me of exploiting her." Christina was very wide awake and very angry. Of all the unmitigated nerve, she fumed. She listened while Jacques Freemont vented his fury after his wife had burst into tears and handed him the phone.

"We are on our way to New York in the morning and will see you the following day. Make yourself available and be prepared to have Nicole taken away from you, you pervert." The expletive, although not profane, offended Christina to no end.

"Yes, and I remind you that I am her legal guardian and she has landed immigrant status. That's as close to being an American citizen as it gets. She has done nothing wrong and won't be deported. Yes, I suggest you take the next plane out of Paris and we'll settle this, once and for all. I can't believe you are attacking me in this manner. I'm going back to bed and I suggest you go back to what the hell you were doing before you interrupted my sleep."

Maggie and Christina discussed the conversation as quietly as they could, but they had no knowledge of the fact that Nicole had heard everything. She had picked up the extension in the bedroom and was near tears when she overheard the terrible tirade. Her parents were livid and determined to end her new found life style. Well, she wouldn't return to France. If they forced her to, she would run away, again and again if necessary. To accuse Christina of such horrible actions was just the way they had always acted. Nicole had run away from their imposing ways. She was expected to act in a demure manner, amuse their guests, and was kept apart from having friends her own age. She was treated as a Dresden doll, or as a prize pet poodle. Nicole wasn't even sure if her parents loved her as their child, or as someone they had chosen as one would choose a pedigree animal. It was negative thinking, but that was how she felt and she had never shared these emotions with anyone, not even Yves. When Christina finally re- entered the bedroom she shared with Nicole, she muttered something to the effect that some people had no respect for the time of night. Nicole pretended to be asleep but after a relative length of time began to cry, her sobs quietly muffled by the heavy bedcovers.

Three very tired people sat at the dining room table the following morning. No one wanted to discuss the angry conversation that had kept Christina from falling into her usual deep sleep. She had tossed and turned with terrible visions of Nicole being dragged out of the apartment and forcefully taken out of the country. Finally, she said, "Nicole, I heard from your parents last night. They wished to join us in a few days to celebrate your sixteenth birthday. They have missed you terribly and expressed the desire to spend some time with you, as well as to see how well you are doing."

"It's been a long time since I saw them. It must be almost a year. I don't know if I want to spend time with them alone. Will you stay with me, Christina, all the while they are here?" Nicole didn't want to let Christina know that she was afraid that they would force her to leave with them and return to her unhappy life in France. She attempted to be unaware of the threat of just that happening, having feigned sleep during the events of last night.

"Of course I will, Nicole. Your free time is limited anyway. We will celebrate your birthday at Sardi's with a wonderful dinner, a cake with all the trimmings, and gifts for you. I made all the necessary arrangements last week. I just have to call and have the staff add two more guests at the table. That will mean nine of us, which is a small crowd in my estimation." Christina exchanged glances with Maggie, and the two read one another's thoughts. Hopefully, the Freemonts wouldn't have the opportunity to continue their serious accusations and threats in a public place as well as ruin Nicole's special evening.

True to their word, the Freemonts were on the scene within the time specified. They were booked in another hotel not two blocks from Maggie's apartment, and had been calling hour upon hour with explicit orders for them to meet. As their hours were often undefined, with Nicole having to finish photo shoots, Maggie to answer her messages, and Christina to finish her designs, the trio always waited for one another so they could leave together. That evening, they didn't arrive home until around seven. The switchboard had been inundated by the Freemont calls and messages, and was happy to finally give them over to Christina.

She ruffled through them rather unconcerned. After reading the first one she had no reason to read the rest. Nicole's face looked a little pale. They had all had a very trying day, and were looking forward to their time together at the dinner table.

They were no sooner within the apartment when the doorman rang. Two very irate people were downstairs asking for their suite number. Should he give it to them?

"Look, the sooner we see them, the sooner this gets cleared up. Nicole, go to your room and we'll call you when they get here and are settled. I guess dinner can wait, although I am a little hungry," Christina said. Maggie prepared a pot of coffee and checked the refrigerator for something light to serve with it. No luck, so she called room service to have something sent up as quickly as possible. Just as she put down the phone, the doorbell rang and Christina motioned for Maggie to answer the door. It was, after all, her apartment.

"Yes, how may I help you?" she asked politely.

"Who are you? We were told that Christina D'Argent and our daughter lived here. Have we come to the wrong apartment?"

"Oh, you must be the Freemonts. Christina has told me so much about you. It was you who telephoned a few nights ago. I'm Maggie Cole, Christina's partner, and it was I who answered the call."

Maggie was stalling and doing her best to be annoyingly polite while Christina collected herself and prepared for whatever was to come. She came out of the kitchen and approached the front door as Maggie ushered the Freemonts into the living room. "Our guests have arrived, Christina."

Christina smiled as pleasantly as her racing emotions would allow. "Come join us. We are about to have a light supper. Room service should be here shortly. Let me take your coats. Maggie will show you to your seats. I'll join you in a minute." Christina took the opportunity to hang their coats in the hall closet, and took the few moments of respite to regain her composure. Gone was the warmth and friendliness that she had experienced when Evan had first introduced her to Carliss and Jacques so many years ago. There was no indication that they had ever been friends; thus, Christina realized that she was facing an uphill battle in the days to come. As she joined the three at the table she asked, "How was your flight? That overseas run can be rather tiring at times, don't you agree?"

Jacques interrupted rudely, "Enough of the small talk. Where is Nicole? We demand to see her, and you have no right to keep her away from us."

"Wait, just a minute. I'll get her. She has no idea you are coming and this will be a shock, I'm sure." Christina lied.

"Nicole, honey, there's someone here to see you." She bent forward and said, "your parents are here, act surprised. I lied and said that you weren't expecting them. Help me out here, will you?"

Nicole nodded, turned, and entered the dining room. She spoke as though she were meeting these people for the very first time. "Hello, it's nice that you could come to celebrate my sixteenth birthday." She did not ask as to their welfare, their state of mind, or why they were really in New York.

"Nicole, it's wonderful to see you." Her mother's eyes glistened with tears and her father's voice sounded choked as he said, "You look incredible. So happy! So grownup." He appeared at a loss for words. Nicole didn't respond or return his kiss and hug. She stepped back from him and took a seat at the table. "When will dinner be served? I'm suddenly very hungry," she said to no one in particular. It was as though she had removed herself from their presence and wished to resume her daily routine with Christina and Maggie, while they remained aloof. There was a distinct chill in the air. The waiter came in wheeling a cart and left it beside the table. Maggie nodded her thank you and dismissed him, saying she would serve everyone. The Freemonts felt the animosity; their attitude had aroused and they thought better of pursuing this facade. As Nicole chose her usual seat her mother attempted to draw her own chair closer to Nicole, but her daughter moved further away. Carliss was hurt but hid her feelings, her emotions churning within as she sent a pleading look to Jacques across the table.

He asked, "Nicole, how have you been? We were frantic when you left home last May. We searched for you for many months and thought the worst. When Christina telephoned us last December, it was with such joy when we learned that you had found your way to her and she promised she would look after you. Why did you run away from us, my child?"

"I'm not exactly the child you think I am, Papa. I have more experience behind me than most young women my age, but that is all in the past. I should not have run away with Yves, it was a very unhappy time and I, for one, am happy that it is over and done with. Christina saved me from falling even further and ending up on the streets. You must thank her, Papa, if it wasn't for her, I would not be here today." Jacques listened quietly as Nicole spoke. He knew then that their threats were meaningless. Christina had taken Nicole in and nurtured her as she would her own child, had she had one. They could find no fault as to Nicole's attitude, her mannerisms, or her attire. She was as normal as the most well-rounded teenager in New York as one would hope to find. For this they were truly grateful.

"Christina, perhaps we were out of line when we accused you of exploiting Nicole. Please accept our apologies. We are very emotional people and when we saw the magazine article, it upset us to no end. Again, we are very sorry."

With great trepidation, Christina nodded in agreement. She coldly accepted the apology for as far as it went. She thought to herself how he had accused her of being a pervert. How soon he forgot! "It's all right, Carliss, I understand. You are her mother and you have every right to question me. I will tell you this though. If you attempt to take Nicole back to France I will seek an injunction against you. She is not only my charge but she is the lifeblood of our company. We are on a tremendous upswing in our popularity and profits, and we cannot allow you to take her from us. The contracts have been drawn up by our team of lawyers, tying her to our company for many years. The door does not swing both ways in this case, I'm afraid. You have as much access to Nicole while you are here in New York as you wish, so long as it doesn't interfere with her schooling or her work. I have to make this clear right from the outset, so that you don't harbour any hopes of her ever returning soon." There, her cards were on the table. Nicole said nothing more. She merely held her breath. Maggie wore her corporate face, waiting for the Freemonts' reply.

Jacques spoke first. "Will we have the freedom to watch Nicole at work? Then we can decide for ourselves what course to follow, if indeed we find one is necessary?"

"By all means, but you mustn't disturb her during her studies. She has a tutor and they spend four hours a day in a room set aside for this purpose. When Nicole finishes her daily studies, we all have lunch together and her work day begins after lunch. I must warn you that some of the photo shoots and personal outings are often noisy, as she is accompanied by an entourage of makeup artists and photographers as well as costume people. The personal appearances are at department stores which carry our products, but Nicole is dressed in day clothes and is available to answer questions from the customers. She is very natural during these sessions. Her audiences are growing in number as her popularity increases. I believe you will be very proud of her, as we are." Christina saw that her speech had made a good impression on Nicole's parents, as their expressions changed from outright suspicion to undivided attention. Christina outlined the plans for Nicole's birthday party and said that the reservations had been changed to include them.

Carliss asked, "Nicole, is there anything special that you would like for your birthday?"

Nicole pondered the question, the tiny frown appeared between her eyebrows then she said something that made Christina's heart almost break. "I would like a gold locket, Maman, with a picture of you and Papa, and I will wear it close to my heart."

Christina remembered the locket that was purchased for her by Adam, which Becka had given to her as a favour to him as they had missed one another that fateful Thanksgiving holiday. Maggie noticed the sudden change in Christina as she bent forward and said behind her hand, "Are you all right? You as though you had seen a ghost."

"It's nothing. I'll tell you later when they've left. Okay?"

The party seated around the table retired to the living room while Christina cleared the table. Maggie excused herself to attend to some small chores in her bedroom, leaving Nicole alone with her parents. Whenever the conversation turned to their life in France, Nicole's face paled and they suddenly changed the subject. She spoke of her new friends, what they did for entertainment, how exciting life was in New York. She was especially enthralled with Central Park, which was located right in the middle of the city. It was the heart and soul of New York and New Yorkers, who used the park with the utmost respect throughout the entire year. She had been taken to the Metropolitan Museum of Art, Fire Island, Staten Island, and the Statue of Liberty up close. After all, the Statue of Liberty was a gift from France. A few hours passed in relative peacefulness with no harsh words or accusations being made.

Carliss and Jacques Freemont finally agreed that they were overcome with jet lag and wished only for a good night's sleep. They were planning a shopping trip the following day, and would meet at Sardi's for the celebration dinner.

Christina was the first to speak after they had taken their departure. "Thank goodness for that. Once they see Nicole at work I'm sure they will be convinced that taking her away would be bad for everyone concerned. A legal battle would ensue and feelings would be hurt. Nicole's career would be shattered and I just can't picture her returning to a schoolgirls' life in France wearing a shapeless, colorless uniform as she joins the fold. I know that she would run away at the first opportunity, and who would be around to save her?"

Maggie agreed. "Now, Ms. Corelli, tell me about the locket."

Christina unlocked and reached into a desk drawer, which held her personal papers. Before she withdrew the locket, she made sure that Nicole was not in the room or within earshot. She heard the shower running and deemed it safe to continue her conversation with Maggie. "Remember how I told you about the photos of the twins? Well, here they are, within this locket, which I haven't opened in five years. I used to wear the locket every day, but for some reason it disturbed Evan. He knew about the twins, and had endeavoured to find them, but all his money and connections were to no avail and we put the matter to rest. At least, he did. Always in my heart I believe I will find them, I just don't know when that will happen."

Maggie hugged her in sympathy. "I suspected that was what was troubling you. You always get such a sad, faraway look in your eyes, and I know you are remembering those precious twenty minutes you had when they were first born. My heart thanks Sister Rose for her compassion in bringing them to you, but in another sense, you have never said goodbye to them. Am I right?"

"I can never say goodbye, Maggie, even if I hadn't been allowed to see them. I just couldn't ever forget them. I realize now why Adam was so angry with me. If I had remained in New York, would we have settled our differences? I just don't know, and I may never know."

"Come on now, Christina, don't beat yourself up. Let's put this to rest for tonight. I don't know about you, but I'm bushed. Goodnight. And incidentally, you handled yourself very well in placating the Freemonts, as well as not giving in to them with regards to Nicole. There's too much at stake, believe it."

An evening at Sardi's always lived up to one's expectations. Nicole's birthday meal was superb, served with the champagne selected by the Freemonts, which was one of the best on the market. Christina was pleased to see that everyone appeared happy and relaxed. The time came for the cake and Nicole shut her eyes and crossed her fingers as she wished with all her might, then promptly blew out all the candles. John, who loved parties, ordered a bottle of wine be sent to all the patrons' tables so that they may drink a toast to the birthday girl. The restaurant took on a festive air with everyone participating. The exchange of gifts was next. Nicole loved the new emerald green angora sweater, a gift from Maggie. Christina had purchased an emerald ring, which was a perfect fit. Next, gifts from Robert and Andrea included accessories for her bed, a heart shaped pillow, a stuffed bear, a picture of her favourite movie star. Ellen and John had consulted with Christina and decided upon a silver charm bracelet with openings where new charms could be added. Finally, the Freemonts, last but not least, presented Nicole with a blue velvet box which without a doubt contained jewellery.

Nicole opened the box and exclaimed with delight. "It's the locket I asked for. How wonderful." She opened it very carefully and discovered a picture of her mother and father holding a tiny baby. "Is that picture of me, *Maman*?"

Christina attempted to cover up her sharp intake of breath. The color drained from her face. How fortuitous, she thought; a locket containing a picture of an infant. Memories flooded back to her time in confinement, of a gift under such differing circumstances. Nicole turned and handed the locket to Christina saying, "Look, Christina, how lovely it is." The inscription on the back of the locket read, "to Nicole, our precious daughter, *Maman* and Papa," and a small "16" placed at the base of the heart-shaped trinket.

"What a gracious gift. One Nicole will treasure all her life, I'm sure." Christina spoke with as much grace as she could muster.

The orchestra had arrived and began to play. Christina noted the time, feeling somewhat tired, but agreed that everyone could enjoy the dancing for an hour or so. The music was of the popular variety and encouraged the patrons to get up and dance. Toe tapping led to hand clapping, and finally the restaurant resounded in many people singing along with the orchestra. Nicole's eyes shone with happiness. This was the most delightful birthday party ever.

The Freemonts left around ten p.m. and the party began to break up. By ten-thirty, all had left the restaurant. Nicole was a little let down by the time they had reached the apartment, but her mood was still high as she unloaded the gifts onto her bed. Christina enjoyed watching her pleasure.

The following day, the Freemonts, as promised, were waiting for Nicole after she had broken for lunch. She was to resume work on an overseas project, which was to feature a summer line for their new lingerie. If the Freemonts promised to remain as quiet onlookers they could stay for the shoot. If any interruptions, unwanted conversations, or other extraneous noise affected the work of the team, they would be removed. They understood the regulations and waited patiently for Nicole to appear. They were speechless when she walked out onto the set. She had been transformed into a vision of loveliness that took their breath away. Her ensemble was not too risqué, but rather demure to match the model. The material was of the highest quality chiffon, glacial green in color, which shimmered in the artificial light. The slightly darker marabou feathers framed the bodice and flounced the hem. Nicole looked right at home wearing this getup. She had taken to this job as a duck to water, and nothing could persuade her to pursue a career other than this. At first glance Carliss was a little shocked at the outfit's short length, but when she finally considered where the frock was to be worn, it made a lot of sense. Nicole's photographer instructed her in many of the poses that he wanted, but she also used her own initiative in creating poses of her own. The first phase of the shoot lasted an hour and a half. Nicole left the set to change and renew her makeup, as well as to relax her body from the poses that were a strain on her muscles. She had no time to chat with her parents, although she knew they were out there watching her every move. Once the lights were focused on her she forgot everything but the work at hand and the voice of her photographer, Domingo.

At long last, the day's work was over. Everyone was satisfied that the afternoon had been very productive, but the prints would ultimately tell the tale. They were examined very carefully and only the perfect were selected. That often meant that out of a hundred or so shots, only a handful would qualify for the magazine features.

Christina poked her head in to see how the day had gone. Jacques and Carliss were amazed at the professionalism of their daughter. She performed under pressure, took direction like a pro, and had conducted herself in a manner befitting a proper young woman. That was all that Christina had to hear. She knew they would not pursue the issue of taking Nicole back to France. Incidentally, she wondered when they were leaving. By the looks of it, most likely it would be soon.

Christina was right. Carliss and Jacques were satisfied that all was well in New York and they had no intention of holding Nicole back from her most lucrative career. Maggie had informed them that Nicole's share of the profits was being put into a trust fund until she turned twenty-one. If all of the predictions were right, the balance would add into the millions when she turned twenty-five. They had expressed their satisfaction as to the conditions of the contract. They did not wish their daughter to become rich overnight and, within a short time, use the same amount of time to spend her entire fortune. Rags to riches to rags! Maggie couldn't agree more.

Within the following two months, Christina urged Nicole to attend more social functions. The weather was becoming downright balmy and the early summer evenings were meant to be enjoyed. She encouraged Nicole to accompany her to the theatre, as well as attend concerts staged by the New York Philharmonic Orchestra. She was becoming extremely popular and The House of Corelli admitted that she must be seen in public, but in quality surroundings and at quality functions.

On the first day of summer, Christina asked Nicole, "How would you like to attend the ballet this evening?" It would last a few hours with a half-hour intermission, so they would probably be home just after eleven. They would alert the press that she was to be attending so a few quality photographs could be taken during the intermission. Christina and Nicole pondered over what she should wear and finally picked out the suit they had purchased at Sak's a few days previous. It was a formal dress of a soft pastel crepe, the sleeves off the shoulder but the bodice still held up by fine spaghetti straps. The dress was tucked in at the waist, but the skirt flowed out in a bias so that when it reached the middle of her knee the hem flared out and around her legs. She wore a white mink-trimmed stole over the dress to ward off the late evening chill. To complement Nicole's outfit, Christina chose a warm, peach-coloured two piece suit, trimmed in sequined detail framing the collar of the jacket. They both embraced the seasons' colors and stood out from the crowd which, for the most stuck to their basic black for evening functions. Some of the society women wore red, but most could not carry off such a strong color.

During the performance Christina began to squirm. She became nervous for no reason at all. Nicole was enthralled by the performance and noticed nothing untoward in Christina's manner.

The feeling persisted and Christina began to glance about. Suddenly her eyes were riveted on the couple seated with others in a special box above them. The man in the box was none other than Adam. Their eyes locked, neither one wishing to be the first to turn away. He was accompanied by his wife Joan, the ice queen. Christina did not return Adam's smile but continued to stare as though mesmerized by the sight of him. Joan noticed her husband's attention was not on the performance, and looked in the direction of his gaze. She noticed Christina at once and her look was deadly. Christina finally looked away, turning her attention once more to the performance. A few minutes later, she stole a quick glance to see if Adam was still there. He certainly was, and this time his smile had turned into a grin of triumph. She felt the color rise to her cheeks as she quickly glanced away. During the intermission, Nicole and Christina were the center of attention. Many people were approaching them, their greetings for Christina but their eyes focused upon Nicole. The press was there as promised, doing what they did best. Through the flash of camera shots, Christina glanced over the heads of the crowd and once again her eyes locked with Adam. This time he was admiring her, the woman he had loved so very long ago. And, damn it, he still loved her. Christina experienced a shock, the emotions coursing through her body. Why did he have to be so damned handsome?

Joan was chatting away with friends, sipping her glass of champagne while pretending not to notice just where her husband's attention was directed. She smiled at Christina, but the smile never reached her eyes. The two women studied one another for a brief moment until Christina decided it was just a waste of time to give this chance meeting another thought. She was delighted that Nicole had been received so well by everyone. She answered all of the public's questions openly and sincerely but gave away nothing of her personal life. She refused to say how old she was, who her parents were, and where she had lived before coming to New York. Christina was very proud of her.

A week passed and the month of July was almost upon them. Christina had spent a very trying day at the office, inundated with overseas calls from *Chez Corelli* and *Casa Christina*. They had received numerous requests from customers asking to meet and speak with Christina as well as Nicole, who had taken Europe by storm. Christina had put them off with a half- promise that when her schooling was over for the term, they just might be able to reserve some time away from New York. At long last the day came to an end. Maggie was off to an evening social, dinner and theatre. Nicole had asked if she and Robert could go out for pizza and a movie. Christina couldn't believe her luck. She was actually going to be alone this evening.

She entered the apartment, placed her bag on the foyer table, hung her suit coat in the hall closet and walked into the kitchen, where she opened the refrigerator door and surveyed the contents. Not much of a choice. She decided that room service was her best bet and called in an order.

The waiter arrived within a half hour and was only too happy to serve his dream girl. Christina still enjoyed the public admiration, more so since she was not so much in the limelight. She nibbled away at the meal, sipped on the wine and began to daydream. She walked over to the desk where she kept her personal items and pulled out the drawer. For no reason that she could identify she began to cry. Was it the poignant memories that Nicole's gift of a locket had triggered and which she had suppressed? Christina could not stop crying. Her own locket lay in the palm of her hand and she cried for the babies she had lost, she cried for Adam who's anger had driven into a loveless marriage and whom she still loved with all her heart, she cried for Evan, who's only wish was that they spend more time together not having to share her with the fashion world. She cried because she was lonely. The only blessings Christina had were that she had many dear friends and was very financially secure. Nicole had come into her life at a crucial time and was beginning to endear herself to Christina, but it wasn't enough. Christina needed fulfillment. To her, that meant a husband, preferably

Adam, and children, preferably the twins. She reached deeper into the drawer and withdrew a notebook. It was her old journal, in which she used to write entries daily but had given up many years ago when Adam had stormed out of the apartment, his accusations ringing in her ears. By now her tears had lessened in intensity, but when she opened the journal they began in earnest. She skimmed over a few of the entries, familiarizing herself with the circumstances. She was about to place the journal back in its place when a piece of paper fell from between the pages. It was the note Sister Rose had thrust into her hand when they said goodbye sixteen years ago. Christina wiped the tears from her eyes as she studied the note. The address of Sister Rose's birth sister was boldly written. She lived in the city of Montreal, Quebec. A phone number was included, along with her address and full name. Christina could not deal with her surging emotions. She replaced the paper within the folds of the journal and placed it in the drawer of her bedroom night table. The effect of the wine was wearing off, so she poured herself a stiff shot of brandy to quell the continuous shaking of her hands. Christina realized that she was at a crossroads. Would it be wise to search for her daughters at so late a date, only to suffer devastating disappointment?

Besides, the address was so old, would the people have moved? Where was Sister Rose? The nuns were often transferred within the order, so she could be anywhere. The brandy began to take effect as Christina pondered the possibilities. She prepared for bed, her mind in turmoil. Christina slept fitfully, awaking once from a dream in which she pictured herself holding two infants as she lovingly sang the lullaby that her mother had once sung to her. Her pillow was wet with tears. It was a good thing that Nicole was sleeping over at the Cole's, because Christina's mood would have disturbed her greatly. She was Nicole's rock, and as her rock she couldn't cry.

It was Saturday morning, and there was nothing to do but have a leisurely breakfast, read the Times, and chat with Maggie. It was still early, and Maggie was not awake. Christina's mood was not improved from her evening sojourn. She had been depressed once before in her life and it was Evan who had saved her. Now there was no one. She would have to deal with her grievous memories by herself.

Chapter Forty-Four

CHRISTINA WAITED UNTIL TEN o'clock that morning before she picked up the phone to place her call. She put the receiver back onto the cradle, stared at the phone for a few more minutes, then, with determination, she placed the call. A woman's voice answered, "Good morning, you have reached the Carmichael residence. To whom do you wish to speak?"

The maid was well-schooled in the proper use of the English language. Christina asked, "I must speak with Dr. Carmichael. Tell him it is most urgent."

"Whom shall I say is calling?" "Just a very old friend."

"Wait one moment, Madame." The maid put the phone down and Christina could hear her footsteps fade away. A few minutes she returned, saying that Dr. Carmichael had left for his office. Would Madame care to speak with Mrs. Carmichael?"

A voice in the background interrupted the maid. "Who is calling at this ungodly hour of the morning? How rude. Take a message or just hang up." A very annoyed Joan Carmichael admonished her maid.

Christina said nothing. She just hung up. She reached for the telephone directory and took some time finding the correct address and phone number. If she didn't follow through with this call, who knew when her determination would be this strong again? She had to speak with Adam.

"Good morning, Dr. Finestad and Carmichael's office. How may I help you?"

"I'm sorry to disturb you, Miss, but I must speak with Dr. Carmichael. It is rather urgent, I may add. Just tell him it's Christina ... he'll know."

"Hold the line, Madame. She buzzed the intercom to his office and said, "A call for you.

Dr. Carmichael. She says it is Christina."

"I'll take it. And please hold all further incoming calls." The receptionist hung up and he continued. "Christina, is it really you?"

"Yes, Adam. I must see you. Where can we meet? Are you free for lunch?"

"What's happened? You sound agitated. I'll meet you in the park by the pretzel stand in half an hour?" Christina said that would be fine, and hung up.

Adam had come into the office to complete many of his patients' charts and to dictate progress reports. He could have done this at any time during the week but he had to escape from his insufferable wife, Joan. She was fast becoming intolerable, especially after she had witnessed the long intimate look that he and Christina had exchanged during the ballet performance. She had been more distant and even colder than usual, but by this time he had become quite used to her moods and couldn't care less if her feelings had been hurt or not. Actually, she was probably more concerned that some of her friends may have witnessed what she had. Adam hadn't been able to take his eyes off Christina and found his eyes returning to study her and Nicole. He had no idea who Nicole might be, and as he watched them together, laughing and whispering, he thought he caught some familiar movements from the young girl. The way she tossed her head as she pushed the curls from her face; the way she held her head and lifted her shoulders. She reminded him of someone, but he couldn't remember who. He hurriedly placed the charts in a neat pile, grabbed his suit coat, and was out of the office without a backward glance.

He was in the park before Christina, simply because his office was on Park Avenue and he had but to walk across an intersection to the park's entrance. He paced in front of the bench near the pretzel stand, all the while glancing at his watch at five minute intervals. She was a few minutes late, but at last he saw her as she walked proudly towards him. He was at a loss for words. What should he say? Sorry was not enough for what he had said years ago, which had driven her away.

Christina extended her hand and said, "Thank you, Adam, for meeting me. It's good to see you. You look well."

He took her hand in his, feeling the warmth and familiarity of her touch. An electric shock ran through him and he was reluctant to let go. Their eyes met as Christina's body pulsed with old emotions. She wanted desperately to throw herself into his arms and stay there forever, but Adam was a married man. "Christina, I can't believe it's really you. When I saw you at the ballet a few weeks ago I couldn't believe my eyes. I haven't been able to get you out of my mind since." He noted the sudden glistening of tears in those incredible emerald eyes. "Come, sit here. What's troubling you?"

She told him about her experience during Nicole's birthday party; how her locket had triggered all the old emotions. She said she had rehashed everything by reading the entries in her old journal, and now the locket, which Adam had given her, was adorned about her neck. She opened the heart, splitting it in two, and extended the contents so that he could get a good look. For a long moment, he said nothing. Christina returned the locket with the precious photos inside to its rightful place around her neck. She said, "I found a piece of paper, which I had completely forgotten about after I left the Grace Hospital. The nun who had befriended me thrust it into my hand as my parents were dragging me out of the building. I put it between the pages of my journal and it wasn't until last evening that I re-discovered it. Here, I want you to have it. I can tell you that it contains the name, address, and telephone of Sister Rose's birth sister whom, she says, will know where to find her if I should ever need her. The Mother House of the Sisters of St. Martha is in Montreal, and that is where Sister Rose's family resides. Adam, if I ever meant anything to you at all, will you try to find them? Because so much time has passed, Sister Rose may be retired and you may find her in Montreal. I can't leave New York without taking Nicole. I am her guardian. That is a long story, though, and doesn't have anything to do with what I am asking. No one knows about the twins except my partner and dear friend, Maggie Cole. My husband Evan knew and did everything in his power to find them. He threw money at the convent, investigators came up with nothing and I guess I gave up for a while."

Adam studied the note she had handed him, trying to still his shaking hands. His voice sounded choked with tears as he answered.

"I'll arrange my practice so that Finestad can take over for as long as it takes, I guess ..."

"What about your wife? Won't she want to know why you're suddenly leaving?"

"What about my wife? She won't miss a hair on my head. I've long given up on her and I'm tired of being her escort to those insufferable social functions that have become the mainstay of her purpose in life. My marriage is a joke, Christina, I don't mind telling you." Trying not to appear too eager he asked, "What about your husband, Evan, isn't it? Won't he mind? Have you discussed this with him?"

Her face took on an ashen pallor so suddenly that it frightened him. She took her time answering. "Evan was killed in a boating accident a year ago tomorrow. I was in the spectator seats and witnessed the entire crash. It was horrific and I still have nightmares. He was thirty- five years old and had his whole life ahead of him. I couldn't stay in France any longer and have been in New York for a year. It must have been fate that brought us to the same ballet." Adam expressed his condolences, but in his heart he was secretly glad that there was no longer a Mr. D'Argent in the picture. "Adam, I know this is sudden, but if you don't wish to pursue this matter, should we just let sleeping dogs lie? I don't want to live with this empty place in my heart for the rest of my natural days. It's too hard to bear."

"No, Christina. I want to do this. It's about time I quit blaming you for their loss. I know now that you were helpless in the wake of your father's anger. You were just a kid. I had no right to attack you the way I did. Lord knows how I've regretted my actions to this very day."

Christina arose from the bench as she prepared to take her leave. Adam wished to prolong the meeting and asked, "Would you care to join me in a New York lunch?" She nodded her head and he asked the vendor, "Two of your largest hot pretzels, sir, as well as two coffees."

He returned to the bench, handing her the pretzel wrapped in a large paper napkin. She said, "It's been years since I had one of these. Thank you, Adam." She smiled as she took a large bite out of the pretzel, "Absolutely delicious."

He returned her smile. He hadn't felt this relaxed in years. She was so easy to be around. No affectations, no false smile, no "How are you darling ... it's been simply ages," as his wife was prone to say. Christina, despite her fame and fortune, was as natural and infectious as she had always been. She was like a breath of fresh air, so different from his world.

They said very little while they ate their lunch. Finally, Christina said, "I must go, Adam, Nicole will be home soon and wondering where I've been. Here's my number. Call me whenever you can. I'll be waiting."

He sat on the bench as he watched her walk away, her head held proud, her long chestnut hair blowing about in the wind. For a split second he thought he had been dreaming, and the meeting hadn't happened, until he looked down and saw the note clutched in his hand. Adam knew then that his life had just taken a turn for the better.

The first thing he had to do was clear his coming absence with his partner, Dr. Finestad. Once that was accomplished he would inform Joan. Adam returned to the office in time to meet Sam as he prepared to catch up on his paperwork. "Could I talk with you for a few minutes? It's rather important."

"Sure thing, Adam. Come on in. What's on your mind?"

"I have to go away for awhile. I don't know for how long. All I can tell you is that it involves something I should have done five years ago, and I can't put it off any longer." Adam's face was the picture of determination.

Dr. Finestad replied, "By the looks of you, you're hell-bent on whatever this is and you'd probably go anyway, whether I agreed to it or not. Am I right so far?"

Adam smiled. His partner knew him so well. "Yeah, you're right. I would like to tell you, but I can't get my hopes up, and I wouldn't want to fail and disappoint a number of people. Can you finish up with my patients? Most of them have already had their surgery and are recovering well. I would really be at a loss to find anyone else and I hate to cut them loose."

"No problem, Adam. When are you leaving?" "Today, if I can get a flight out."

"Have you told Joan?"

"No, not yet. I'll do that while I'm packing," Adam said, his lips pressed tightly, as though he were about to enter the ring. "I've left my charts on my desks. One pile has been dictated and the other I was about to do this morning when this problem arose."

He left the office, his thoughts in turmoil. Where should he begin? If he flew to Edmonton, most likely the records would be filed in some dark, dank basement and the staff would have left or retired over the sixteen-year gap. He decided that he would follow up with the name and address that Christina had given to him. If this nun's sister was still in Montreal, she would probably be his best lead. He drove the car into the garage, withdrew his briefcase from the front seat, and hurried toward the entrance to his building. Joan was still at the breakfast table, nibbling on a slice of dry toast and drinking her innumerable cups of coffee. The air was thick with smoke, a habit she had been adamant about not breaking. It was her only vice, or so she said. "Good morning, Joan. We have to talk." Adam tried to gauge her mood.

"What's on your mind, Adam? You look so serious," she asked.

He walked into the adjoining bedroom and withdrew his suitcase from the closet. She had followed him, and her eyes widened in consternation. "Are you leaving me? I don't believe it. After all I've done for you, how dare you."

"You haven't even asked where I might be going, and after what you just said, it's really none of your concern. I have to go away for a while, and I don't know for how long. That's about all I can tell you."

"Are you going away with another woman? That's it, isn't it?" Joan had the annoying habit of answering her own questions, not ever allowing him to get a word in edgewise. He decided to torment her.

"You might say it involves a woman. But I'm not going away with her. I'm going alone." "Why won't you tell me? What will I tell my friends?" she asked.

"Tell them whatever you think they'll believe. I really don't give a damn." "How dare you talk to me in that tone of voice. I'm your wife."

"Yeah, don't remind me. Your idea of being a wife is having someone to escort you to all your boring social functions and gossip parties. I just don't have the stomach for it any longer. This mission I'm on is very important to me, and I don't really care if you approve or not. Suck it up, my ice queen, I'm going and that's that."

The argument became more heated as Joan replied. "Fine, go, you miserable excuse for a husband. You think more of your patients than you ever think of me. And don't deny it!"

"I'm denying nothing. Those patients keep you in jewels and furs and memberships to your women's clubs. Who do you think paid for that car in the garage?"

"Now that's hitting below the belt. You knew when you married me that I had to be kept in high style. Why complain now?"

"I've had enough of this. I'm through discussing this, goodbye Joan."

"If you leave now, Adam Carmichael, don't come back."

"That's the best news I've had all day. I just might do that."

Joan's eyes glistened with angry tears, "I'm filing for divorce on Monday. I'll be free of you in six months."

"Yes, and I'll be out from under you and your insufferable arrogance and pride. All I ever wanted from this marriage is to have a loving partner, and I expected a child or two to come from this union. Instead, all I got from you were excuses. 'The time wasn't right,' 'Perhaps in a year or so,' 'A pregnancy would ruin my figure,' 'Children are a burden. They would interfere with my schedule.' And the list goes on and on. Well, I've had it too. Take this life and shove it, and you have my permission to change your name back to Joan Finestad. As a favour, include that in your divorce proceedings."

Joan was stunned. She had never seen Adam so incensed. Something was driving him. She had been bluffing about filing for divorce on Monday, but after suffering through his tirade she was more determined than ever to follow through. He was right. They had nothing left. They had trouble carrying on a conversation over the dining table, before it became intolerable. She cared nothing about his latest surgery success, and he didn't give a rat's ass about which of her friends was having an affair.

As he left the stately home he had shared with Joan, he didn't even give a backward glance. Actually, Adam felt as though he had sprouted wings. A great weight had been lifted from his shoulders, and his newly found freedom felt incredible. Lord knows he should have done this a long time ago, but he had resigned himself to life with Joan as opposed to life alone. He drove to the airport and arranged to leave his car in the airport storage until his return, and left the clerk with his credit card number in case they would have to bill him. Having called ahead of time, he knew that the airport had had a last-minute cancellation on the noon flight, and had jumped at the offer. He glanced at his watch; he had a half hour before he would be airborne. Montreal wasn't far, and he probably should have driven the distance, but he was so excited from his meeting with Christina that he couldn't have contained himself driving along congested highways. As planned, Adam was airborne and comfortably seated by noon. The plane would arrive in an hour's time, but by the time he was actually at the terminal for unloading, another hour would be used up. Because he had checked one large suitcase, he had to spend some time at the baggage collection area. He hailed a cab from the line-up outside the airport and directed him to the best hotel in town. The driver recommended the Hotel Frontenac, which very posh, very expensive, and had the very best of service. Adam didn't mind, so long as he was comfortable and could access the city within minutes. He paid the cabbie and registered at the hotel desk. He made arrangements to have a rental car sent over for his use. The hotel had underground parking and would reserve a stall.

Approximately at three o'clock that afternoon, Adam sat on the luxurious bed in his hotel room, and with shaking hands dialled the number on the scrap of paper Christina had given him.

"*Allo.*" A female voice on the line answered.

"Yes, I'm looking for Madame Benoit? Have I the correct number?" "*Oui,* you do. I must call Madame to the telephone. Please wait." "*Allo.* This is Madame Benoit speaking? Who's calling?"

"Madame, you don't know me, but I am a friend of a friend of your sister, the nun. I was given your number as a contact if my friend was ever in need. Rather than speak with you about this matter, may I meet with you? My name is Dr. Adam Carmichael and the matter is of great importance. Shall I come to your home?"

The line was quiet for a moment. Finally, Madame Benoit said, "*Oui,* Doctor. You may come to my residence at the following address. I will meet with you around four o'clock, if that is convenient for you?"

As she read the address to him, he noted that it was exactly the one on the note. As he thanked Madame Benoit and broke off the connection, he lay back upon the bed and his first thoughts were about how the search had finally begun. He thought about how not only needed to do this for Christina, but for himself as well.

Chapter Forty-Five

After her meeting with Adam in the park, Christina couldn't believe that she had actually summoned the courage to meet with him. The emotions which coursed through her body had frightened her. Obviously, he still had the charm that had drawn her to him so many years ago. She did admit to herself that she loved him and always would, whether there was a future for them or not. When she returned to the apartment, Maggie and Nicole asked her where she had been. Because she was a creature of habit, her absence from the suite on a Saturday morning in July caused them to worry. Christina merely said, "Maggie was asleep, Nicole hadn't returned from the Coles', and the day was so lovely that I decided a walk in the park was exactly what I needed. We are stuck in the office all day and often long into the evening, and it felt nice to feel the sun on my face and no phone in front of me needing my attention." Her color was still high from her meeting with Adam and she hoped the two wouldn't notice. She poured herself a cup of coffee and asked them to sit down.

"Okay, we're sitting down. What's on your mind?" Maggie asked.

"I have turned this matter over in my mind and have reached the following conclusion." "Oh boy, this sounds serious." Nicole remarked as she pressed Christina for more details.

"In a way, you could say it is. Our overseas outlets have been pestering me to allow them to meet Nicole in person. They want to set up appearances for the two of us during peak business hours so that our customers will be able to question us one on one. Most likely the topics will zone in on makeup, perfume, and lingerie. If they become too personal, we can always cut short the appearance by requesting a break. Paris wants us, Barcelona has called a number of times, and Milan has sent memos. What do you think? Do you want to spend a month or so roaming about Europe with me, Nicole? And Maggie, will you relish the break from the two of us constantly cluttering up your apartment?"

"Don't be silly. I love your clutter." Maggie continued, "I think it would do you both some good. Do you plan on visiting the Freemonts?"

"Only if Nicole wishes to."

"I would like very much to visit and meet with our companies, Christina. It's a splendid idea. As for my parents, I suppose we could spend a day or two with them, but only after we have finished our tour. Then we can beg off by telling them that we must return to New York, as the tour took longer than anticipated." Nicole waited for an answer.

"She sure is learning the ropes. Your parents are lovely people, Nicole, but the choice is entirely up to you. Their visit here in May was a good idea, and I don't think that they are as worried about you now as they were when they first saw that feature article of you in the Italian magazine. I guess it came as quite a shock. They still think of you as that beautiful, precocious little girl I first met six years ago." Christina smiled as she recalled the meeting. I also remember another little girl saying *'Bellisimo'* when she caught sight of me leaving a taxi during our stay in Milan for a runway show."

Christina said that she had a few important matters to clear up early in the week, but they could plan their trip beginning on Wednesday. With luck, they could finish the necessary business dealings and still have time to take in a few side trips. Maggie and John would hold down the fort in New York.

"I'm sorry to have taken up much of your first summer in New York, but we'll be back in August and the weather stays warm and balmy right into November." Christina said.

"It's just fine, Christina. I'm getting excited already. Could we see more of Italy? France is all too familiar to me, and I hope we can spend some in the south of Spain. Costa del Sol, from what my friends always said, really and truly is the Sun Coast. They spent many weeks there with their parents, while mine were too busy with the vineyards to vacation in the summer. Should I pack a lot of clothes, Christina, or shall we round out my wardrobe with some European designs?"

"Pack whatever you please, and yes, we'll buy whatever we need. I'd like this to be a working holiday, whereby work will take a backseat to the holiday aspect."

Maggie said, "It sounds wonderful. I only wish I could join you, but perhaps another time."

They continued to talk about the upcoming vacation while the afternoon drifted by. Nicole was on the telephone with Robert and Maggie was immersed in the Wall Street Journal, while Christina rifled through the latest editions of Fashion magazine. From time to time they would share a news item or feature article with one another. "What shall we do about dinner this evening?" Maggie asked.

"Seeing that it is going to be our last Saturday night together, why don't we go out and celebrate? It's been awhile since I've had lobster and champagne," Christina replied.

"Nicole, come in here a minute, please?"

"Be right with you," was the reply. She soon entered the room. "What's up?" she asked. "What do you think of us getting dressed up and going out to a fine restaurant for dinner tonight? Did you make any plans with Robert?" they asked.

"No, I was just telling him of our plans to leave on Wednesday, and I told him how much I would miss his company." Nicole had indeed been sincere about that last statement. Robert was actually her best friend and confidante. He had listened when she told him about her parents' threat to take her back to France, and he had been as worried as she. They had weathered that storm together. He had said that he would definitely miss her, but they could make up for lost time during the month of August. Andrea said that she would save up lots of good things for them to do when she returned. She asked if Nicole would bring her back some perfume from Paris. A Summer's Evening, it was called.

Their Saturday evening was a huge success. The restaurant which they had chosen was filled with business acquaintances, friends, and relatives of friends, whom they had met on many occasions. The night out lasted well after ten before someone noticed the time and decided that it was getting late.

Saturday's weather had spilled over into Sunday. Christina asked Nicole if she would like to walk in the Park, feed the swans, and get her first taste of a giant hot pretzel. Nicole asked if Andrea and Robert could come along. "What a good idea. Of course, call them and invite them."

Ellen and John had no plans for the day, and Christina invited them as well. Before long, Maggie was included as well, and they made quite an entourage as they strolled through the park. Christina loved to people-watch, and the weather had brought out a crowd composed of people from all walks of life. The younger half did their own thing, and the adults chatted and laughed while everyone enjoyed their lunch breaks. The pretzel stand operator said to Christina, "Hello again, Miss. It's nice to see you."

Maggie looked at her sideway, confused as to what Christina had been up to. "Don't look so suspicious." She made up a story saying that she had asked for directions to the central fountain. "He said he recognized me from the cover magazines, and didn't ever forget a beautiful woman."

Maggie said, "Don't you ever get tired of the fame and intrusion upon your privacy? I think that if it was me, I just might begin to resent it."

"Not in the least. I love people, and if they delight in talking to me and admiring what I do, then I am happy for them. Being in the limelight can't last forever you know, so why not bask in it while I'm still young enough?"

"Yes, you have a point. Enjoy the moment. Speaking of which, will you visit with Andre and Marie? If you do, will you tell Jean that I send my regards?"

"You do have a thing for that man, Maggie Cole. I don't blame you. Jean is an exceptional human being. He was compassionate, caring, and attentive after Evan's accident while attempting to deal with his own personal loss. I was completely out of it for a day or two and Jean took care of everything. I only wish his personal life was happier. His wife will not budge on the divorce. Why keep on with a hopeless situation? I guess it's true when people refer to 'the ties that bind,' as Jean can surely attest to. Why don't you write to him, Maggie?"

"I have wanted to, Christina, but what would I say? He knows how much I care for him as he for me, so what else is there to say? Of course I miss him, and it would be a welcome pleasure to see him again, but we have covered that as well. I just don't know. My last few dates have left me comparing the guy to Jean, and the guy never comes out on top." Christina noticed that her friend's eyes were sad as she lamented upon her loneliness.

"I'll do my best. Maybe I can light a fire under him and induce him to come to see us in New York. He has pledged his devotion to the D'Argents, but everyone deserves a break from their routine, don't you agree?" Maggie's smile of approval was answer enough.

Nicole and Christina left on Wednesday as planned. Maggie wandered around the office for the first few days, missing them terribly, until her work began to pile up. She welcomed the extra tasks, as they made her days literally fly by. She missed them most in the evening, when she realized just how lonely and drab her life had become before they had come to live with her. They had promised to call at regular intervals to bring her up to date on what they had accomplished, or just to chat. By Friday evening Maggie was pacing the apartment, totally at loose ends. Should she call John and Ellen and invite them out to dinner, her treat? Should she attend the dinner and theatre fundraising function? Or should she just stay home and wait for Christina's call? She chose the latter, prepared a light supper, and with this in hand sat down in front of the television, cruising through the channels with hopes of finding something interesting.

True to her promise, Christina called around nine. Maggie was very happy to hear her voice.

"I've missed you two so damned much, you have no idea."

"We've missed you too, Maggie. We're here in Paris for a few extra days, and the response to Nicole has been extraordinary. She has been inundated with invitations to attend all types of functions, but we have to turn many of them down with the promise that maybe next time we'll accept. I tell you, it's been absolutely fascinating to see the admiration on the faces of young women who aspire to be just like her. She loves every minute of it."

Christina went on to tell her of the sales contracts that would be arriving by air mail and that Maggie had better be prepared to be busy for the next few months. Nicole got on the line and said how much she missed her, although it had just been a few days. She ended with "Love you, Maggie, take care." Maggie got a little choked up when she heard Nicole send her love. She had grown as fond of Nicole as she would her own daughter, if she had one. The phone call made her day, so she prepared for bed.

* * * * *

NICOLE AND CHRISTINA CONTINUED on their hectic schedule over the next few days. Christina took time out to visit the Dior House and say hello to her old friends. They were delighted to see her, and invited them to lunch. That event pretty much took care of a long summer afternoon. Christina was giddy from two glasses of wine, as well as from the warmth of their reception. The workers had expressed their concern as to how she was faring with the loss of her husband. Christina knew that they were sincere. She told them that she was coping well, mainly by keeping busy. As time healed all wounds, she found herself remembering just the happy times. The memory of the explosion was fading, her nightmares occurring less and less. Nicole kept in the background on occasions such as the lunch. These were Christina's friends and she didn't want to take over the limelight. Her respect for Christina grew daily.

They left Paris in a rental car, which would give them the freedom to stop whenever the mood struck. The scenery changed over the hours as they experienced rolling hills, large expanses of vineyards, small villages where the lifestyle never seemed to change, and enjoyed lunch at a very quaint roadside inn. Nicole had never experienced France at this level. Whenever they traveled, they either flew or rushed to their destination, not stopping to enjoy the ambience of the country. They arrived at the D'Argent estate within hours. It being Saturday, everyone was at home and overjoyed to see them. They vaguely remembered Nicole from when she had been Christina's flower girl, but they were not expecting such a beautiful, warm hearted, friendly young woman in place of the little girl. Christina's pride swelled as she captured their hearts. Andre was looking a little tired, but he was well. Marie was thinner than she had been. Apparently she still had trouble sleeping through the night, but would not accept or follow her doctor's advice and take a sleeping potion to overcome her lack of sleep.

They were taken on a whirlwind trip through the shipyards the next day. Christina was amazed at the progress and expansion that had taken place during the past year. Everyone had put their hearts into rebuilding, and it had paid off. After church services the family settled into spending their day relaxing on the grounds. A game of lawn bowling kept them occupied for a few hours, while Nicole spent time with Andre and Marie's grandchildren playing tennis. Christina relaxed in the shade of one of the huge elm trees, content to be in a familiar place with people whom she loved and would always love.

With sadness they took their leave the following morning. They were flying to Rome out of Paris. They were going to visit the Freemont vineyard, but it was very much out of their way, as Nicole pointed out. "Perhaps next time," she said. Christina didn't argue. She didn't want any confrontation with them in regards to Nicole, as they were much too busy to become involved in anything serious. Christina confessed to herself that she had no wish to hear them say that they wanted Nicole back in their care.

They had plenty of time before their early evening flight to Rome. Christina left the rental car at the airport. Their luggage was checked and they had time to browse through the duty-free shopping stores in the airport terminal. Nicole purchased the small vial of perfume which Andrea had asked for, but she had no idea what to buy for Robert. Christina told her to wait. Rome had much to offer, especially in the line of Italian leather goods.

Once again, they were received by the staff of La Casa Corelli with warmth and admiration. A few of the young and very handsome Italian men couldn't take their eyes off Nicole. They invited her to dinner, for a fast ride on their Vespa scooters, a night on the town, but Nicole thanked them and declined. She much enjoyed the Italian custom of meeting for dinner at eight p.m. where they enjoyed a hearty meal, drank fine wine, listened to the music, and later walked through the square. They often stopped to visit with acquaintances or talk to strangers who approached them, having recognized both of the women, one who was already famous and the other fast becoming famous. Nicole couldn't help comparing this slow pace of life with the rushed style of New York. She had always wondered upon her arrival in the Big Apple just where everyone was going, as they were in such a hurry to get there and in a rush to return. What a difference. Actually, she preferred the European pace much more.

The following week they were in Milan. Christina was captivated by the fashion houses' window displays. She did regret their own decision to leave high fashion, substituting the line for lingerie, but she knew they couldn't have it all. Better to focus all their energies on one fine product than turn out second-best merchandise just to stay in the swim of things. She and Nicole bought some very fine ensembles, filling many couture shopping bags as they made their way through the streets and avenues. Nicole bought Robert a finely tooled leather belt. Friday came around soon enough. They were in their hotel room for one last evening and they were leaving for Barcelona the next day. Christina placed the usual call to Maggie in New York.

"Hello, Maggie, it's Christina. How's everything? We're leaving tomorrow for Spain.

Italy has been absolutely enchanting."

"Christina, good to hear your voice. I'm fine, just very busy and missing you both like blazes."

Christina asked, "Did I get any messages, Maggie?" She was hoping against hope that Adam had called.

"No, sorry dear. Were you expecting some?"

"Well, there was one person I was hoping to hear from, but I guess it didn't pan out."

Maggie asked. "Is there something that needs to be handled quickly, or that I can help with?"

"Don't worry about it. I'll check with you again next Friday." Christina went on to tell Maggie of their work week, the warm receptions, the promise of large contracts, and their side shopping trips. She didn't tell Maggie that she had a gift from Jean for her. He had been surprised by their visit but disappointed that Maggie was not with them. She did tell Maggie that Jean's wife was not well. She had been failing now for the past few months. They did not know if she would recover soon. Jean was saddened, but because of their estrangement he didn't appear to be heartbroken over the news. Instead, he sent his love to Maggie, hoping that they could be together in the near future if just for a few days. He would take whatever time he could get. Maggie's voice changed when Christina told her the news. She could hear the happiness in the lilt of Maggie's happy laughter when Christina told her that Jean "sends his love."

Christina was the first to say goodnight, trying to hide her own disappointment when Maggie said there were no messages. Three weeks had gone by and nothing. Maybe Adam had given up and didn't have the heart to tell her by leaving an impersonal message on the machine. That must be it. But no, the trail was cold, at sixteen years old. He had his work cut out for him just trying to find anyone who had been personally involved with the adoption. Nicole emerged from the bathroom refreshed from her bubble bath, her thick hair under a turban- wrapped towel. "Did I hear you on the telephone, Christina?" she asked.

"Yes, I'm sorry you didn't speak to Maggie. I told her you sent your love."

"That's all right. I'll talk to her next time. Are you okay? You seem sad. Did something happen in New York?"

"No, I guess I'm getting a little homesick. I can't imagine why. The European lifestyle is relaxing, healthy, and very comfortable, but it's just not home," Christina answered.

"Well we're off to Spain tomorrow, so let's get to bed, shall we?" Christina said, "You go ahead, I'll be along soon. Goodnight, Nicole." "'Night. See you in the morning."

They were on schedule, as their flight was met by company staff in Barcelona. Again, they became immersed in a different culture. Everything, from the food, to the hand clapping and toe tapping of the Spanish Flamenco dancers, was fiery and exciting. They attended the business for the first few days, but took time to relax for the following three. They had been invited to attend a bullfight on Saturday. The day was hot and dusty with very little wind, and the bullfight was to begin at two p.m. The crowd was already worked up, shouting to the occupants of the bullring, who were teasing the bull and tiring him, placing sharp lancets in his shoulders to weaken him so that he could not raise his head to charge the matador. It was all very barbaric, but Christina and Nicole were totally fascinated. Because the sun was beating down upon them, Nicole removed her bolero top from her sundress. Christina gasped in shock. She was stunned, unable to speak. Nicole didn't realize anything was wrong, as she was focused on the events in the ring. Christina shook her head, her eyes riveted upon the three dark spots on Nicole's shoulder, which formed a perfect heart. All she could think was that the mark must a coincidence, that her reaction was unnecessary. But no, the shape's signature formation was printed indelibly in her mind. She tried to calm herself, but to no avail. Her eyes remained focused upon the birthmark. Nicole's laughter and loud "Ole!" broke through her turmoil. Christina attempted to join in, unable to cope with this heart-wrenching knowledge. Could Nicole be her long lost daughter? She had been born in May sixteen years ago. She had been adopted from a convent in Montreal by the Freemonts. But Christina had given birth to the twins in Edmonton. How old was Nicole when the Freemonts obtained custody? Were the twins taken to Montreal a few weeks after their birth? Adam had to be told. Dozens of thoughts raced through Christina's mind.

Maybe she was grasping at straws in her desperation to find them. Her reverie was broken by the loud cries of the crowd as the bull lifted the matador high into the air. The bullfighter was luckily not impaled by the sharp curving horns, but rested on the bull's forehead. He was tossed a good distance, but had time to come to his feet and pick up the cape. The bull was pawing the dirt in front of him, his head down, ready for the next onslaught. All his horns encountered was an empty cape, the matador turning expertly as the bull thundered past. Christina watched in fascination, grateful for the respite from her tumultuous suspicions. The bull fought bravely, spurred on by the crowd's hysteria as they cried, "Toro! Toro!"

The matador pierced the heart of the bull with the sword he had hidden in the top roll of his cape. Because he had been such a brave bull an ear was cut off and the matador approached the spectator seats in the direction of Nicole and Christina. He motioned for Nicole to stand. She did so, as the crowd cheered. The handsome matador extended the ear and a rose for the beautiful *señorita* with the raven hair and emerald eyes. Nicole didn't understand all of the Spanish as this honour was being placed upon her. Her cheeks flushed with the attention and her eyes met the intense deep brown eyes of the matador. She smiled and nodded her thanks, saying *"Gracias, señor, muchos gracias."* He returned her smile and bowed deeply from the waist, in a gesture to accept applause from a beautiful woman. The experience left Nicole shaken, it had been so intense. Christina delighted in her pleasure and the fact that her charge had been singled out for this compelling honour.

This was an afternoon to remember, considering Christina's discovery of the telltale birthmark and the accolades of the bullfight. Nicole's spirits remained high throughout the remainder of the day, and Christina was preoccupied with her thoughts. She began to really study Nicole. The way she held her head, how she responded with sudden laughter, and her infectious manner. Of whom did she remind Christina? Nicole's hair was her shining glory; the thick dark tresses often became unruly even with the application of hairspray. Christina was reminded of her mother. Yes, of course, the hair. She had loved her mother's hair. How often when she had cuddled in her mother's lap had Angela's hair fallen forward to brush Christina's cheek. Nicole broke her reverie, "Christina, it's getting late. Shall we go out for dinner? You've been so quiet since the bullfight."

"I'm sorry, Nicole. I've just been preoccupied with my thoughts. There's nothing to worry about. Let's change and go to Carlos tonight. Their ribs are apparently out of this world."

"That sounds wonderful. I'll be ready in a few minutes."

Everything that occurred after the day of the bullfight paled in comparison to what had happened before it. They settled down encompassing the tasks at hand. Christina was involved with the selection and ordering of their designs. Nicole was immersed in the personal attention of her growing young fans. She answered their questions as best she could but relied heavily on an interpreter. When she mispronounced a word everyone laughed, as well as Nicole, who was learning from her mistakes.

Christina could hardly wait until Friday. She was losing sleep with the knowledge that Nicole could be her and Adam's child. He must have called by this time. The month was almost over and they would have to return to New York. "Hi, Maggie, it's me again. We're really very busy here. The week has been full of appearances, meeting key staff, and filling orders; it's just been so hectic. How are things there?"

Maggie said, "Christine thank goodness you've called. That message that you were expecting finally came."

"What did it say?" Christina held her breath.

"I can't begin to understand it, it's all very mysterious. Maybe you can decipher it." "Go ahead, Maggie, I'm listening."

"Christina, I have made some progress in my investigation, but have hit a snag. My number is 555-7919. Can you give me a call within the next few days as I have to leave soon?" Maggie paused. "Does any of that make sense to you?"

"Oh, yes it does, Maggie. I'll fill you in when we get back on Sunday. Love you. Bye."

As soon as she had hung up, Christina called the overseas operator and placed the call. She gave instructions for the operator to keep trying, for as long as it would take, to reach Dr. Adam Carmichael. The operator agreed. Because she had to be available to take the call at any time, Christina begged off going out to dinner. She urged Nicole to go down to the hotel restaurant by herself. She had made friends with a few of the staff and they were on a first-name basis. Nicole agreed rather unhappily, but left the hotel room. Christina couldn't keep still. She ordered room service along with a bottle of brandy. If she was right, it would become her fortitude for the rest of the evening, as well as her sleep aid.

Nicole had been gone for nearly an hour and Christina began to worry that she would be present when Adam finally returned her call. Luckily, the phone rang. "Hello, yes this is Christina Corelli." The operator stated that she had her party on the line and to go ahead with her call. "Hello, Adam?"

"Yes, Christina, I'm glad you got my message."

Before he could continue on with polite small talk Christina said, "Adam, I want you to check with the Sisters of St. Martha Mother House in Montreal. Ask them if a couple by the name of Jacques and Carliss Freemont were the adoptive parents of a little girl just a few months old."

"I found Sister Rose through her birth sister. She is much older but very well, retired, and living in the Mother House. She was guarded when I asked her a few pointed questions, afraid of opening up to me. Could you call her from Spain and tell her that she can trust me? She needs to know that I'm doing this for the both of us, and not for any selfish reasons that I might harbour for the custody of the child."

"I'll call tomorrow morning. We're leaving around eleven and should be in New York by late Sunday. Call me when you hear anything. You have my number at home. We live with my partner, Maggie Cole. Adam, I have some news but I'd rather tell you when we meet. I have to go now, Nicole has just returned. Thank you so much."

"You're welcome, Christina. Take care of yourself. I don't know if I'll be back by Sunday, I have something else to do. Talk to you soon. Bye."

"Hi, who were you talking to?" Nicole asked, just out of normal curiosity.

"Oh, I missed you and decided to call Maggie. I told her we were coming home on Sunday and to expect us on Flight 717. She said she would be there to meet us."

"Gosh, I can't believe a month has gone by so fast. It seems like yesterday we arrived in Europe. This has been a very special time for me, Christina; I can't thank you enough. I'm ready now to work my body to the bone when we get home. The reception here has been so much more than I could ever have imagined. It's feels good to be able to set an example for girls my own age. No one thinks that my modeling lingerie is any way degrading, or too explicit. You have seen to that. Everyone applauds your good taste and decorum when my photos are selected for advertisements. We all know that sex sells, but it shouldn't be marketed by someone as young as I am. That's the message everyone sends, and they are satisfied that I am not being exploited by big business and the promise of wealth and fame. Thanks so much." Nicole crossed the room and gave Christina a resounding kiss on the cheek and embraced her in a big hug.

Tired from the long day, Nicole then went to bed. Christina waited until she was sure that the young girl was sleeping soundly. The time change was just right for her to make the call to Montreal, Canada.

It seemed like an eternity had passed before she heard someone answer the phone in a heavily French accent. "*Allo.* Who is it you wish to speak with?"

Christina asked, "May I speak with Sister Rose?" "*Oui*, Madame. Who is calling please?"

"Just tell her it is Christina Corelli. We met many years ago in the Grace Hospital in Edmonton. Please tell her I must speak with her on a matter of great urgency."

"Just please wait. I will call her to the telephone."

Another eternity passed as Christina paced about the hotel room, clutching the receiver so tightly her knuckles were white. Finally a gentle voice said, "Hello, Christina. This is Sister Rose. You wished to speak with me?"

"Thank God, Sister, is it really you? I thought you had forgotten me. It was such a long time ago."

"I have never forgotten you or your babies. You have been in my prayers throughout these past years. Why have you called after so much time has passed?"

"Sister, I have a great favour to ask of you. There was a young doctor who came to see you last week. I gave him the note, which you thrust into my hand when I was leaving the hospital. It contained the name and address of your birth sister, Madame Benoit. He called me and said that he had met with you, but that you were reluctant to give him any information regarding the whereabouts of the babies. He is the babies' father."

"Yes, I was reluctant to speak of them. I didn't know if he was acting alone or not on your behalf. Now that I know that you have spoken with him, I will try to give him more information, as much as is permitted."

"Please Sister, I'm begging you. I can no longer go on not knowing where they are, if they are well, if they are happy." She waited with bated breath.

"Christina, I understand the anguish and heartache you have been going through, but if I open the file, I will be in very bad trouble with my order."

"Sister, could you just check on one small piece of information for me. I think I may have found one of the twins, but I have to be absolutely sure before I can approach her with the news that I am her birth mother. Can you tell me if a young couple by the name of Jacques and Carliss Freemont from France adopted a baby girl around late August or early September of 1957? I'm desperate, and I have no one else to turn to. You are my one and only hope. Please, Sister, if you have any compassion for me, will you help us?"

Sister Rose's heart wrenched as she heard the anguish in Christina's voice. She had grown very fond of the young girl and had taken her under her wing during her time of confinement. The memory of their last few minutes together became very clear. Finally, she said, "Christina, I believe you. You have endured enough heartache to last a lifetime. I promise I will do whatever it takes to help you both. Please have the young doctor Carmichael return and we will meet at my sister's home. That way, I will be able to give him the information that he seeks without anyone finding out. I will pray for you both. Just know that this is going against my vows, but as I said, you have suffered enough."

"Thank you, Sister. God bless you. If and when I do find them, I promise that I won't interfere with their lives. I just want to meet them and to let them know that I love them, I have always loved them, and I didn't want to give them up."

"Yes, I understand, Christina. I must hang up now. Bless you. You are in my prayers.

Goodbye."

Christina managed a grateful goodbye and heard the click at the other end of the line. Sister Rose was gone. Christina's eyes filled with tears of gratitude. For the first time, she actually began to hope that all was not lost. If they could get just a name, or an address for Adam to follow up on, it just might lead them to the girls. She looked skyward and softly said, "Thank you God."

Before retiring for the night, Christina called the number Adam had given her. He was not available so she left a message saying, "Adam, I spoke with Sister Rose. She will trust you with the necessary information. Call Madame Benoit, and arrange a meeting with Sister Rose as soon as possible. And Adam, good luck. I'll be home on Sunday."

For the first time in many months, Christina slept as soundly as a hibernating bear. When she awoke she found Nicole already dressed. "What time is it? Have I overslept?"

"You have plenty of time before we have to be at the airport. I ordered our breakfast so you had better shake a leg." Nicole enjoyed bossing Christina about.

"Don't get sassy with me, young lady. I'll be ready in a jiffy," she said over her shoulder as she entered the bathroom. Christina consciously, and for no apparent reason, studied the heart-shaped birthmark that was the exact replica as Nicole's. Her heart soared with hope. All she needed now were the adoptive parents' names and she could have a heart to heart talk with Nicole. She didn't know how she would break the news to Adam of her findings, but she trusted him this time. He had left his practice, he had left his wife, and he had come to her aid all at the drop of a hat. That was evidence that he still cared, wasn't it? She pondered the question.

They got through customs with little distress. Nicole declared all of her gifts, as well as her personal items, and answered the customs officers' questions honestly. Christina did likewise and they were soon aboard their flight, their last flight for a very long time, Christina promised herself.

Maggie was at the airport to meet them. She hugged them tightly, kissed them on both cheeks and wiped the tears from her eyes. "My goodness, you look absolutely fantastic. The trip has done wonders for you. Christina, I haven't seen you look this rested in a very long time. And Nicole, the European climate has put new rose coloring in your cheeks and a definite glow to your skin."

Christina laughed as she said, "Now Maggie, what have you been up to? This is too much praise at one time. What are you hiding?"

"Nothing, I swear. I'm just so glad to see you both."

"Okay, I believe you. Let's go home. I have a message for you from Jean, but you will have to wait until we are back at the apartment. We have gifts for everyone."

"You sure know how to make me squirm. Was he well? How did he look? As handsome as ever, I'll bet."

"No clues. Behave yourself. I'll tell you once we have Nicole settled. The first thing she'll want to do is call Robert and Andrea."

The ride home took about twenty minutes and they made their way into the apartment complex quickly, their arms laden with suitcases and carry-on bags. As Christina had predicted, Nicole rushed into the bedroom and lay back upon her bed as she picked up the telephone to dial Robert.

Maggie asked, "Okay, Ms. Corelli. Give me my message."

She explained that Jean's wife was very ill and may not recover. He spent only a small amount of time at her bedside because they were still estranged. He felt obligated to hear her last wishes and promise to carry them out, but that was his only responsibility. She had tormented him and kept him chained to her for too long for him to feel any love. He was a compassionate man and didn't wish her suffering on anyone, but that was about the extent of his feelings. To Christina, Jean had said, "Tell Maggie I love her and miss her very much. If it is possible, I will try to come to New York to be with her. There is much to do here and it may not be for perhaps six months, but I will come."

"That's good enough for me, Christina. That should get me through the fall and winter, don't you think?" She hugged Christina as she said, "Thank you, my dear friend. I don't know what I'd do without you."

"Just try doing without me, Madame Cole." Christina chided her. "Jean is in a bad place right now, but he is coping. Marie and Andre could manage without him. They have many relatives who care about them and would look after them if anything should befall either one of them. As for Jean's wife, the Lord will take care of her, and Jean will be free." She paused briefly, then as an afterthought she asked, "Any messages come for me?"

"No, not since the other day, but you could check the machine. There might be something over the past few hours."

Christina checked but there was nothing. Adam must be following her orders to meet with Sister Rose. She crossed her fingers behind her back then joined Maggie in the living room.

"I guess it is back to business tomorrow. If we call all the department heads for a general meeting, I'll fill everyone in on our most productive travels. I'm really tired, Maggie, I should get some sleep. Jet lag has never been my best friend. Wake me in the morning."

"'Night, Christina. And thank you."

In the morning Christina padded her way to the bathroom, still half asleep. Maggie was sitting at the table reading the morning paper. Before Christina could enter the bathroom, Maggie raised her voice saying, "Christina, come read this. Well, I'll be damned. I don't believe it."

"Don't believe what?" Christina asked now fully awake.

"Here, let me read it to you. The article says, "This reporter has just discovered that Mrs. Joan Carmichael has just filed for divorce from her husband, renowned plastic surgeon Dr. Adam Carmichael. She claims it's due to irreconcilable differences. What the hell brought that on, I wonder? There's no mistake. Here's a picture of the ice queen. The caption reads, 'One of New York's most prominent socialites, the former Joan Finestad.' All that's missing is the tiara."

Christina had a funny look on her face. It was as if she was attempting to hide her pleasure at the news. She said, "Well, I'm really not surprised. She's not at all his type. Apparently, from the rumours, all Joan Finestad wanted was a trophy husband and handsome escort. There was nothing else holding that marriage together."

"And how do you know this much?" Maggie asked suspiciously.

"Well, when Adam dumped me three weeks before our wedding

I tried to forget him. But, as you know, I subscribe to the New York Times and the society page kept me well informed."

"Aren't you the sly one?" Maggie mused.

"Well, enough gossiping. We'll be late for that very important meeting this morning."

Nicole was already up and dressed, ready to face the day. She didn't have to be tutored, as this was the summer break, but she wanted to hang out at the office to catch up on the latest news, as well as satisfy her curiosity regarding the new designs.

The trio set off as usual, each preoccupied with her own thoughts.

Chapter Forty-Six

C HRISTINA DID NOT HEAR a word from Adam for the next two weeks. She was beside herself. What could have happened to him? The gossip column in the Times did a follow-up on Joan's divorce proceedings. The reporters had asked her where he was, was it true he had given up his practice, if there was there another woman, and all the usual smut questions. All Joan did was to say very firmly, "No comment."

"How do you intend to serve him with divorce papers?"

To this, her lawyer replied that they would proceed in absentia. The divorce would go ahead and would be final within six months. If the good doctor did happen to return to New York, he would then be informed as to the expected settlement and could contest it if he wished. Christina absorbed all the information regarding Adam's predicament that she could. Was he deliberating avoiding a confrontation with Joan, or was he determined to not provide the paparazzi with any more gossip that could damage his reputation? Christina did not realize how much Adam had changed over the past six years. He had become hardened to his life with Joan and had learned to dodge many questions during the course of their marriage. The press had accused Joan of having numerous affairs, all the while blaming Adam because he was such a workaholic that he didn't have time for a wife.

Christina didn't think that she should trouble Sister Rose any further. Repeated calls to the Mother House would likely arouse suspicion and Sister Rose would have to answer truthfully as to what had transpired. She had to just wait until Adam surfaced. In the meanwhile, Christina found escape in her work. The department heads were extremely excited at the enormity of orders that were coming in almost daily. The entire company shifted into high gear. Maggie, John, and Christina tossed around the possibility of Christina's suggestion to hire two additional models, older than Nicole and with more experience. Her reasoning was that one of them could be used to compliment Nicole. Also, some of the ensembles were seductive and very sensual, and an older model would have to be used, as Nicole was a minor. They decided on searching for a platinum blonde and a black American. The trio would make a picture worth a thousand words, the contrast would be so daring. Resumes were reviewed for a few weeks, until finally they were down to a handful of girls. Nicole wanted to sit in on the interviews, just to observe. Maggie could see no harm and having her main model in the room would give her the chance to compare the aspiring interviewees with Nicole.

Maggie asked the platinum blonde. "Miss Erica Nilson, I see? I've looked over your portfolio and I am very impressed. How long have you been modeling professionally?"

"For about six years now. I started out with a small modeling agency and as my popularity grew, so did the work. I love what I do."

"Have you ever modeled lingerie before this?"

"No, but I have no inhibitions regarding the product. I realize that I won't be required to walk down a runway in my underwear, so to speak, so I wouldn't be embarrassed in front of a crowd. I prefer the camera, as the best pictures are always selected for publication."

Maggie appeared satisfied with the interview and said, "You'll be hearing from us within a few days. Thank you so much for coming in."

Erica nodded, smiled politely, and left the office.

The next interview began with the entrance of a willowy, striking black woman who appeared to be in her early twenties. Her complexion was not extremely dark, but more of a deep golden brown. This was what they were seeking. Maggie began, "Please have a seat, Miss Washington."

She began the questioning much along the same line as she had taken with Erica. Delia was natural, friendly, and had a charismatic charm. She had taken special classes in decorum, posture, and polite conversation. She spoke when spoken to, and answered the questions clearly, making eye contact with Maggie at all times. Maggie glanced over at Nicole. The milk-white complexion and raven hair of her top model would contrast beautifully with Delia and Erica. She seemed completely satisfied at her luck in finding exactly what they needed. "You'll be hearing from us within a few days. Thank you so much for coming in, Miss Washington."

"The pleasure has been mine. Thank you, Ms. Cole." She left the room.

"Well, Nicole, what do you think? I know they are older than you, but just picture you in the center, flanked by a platinum blonde and a dusky black American. I think the photo promises to be sensational."

"I don't know that much about it, but I liked both of them. If the outfits are too sexy, let them wear those and leave the demure ones to me. I think that would suit us all just fine." Nicole waited for Maggie's reply.

"Looks like we have two new members on staff. We'll talk to Domingo and show him their portfolios. If he thinks it will work, and Christina also approves, then we're in business. Personally, I believe the European markets will eat up our new image."

Christina walked in at the last bit of the conversation. "What will eat what up?" she asked. "Here, have a look at these last two interviewees. Their portfolios are pretty outstanding.

Get a picture of Nicole and we'll put her between these two. There, now what do you think?"

"Maggie, you're an absolute genius. I really didn't think you would take my suggestion seriously, but now that I see the trio, I'm impressed. Now, if Domingo approves, as well as John, we can go ahead with the campaign for the fall line."

As expected, John and Domingo were duly impressed by the portfolios and excited to get to work on the new shoots. John said he would call the models on Wednesday and schedule a practice shoot on Thursday morning, if that suited everybody.

They had accomplished much that very morning. Everyone was in high spirits, anticipating a successful season and increased profits. They broke for lunch at half past twelve. Maggie and John went in one direction while Christina and Nicole went in another.

When they were seated in the restaurant and had ordered their lunch Nicole looked directly into Christina's eyes and asked, "Christina, I have something to ask you. Is there something I have done to displease you?" she asked worriedly.

Christina was taken aback by the question. "No, of course not, Nicole, why do you ask?"

"I don't know. Maybe I'm wrong but you seem to be holding something back. We used to talk about anything, but now you seem to be more reserved with me."

Christina didn't know how to answer her young charge's question without giving way to her emotions. She could not say, in all honesty, "I think you are my long lost daughter, and if you are, I am so very fortunate to have found you when I did." She had to wait until she heard from Adam. If he didn't call soon, she feared she would go a little crazy. Instead she said, "No, Nicole there's nothing wrong. I've had so much on my mind that I didn't realize that my attitude had changed and that I made you uncomfortable. Know that I love you very much and would do nothing to hurt you. You do believe that, don't you?"

Nicole's wide smile and the sudden tears in her eyes were answer enough. "I love you too Christina, I wish you were my mother, and not just my guardian. There, I've said it, and I meant every word."

The waiter broke into their poignant conversation just in time. Christina almost broke down and blurted out that she could very well be Nicole's mother, but instead she welcomed the respite and they ate their lunch quietly, enjoying the pleasure of one another's company without the need for constant conversation. Lunch behind them, Nicole and Christina returned to complete the rest of the work day.

Christina's thirty-third birthday had come and gone without very much fuss. Marking another year was the last thing on her mind. It was nearing the end of August and there was still no word from Adam. She was absolutely beside herself with worry. Where the hell was he?

Maggie had gone out to a business dinner, Nicole was with her friends, and Christina was going mad in the apartment. She tried relaxing in a long, hot bubble bath with a bottle of wine. The bubble bath worked wonders for about a half hour, and then the wine gave her a splitting headache. She checked the time. Half past seven. The whole damn evening was staring her in the face. She was about to leave when the phone rang.

"Hello. This is Christina speaking." "Christina. Hi, it's Adam."

"Adam, finally, you're calling. Where the hell have you been? Why haven't you called? I've been absolutely frantic wondering when you'd call. Did you find out about the Freemonts?"

"Just listen, all right? I want you to meet me in Boston at the Ritz on September 19. It's very important that you don't be late. I'll call you at the hotel after you check in. I have reservations for eight o'clock. I also want you to bring Nicole. You will have to pack evening wear, as this is a formal affair."

"Why would I want to go to Boston and attend a formal event, just to please you? I don't understand you. You've been away almost two months, God knows where, doing God knows what, and now this? What are you on, drugs?" Her exasperation at his request knew no bounds.

"Christina, if you ever loved me, I'm asking you to trust me. This is very important. You have to say yes. I don't know what else to do."

"Adam, are you in some kind of trouble? Does it have to do with the divorce?" "What divorce?" he asked.

"Your divorce. Joan filed the papers two months ago. Haven't you called home?"

"What home? I don't call that ice palace a home, as you well know. So the bitch filed for divorce. You have no idea how relieved that makes me. Sounds rather cold, but she had to put an end to our miserable co-habitation. Maybe now I can look forward to the future."

He sounded so cold, so detached, and happier than he should have been for someone who had just been told that he was being dumped. She didn't pursue the subject but instead returned to his bizarre request. "All right, so what if I agree to meet you on September 19? Why do I have to bring Nicole?"

"I can't tell you any more. Please, Christina, I'm begging you, and if you must know I've had two months to brood over the stupid mistake I made so many years ago. I should have never let you go. If you must know, I love you, I have always loved you, and I always will. There, I've said it and we don't have to discuss it. Now, yes or no, are you coming to Boston, or not?"

Her heart soared at his words. She reserved her own feelings about being in love with him. That was something she had to come to terms with before she made any commitment. "Yes, Adam, we'll be there. It's only a week away. Are you sure you can't tell me anything more? What shall I tell Nicole?"

"Just tell her that you may have a potential new sales opportunity and the company president wanted to meet her. Tell her whatever you think she'll believe, but just come to Boston."

"Yes, we will. And Adam, thank you for finally calling. It's been wonderful just hearing your voice. Good night." That was the closest thing to an endearment as he was going to get. She promised herself she would proceed with caution.

The apartment seemed to close in on her, so Christina grabbed a sweater and her purse, thinking that now would be a good time to take in a movie. She would be surrounded by people, but in essence she would be alone in a group of strangers. The darkness of the movie would hide any tears if she felt the need to cry. It was public, but it was also private, and she would not feel alone. Adam's confession had shaken her to the core. Many years ago he had confessed his love by saying to her, "I will love you all the days of my life," and she had believed him beyond any doubt. Now that she was older and hopefully wiser, could she put herself through another round of Dr. Carmichael and the prospect that he just might leave her in the lurch once again? Her mind was so preoccupied throughout the entire movie, if anyone was to ask her what the movie was about she would be at a loss to tell them. She had no idea.

The following evening, Christina sat opposite Nicole at the dining table. She said, "Nicole, I want you to come to Boston with me on September 19th. We'll have to stay overnight, but we will be back the next day."

"Why are we going to Boston, Christina?" Nicole asked.

"I received a call from a potential buyer with a huge outlet situated in Boston and the surrounding region. Before they commit to our lingerie line they wanted to meet us in person." Christina lied through her teeth.

"Sounds okay to me. What shall I pack?"

"Apparently we have to attend a formal affair, so we must be dressed for it. He would give me no further details other than we would be picked up in front of the Ritz Hotel and whisked away in a limousine. Sounds pretty posh and mysterious, don't you think?"

"Yes, it does. I'm already looking forward to it."

Maggie appeared on the scene. "Guess what, Maggie, Christina and I are going to Boston on September 19th."

"What's going on in Boston?" Maggie asked.

Christina once again lied through her teeth and explained about the formal affair with the potential buyer. Maggie asked again, "Why wasn't I told about this?"

"It just came up, and we're telling you now." Christina hoped that this would placate Maggie and she would accept the explanation.

"Okay, who's the mysterious buyer?"

Christina said, "Apparently, it involves a conglomerate located in Boston and the surrounding area. They have seen our advertisements and catalogue and are extremely interested. They don't want to commit to any contract until they have met with me and Nicole. Sounds okay to me, so I said yes."

"Well, if it doesn't pan out, at least you'll have had a quick trip out of town," Maggie replied.

Before they knew it the time had passed quickly and it was time to leave. The two departed on the evening of September 18th in order to arrive in Boston, check in at the hotel, and hopefully meet the potential clients. Nicole was excited. Travel always got her adrenaline pumping. Christina had chided her on being a travel addict. She became alive, meeting new people, talking about her career, and making new friends.

They were settled in the Ritz that evening with time on their hands. Christina asked if Nicole would like to eat dinner in the hotel dining room, and later on inspect some of the shops within the confines of the hotel. That's exactly what they did. For at least three hours they were busy. Christina stopped at the hotel hair salon and made appointments for them both at three p.m. the next afternoon, explaining that they must be ready for an evening out. The car was to pick them up at seven-thirty, which wouldn't be a problem, according to the clerk. They browsed through the dress shops; Nicole fell in love with an amazing white crepe top that would go well with a number of her slacks and skirts. Christina also purchased a top, which was exquisitely embroidered in finely stitched eyelet that was especially eye-catching. They retired at ten that night, exhausted from sightseeing and shopping.

The following day, Christina suggested that they venture out to the harbour and dine on lobster and shrimp. She loved seafood. Nicole wasn't really into it, but she went along with the idea. They spent at least two hours over lunch, chatting and people-watching as the crowds strolled along the pier. The handsome young waiter was totally enamoured with

Nicole by the time the two hours had passed. Christina noticed the time. It was a little past two and they had to make their hair appointments.

The remainder of the afternoon was filled with having their hair and nails done, long bubble baths in the hotel suite, and a short nap to refresh them before they had to dress for their date.

Christina surveyed herself in the full-length mirror. The deep emerald sequined evening gown clung to her body in all the right places. As she turned to survey the back of the dress, it caught the light and shimmered as if lit by a thousand candles. The tiny spaghetti straps held the bodice in place and an emerald necklace rested in the subtle cleavage of her perfectly shaped bosom. Her hair was pulled back from her face, clasped together firmly with a sparkling circle- shaped barrette, and the curls cascaded down her back.

When Nicole came out of the bedroom she gasped at the sight of Christina standing before her. "I have never seen you look so beautiful, Christina. You're dazzling, just dazzling."

"You don't look half bad yourself, my dear. That white dress is a perfect contrast against your long black hair. Those tiny rosebuds that trail from the bodice to your waist are a nice touch against the soft chiffon. Why don't you wear that three strand pearl necklace that I brought along? There are matching earrings if you want to borrow those as well."

"That would be perfect. You don't mind?" Nicole asked, happy to be able to wear one of Christina's favourite necklaces.

The telephone rang, suddenly interrupting their mutual admiration. It was the hotel desk clerk. "Ms. Corelli, your driver is here to collect you."

"Thank you. We'll be right down."

When they left the elevator, all heads turned as the small crowd in the waiting room whispered to one another, "Absolutely stunning. Who are they? They must be celebrities." Christina heard her last name whispered to another woman and smiled to herself.

Adam was waiting outside on the sidewalk and he helped each of them into the back of the limousine. He joined and instructed the driver to take them to the concert hall. They made small talk on the way, Christina introducing Adam to Nicole. Adam and Christina chatted away, much to Nicole's surprise. She wondered if they had known one another for a long time. It sure looked that way, she thought.

They had excellent seats about a dozen rows back from the stage. Christina surveyed the concert hall. It was magnificent, with tiers of private boxes to the left and right of the center floor. Behind them were additional rows reaching well up the back wall of the concert hall. Nicole said, "This is a beautiful concert hall. What are we going to hear?"

Adam replied, "It's a surprise. I think you'll like her. I know I do."

Christina by this time was totally confused. What in the world was Adam thinking, dragging them all the way here, to hear a concert by an unknown artist? She gave up trying to understand the situation. A distinguished couple in their early forties joined them. Adam introduced them as Tom and Elizabeth Bennett. It was their daughter who was the featured artist. She was very young, but already becoming a household name in the music world. She played the piano as though the keys were an extension of her fingers, her skill phenomenal. After the introduction there was a round of applause, and the conductor bowed then motioned to the orchestra to continue with the second portion of the performance. The young lady had chosen four well-known concertos, which were well received by the audience. Christina overheard Mrs. Bennett say to her husband, "I'm so proud of Sarah, Tom. Isn't she wonderful?"

After the concert was over, Adam informed them all that they would meet Sarah backstage, and later fill the reservations he had made in the private dining room in the Ritz. Christina was still baffled. Why were these people so important? Adam was treating them as though they were royalty. Well, maybe they were for all she knew. Nicole looked as bewildered as she.

By ten o'clock they were finally seated at a large round table, the white linen sparkling like new fallen snow under the massive chandelier. Adam ordered drinks all around, with soft drinks for Sarah and Nicole. Finally, he cleared his throat and began to speak. "I've gathered you here tonight to discuss and disclose some very important news. I'll begin by saying that whatever I have to tell you should not change the direction of your lives or how you wish to conduct yourselves. To get to the point! This lovely lady on my right is Christina Corelli of the House of Corelli. Many years ago when she was a young girl she found herself in a compromising situation, pregnant at a young age. She was abandoned by the young father of the children and left to fend for herself. Ms. Corelli gave birth to twin daughters. As she was alone and had no way to care for the infants, she gave them up for adoption. Sarah, I would like you to meet your mother. Christina, Sarah is our daughter." Christina's eyes opened wide as she gasped for air. Her hand she placed over her heart as she tried to find the right words. Sarah smiled and reached out her hand. Christina grasped her hand in her own and felt the warmth of flesh on flesh, but also something else. A tingling began to course through her fingers as she held onto Sarah's hand. Tears of happiness began to course down her cheeks. She finally said, "Hello, Sarah, my darling girl. I have searched long and hard for you, never, ever expecting to find you, but here you are."

She looked across the table at Tom and Elizabeth. "Thank you for bringing her up to be such a fine young woman."

Adam took Christina aside for a moment while the other four members of the party chatted. "Sister Rose told me that the adoptive parents were named Jacques and Carliss Freemont, and the baby was taken to France. How did you know that?"

Christina cleared her throat, choking back tears of joy, and said, "I too have an announcement which will be a complete surprise to everyone here." She brought Adam back to the table and announced, "Adam, I would like you to meet your daughter, Nicole. Nicole, it is time for you to know that I am your mother, and Sarah is your sister."

Now it was Adam's turn to become speechless. His face turned white, and then the color returned as his eyes shone with pride and happiness. He extended his hand to Nicole and said, "I couldn't ask for a more beautiful daughter. I'm proud to be your father, Nicole."

Nicole began to cry. She said, "Oh my God, oh my God, you really are my mother?

Christina, is it true?"

"Yes, Nicole. I couldn't tell you until I knew for a fact that your parents were the Freemonts who had taken you from the Mother House in Montreal. This man is indeed your father. He has been looking for you almost as long as I have. Now I have to show you the final proof, if anyone here doubts what we have said. Sarah, please pull down your right sleeve and bare your shoulder. Nicole, I want you to do the same." As she said this, Christina turned so that all could see the triangular birthmark on her shoulder. Sarah and Nicole each stared in turn, each at one another's exact mark and then at Christina's. They began to laugh through their tears. Tom and Elizabeth were amazed at the evidence. Christina began to study Sarah. She was the spitting image of Adam. She had his strawberry blonde hair, his grey eyes, and the shape of his lips. That was where their similarities ended. She recognized herself in the girl's profile, high cheekbones, almond shaped eyes, and perfect eyebrows. When she smiled it was as though Christina was smiling in the mirror. There was no mistaking who Sarah's birth parents were.

Although they had been introduced, the party of six made no future plans concerning Sarah. She was given the opportunity to choose to remain in contact with them either in the near future or well beyond it. She would always be welcome in New York to visit or stay, but it would be her choice. Sarah dearly loved her adoptive parents and was reluctant to uproot her life, which was centered on the music world in Boston. Furthermore, her friends and extended relatives were all in Boston, and she just couldn't leave. Adam and Christina assured her that they had no right to make any demands upon her. They had abandoned her when she was an infant and she had no obligation towards them. She acknowledged that they were her biological parents, but her love and devotion remained with the Bennetts.

Nicole was beside herself. Here she was, already living with her mother and hadn't even guessed. She had never been so happy in her entire life. Also, the fact that she had a twin sister was the best news she had ever heard. They didn't look at all like twins, but they were blood relatives nevertheless and promised faithfully to keep in touch at all times. By the time the evening was coming to a close, everyone was emotionally exhausted. It had been an experience no one would ever forget, or wished to forget. Nicole had one problem left to solve. She asked Christina if she could be the one to break the news to her adoptive parents. Christina felt that they should do it together, and when the Freemonts visited her in New York they could meet Nicole's father, Adam.

Although Adam wished to stay and talk with Christina well into the night, he thought better of it. They bid goodnight to the Bennetts, Nicole hugged Sarah and kissed her on the cheek. Christina hugged her tightly, relishing the feel of her body in her arms. She looked over Sarah's shoulder and locked eyes with Adam, hers filled with gratitude and his filled with love. At last the evening was over. Adam would call for them the following morning and they would travel together to New

York. Nicole said to Christina, "Shall I call you mother, or shall I still call you Christina?"

"How about you call me mother when we're not at work. I don't want to be the mother of a beautiful teenage daughter and still maintain my place in the fashion world. Age is the demise of all models sooner or later. Just wait until we tell Maggie the news. Do you want to or shall I?"

"Please, let me tell her. It will knock her socks off."

They were homeward bound the following morning in Adam's company. Nicole sat across from her parents on the plane, content to share a seat with someone her own age, in this case a young man.

Christina said to Adam, "I've been dying to ask you this." She paused for a moment then continued. "You never did tell me how you found Sarah. How did you find her?"

"After I realized that dealing with the Sisters in Edmonton was like attempting to communicate with a brick wall, I was finally able to learn that she, too, had been sent to Montreal. Rather than place Sister Rose in jeopardy I met with the Archbishop and Mother Superior Sister Consalata. I made some cockamamie story about the birth mother having a rare and very serious genetic disease, and her wish was to find the baby so that she could be tested before she passed the point of no return, which is what would happen if she did have the disease and wasn't treated immediately. Well, I suppose I'm going to hell for lying to people of the cloth, but I did what I had to do. It was easy to follow her trail, the records were correct, and Sarah was well adjusted and happy with the Bennetts. You are the one who surprised me the most, springing Nicole on me the way you did. Not that I wasn't happy about it, but as it turned out we both got what we wanted, didn't we?"

"I still want to pinch myself to see if I'm not dreaming. It's like a fairy tale, where everyone lives happily ever after. I'm not saying that everything is going to be roses, because everyone has their bad patches, but I intend to see that Nicole stays on the straight and narrow."

Adam became very serious then as he took Christina's hand in his. "I want you to know that what I am about to tell you is in our best interests. Because Joan has filed for divorce with the reason of irreconcilable differences, the press will be looking for another woman. I don't want to put you into the middle of our problems. The media would eat it up, and the House of Corelli couldn't take on a scandal.

You are just picking up the pieces from the Cole disaster and this would be a definite setback. We can't see one another at all once we leave this plane. I intend to go my way and I want you and Nicole to walk away on the tarmac as though we are complete strangers. I'm very serious about this, Christina, you have to promise me."

"But Adam, couldn't we just meet to talk over lunch or dinner?

"No, we can't. Joan would jump on it, as sure as I live and breathe. If something comes up that is urgent, I'll send a message to meet me at the pretzel stand in the Park. That's about it."

Christina had anticipated the possibility that they would rekindle their relationship once they returned to New York. She did see the hurdles ahead and finally had to admit that he was right. They could speak on the phone but not meet anywhere in public. All things considered, this would just last until early January, which was only three months away. She would concentrate on work and the time would pass quickly. Having settled their dilemma, Christina and Adam reclined their seats and sat quietly, holding hands in comfortable silence. This was not the time to discuss any possible future they might have, as Adam was not free.

They said a cursory goodbye at the airport. Maggie had sent a car to collect them, so it was with heavy hearts that Christina and Nicole watched Adam stroll out through the entrance doors and disappear into the crowd.

Nicole burst into the apartment, all smiles as she hugged Maggie. "Maggie, I have the best news of my entire life. Just wait 'till I tell you."

"What? The business trip was more successful than you could have possibly imagined?" Maggie attempted a guess.

"No silly. It's much better than that. Wait for Christina. She'll be along in a minute. Here she is. All right, everybody sit down, except me of course."

Christina said hello to Maggie and asked her to indulge Nicole while she delivered the news. "You know about this, Christina? Of course you must, you were with her." Maggie waited in anticipation.

"Maggie, did you know that you are sitting beside my mother?"

Christina's face broke out in a wide smile as her eyes met Maggie's, which were now wide and incredulous. "What are you saying? Christina is your mother?"

"Yes, yes, Christina is my real mother, and I also met my father, Adam Carmichael." Her eyes shone with happiness.

Christina nodded her head and said to Maggie, "It was Adam who began the search, but it was Sister Rose who gave me the name of Nicole's adoptive parents, Jacques and Carliss Freemont, Evan's friends."

"What are the odds, Christina? It's a miracle, is all, a real miracle."

Nicole was still bubbling away as she said, "Wait, there's more. I have a twin sister, although we don't look the same we are twins. Her name is Sarah Bennett, and she is the most talented concert pianist I have ever met, not that I have met that many. Actually she's the first."

Christina explained how Adam had tricked the Archbishop into releasing the name of Sarah's adoptive parents, and the rest had been easy. It was he who had arranged the meeting in Boston so that they could all be together. Maggie was speechless. Finally she said, "To think you found both of them. I can't believe it."

Christina said that neither Adam nor Nicole knew anything about their mother-daughter relationship until she sprang it upon them after they had recovered from the news of Sarah. "There were tears all around that table, I can assure you," she said.

"What a wonderful happy ending. Will Sarah be coming to New York to live?"

"No, her life is with her loving parents, the Bennetts, and her career is just getting started. You should hear her play, Maggie. She's absolutely captivating. I know we will be watching her play here in New York in a few years' time. You know, she looks like Adam. She's tall and fair-haired, with his grey eyes, but her profile and stature resemble mine. Being fair, she is the opposite of Nicole, but we all have the birthmark on our shoulders. The waiter in the private dining room probably thought we had lost our marbles baring our shoulders the way we did, but I think he got the idea when everyone remarked on their existence. Well, my dear, all that's left is for me to break the news to the Freemonts. I can well imagine how they are going to react. We'll just have to watch it play out, I guess."

"What about Adam? Are you two going to get back together? The divorce proceedings are well in the works, so he will be a free man soon. We won't be able to see one another until the divorce is final. Adam doesn't want me to be in the middle of the divorce, as it could get rather ugly. He said he would only call if something came up ... we agreed it was for the best ... but he did tell me in a private moment that he still loved me and always had. He did end up apologizing for leaving me in such an emotional mess. I believe he is sincere, but I still have a few reservations. Once bitten, twice shy, Maggie."

"So, it looks like it's back to the grindstone as usual," Maggie said to no one in particular.

Nicole asked, "Would you mind if I shared my news with Robert and Andrea? They are my very best friends."

"Not at all. But I would like to speak with John and Ellen after you have finished your call.

I don't think they should hear the news from their children."

Nicole rushed off to the bedroom to use the phone on the night stand. Maggie rolled her eyes at Christina, revelling in the wonder of it all. "If that doesn't beat all. I still can't wrap my head around it."

"Well, enough said. I have two teenage daughters and I'm only thirty-three years old. Don't spread the word at work, will you? Nicole will continue to call me Christina at work but she insists on calling me Mom when we're at home, which will take some getting used to."

* * * * *

THE FOLLOWING TWO MONTHS passed swiftly. Soon it was early December and they were making plans for Christmas, lost in a flurry of shopping, and making last minute plans for where they would have Christmas dinner. John and Ellen insisted they spend it with them. Christina and Nicole wanted to make a quick trip to Boston to visit Sarah and exchange early gifts. They thought they would surprise her. The Freemonts had, very begrudgingly, taken the news of Christina being Nicole's birth mother. Jacques had said, "After all we did for that child, this is how we are repaid. She was difficult from the beginning and I'm not surprised that she would choose to stay with Christina."

It was strange. They didn't appear to be happy for Nicole, but more concerned with themselves and their sacrifices. Christina thought they were being very selfish. They did agree that it would be of little use to have Nicole return to them, and Christina heard the definite note in Carliss' voice as she washed her hands of all responsibility regarding their adopted daughter. In other words, she could not care less that

Nicole had chosen to stay in New York. Nicole had been crushed at first, but after having time to think about it, she accepted the fact that they hadn't really wanted Nicole; they had just wanted any child. It was a hard pill to swallow but having found her real parents, she thanked her lucky stars that they were the best of the best and that she felt loved and wanted for the very first time.

On Christmas morning Christina received a bouquet of two dozen yellow roses. The card read, "To my love, Happy Christmas, it won't be long now," and it was signed "Always, Adam."

Christina buried her face in the roses, and a few happy tears fell upon the delicate flowers. Maggie also received a surprise. She too was the recipient of a large package. After signing for the delivery, she stood in the doorway wondering who had sent it. Her eyes widened as she read out loud, "It's from France. It must be from Jean."

She tore open the package and found that it contained the most delicate silk scarf, a pair of Gucci leather gloves, a vial of the finest French perfume, and a letter from Jean. In it he expressed his longing to be with her once more. His wife had died recently and he was in the process of clearing her estate. Would she like him to come to New York in the New Year, perhaps to stay for good? Maggie said, "Christina, he loves me, he wants to come to New York for keeps. This is the best Christmas present I have ever gotten. What shall I do?"

"You shall get him on the telephone and tell him you love him, and wish him the happiest Christmas ever. We still have a few hours before we leave for John and Ellen's."

Christmas Day at the Coles' was as wonderful as always. Maggie and Christina had arrived in high spirits, which carried them throughout the day. They were tired when they returned to the apartment later that evening, but everyone was happier than they had ever dreamed.

Sarah had called to thank them for the wonderful gifts and to send her love. Nicole and she chatted for a long time, discussing the latest in clothes, boys and movies.

Returning to a regular work routine was a welcome respite from all the excitement of the past few weeks, but it was also a definite letdown.

On January tenth Christina received a call at the office from a gentleman who wouldn't give his name, according to her secretary.

When she answered, Christina heard Adam's voice and her heart began to beat faster, "Adam, what is it?"

"Just meet me at the pretzel stand at four o'clock. I have news."

"I'll be there, I promise." She hung up the phone and found that she was unable to concentrate or focus on anything for the remainder of the day. At long last it was three-thirty and Christina hurried out of the office without a backward glance. Adam was seated on their bench waiting for her. When he saw her he arose and began walking towards her, as Christina increased her own pace. He grabbed her and held her tightly in her arms saying, "My darling, it's over. I'm a free man. Will you marry me, Christina?"

She pulled away from him to look deep into his eyes. All she saw was the love shining there as they stood together for what seemed like an eternity. She didn't answer him but asked instead, "What happened with the divorce settlement?"

"She took me to the cleaners, as I expected. I gave her the mausoleum she called our home. No loss there. The worst thing and the least expected was when her father Sam, called me into the office. He explained that he was under much pressure from Joan to cut me loose. Unfortunately he was made to choose, and explained that he had to choose his daughter. You know, 'blood is thicker than water.' I was shocked until he said, "I'd like to buy you out if you allow it. I'm offering you twenty million dollars for your half. What do you say?"

"Well, what did you say, silly?" Christina waited with bated breath.

"I said, no, and I held out for twenty five million. Samuel Finestad wrote the check right then and there, and it most likely didn't make a dent in his finances. Now, my problem is that I have to set up a clinic and begin a new practice all over again. It won't be easy and it will be expensive. I hope you can understand that I'll be working long hours and won't have much time to spend with you."

"I think you will be successful a lot sooner than you think. Your previous patients will spread the word and your office will be filled to capacity. Also, I know many beautiful women in my field who incidentally want to remain beautiful as long as they can, and I will recommend my dear friend, Dr. Adam Carmichael." She returned his hug.

"You haven't answered me, Christina. Will you marry me?"

"Adam, I need time. Let's take this slowly. We've become the best of friends over the past few months and I know what will follow, but I want it to happen spontaneously. I'm not the same person I was six years ago. I did love Evan, not in the way I loved you, but he gave me strength and purpose and adored me right up until the time of his death. Can you understand what I'm saying? I do love you, don't ever doubt that, but I have to be sure this time."

He smiled when she told him she loved him. "I can live with that, Christina, for as long as it takes. I have to leave now, but I'll call you soon."

She nibbled on the hot pretzel and looked out upon the park. Last night's snowfall had clothed the park in sparkling wonder. The trees were coated with frost and the sight before her resembled a fairytale land. The sun shone through the trees and bathed her in warmth. She snuggled deeper into her full length fur coat and pulled the scarf tighter around her throat. Deciding to leave, she arose from the bench, said goodbye to the pretzel man, and made her way out of the park. She thought that they could have walked out together but they both had to be alone, he to attend to his work, and Christina to think about the proposal.

* * * * *

THE HOUSE OF CORELLI employees became caught up in the rush of another Valentine's Day. Nicole was the center of attraction, making personal appearances at their major outlets in the city. She was featured on several magazine covers alone, while the feature article inside included Erica and Delia. Sarah had called and congratulated her saying that she had bought up half the magazines in Boston which featured her picture. Nicole laughed and thanked her. As Sarah was still attending school she wasn't as free as Nicole, and as much as they wanted to visit it would be impossible until the Easter Break. The girls made tentative plans for Sarah to come to New York.

Adam received wonderful news on Valentine's Day. Christina sent him two dozen red roses with a card attached saying, "Yes, my darling, I will marry you. Happy Valentine's Day. Always, Christina."

She had been right in her predictions about the success of his new clinic. Adam practically emptied Sam Finestad's office. The women had flocked to him for advice and possible surgical procedures, which he always explained in detail, outlining the positive but cautioning them of the risks.

Today, he directed his receptionist to cancel the remainder of his appointments telling her had an emergency. She wished him good luck as he rushed out the door.

He found Christina in the drafting room at the office. He had hugged her secretary and burst past her without being announced. "Happy Valentine's Day, my love. You just made me the happiest man on the planet." She was still seated at the design table and he swivelled her chair about to face him while he went down on bended knee. He said, "I know you'll marry me. So now I ask, when will you marry me?" He pulled a navy blue velvet box from his pocket. He placed it in her hand. "This is a token of my love for you, Christina. I hope you like it."

"Like it, it's downright gorgeous. Oh, Adam, I can't believe my eyes. It's enormous, awesome, dazzling. What else can I say? Thank you." Christina couldn't take her eyes off the diamond ring.

Maggie came in at that moment and was about to back out of the room when Christina said, "Maggie look. Have you ever seen anything so gorgeous? Oh, and I said yes."

"Congratulations, you two. It's about time, don't you think? I've been waiting for this a very long time, years in fact." She kissed them both, hugging Christina tightly as she whispered, "You lucky, lucky woman. Be happy, Christina."

A few weeks later, Adam called Christina asking if she was free for the afternoon, as he had somewhere to take her and it couldn't be put off any longer. She cleared her desk, delegating her work to Nicole and Domingo. Adam helped her into his car and they sped away.

"Where are we going, or dare I ask?"

"You'll see. Just be patient. We'll be there in about twenty minutes." He drove skilfully through the traffic until they were on the outskirts of the great city. She noticed that they were heading for upstate New York. She gave up trying to coax him into giving up their destination.

Finally, he turned the car onto a road which was fronted with large iron gates. Her heart skipped a beat. Christina vaguely remembered the area, but since the facade had been changed she wasn't quite sure. They drove along a magnificent driveway flanked by massive oak trees. He said, "Look straight ahead. Yes, there it is." Adam confirmed as they approached a house that would impress royalty. They had stopped at the entrance and Adam helped her out of the car. "Who do you know that lives here?" she asked. He turned the key in the massive oak front door and gestured for her to enter.

"Oh my God, Adam. This is the house we were going to buy before we broke up, isn't it? I remember now. Why are we here?"

"Because my darling, this is our home. I bought it on Valentine's Day after you said you would marry me. Did I do something wrong?"

"Wrong? No, never wrong. This is the most unexpected gift I have ever received." She twirled around within the great foyer, dashed about opening doors, and threw back dusty drapes.

She called to him to come and join her in the great room. "Oh, Adam, it's absolutely magnificent. There's so much room. How in the world did you find it?"

"Luckily it had been listed for some time, but the real estate agent said that it was difficult to sell such a large and expensive property during the winter months, so they had taken it off the listing. I finalized the sale a few days later and have been waiting for the right time to tell you."

They embraced in the great room, the sun shining through the fifteen high windows bathing in a warm magical spotlight. "Oh, Adam I am so happy," Christina said, her eyes filled with tears of happiness.

"I know, my love. It's wonderful, isn't it?"

"I can't wait to tell Maggie and Nicole. Let's go."

The cleaning, painting, and redecorating of the house lasted well into the month of March, but all was completed on the date the contractor had promised.

Sarah did come to visit during the Easter Break, but it was for a different reason entirely. The Bennetts were special guests invited to attend the wedding of Sarah's real parents. Spring had turned the grounds of the estate into lush greenery and the leaves were bright and new on the stately oak trees. Christina and Adam were married in the great hall of their new home. The guests included Adam's parents, Tonio and Becka's family from Cranston, John and Ellen, and their children Robert and Andrea. Maggie brought Jean, who had come to New York early on in the year and was already successful as staff instructor for the Hilton chain of hotels. Also in attendance were Christina's Aunt Maria and Uncle Guido Corelli from Toronto, Nicole and Sarah as bridesmaids, and Becka as Christina's maid of honour. Many members of the company rounded out the guest list and fifty very important people witnessed the ceremony whereby Christina Corelli became Christina Carmichael. Everyone agreed that her new name had a nice ring to it. Following the ceremony, everyone retired to the massive dining room where they were served a most delicious seven course dinner. The champagne flowed for hours. The orchestra arrived and the great room became a makeshift ballroom. Such a festive celebration hadn't been enjoyed by their friends and family for a very long time. The best part of it all was that there were no members of the press to invade their privacy. The gates were totally secured by hired security guards, and they did a great job.

The hour approached eleven and the party was still going strong when Adam said, "My love, I think we should bid our guests good night and go upstairs. What do you say to that?"

Christina smiled up into his eyes and her passion matched his. "Hey everyone, gather around. I'm going to throw this bouquet and I want the best woman to win." With those words she turned her back on the crowd at the foot of the stairs and threw the bouquet over her shoulders. She heard a gasp, turned around, and discovered that Maggie had caught the coveted bouquet. Christina winked at her and Maggie mouthed "Thank you, Christina" to her friend.

Adam and Christina waved goodnight from the landing and continued up the long staircase. Part way up, he scooped Christina up into his arms and carried her to the top floor. He approached their bedroom and stopped to give her a long kiss, as Christina reached for the doorknob. Adam carried her into the room, where he placed her on the four poster bed. They closed the door on the world below and entered a world of their own. A world filled with everlasting love, the promise of a lifetime of joy and happiness.

"Adam, I'm so happy, darling."

"I know, I feel it too. We're the two luckiest people in the world. Now, my love, enough talk, it's time for action."

She laughed as she replied, "I couldn't agree with you more. Love me and never let me go, Adam."

Her answer was his lips meeting hers in a long, very passionate kiss, his hands moving expertly over the curves of her body. Their lovemaking was the culmination of all that they had been through, finally resulting in their discovery of paradise.

Thus began the life they had promised one another so many years ago during a warm summer evening in August, so long ago and far away.

THE END

About The Author

MARILYN C. MILLEY

Born in Northern Ontario, Marilyn, at the age of nine, moved to a small community in the Rocky Mountain Region of Alberta, in the Crowsnest Pass. After many years working as a professional in the Medical field of Laboratory Medicine, Marilyn retired and embarked upon a new career compelled to pursue her love of writing. Her characters and situations evolve from a vivid imagination and are set within a factual and well researched environment. She has successfully two other novels over the last five years plus a current novel for ebook publication.

www.ingramcontent.com/pod-product-compliance
Lightning Source LLC
Chambersburg PA
CBHW051504120626
46551CB00012B/768